Lecture Notes in Computer Sc

T0238251

Edited by G. Goos, J. Hartmanis and J. van Leeuwen

Springer

Berlin
Heidelberg
New York
Barcelona
Hong Kong
London
Milan
Paris
Singapore
Tokyo

Oliver Rüthing

Interacting Code Motion Transformations: Their Impact and Their Complexity

Springer

Series Editors

Gerhard Goos, Karlsruhe University, Germany
Juris Hartmanis, Cornell University, NY, USA
Jan van Leeuwen, Utrecht University, The Netherlands

Author

Oliver Rüthing
Universität Dortmund, Lehrstuhl Informatik V
Baroper Str. 301, D-44221 Dortmund, Germany
E-mail: ruething@ls5.cs.uni-dortmund.de

Cataloging-in-Publication data applied for

Die Deutsche Bibliothek - CIP-Einheitsaufnahme

Rüthing, Oliver:
Interacting code motion transformations : their impact and their complexity / Oliver Rüthing. - Berlin ; Heidelberg ; New York ; Barcelona ; Hong Kong ; London ; Milan ; Paris ; Singapore ; Tokyo : Springer, 1998
(Lecture notes in computer science ; Vol. 1539)
ISBN 3-540-65510-7

CR Subject Classification (1998): F.3.2, D.3.4, D.2.4

ISSN 0302-9743
ISBN 3-540-65510-7 Springer-Verlag Berlin Heidelberg New York

This work is subject to copyright. All rights are reserved, whether the whole or part of the material is concerned, specifically the rights of translation, reprinting, re-use of illustrations, recitation, broadcasting, reproduction on microfilms or in any other way, and storage in data banks. Duplication of this publication or parts thereof is permitted only under the provisions of the German Copyright Law of September 9, 1965, in its current version, and permission for use must always be obtained from Springer-Verlag. Violations are liable for prosecution under the German Copyright Law.

© Springer-Verlag Berlin Heidelberg 1998
Printed in Germany

Typesetting: Camera-ready by author
SPIN 10693009 06/3142 – 5 4 3 2 1 0 Printed on acid-free paper

Foreword

Is computing an experimental science? For the roots of program optimization the answer to this question raised by Robin Milner ten years ago is clearly yes: it all started with Donald Knuth's extensive empirical study of Fortran programs. This benchmark-driven approach is still popular, but it has in the meantime been complemented by an increasing body of foundational work, based on varying idealizing assumptions ranging from 'space is for free' over 'there are sufficiently many registers' to 'programs consist of 3-address code'. Evaluation of the adequacy of these assumptions lacks the appeal of run-time measurements for benchmarks, which is so simple that one easily forgets about the difficulties in judging how representative the chosen set of benchmarks is. Ultimately, optimizations should pass the (orthogonal) tests of both communities.

This monograph is based on foundational, assumption-based reasoning, but it evolved under the strong pressure of the experimental community, who expressed doubts concerning the practicality of the underlying assumptions. Oliver Rüthing responded by solving a foundational problem that seemed beyond the range of efficient solutions, and proposed a polynomial algorithm general enough to overcome the expressed concerns.

Register Pressure:. A first formally complete solution to the problem of register pressure in code motion – hoisting computations enlarges the corresponding life-time ranges – was proposed for 3-address code. This assumption allowed a separate treatment of single operator expressions in terms of a bitvector analysis.

The algorithm, although it improves on all previous approaches, was criticized for not taking advantage of the flexibility provided by complex expression structures, which essentially boils down to the following trade-off patterns:

- if (two) operand expressions are only used once, within one large expression, one should hoist its evaluation and release the registers holding the operand values;
- if there are multiple uses of the operand expressions, then one should keep the operand values and delay the evaluation of the large expressions.

Based on matching theory, Rüthing proposes an algorithm that optimally resolves this 'trade-off' problem in polynomial time.

Interacting Transformations:. Optimizing transformations may support and/ or impede each other, as illustrated by the two trade-off patterns in the previous paragraph: hoisting a large expression is supportive in the first but impeding in the second. In this sense, the corresponding optimal algorithm can be regarded as a complete solution to a quite complex interaction problem. In this spirit, Oliver Rüthing additionally investigates the complexity and the interaction potential of assignment motion algorithms comprising both hoisting and sinking, and establishes a surprisingly low complexity bound for the 'meta-iteration' cycle, resolving all the so-called *second-order effects.*

Finally, the monograph sketches how these two results can be combined in order to achieve independence of the assignment granularity. In particular, the combined algorithm is invariant under assignment decomposition into 3-address code, as required for many other optimization techniques. This is of high practical importance, as this increased stability under structural changes widens the range of application while maintaining the optimizing power. I am optimistic that conceptual results like this, which seriously address the concerns of the experimental community, will help to establish fruitful cross-community links.

Summarizing, this monograph, besides providing a comprehensive account of the practically most accepted program analysis and transformation methods for imperative languages, stepwise develops a scenario that overcomes structural restrictions that had previously been attacked for a long time with little success. In order to do justice to the conceptual complexity behind this breakthrough, Rüthing provides all the required formal proofs. They are not always easy to follow in full detail, but the reader is not forced to the technical level. Rather, details can be consulted on demand, providing students with a deep, yet intuitive and accessible introduction to the central principles of code motion, compiler experts with precise information about the obstacles when moving from the 3-address code to the general situation, and the algorithms' community with a striking application of matching theory.

Bernhard Steffen

Preface

Code motion techniques are integrated in many optimizing production and research *compilers* and are still a major topic of ongoing research in *program optimization*. However, traditional methods are restricted by the narrow viewpoint on their immediate effects. A more aggressive approach calls for an investigation of the *interdependencies* between distinct component transformations.

This monograph shows how interactions can be used successfully in the design of techniques for the movement of expressions and assignments that result in tremendous transformational gains. For *expression motion* we present the first algorithm for computational and lifetime optimal placement of expressions that copes adequately with composite expressions and their subexpressions. This algorithm is further adapted to situations where large expressions are split into sequences of assignments. The core of the algorithm is based upon the computation of maximum matchings in bipartite graphs which are used to model trade-off situations between distinct lifetime ranges.

Program transformations based upon *assignment motion* are characterized by their mutual dependencies. The application of one transformation exposes additional opportunities for others. We present simple criteria that guarantee *confluence* and fast *convergence* of the exhaustive transformational process. These criteria apply to a number of practically relevant techniques, like the elimination of partially dead or faint assignments and the uniform elimination of partially redundant expressions and assignments.

This monograph is a revised version of my doctoral dissertation which was submitted to the Faculty of Engineering of the Christian-Albrechts University at Kiel and accepted in July 1997.

Acknowledgements

First of all, I would like to thank Prof. Dr. Hans Langmaack for giving me the opportunity to work in his group and doing the research that finally found its result in my doctoral thesis, on which this monograph is based. I thank him for sharing his wealth of experience on the substance of computer science.

I am particularly grateful to Bernhard Steffen, who raised my interest in the field of program optimization and abstract interpretation. I certainly benefited most from the excellent cooperation with him and his group, among whom Jens Knoop had a predominant role. Our close cooperation started in Kiel and continued uninterrupted after he joined Bernhard's group in Passau. Jens was always willing to discuss my sometimes fuzzy new ideas and finally took on the proof-reading of earlier and mature versions of the book, which would not be as it is without his support. Finally, I thank Alan Mycroft for acting as the third referee of my thesis and for giving me lots of valuable comments.

In addition, I would like to thank Preston Briggs, Dhananjay Dhamdhere, Vinod Grover, Rajiv Gupta, Barry Rosen, Mary Lou Soffa, and Kenneth Zadeck for several stimulating discussions, mostly at conferences or via email exchange. I owe special thanks to Preston Briggs, as he was the one who called my attention to the problem of lifetime dependencies in code motion.

Last but not least, I want to thank my wife Sabine for steadily encouraging me, and, together with our children Laura, Thore, and Aaron, providing the pleasant and lively atmosphere in which I could relax from the up and downs during writing this book.

Dortmund, September 1998 Oliver Rüthing

Table of Contents

1. Introduction 1
1.1 Interacting Program Optimisations 2
1.2 Interacting Code Motion Transformations 3
1.2.1 Interactions in Expression Motion 4
1.2.2 Interactions in Assignment Motion 5
1.3 Code Motion in the Presence of Critical Edges 6
1.4 Structure of the Monograph 7

2. Basic Formalisms and Definitions 9
2.1 Graph Theoretical Foundations 9
2.1.1 Undirected Graphs 9
2.1.2 Directed Graphs 10
2.2 Programs and Flow Graphs 10
2.2.1 Expressions 10
2.2.2 Statements 11
2.2.3 Flow Graphs 12
2.2.4 Program Points 12
2.2.5 Code Patterns 13
2.2.6 Critical Edges 14
2.3 Program Transformations 15
2.3.1 Admissibility 15
2.3.2 Optimality 15

Part I. Expression Motion

3. Optimal Expression Motion: The Single-Expression View 21
3.1 Expression Motion 22
3.1.1 Safety and Correctness 22
3.2 Busy Expression Motion 24
3.2.1 Computational Optimality 24
3.2.2 The Transformation 25
3.3 Lazy Expression Motion 26
3.3.1 Lifetime Optimality 26

3.3.2 The Transformation 27
3.4 A Classification of $\mathcal{COEM}_\varphi$ 30
3.5 Computing $\mathtt{BEM}_\varphi$ and $\mathtt{LEM}_\varphi$ 31
3.6 The Complexity 35

4. Optimal Expression Motion: The Multiple-Expression View 37
4.1 Flat Expression Motion 37
4.1.1 Flat Busy and Lazy Expression Motion 38
4.2 Structured Expression Motion 39
4.2.1 Defining Structured Expression Motion 40
4.2.2 Computationally Optimal Structured Expression Motion 41
4.2.3 Lifetime Optimal Structured Expression Motion 46
4.3 A Graph Theoretical View on Trade-Offs between Lifetimes .. 50
4.3.1 Motivation 50
4.3.2 Tight Sets in Bipartite Graphs 51
4.3.3 An Efficient Decision Procedure 51
4.3.4 Efficient Computation of Tight Sets 53
4.4 Levelwise Flexible Expression Motion 59
4.4.1 Defining $\mathtt{LFEM}_\Phi$ 60
4.4.2 Proving Admissibility 62
4.4.3 Proving Computational Optimality 67
4.4.4 Proving Inductive Lifetime Optimality 70
4.4.5 Computing $\mathtt{LFEM}_\Phi$ 83
4.5 Fully Flexible Expression Motion 84
4.5.1 A Classification of Expressions 85
4.5.2 Limitations of Inductive Lifetime Optimality 88
4.5.3 General Trade-Offs 88
4.5.4 Defining $\mathtt{FFEM}_\Phi$ 93
4.5.5 Proving Admissibility 95
4.5.6 Proving Computational Optimality 98
4.5.7 Proving Lifetime Optimality 98
4.5.8 Computing $\mathtt{FFEM}_\Phi$ 105
4.6 The Complexity 109
4.6.1 The Complexity of $\mathtt{BEM}_\Phi$ and $\mathtt{LEM}_\Phi$ 109
4.6.2 The Complexity of $\mathtt{LFEM}_\Phi$ 109
4.6.3 The Complexity of $\mathtt{FFEM}_\Phi$ 110
4.6.4 Bit-Vector Complexity of $\mathtt{BEM}_\Phi$, $\mathtt{LEM}_\Phi$, $\mathtt{LFEM}_\Phi$ and $\mathtt{FFEM}_\Phi$ 111

5. Expression Motion in the Presence of Critical Edges 113
5.1 The Single-Expression View 113
5.1.1 Computational Optimal Expression Motion 114
5.1.2 Busy Expression Motion 115
5.1.3 Lazy Expression Motion 117
5.1.4 Computing $\mathtt{CBEM}_\varphi$ and $\mathtt{CLEM}_\varphi$ 118
5.1.5 The Complexity 122

5.2 The Multiple-Expression View ... 126
5.2.1 Flat Expression Motion ... 126
5.2.2 Structured Expression Motion ... 126
5.2.3 The Complexity ... 128

Part II. Assignment Motion

6. Program Transformations Based on Assignment Motion .. 137
6.1 Assignment Motion ... 137
6.1.1 Admissibility ... 138
6.2 Partial Dead Code Elimination ... 140
6.2.1 Motivation ... 140
6.2.2 Defining Partial Dead Code Elimination ... 141
6.2.3 Second Order Effects in Partial Dead Code Elimination 142
6.3 Partial Faint Code Elimination ... 145
6.4 Partially Redundant Assignment Elimination ... 146
6.5 The Uniform Elim. of Part. Redundant Assignments and Expressions ... 147

7. A Framework for Assignment Motion Based Program Transformations ... 153
7.1 The Setting ... 153
7.1.1 Motion-Elimination Couples ... 153
7.1.2 A Note on the Correctness of Motion-Elimination Couples ... 154
7.1.3 Notational Conventions ... 155
7.1.4 Uniform Motion-Elimination Couples ... 156
7.2 Confluence of Uniform Motion-Elimination Couples ... 157
7.2.1 The General Case ... 157
7.2.2 Consistent Motion-Elimination Couples ... 157
7.2.3 Confluence of Consistent Motion-Elimination Couples . 166
7.2.4 The Applications ... 169
7.3 The Complexity of Exhaustive Iterations ... 171
7.3.1 Simultaneous Iteration Steps ... 173
7.3.2 Conventions ... 175
7.3.3 The General Case: Weakly Consistent UMECs ... 175
7.3.4 Consistent UMECs ... 178
7.4 $\mathcal{UPRE}$ as an Advanced Application of MECs ... 187
7.4.1 Computationally Optimal $\mathcal{UPRE}$ ... 188
7.4.2 $\mathcal{UPRE}$ and Code Decomposition ... 194
7.4.3 $\mathcal{UPRE}$ with Trade-Offs between Lifetimes of Variables 194

8. Assignment Motion in the Presence of Critical Edges 199
8.1 Straightforward Adaption of MECs 199
8.1.1 Adequacy 199
8.1.2 Confluence 200
8.1.3 Efficiency 201
8.2 Enhanced UMECs 202
8.2.1 Adequacy 203
8.2.2 Confluence 204
8.2.3 Efficiency 205

9. Conclusions and Perspectives 211
9.1 Summary of the Main Results 211
9.2 Perspectives 212

References 214

Index 221
Index 221
Index of Symbols 224

1. Introduction

Traditionally, *program optimisation* stands for various kinds of program transformations intended to improve the run-time performance of the generated code. Optimising transformations are usually applied as intermediate steps within the compilation process. More specifically, an *optimising compiler* principally proceeds in three stages [Muc97]:

- The *front end* translates the source program into an intermediate form. Usually, intermediate level programs are represented in terms of flow graphs built of quite elementary, yet machine-independent instructions.
- The *optimiser* performs several transformations on the intermediate level, each addressing a particular optimisation goal of interest.
- The *back end* finally translates the transformed intermediate program into machine-specific code. This stage particularly comprises typical machine-dependent tasks like *register allocation* [Cha82, CH90, Bri92b] and *instruction scheduling* [BR91, GM86].

Optimising program transformations should preserve the *semantics*[1] of the argument program, while improving its run-time *efficiency*. Ideally, the improvement is witnessed by a formal *optimality criterion*. Since the intermediate level languages under consideration are computationally universal, almost all program properties of interest are in general undecidable. For many program properties this is even true, if conditions are treated in a non-deterministic way [RL77], i. e. the conditions are not evaluated and each program path is considered executable. To force decidability and furthermore to gain efficiency further assumptions are introduced that abstract from certain aspects of the program behaviour. Common assumptions are for instance:

- Assignments change the values of all expressions having the left-hand side variable as an operand.
- There is an infinite number of (symbolic) registers.
- Operations are significantly more expensive than register transfers.

[1] This requirement addresses both the preservation of *total correctness* and the preservation of *partial correctness*. A more detailed discussion on this topic with respect to the transformation presented in the monograph can be found in Chapter 7.

The usage of such assumptions has a number of advantages. First it allows us to gather information by means of efficient standard techniques for static program analysis [Hec77, MJ81, CC77, Nie86]. Moreover, the assumptions can often be organised in a way that expresses a hierarchical structure of concerns. Certain aspects are neglected in a first approximation, but investigated separately later on. Finally, the use of formal optimality criteria makes alternative approaches comparable on a clean abstract basis.

1.1 Interacting Program Optimisations

It is well-known that in program optimisation one is often faced with massive interactions between distinct optimisation techniques. One optimising transformation can create as well as destroy opportunities for other optimising transformations. Usually the dependencies are resolved at most heuristically: an ad-hoc *phase ordering* [Muc97, ASU85] among the pool of optimisations is chosen based upon the most striking dependencies, often resulting from empirical observations. In some cases the same optimisation technique may be applied several times in order to cover the potential introduced by other transformations. In fact, there are almost no approaches that systematically exploit the dependencies between distinct optimisations. Whitfield and Soffa [WS90, WS97] use pre- and post-conditions of optimisations as interface specifications in order to capture those optimisations that are enabled or disabled by other ones. Unfortunately, their proposal reveals application orders that do not take into account cyclic dependencies between distinct optimisations.[2] Click and Cooper [CC95, Cli95] present a framework for combining optimisations by combining their underlying data flow analyses. They demonstrate their framework for an extension of Wegman's and Zadeck's algorithm for computing *conditional constants* [WZ85, WZ91], where constant propagation is combined with the elimination of unreachable branches of conditional statements. Both transformations mutually benefit from each other: the detection of constants may exhibit more accurate information on branching conditions, while the detection of unreachable branches may lead to the detection of further constants. Essentially, their proposal is based on the combination of two monotone data flow analyses [KU77] by means of monotone transfer functions. Under these conditions a combination can reach results that cannot be obtained by exhaustive application of the individual transformations.[3] However, Click's and Cooper's approach is only applicable to optimising transformations where the underlying data flow informations are

[2] Except for the repeated application of a single technique in isolation.

[3] Such phenomena have been observed before. Giegerich et. al [GMW81] showed that repeated dead code elimination can be collapsed to a single data flow analysis (*faint code analysis*) that outperforms the results of iterated dead code elimination in some cases.

pinned to fixed program points, and thus cannot be used for *code motion transformations.*

This monograph focuses on interactions in code motion. In particular, we examine the question how the optimisation potential can be exhausted completely, and if so, if the results are independent from the application order, and what the costs are in terms of computational complexity.

1.2 Interacting Code Motion Transformations

Code motion is an important technique in program optimisation whose impact rests on the idea to move code to program places where its execution frequency is reduced or, more importantly, it can be eliminated since the movement exposes opportunities for suitable elimination techniques to become applicable. Nowadays, code motion algorithms have found their way into many production compilers and are still a main concern of actual research in program optimisation.

Nonetheless, traditional methods are often limited by the narrow view on their immediate effects. On the other hand, a more aggressive approach to code motion requires to investigate the interdependencies between distinct elementary transformations, too. In essence, interdependencies show up in two different flavours:

Order dependencies: this addresses situations where an improvement that can be reached by the sequential execution of two component transformations is out of the scope of their individual impacts. Typically, this happens if one transformation exposes opportunities for the other one. Commonly, such phenomena are known as *second order effects* and their resolution provides an enormous potential for transformational gains.

Structure dependencies: this addresses situations where the result that can be reached by investigating a more complex structure[4] cannot naively be combined from transformations operating on smaller entities. This kind of interdependencies is even more serious, as often the "naive" combination is not only suboptimal but even inadequate.

We will investigate prominent and practically relevant examples for both kinds of interactions and present how their interdependencies can be resolved completely exploiting the optimisation potential as far as possible. To this end we give a taxonomy of (syntactic) code motion and present powerful extensions to standard methods where dependencies among elementary transformations play a crucial role.

---

[4] That means the object of the transformation under investigation, e.g., a single expression (assignment) or a set of expressions (assignments).

1.2.1 Interactions in Expression Motion

Expression motion, which addresses techniques that are concerned with the movement of right-hand side parts of instructions in a program only, has thoroughly been studied in program optimisation [Cho83, Dha83, Dha88, Dha89b, Dha91, DS88, JD82a, JD82b, Mor84, MR79, MR81, Sor89]). Its primary goal is to eliminate partially redundant expressions, i. e. expressions that are unnecessarily reevaluated on some program paths at run-time. This is achieved by replacing the original computations of a program by temporary variables (symbolic registers) that are initialised *correctly* at suitable program points. It is known for decades that partial redundancies can be eliminated as far as possible.[5] The resulting programs are *computationally optimal*, i. e. on every complete program path the number of evaluations of a program term is reduced to a minimal amount. On the other hand, the primary goal leaves plenty of room for distinct computationally optimal programs. At this point a secondary aspect of expression motion comes into play. By definition, the gain of expression motion comes at the price that values have to be stored in a private symbolic register. In fact, using the idea to separate the concerns of expression motion, the primary goal, i. e. reaching computational optimality, is investigated under the assumption that there is an unbounded number of such symbolic registers. More realistically, however, registers - like other resources - are limited. Symbolic registers finally have to be mapped onto the set of available machine registers. This task is commonly known as *register allocation* [Cha82, CH90, Bri92b]. Therefore, an uneconomic usage of symbolic registers would reveal its fateful impact at the register allocation phase leading to register pressure that finally causes the generation of spill code[6] slowing down the program. Therefore, a secondary goal of expression motion is to use the resource of symbolic registers as economically as possible. In more technical terms this requirement means to keep the lifetime ranges of the symbolic registers as small as possible. In [KRS92] we developed an algorithm for *lazy expression motion* which was the first one being computationally as well as lifetime optimal for a single expression under investigation. This single-expression view is typical for algorithms in expression motion. It is motivated by the fact that an extension to multiple expressions is straightforward, if the set of expressions is *flat*, i. e. the set does not contain both expressions and their subexpressions at once. In this case a simultaneous algorithm is essentially determined as the independent combination of all individual transformations. Such a situation is for instance given for intermediate representations of programs where expressions are completely decomposed into three-address format. Even though such an assumption seems attractive at first glance, one should keep in mind

[5] Indeed, this means under a formal optimality criterion that is commonly accepted for syntactic expression motion.

[6] That is, code used in order to store registers into main memory and to reload them.

that splitting up large expressions comes at the price of weakening the potential for expression motion. This is because the decomposition introduces a bunch of assignment statements which may block the movement process.

To this end extensions that are able to cope with expression sets with a non-flat structure are much more appealing. Whereas the primary focus on computational optimality is easy to preserve with a careful combination of elementary transformations, considerations with respect to lifetimes of symbolic registers are heavily affected. Here we are faced with subtle trade-offs between the lifetimes of different symbolic registers that cannot be resolved from the isolated point of view with respect to single-expression transformations. Hence this problem is a model for structure dependencies in code motion.

As a main result we present the first algorithm for lifetime optimal expression motion that adequately copes with composite expressions and their subexpressions at once. The central idea is to model trade-off situations among expressions at each program point by means of *bipartite graphs* and then to determine optimal trade-offs by means of graph *matching* techniques [LP86]. Fortunately, the local view on trade-offs between lifetimes of temporaries is well-behaved with respect to its globalisation leading to a *refinement* based approach that can be sketched as a three-step procedure:

1. Perform the traditional data-flow analyses gathering the information for the computationally and lifetime optimal movement of a single expression.
2. Compute for each program point a most profitable trade-off between lifetimes of symbolic registers. Informatively, such a trade-off is based on two sets of expressions:
   i) The set of expressions R that definitely occupy a symbolic register on entering the given program point, but whose registers can be released, since they are only used for initialisations of expressions of kind ii).
   ii) The set of expressions I that may be initialised at the program point such that their values have to be stored in a symbolic register for a later usage.

   If R is larger than I, it is profitable to release the R-associated lifetimes at the costs of introducing new I-associated ones. Moreover, a most profitable trade-off addresses one for which the difference between the cardinalities of the sets R and I gets maximal.
3. Adjust the information computed in the first step by means of the local information gathered in the second step.

1.2.2 Interactions in Assignment Motion

Assignment motion complements expression motion by incorporating the movement of left-hand side variables of assignments as well. Although such an extension may appear straightforward at first glance, the movement of left-hand sides of assignments induces *second order effects*, i. e. one is now faced with order dependencies whose resolution requires the iterated application of the component transformations. The consequences are twofold: on the one hand the iterated application reveals much more optimisation potential then a one-step procedure, on the other hand iteration has its price in terms of extra costs.

Another essential difference to expression motion is the fact that not only code hoisting, i. e. backward movement of code, but also code sinking, i. e. forward movement of code becomes important. This observation led to the development of a technique for *partial dead code elimination* and *partial faint code elimination* [KRS94b] that complements expression motion.
This monograph gives a systematic approach to the phenomena of interacting program transformations that are based upon assignment motion. To this end a general framework is developed in which criteria for the following two questions of interest are examined:

Confluence: do different iteration sequences eventually collapse in a unique result?

Complexity: what are the extra costs in terms of a penalty factor compared to a single-step application of the elementary components?

We provide simple criteria that grant confluence and fast convergence for the exhaustive iteration of elementary transformations.

Finally, we also investigate structure dependencies in assignment motion by adapting the lifetime considerations in expression motion to the situation in assignment motion. In fact, our technique for minimising lifetime ranges can be directly adapted to the assignment motion situation. This way our method becomes applicable even if large expressions are already split at the intermediate level, which is the situation of highest practical relevance. Even better, the phase that is responsible for minimising the lifetime ranges of temporaries can be completely decoupled from the setting of partial redundancy elimination. This results in a stand-alone technique for resolving register pressure before register allocation takes place. At each program point the number of symbolic registers that are required to hold values is reduced to a minimum which tremendously eases the starting situation of the register allocator.

1.3 Code Motion in the Presence of Critical Edges

Critical edges [MR79, Dha88, SKR90, Dha91, DRZ92] in flow graphs, i. e. edges leading directly from branch-nodes to join-nodes, are known to cause massive problems for code motion. Essentially, the reason for all these problems is that critical edges prevent to decouple run-time situations arising on distinct program paths properly. From a theoretical point of view the problem can be easily overcome by introducing an empty synthetic node on every critical edge, a technique that is commonly known as *edge splitting*. On the other hand, in practice moving code to split nodes has also some drawbacks, as, for instance, additional unconditional jumps are introduced. In the light of this dilemma implementors are sometimes unwilling to split critical edges. Therefore, the problems due to critical edges are well-studied. The most prominent two drawbacks are:

- Critical edges may cause poor transformations due to the lack of suitable placement points.
- Critical edges may impose higher solution costs of the associated data flow analyses due to the usage of bidirectional equations.

Whereas the first drawback cannot be remedied, a lot of research [Dha88, DK93, DP93, KD94] has addressed the second deficiency. While a restricted class of *weakly bidirectional* problems can be solved as easily as undirectional ones, it was recently shown that bidirectional code motion algorithms are inherently more complex than their undirectional counterparts when following a naive round-robin schedule [DP93, KD94]. Surprisingly, the latter result is diminished in the light of a new technique presented here: bidirectional data flow analyses can completely be avoided if the flow graph is (virtually) enriched by shortcuts that are used to bypass nests of critical edges which are the reason for slow information flow along "zig-zag" paths.

While the "classical" deficiencies all address standard non-interacting code motion algorithms, here, in addition, we further investigate the impact of critical edges for interacting code motion transformations. However, our main findings are negative:

- Critical edges ruin the existence of lifetime optimal expression motion for structured sets of expressions.
- Critical edges significantly slow down the exhaustive iteration process for assignment motion based transformations.

These new results strengthen the argument for splitting critical edges, especially since at least the latter deficiency must be apparent in all assignment motion based implementations of partial redundancy elimination that do not split critical edges.

1.4 Structure of the Monograph

The monograph starts with a preliminary chapter being devoted to fundamental notions and concepts. The remainder is split into two parts reflecting our two major themes on interacting code motion transformations. **Part 1** comprises Chapter 3 to 5 and deals with expression motion. Chapter 3 starts by investigating the standard situation for the single-expression view of expression motion. This chapter essentially provides a survey on the main results of [KRS94a]. Chapter 4 then deals with the extension to the multiple-expression situation. As the major achievement we present an algorithm for computationally and lifetime optimal expression motion that works for arbitrary structured sets of expressions. To this end, a significant part of the chapter prepares the graph theoretical background on which our local trade-off decisions are based upon. Central is the development of a simple graph theoretical algorithm for computing *tight sets* in a bipartite graph. For the sake of presentation the algorithm reaching full lifetime optimality is preceded by a weaker variant that advances level by level within the universe of expressions starting with the minimal ones. In this process each transition between levels is optimised on its own, i. e. based on the assumption that decisions made for prior levels are fixed. As a key observation we found out that the central ideas of the levelwise approach could be also utilised to solve the full problem which, at first glance, seemed to be much more intricate. In fact, the central idea for this generalisation is a reduction of an arbitrary structured universe of expressions to a two-level situation that actually suffices for the entire reasoning on register trade-offs. Chapter 5 closes the first part by investigating the impact of critical edges for both the single-expression view and the multiple-expression view.

Part 2 which comprises Chapter 6 up to Chapter 8 deals with assignment motion and is organised similarly as the first part. In Chapter 6 we start by presenting the main applications of assignment motion, among which *partial dead code elimination* [KRS94b] and the *uniform elimination of assignments and expressions* [KRS94b] have a predominate role. Afterwards Chapter 7 introduces a uniform framework for assignment motion based program transformations that is applicable in all relevant situations. Like in the first part the final chapter of the second part is devoted to the impact of critical edges.

Chapter 9 provides a summary of the results, and investigates directions for future research.

2. Basic Formalisms and Definitions

This chapter introduces into the basic formalisms that are used throughout this monograph.

2.1 Graph Theoretical Foundations

Because graph theoretical concepts play an important role for various tasks, for instance for modelling programs or for the reasoning on the lifetimes of symbolic registers, we briefly sum up the most relevant basic notions and concepts.

2.1.1 Undirected Graphs

An *undirected graph* is a pair (V, E), where V is a set of *vertices* and $E \subseteq \mathfrak{P}_{1,2}(V)$ a set of *edges*.[1] For an undirected graph $G = (V, E)$ and a vertex $v \in V$ the set of *neighbours* of v is defined by

$$neigh_G(v) \stackrel{\text{def}}{=} \{w \mid \{v, w\} \in E\}$$

If the underlying graph G is understood from the context the index might be omitted. Moreover, $neigh_G$ is naturally extended to sets of vertices $M \subseteq V$.

$$neigh_G(M) \stackrel{\text{def}}{=} \bigcup_{v \in M} neigh_G(v)$$

An undirected graph (V, E) is called *bipartite*, if and only if there are two sets of vertices S and T such that $V = S \uplus T$ and every edge in E is incident to both a vertex in S and a vertex in T.[2] For convenience, bipartite graphs will often be given in a notation $(S \uplus T, E)$ that already reflects the bipartition of the set of vertices.

---

[1] $\mathfrak{P}_{1,2}(V)$ denotes the set of one- and two-elementary subsets of the power set of V. Hence an edge of an undirected graph is a subset like $\{v, w\}$ with $v, w \in V$.

[2] $\uplus$ stands for set union of disjoint sets.

2.1.2 Directed Graphs

A *directed graph* is a pair (V, E), where V is a set of *vertices* and $E \subseteq V \times V$ is a set of *directed edges*. For a directed graph the set of neighbours of a vertex v is divided into two classes: the set of *successors* $succ_G(\varphi)$ defined by

$$succ_G(v) \stackrel{\text{def}}{=} \{w \in V \mid (v, w) \in E\}$$

and the set of *predecessors* $pred_G$ defined by

$$pred_G(v) \stackrel{\text{def}}{=} \{w \in V \mid (w, v) \in E\}$$

By analogy to $neigh_G$ also $succ_G$ and $pred_G$ can be extended to sets of vertices.

2.1.2.1 Paths. A *finite path* p in a directed graph $G = (V, E)$ is a sequence of vertices $\langle v_1, \ldots, v_k \rangle$ $(k \geqslant 0)$, where

$$\forall 1 \leqslant i < k.\ v_{i+1} \in succ(v_i)$$

$\langle\rangle$ is the *empty path* and we use $|p|$ to refer to the *length* of path p, which is k for $p = \langle v_1, \ldots, v_k \rangle$. The set of all finite paths of G is denoted by $\mathbf{P}_G$ and the set of finite paths leading from a vertex v to a vertex w is denoted by $\mathbf{P}_G[v, w]$. Furthermore, we define

- $\mathbf{P}_G[v, w[\stackrel{\text{def}}{=} \bigcup_{w' \in pred(w)} \mathbf{P}_G[v, w']$
- $\mathbf{P}_G]v, w] \stackrel{\text{def}}{=} \bigcup_{v' \in succ(v)} \mathbf{P}_G[v', w]$

In situations where G is understood from the context the index G may be omitted.

For a given path $p \in \mathbf{P}_G$ and an index $1 \leqslant i \leqslant |p|$ the i-th component of p is addressed by p_i. A path $q \in \mathbf{P}_G$ is said to be a *subpath* of p, in symbols $q \sqsubseteq p$, if there is an index $1 \leqslant i \leqslant |p|$ such that $i + |q| - 1 \leqslant |p|$ and $q_j = p_{i+j-1}$ for all $1 \leqslant j \leqslant |q|$.

A path p is a *cycle* if $p_1 = p_{|p|}$. A directed graph G for which $\mathbf{P}_G$ does not contain any cycle is called *acyclic* or for short a DAG (Directed Acyclic Graph).

2.2 Programs and Flow Graphs

2.2.1 Expressions

We consider *expressions* $\mathcal{E}$ that are inductively built from variables, constants and operators. The set of *immediate subexpressions* of an expression φ

is denoted by $SubExpr(\varphi)$. Moreover, this notion can be extended straightforwardly to sets of expressions. Then the set of *mediate subexpressions* of an expression φ is given by

$$SubExpr^*(\varphi) \stackrel{\text{def}}{=} \bigcup_{i \in \mathbb{N}} SubExpr^i(\varphi),$$

where $SubExpr^i(\varphi)$ is inductively defined by $SubExpr^0(\varphi) \stackrel{\text{def}}{=} \{\varphi\}$ and $SubExpr^{i+1}(\varphi) \stackrel{\text{def}}{=} SubExpr^i(SubExpr(\varphi))$. For instance,

$$SubExpr^*((a+b)*(c+d)) = \{(a+b)*(c+d), a+b, c+b, a, b, c, d\}$$

Complementary, the notion of *superexpressions* is defined by

$$SupExpr(\varphi) \stackrel{\text{def}}{=} \{\psi \in \mathcal{E} \mid \varphi \in SubExpr(\psi)\}.$$

Mediate superexpressions $SupExpr^*(\varphi)$ of φ are defined analogously to mediate subexpressions $SubExpr^*(\varphi)$.

For a set of expressions Φ we use $SubExpr_\Phi(\psi)$, $SubExpr^*_\Phi(\psi)$, $SupExpr_\Phi(\psi)$ and $SupExpr^*_\Phi(\psi)$ as shorthands for $SubExpr(\psi) \cap \Phi$, $SubExpr^*(\psi) \cap \Phi$, $SupExpr(\psi) \cap \Phi$ and $SupExpr^*(\psi) \cap \Phi$, respectively.

Finally, the minimal and maximal expressions with respect to Φ are defined by

$$\Phi^{min} \stackrel{\text{def}}{=} \{\varphi \in \Phi \mid SubExpr_\Phi(\varphi) = \emptyset\} \text{ and}$$

$$\Phi^{max} \stackrel{\text{def}}{=} \{\varphi \in \Phi \mid SupExpr_\Phi(\varphi) = \emptyset\},$$

respectively.

2.2.2 Statements

Expressions are used in order to construct *statements*. With respect to our application, code motion, statements are classified into three groups:

- *Assignment statements* of the form $v := \varphi$, where v denotes a program variable and φ an expression. Assignment statements are responsible for the transfer of values.
- *Immobile statements* that are assumed to be the unmovable determinants within the program. This, however, only excludes the movement of the statement itself, while its expressions may be subjected to expression motion. For the sake of presentation we consider two types immobile of statements. Output statements of the form *out*(φ) are immobile, since they influence the observable behaviour of the program. Conditional branches of the form *cond*(φ) are immobile, since we assume that the branching structure of the program is preserved.[3]

[3] In practice, also some assignment statements, for instance assignments to global variables (variables out of the scope of the flow graph under consideration), should be treated as immobile statements for safety reasons.

- *Irrelevant statements*, i. e. statements that are irrelevant for code motion. For the sake of simplicity we will use the *empty statement skip* as the only representative.

2.2.3 Flow Graphs

As it is common imperative programs are represented in terms of *directed flow graphs* $G=(N,E,\mathbf{s},\mathbf{e})$, where (N,E) is a directed graph and $\mathbf{s} \in N$ and $\mathbf{e} \in N$ denote the unique *start node* and *end node* of G. The *nodes* $n \in N$ represent statements and the directed edges $(m,n) \in E$ represent the nondeterministic branching structure of G. $\mathbf{s}$ and $\mathbf{e}$ are both assumed to represent the empty statement and not to possess any predecessors and successors, respectively. Moreover, every node $n \in N$ is assumed to lie on a path in $\mathbf{P}[\mathbf{s},\mathbf{e}]$.[4] Finally, we define the program size $|G|$ which is important for reasoning about complexity issues by $|G| \stackrel{\text{def}}{=} |N| + |E|$. Note that for real life programs it is reasonable to assume that the edges of a flow graph are somehow sparse,[5] i. e. $\mathcal{O}(\,|N|\,) = \mathcal{O}(\,|E|\,)$.

Basic Blocks Considering nodes that represent *basic blocks* [Hec77], i. e. maximal linear sequences of statements, reveals an alternative view of the flow graph. Basic block nodes are more appropriate from a practical point of view, while nodes with elementary statements are more appealing for the theoretical reasoning. Moreover, basic blocks are more suitable for assignment motions that are applied repeatedly, since as opposed to the position of statements within the program which may change significantly the general branching structure in terms of the basic block flow graph is preserved. To distinguish basic blocks from elementary nodes we will use bold-faced symbols like $\mathbf{n}, \mathbf{m}, \ldots$ for them. Finally, the terms *first*$(\mathbf{n})$ and *last*$(\mathbf{n})$ refer to the first and the last instruction associated with a basic block $\mathbf{n}$.[6]

2.2.4 Program Points

For a code motion under consideration relevant program properties refer to the entries and exits of the nodes of N. To this end we introduce the set of *program points* $\dot{N}$ which contains all entries and exits of nodes in N. The usage of program points significantly simplifies our reasoning, because program properties can be specified in a uniform way and we do not have to

---

4 This assumption is fairly standard in data flow analysis. On the one hand, nodes that are not reachable from $\mathbf{s}$ can always be eliminated. On the other hand, nodes that do not reach $\mathbf{e}$ can be directly connected to $\mathbf{e}$ resulting in a program where each path originating in $\mathbf{s}$ is made terminating.

5 This condition can always be forced by assuming that the maximum out-degree of branching nodes is bound by a constant.

6 An empty basic block is at least considered to be associated with the empty statement *skip*.

cope with an artificial distinction between entry- and exit- situations. In order to distinguish program points in $\dot{N}$ from nodes in N we follow the convention to use dotted symbols like $\dot{n}, \dot{m}, \ldots \in \dot{N}$ for the former ones. In particular, the entry of $\mathbf{s}$ and the exit of $\mathbf{e}$ are denoted by $\dot{\mathbf{s}}$ and $\dot{\mathbf{e}}$, respectively. Regarding the exit point of a node as the immediate successor of its entry point makes the program points $\dot{N}$ a directed graph, too, which implies that notions for *pred*, *succ* and for paths apply as well. Moreover, from a conceptual point of view the statement of a node will be considered to be attached to the entry point, while the exit point is considered associated with the empty statement *skip*.

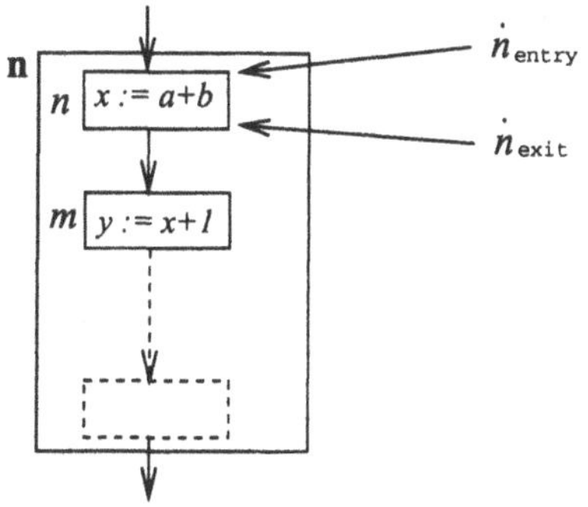

Fig. 2.1. Granularity of a flow graph: nodes in form of basic blocks, elementary statements or program points

2.2.5 Code Patterns

Code patterns refer to the syntactical shape of a piece of code in a flow graph G. Important for code motion are code patterns that can be subjected to a movement. In this monograph code patterns of particular interest are *expression patterns* $\mathcal{EP}(G)$ and *assignment patterns* $\mathcal{AP}(G)$.[7] Typically, $\varphi, \psi, \ldots$ are used to range over expression patterns and $\alpha, \beta, \gamma, \ldots$ to range over assignment patterns. For an assignment pattern $\alpha \in \mathcal{AP}(G)$ the set of *α-occurrences* in G is denoted by $Occ_\alpha(G)$. Typically, symbols like $occ_\alpha, occ_\beta, occ_\gamma, \ldots$ are used to range over elements of $Occ_\alpha(G)$, where the index refers to the corresponding assignment pattern. In some situation we are explicitly addressing *path occurrences* of an assignment pattern. In contrast to program occurrences such occurrences refer to an occurrence at a particular position on a path. For a given path p we use $occ_{\alpha,p}, occ_{\beta,p}, occ_{\gamma,p}, \ldots$ for path occurrences of $\alpha, \beta, \gamma, \ldots$, respectively, and denote the set of p-path occurrences of α in G by $Occ_{\alpha,p}(G)$. Finally, a given path occurrence $occ_{\alpha,p}$ is projected to its corresponding program occurrence occ_α by omitting the path parameter.

[7] Some of the results can also be adapted to more complex code patterns as discussed in [CLZ86].

2.2.6 Critical Edges

It is well-known that in completely arbitrary graph structures the code motion process may be blocked by *critical edges*, i. e. by edges leading from nodes with more than one successor to nodes with more than one predecessor (cf. [Dha88, Dha91, DS88, RWZ88, SKR90, SKR91]).

In Figure 2.2(a) the computation of $a+b$ at node 3 is partially redundant with respect to the computation of $a+b$ at node 1. However, this partial redundancy cannot safely be eliminated by moving the computation of $a+b$ to its preceding nodes, because this may introduce a new computation on a path leaving node 2 on the right branch. On the other hand, it can safely be eliminated after inserting a synthetic node $S_{2,3}$ on the critical edge $(2,3)$, as illustrated in Figure 2.2(b).

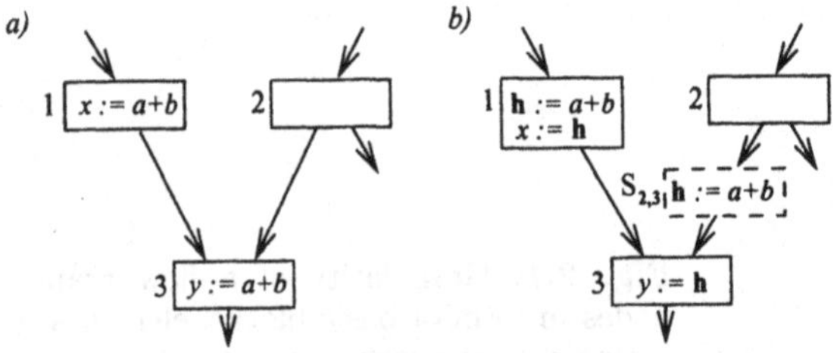

Fig. 2.2. Critical edges

We distinguish between flow graphs possibly with or definitely without critical edges. Accordingly, these two classes of flow graphs are denoted as $\mathfrak{FG}_{\mathtt{Crit}}$ and $\mathfrak{FG}$, respectively. Throughout this book we will usually consider flow graphs without critical edges. This is for the reason that every flow graph G with critical edges can be transformed into a corresponding flow graph without critical edges G^{Σ}. This procedure that is known as *edge splitting* is accomplished by inserting a synthetic node being associated with the empty statement on every critical edge.

Nonetheless, we will carefully examine the impact of critical edges for most of the presented results. Besides the well-known drawbacks we also found strong new arguments giving evidence for the importance of edge splitting.

Fundamental for the differences between flow graphs with and without critical edges is the following structural property that exclusively applies to flow graphs in $\mathfrak{FG}$:

Lemma 2.2.1 (Control Flow Lemma).

1. $\forall n \in N. \ |pred(n)| \geqslant 2 \Rightarrow succ(pred(n)) = \{n\}$
2. $\forall n \in N. \ |succ(n)| \geqslant 2 \Rightarrow pred(succ(n)) = \{n\}$

Proof. For the proof of the first property consider a predecessor m of a node n with $|pred(n)| \geqslant 2$. Suppose $|succ(m)| \geqslant 2$ then (m, n) is a critical edge in contradiction to the assumption. Hence $succ(pred(n)) = \{n\}$ as desired. The second property is symmetric. □

2.3 Program Transformations

2.3.1 Admissibility

Considering an optimisation goal of interest a universe of *admissible* program transformations is usually determined by means of a general syntactic scheme for the transformations and additional constraints capturing semantic properties that have to be preserved.

Program transformations considered here do not modify the branching structure of a program.[8] Therefore, every program path p in a program G has an associated program path in the transformed program G_{TR} that is denoted by p_{TR}.

2.3.2 Optimality

The concern to prove a particular program transformation optimal within a universe of admissible transformations $\mathcal{T}$ requires to make a criterion explicit that is suitable to compare the "quality" of distinct program transformations with respect to some optimisation goals of interest. This comparison is accomplished by means of a suitable relation $\precsim\ \subseteq\ \mathcal{T} \times \mathcal{T}$ that in general will be a *preorder*, i. e. a relation that is transitive and reflexive. However, usually $\precsim$ will not be antisymmetric, which is due to the fact that most optimality criteria are quite liberal allowing different programs of equal quality. Based on $\precsim$ a transformation $\mathrm{TR} \in \mathcal{T}$ is then called $\precsim$-optimal, if and only if $\forall\, \mathrm{TR}' \in \mathcal{T}.\ \mathrm{TR}' \precsim \mathrm{TR}$.

8 Steffen [Ste96] and later Bodík, Gupta and Soffa [BGS98] presented approaches that expand the original program in order to eliminate partial redundancies completely, however, at the price of a potential exponential blow-up of the program.

Part I

Expression Motion

Overview

Expression Motion

Expression motion is a technique for suppressing the computation of partially redundant expressions where possible, i. e. expressions that are unnecessarily reevaluated on some program paths at run-time. This is achieved by replacing the original computations of a program by temporary variables (registers) that are initialised *correctly* at suitable program points. A major advantage of expression motion is the fact that it uniformly covers *loop invariant expression motion* and the *elimination of redundant computations.*

In their seminal paper [MR79] Morel and Renvoise were the first who proposed an algorithm for expression motion being based upon data flow analysis techniques. Their algorithm triggered a number of variations and improvements mainly focusing on two drawbacks of Morel's and Renvoise's algorithm [Cho83, Dha83, Dha88, Dha89b, Dha91, DS88, JD82a, JD82b, Mor84, MR81, Sor89]). First, their algorithm was given in terms of bidirectional data flow analyses which are in general conceptually and computationally more complex than unidirectional ones, and second, expressions are unnecessarily moved, a fact which may increase register pressure. In [DRZ92] Dhamdhere, Rosen, and Zadeck showed that the original transformation of Morel and Renvoise can be solved as easily as a unidirectional problem. However, they did not address the problem of unnecessary code motion. This problem was first tackled in [Cho83, Dha88, Dha91] and more recently in [DP93]. However, the first three proposals are of heuristic nature, i. e. code is unnecessarily moved or redundancies remain in the program, and the latter one is of limited applicability: it requires the reducibility of the flow graph under consideration.

In [KRS92] we developed an algorithm for *lazy expression motion* which evolved from a total redesign of Morel's and Renvoise's algorithm starting from a specification point of view. In fact, our algorithm was the first that succeeded in solving both deficiencies of Morel's and Renvoise's algorithm optimally: the algorithm is completely based on simple, purely unidirectional data flow analyses[9] and suppresses any unnecessary code motion.[10] In fact, for a given expression this placing strategy *minimises* the lifetime range of the temporary that is associated with the expression: any other computationally optimal expression motion has to cover this lifetime range as well.

Expression Motion of Multiple Expressions

Typically, algorithms for expression motion are presented with respect to a fixed but arbitrary expression pattern. This is due to the fact that an

[9] The idea for this was first proposed in [Ste91].

[10] This algorithm was later interprocedurally generalised to programs with procedures, local and global variables and formal value parameters in [KS92, Kno93, KRS96b].

extension to multiple expression patterns is straightforward for sets of expressions with a flat structure, i. e. sets of expressions that do not contain both expressions and their subexpressions. In this case a simultaneous algorithm is essentially determined as the independent combination of all individual transformations. Such a situation is for instance given when considering programs whose expressions are completely decomposed into three-address format. Even though such a decomposition severely weakens the power of expression motion, it is fairly standard since Morel's and Renvoise's seminal paper [MR79]. In fact, all relevant algorithms are based on this separation paradigm of Morel/Renvoise-like expression motion. Whereas giving up this paradigm does not severely influence considerations with respect to computational optimality, it affects lifetime considerations. This observation did not yet enter the reasoning on the register pressure problem in expression motion papers. In fact, this does not surprise, as the problem requires one to cope with subtle trade-offs between the lifetimes of different temporary variables. Nonetheless, the problem can be tackled and solved efficiently: in Chapter 4 we present the first algorithm for lifetime optimal expression motion that adequately copes with large expressions and their subexpressions simultaneously.

Expression Motion and Critical Edges

It is well-known that critical edges are the reason for various problems in expression motion. The major deficiencies are that critical edges may cause poor transformations due to the lack of suitable placement points and higher solution costs of the associated data flow analyses. In Chapter 5 we investigate the reasons for known and for new difficulties caused by the presence of critical edges.

Conventions

As in [KRS92] we consider flow graphs whose nodes are elementary statements rather than basic blocks. Following the lines of [KRS94a] we can easily develop algorithms where the global data flow analyses operate on basic blocks whose instructions are only inspected once in a preprocess.[11] Moreover, we primarily investigate the global aspects of lifetimes, i. e. we abstract from lifetimes of temporaries that do not survive the boundaries of a node in the flow graph. However, local aspects of lifetimes can be completely captured within a postprocess of our algorithm that requires one additional analysis (cf. [KRS92, KRS94a]). The whole part refers to a fixed flow graph G which, however, in Chapter 3 and Chapter 4 is assumed to be out of $\mathfrak{FG}$ and in Chapter 5 to be out of $\mathfrak{FG}_{\mathtt{Crit}}$.

[11] Note that such an adaption is only superior from a pragmatic point of view but does not reduce the asymptotic computational complexity.

3. Optimal Expression Motion: The Single-Expression View

In this chapter we investigate expression motion for an arbitrary but fixed expression pattern φ. In particular, we recall busy and lazy expression motion as introduced in [KRS94a] which are of major importance due to their role as the basic components for the multiple-expression approaches presented later. Throughout this chapter Figure 3.1 serves as a running example, as it is complex enough to illustrate the essential features of our approach.[1]

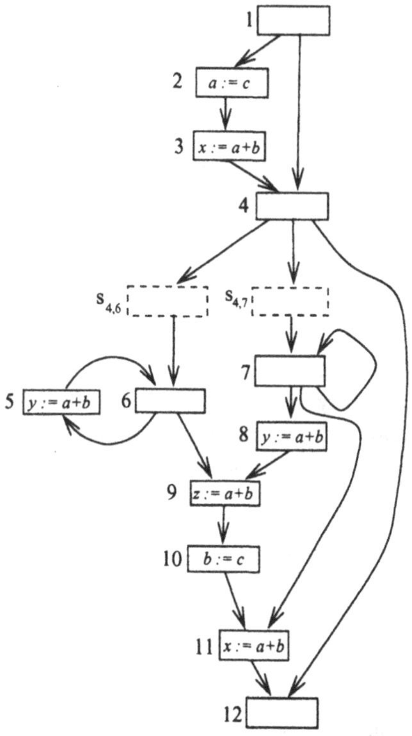

Fig. 3.1. The motivating example

[1] We left out synthetic nodes on the critical edges $(1,4)$, $(4,12)$, $(7,7)$ and $(7,11)$, since they are irrelevant for the expression motions presented.

3.1 Expression Motion

Following [KRS92, KRS94a] we introduce:

Definition 3.1.1 (Expression Motion).
An expression motion *is a program transformation that*

- *inserts some instances of initialisation statements* $\mathbf{h}_\varphi := \varphi$ *at program points, where* $\mathbf{h}_\varphi$ *is an* temporary variable *(or* symbolic register *) that is exclusively assigned to the expression pattern* φ *and*
- *replaces some original occurrences of* φ *by a usage of* $\mathbf{h}_\varphi$.

Hence an expression motion $\mathtt{EM}_\varphi$ is completely characterised by two on program points in $\dot{N}$:

- $\mathtt{EM}_\varphi$-*Insert*, determining at which program points initialisations $\mathbf{h}_\varphi := \varphi$ are inserted and
- $\mathtt{EM}_\varphi$-*Replace*, specifying those program points where an original occurrence of the expression pattern φ is replaced by $\mathbf{h}_\varphi$.

Local Predicates For each node $n \in N$ two local are defined indicating whether φ is computed or modified by n, respectively.

- $Comp_n$: φ occurs as an original computation within n.
- $Transp_n$: φ is transparent at n, i.e. the left-hand side variable of n is not an operand of φ.

The two local are extended to program points as well. To this end we define $Comp_{\dot{n}} \stackrel{\text{def}}{=} Comp_n$ for the entry point $\dot{n}$ of a node n and $Comp_{\dot{n}} \stackrel{\text{def}}{=} false$ for any exit point $\dot{n}$. Similarly, $Transp_{\dot{n}} \stackrel{\text{def}}{=} Transp_n$ for the entry point $\dot{n}$ of a node n and $Transp_{\dot{n}} \stackrel{\text{def}}{=} true$ for any exit point $\dot{n}$.

The local are the propositions used for specifying global program properties of interest. This is usually done by means of path formulas in predicate logics.[2] Therefore, we assume that the priority pr of operators and quantifiers[3] is ordered by

$$pr(\neg) > pr(\wedge) > pr(\vee) > pr(\Rightarrow) = pr(\Leftrightarrow) > pr(\forall) = pr(\exists) = pr(\dot{\exists})$$

3.1.1 Safety and Correctness

In order to guarantee that the semantics of the argument program is preserved, we require that the expression motion must be *admissible*. Intuitively, this means that every insertion of a computation is *safe*, i.e. on no program

[2] Steffen [Ste91, Ste93] considers similar specifications in terms of modal logic formulas that can be automatically transformed into corresponding analysers.
[3] $\dot{\exists}$ stands for definite existential quantification.

path the computation of a new value is introduced at initialisation sites, and that every substitution of an original occurrence of φ by $\mathbf{h}_\varphi$ is *correct*, i.e. $\mathbf{h}_\varphi$ always represents the same value as φ at use sites. This requires that $\mathbf{h}_\varphi$ is properly initialised on every program path leading to some use site in a way such that no modification occurs afterwards.[4] For a formal definition we introduce two capturing if a potential insertion of an initialisation statement $\mathbf{h}_\varphi := \varphi$ at program point is safe or if a potential replacement of an original occurrence of φ at a program point is correct, respectively.[5] The correctness predicate, however, is relative to an expression motion under consideration.

Definition 3.1.2 (Safety & Correctness).
Let $\mathtt{EM}_\varphi$ *be an expression motion and* $\dot n \in \dot N$. *Then*

1. $$Safe_{\dot n} \overset{def}{\Leftrightarrow} \forall p \in \mathbf{P}[\dot{\mathbf{s}}, \dot{\mathbf{e}}]\ \forall i \leqslant |p|.\ p_i = \dot n \Rightarrow \underbrace{\exists j < i.\ Comp_{p_j} \wedge \forall j \leqslant k < i.\ Transp_{p_k}}_{i)} \vee \underbrace{\exists j \geqslant i.\ Comp_{p_j} \wedge \forall i \leqslant k < j.\ Transp_{p_k}}_{ii)}$$
2. $$\mathtt{EM}_\varphi\text{-}Correct_{\dot n} \overset{def}{\Leftrightarrow} \forall p \in \mathbf{P}[\dot{\mathbf{s}}, \dot n]\ \exists i \leqslant |p|.\ \mathtt{EM}_\varphi\text{-}Insert_{p_i} \wedge \forall i \leqslant j < |p|.\ Transp_{p_j}$$

Restricting the definition of safety only to the term marked (i) or (ii) induces for *up-safety* and *down-safety*, respectively, which are denoted *UpSafe* and *DnSafe*.

Based upon Definition 3.1.2 we now formally define the notion of admissibility.

Definition 3.1.3 (Admissible Expression Motion). *An expression motion* $\mathtt{EM}_\varphi$ *is* admissible, *if and only if it satisfies the following two conditions:*

1. *Insertions of assignments* $\mathbf{h}_\varphi := \varphi$ *are restricted to* safe *program points, i. e.*
$$\forall \dot n \in \dot N.\ \mathtt{EM}_\varphi\text{-}Insert_{\dot n} \Rightarrow Safe_{\dot n}$$
2. *Original occurrences of* φ *are only replaced at program points where their replacement is correct:*
$$\forall \dot n \in \dot N.\ \mathtt{EM}_\varphi\text{-}Replace_{\dot n} \Rightarrow \mathtt{EM}_\varphi\text{-}Correct_{\dot n}$$

---

[4] As usual we are exclusively dealing with syntactic expression motion here, where every left-hand side occurrence of an operand of φ is assumed to change the value of φ. For an expression motion algorithm that also captures semantic properties see [SKR90, SKR91, KRS98].

[5] Recall that every node lies on a path from $\mathbf{s}$ to $\mathbf{e}$.

The set of all admissible expression motions with respect to φ is denoted by $\mathcal{AEM}_{\varphi}$.

Let us now take a look at some important properties of safety and correctness. The first one is that safety can perfectly be decomposed into up-safety and down-safety, a fact which is important for the actual computation of this property (cf. Section 3.5).

Lemma 3.1.1 (Safety Lemma). $\forall \dot{n} \in \dot{N}.\ \mathit{Safe}_{\dot{n}} \Leftrightarrow \mathit{UpSafe}_{\dot{n}} \vee \mathit{DnSafe}_{\dot{n}}$

Moreover, for an admissible expression motion correctness also ensures safety, as we can exploit the implication of Definition 3.1.3(1) for the path characterisation of correctness.

Lemma 3.1.2 (Correctness Lemma).

$$\forall\, \mathtt{EM}_{\varphi} \in \mathcal{AEM}_{\varphi},\ \dot{n} \in \dot{N}.\ \mathtt{EM}_{\varphi}\text{-}\mathit{Correct}_{\dot{n}} \Rightarrow \mathit{Safe}_{\dot{n}}$$

The formal proofs of Lemma 3.1.1 as well as of Lemma 3.1.2 can be found in [KRS94a].

3.2 Busy Expression Motion

In this section we recall busy expression motion as introduced in [KRS92, KRS94a]. This transformation is of particular importance, since it provides the key for the characterisation of all other computationally optimal expression motions.

3.2.1 Computational Optimality

The primary goal of expression motion is to minimise the number of computations on every program path. This intent is reflected by the following relation. An expression motion $\mathtt{EM}_{\varphi} \in \mathcal{AEM}_{\varphi}$ is *computationally better*[6] than an expression motion $\mathtt{EM}'_{\varphi} \in \mathcal{AEM}_{\varphi}$, in symbols $\mathtt{EM}'_{\varphi} \precsim^{\varphi}_{exp} \mathtt{EM}_{\varphi}$, if and only if

$$\forall p \in \mathbf{P}[\dot{\mathbf{s}}, \dot{\mathbf{e}}].\ \mathit{Comp\#}(p, \mathtt{EM}_{\varphi}) \leqslant \mathit{Comp\#}(p, \mathtt{EM}'_{\varphi}),$$

where $\mathit{Comp\#}(p, \mathtt{EM}_{\varphi})$ denotes the number of computations of φ that occur on the path $p \in \mathbf{P}[\dot{\mathbf{s}}, \dot{\mathbf{e}}]$ after applying the expression motion $\mathtt{EM}_{\varphi}$, i. e.

$$\mathit{Comp\#}(p, \mathtt{EM}_{\varphi}) \stackrel{\text{def}}{=} |\{i \mid \mathtt{EM}_{\varphi}\text{-}\mathit{Insert}_{p_i}\}| + |\{i \mid \mathit{Comp}_{p_i} \wedge \neg \mathtt{EM}_{\varphi}\text{-}\mathit{Replace}_{p_i}\}|$$

Obviously, $\precsim^{\varphi}_{exp}$ defines a preorder on $\mathcal{AEM}_{\varphi}$. Based on this preorder we now define:

[6] Note that this relation is reflexive. In fact, *computationally at least as good* would be the more precise but uglier term.

Definition 3.2.1 (Computational Optimality). *An admissible expression motion* $\mathtt{EM}_\varphi \in \mathcal{AEM}_\varphi$ *is* computationally optimal, *if and only if it is computationally better than any other admissible expression motion.*

Let us denote the set of computationally optimal expression motions with respect to φ by $\mathcal{COEM}_\varphi$.

3.2.2 The Transformation

Busy expression motion is characterised by introducing its insertions at those program points that are safe and where an "earlier" computation of φ would not be safe. Thus *earliest* program points can be considered as the upper borderline of the region of safe program points.

Definition 3.2.2 (Earliestness). *For every* $\dot{n} \in \dot{N}$

$$\mathit{Earliest}_{\dot{n}} \stackrel{\text{def}}{=} \underbrace{\mathit{Safe}_{\dot{n}}}_{(\star)} \wedge \; ((\dot{n} = \dot{\mathbf{s}}) \vee \exists\, \dot{m} \in \mathit{pred}(\dot{n}).\ \neg \mathit{Transp}_{\dot{m}} \vee \neg \mathit{Safe}_{\dot{m}})$$

Formally, busy expression motion ($\mathtt{BEM}_\varphi$) is then defined as follows:

- Insert initialisation statements $\mathbf{h}_\varphi := \varphi$ at every program point $\dot{n}$ satisfying *Earliest*.
- Replace every original occurrence of φ by $\mathbf{h}_\varphi$.

Remark 3.2.1. As shown in [KRS94a] Definition 3.2.2 can be strengthened without loss of generality by using $\mathit{DnSafe}_{\dot{n}}$ instead of ($\bigstar$) and universal instead of existential quantification.

As a result we have (cf. [KRS94a]):

Theorem 3.2.1 (Optimality Theorem for $\mathtt{BEM}_\varphi$).
$\mathtt{BEM}_\varphi$ *is computationally optimal, i. e.* $\mathtt{BEM}_\varphi \in \mathcal{COEM}_\varphi$.

Figure 3.2 presents busy expression motion for our running example of Figure 3.1.[7] In particular, the algorithm eliminates the loop invariant computation of $a + b$ at node 5 and succeeds in removing the partially redundant recomputation of $a + b$ at node 9.

Finally, for $\mathtt{BEM}_\varphi$ an interesting correspondence between safety and correctness can be established which complements Lemma 3.1.2.

Lemma 3.2.1 ($\mathtt{BEM}_\varphi$-Correctness Lemma).

$$\forall\, \dot{n} \in \dot{N}.\ \mathtt{BEM}_\varphi\text{-}\mathit{Correct}_{\dot{n}} \Leftrightarrow \mathit{Safe}_{\dot{n}}$$

Whereas the forward-implication is due to Lemma 3.1.2, Lemma 3.11(1) of [KRS94a] proves an alternative formulation of the backward-direction.

[7] The index $a + b$ of the temporary variable $\mathbf{h}$ is omitted in the interest of brevity.

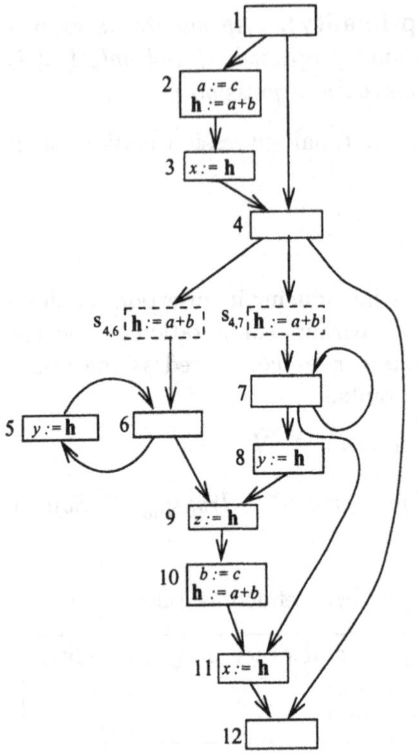

Fig. 3.2. BEM_{a+b}

3.3 Lazy Expression Motion

The busy approach to expression motion of the previous section minimises the number of computations of φ at run-time, however, it does not take into account the *lifetime ranges* of the temporary variable $\mathbf{h}_\varphi$. Since unnecessarily large lifetime ranges of temporaries may cause superfluous *register pressure*, we are interested in a computationally optimal expression motion whose register usage is as economical as possible.
Thus we need to provide a reasonable definition for the lifetime range that is associated with $\mathbf{h}_\varphi$ under a particular expression motion. Since we will separate the global aspects of lifetimes from the local ones an alternative, yet simpler definition compared to the one in [KRS94a] is sufficient.

3.3.1 Lifetime Optimality

Let us first introduce the set of paths leading from an insertion point to a replacement site, which shall be called *insertion-replacement paths*. For $\text{EM}_\varphi \in \mathcal{AEM}_\varphi$ we have[8]

[8] Of course, the path is built of program points.

$$\mathbf{IRP}(\mathtt{EM}_\varphi) \stackrel{\text{def}}{=} \{p \in \mathbf{P} \mid |p| \geqslant 2 \wedge \underbrace{\mathtt{EM}_\varphi\text{-}\mathit{Insert}_{p_1}}_{i)} \wedge \underbrace{\mathtt{EM}_\varphi\text{-}\mathit{Replace}_{p_{|p|}}}_{ii)} \wedge \underbrace{\forall\, 1 < i \leqslant |p|.\ \neg \mathtt{EM}_\varphi\text{-}\mathit{Insert}_{p_i}\}}_{iii)}$$

In the above characterisation term (i) describes an initialisation at program point p_1, term (ii) addresses a replacement at $p_{|p|}$, while term (iii) ensures that the initialisation according to (i) is actually one that belongs to the replacement according to (ii). Then the *lifetime range* with respect to an expression motion $\mathtt{EM}_\varphi \in \mathcal{AEM}_\varphi$ defines the set of program points where the value of φ is kept in the temporary $\mathbf{h}_\varphi$ and cannot be released:

Definition 3.3.1 (Lifetime Range).

$$\mathit{LtRg}(\mathtt{EM}_\varphi) \stackrel{\text{def}}{=} \bigcup_{p \,\in\, \mathbf{IRP}(\mathtt{EM}_\varphi)} \{p_i \mid 1 \leqslant i < |p|\}$$

Based upon this definition we obtain a notion of lifetime optimality.

Definition 3.3.2 (Lifetime Optimality).

1. *An expression motion* $\mathtt{EM}_\varphi \in \mathcal{COEM}_\varphi$ *is* lifetime better *than an expression motion* $\mathtt{EM}'_\varphi \in \mathcal{COEM}_\varphi$*, in symbols* $\mathtt{EM}'_\varphi \precsim^{\varphi}_{lt} \mathtt{EM}_\varphi$*, if and only if*

   $$\mathit{LtRg}(\mathtt{EM}_\varphi) \subseteq \mathit{LtRg}(\mathtt{EM}'_\varphi)$$

2. *An expression motion* $\mathtt{EM}_\varphi \in \mathcal{COEM}_\varphi$ *is* lifetime optimal*, if and only if*

   $$\forall\, \mathtt{EM}'_\varphi \in \mathcal{COEM}_\varphi.\ \mathtt{EM}'_\varphi \precsim^{\varphi}_{lt} \mathtt{EM}_\varphi$$

It should be noted that $\precsim^{\varphi}_{lt}$ is a preorder like $\precsim^{\varphi}_{exp}$. However, we can easily see that lifetime optimal expression motions may only differ in insertions that are solely used immediately afterwards.

Figure 3.3 shows the lifetime range of busy expression motion for our running example.[9]

3.3.2 The Transformation

Whereas $\mathtt{BEM}_\varphi$ realizes an *as early as possible* strategy for the movement of expressions, lazy expression motion aims at placing computations *as late as possible*, but *as early as necessary* (in order to yield computational optimality). Technically, this is accomplished by delaying the $\mathtt{BEM}_\varphi$-initialisations on every program path reaching $\mathbf{e}$ as long as no redundancies are reestablished. Therefore, we introduce a predicate that captures, whether the $\mathtt{BEM}_\varphi$-insertions can be "delayed" to a program point.

[9] For the sake of presentation lifetime ranges are displayed as continuous ranges including entries of use-sites.

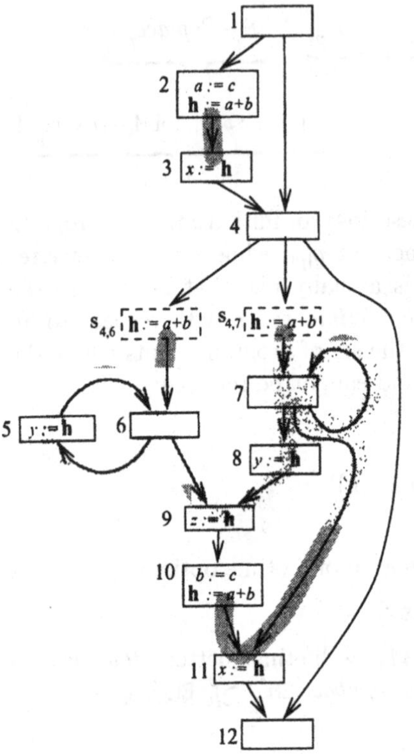

Fig. 3.3. The lifetime range associated with $\mathtt{BEM}_{a+b}$

Definition 3.3.3 (Delayability). *For any $\dot{n} \in \dot{N}$*

$$\mathit{Delayed}_{\dot{n}} \overset{\mathrm{def}}{\Leftrightarrow} \forall p \in \mathbf{P}[\dot{\mathbf{s}}, \dot{n}]\ \exists i \leqslant |p|.\ \mathit{Earliest}_{p_i} \wedge \forall i \leqslant j < |p|.\ \neg \mathit{Comp}_{p_j}$$

Similar to earliest computation points, which were considered upper borders of the region of safe program points, *latest* computation points are defined as the lower borders of the region of "delayable" program points.

Definition 3.3.4 (Latestness). *For any $\dot{n} \in \dot{N}$*

$$\mathit{Latest}_{\dot{n}} \overset{\mathrm{def}}{\Leftrightarrow} \mathit{Delayed}_{\dot{n}} \wedge (\mathit{Comp}_{\dot{n}} \vee \exists \dot{m} \in \mathit{succ}(\dot{n}).\ \neg \mathit{Delayed}_{\dot{m}})$$

Then lazy expression motion ($\mathtt{LEM}_{\varphi}$) is formally defined as follows:

- Insert initialisation statements $\mathbf{h}_{\varphi} := \varphi$ at every program point $\dot{n}$ satisfying *Latest*.
- Replace every original occurrence of φ by $\mathbf{h}_{\varphi}$.

As a result we have (cf. [KRS94a]):

Theorem 3.3.1 (Optimality Theorem for LEM_φ).

1. *LEM_φ is computationally optimal, i. e. $\text{LEM}_\varphi \in \mathcal{COEM}_\varphi$.*
2. *LEM_φ is lifetime optimal.*

Figure 3.4 shows the program that results from applying LEM_{a+b} to our running example of Figure 3.1. In fact, we can see that the corresponding lifetime range is now significantly smaller than the one of BEM_{a+b} (see Figure 3.3).

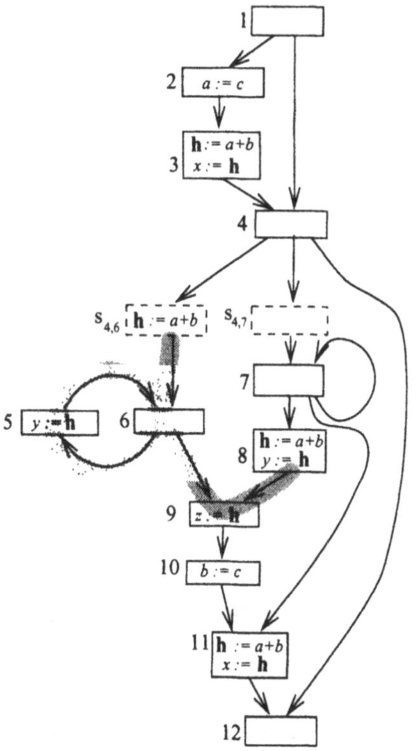

Fig. 3.4. LEM_{a+b} and the corresponding lifetime range

In [KRS94a] LEM_φ as presented here is called *almost lazy code motion.* This is due to the fact that the notion of lifetime ranges used there also incorporates purely local parts where initialisations are only used at the same program point immediately afterwards. In [KRS92, KRS94a] such initialisations are called *isolated* and are identified by means of an additional analysis. As mentioned before, in this monograph we abstract from local aspects of lifetime ranges for the sake of presentation. This, however, does not mean any restriction, since the local aspects can independently be treated by means of a postprocess. For instance, in Figure 3.4 we could eliminate the isolated initialisations at node 3 and 11 by reestablishing the original assignments

$x := a + b$. In contrast, the initialisation at node 8 cannot be eliminated, since **h** is also used at node 9.

3.4 A Classification of $\mathcal{COEM}_\varphi$

Busy and lazy expression motion are the two extremal computationally optimal strategies in expression motion, where delayability provides the interface between them. In fact, delayability is the key for a general characterisation of expression motions in $\mathcal{COEM}_\varphi$. This section provides some useful properties stressing this connection. As a first result we have:

Lemma 3.4.1 (Delayability Lemma).

1. $\forall\, \dot{n} \in \dot{N}.\ \mathit{Delayed}_{\dot{n}} \;\Rightarrow\; \mathit{DnSafe}_{\dot{n}}$
2. $\forall\, \dot{n} \in \dot{N}.\ \mathtt{BEM}_\varphi\text{-}\mathit{Correct}_{\dot{n}} \;\Rightarrow\; \mathit{Delayed}_{\dot{n}} \vee \mathtt{LEM}_\varphi\text{-}\mathit{Correct}_{\dot{n}}$

Proof. Part (1) can be found as Lemma 3.16(1) in [KRS94a]. For the proof of the second part let us assume

$$\neg \mathit{Delayed}_{\dot{n}} \tag{3.1}$$

Then it is left to show that $\mathtt{LEM}_\varphi\text{-}\mathit{Correct}_{\dot{n}}$ holds. The premise $\mathtt{BEM}_\varphi\text{-}\mathit{Correct}_{\dot{n}}$ implies by definition

$$\forall\, p \in \mathbf{P}[\dot{\mathbf{s}}, \dot{n}]\ \exists\, i \leqslant |p|.\ \mathit{Earliest}_{p_i} \ \wedge\ \forall i \leqslant j < |p|.\ \mathit{Transp}_{p_j}$$

As Definition 3.3.3 ensures that earliestness implies delayability the above characterisation particularly yields

$$\forall p \in \mathbf{P}[\dot{\mathbf{s}}, \dot{n}]\ \exists i \leqslant |p|.\ \mathit{Delayed}_{p_i} \ \wedge\ \forall i \leqslant j < |p|.\ \mathit{Transp}_{p_j} \tag{3.2}$$

Let us consider a path $p \in \mathbf{P}[\dot{\mathbf{s}}, \dot{n}]$ that meets the condition of Property (3.2). Then due to Assumption(3.1) there must be a largest index $i \leqslant j < |p|$ satisfying $\mathit{Delayed}_{p_j}$. Since this also implies Latest_{p_j} Property (3.2) delivers

$$\forall p \in \mathbf{P}[\dot{\mathbf{s}}, \dot{n}]\ \exists j \leqslant |p|.\ \mathit{Latest}_{p_j} \ \wedge\ \forall j \leqslant k < |p|.\ \mathit{Transp}_{p_k}$$

which means $\mathtt{LEM}_\varphi\text{-}\mathit{Correct}_{\dot{n}}$ as desired. □

The following lemma provides the proposed strong characterisation of an arbitrary computationally optimal expression motion $\mathtt{EM}_\varphi$ in terms of delayability. While the first part grants that $\mathtt{EM}_\varphi$-insertions are always within intervals of delayable program points, the second part ensures that there is exactly one insertion inside of such an interval.

Lemma 3.4.2 (Computational Optimality Lemma).
Let $\mathtt{EM}_\varphi \in \mathcal{COEM}_\varphi$. Then we have

1. $\forall \dot{n} \in \dot{N}.\ \mathtt{EM}_\varphi\text{-}Insert_{\dot{n}} \Rightarrow Delayed_{\dot{n}}$
2. *If p is an interval of program points between the earliest and latest program point, i. e. p is a path with $Earliest_{p_1}$, $Latest_{p_{|p|}}$ and $Delayed_{p_k} \wedge \neg Latest_{p_k}$ for any $i \leqslant k < |p|$, then p contains exactly one computation of φ after an application of $\mathtt{EM}_\varphi$:*

$$\dot{\exists}\ 1 \leqslant i \leqslant |p|.\ \mathtt{EM}_\varphi\text{-}Insert_{p_i} \vee (Comp_{p_i} \wedge \neg \mathtt{EM}_\varphi\text{-}Replace_{p_i})$$

Proof. Both parts are proved in [KRS94a], where they can be found in a slightly different formulation as Lemma 3.16(3) and Lemma 3.12(3). □

Remark 3.4.1. The condition in Lemma 3.4.2(2) can even be strengthened towards

$$\dot{\exists}\ 1 \leqslant i \leqslant |p|.\ \big(\mathtt{EM}_\varphi\text{-}Insert_{p_i} \vee (Comp_{p_i} \wedge \neg \mathtt{EM}_\varphi\text{-}Replace_{p_i})\big) \wedge \forall i \leqslant k \leqslant |p|.\ \mathtt{EM}_\varphi\text{-}Correct_{p_k}$$

This is obvious for $k = i$. Otherwise, we shall proceed by induction exploiting that no further insertions are allowed at program points p_k with $k > i$.

Remark (3.4.1) ensures that $\mathtt{EM}_\varphi\text{-}Correct_{\dot{n}}$ holds for any $\dot{n}$ being latest. Hence we particularly have:

Corollary 3.4.1 (Computational Optimality Corollary).

$$\forall\, \mathtt{EM}_\varphi \in \mathcal{COEM}_\varphi,\ \dot{n} \in \dot{N}.\ \mathtt{LEM}_\varphi\text{-}Correct_{\dot{n}} \Rightarrow \mathtt{EM}_\varphi\text{-}Correct_{\dot{n}}$$

Figure 3.5 shows the range of program points sharing the delayability property for our running example. According to Lemma 3.4.2(1) this predicate also fixes the range where any computationally optimal expression motion is restricted to in its choice of initialisation points. Note, however, that not every program point in this range is actually an insertion point of a computationally optimal expression motion. For instance, an insertion at node 7 or at the synthetic node $s_{7,7}$ would establish a loop invariant being absent in the original program. In contrast, the synthetic node $s_{7,11}$ is a possible insertion point of a computationally optimal expression motion that is neither earliest nor latest.

3.5 Computing $\mathtt{BEM}_\varphi$ and $\mathtt{LEM}_\varphi$

In this section we will briefly present the algorithms that are applied in order to actually compute busy and lazy expression motion. Both algorithms rely

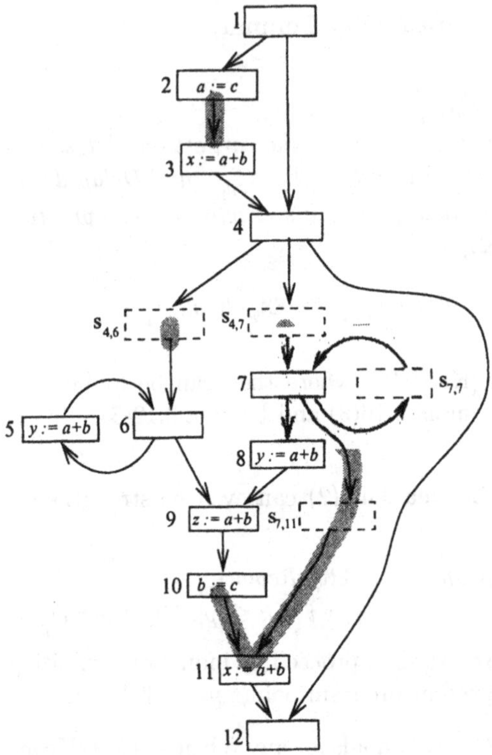

Fig. 3.5. Delayability as the range for valid insertions within $\mathcal{AEM}_{a+b}$

on the solution of appropriate unidirectional data flow analyses. The Boolean equation systems for both transformations are given in Table 3.1 and Table 3.2, respectively.

The equations are formulated in terms of a standard notation (cf. [MR79]), where "+", "." and "overlining" denote disjunction, conjunction and negation, respectively. Predicates refer to nodes of the flow graph and are divided into an entry- and exit-predicate, which is indicated by a preceding N and X, respectively. To distinguish involved in the fixed point iteration from the specified solutions the former ones are emphasised in a bold faced style. A proof of the coincidence of the computed solutions with their corresponding specified definitions is omitted, since it is straightforward along the lines of [KRS94a].

1. Safety Analyses:

a) Down-Safety Analysis

$$\mathbf{NDNSAFE}_n = Comp_n + Transp_n \cdot \mathbf{XDNSAFE}_n$$

$$\mathbf{XDNSAFE}_n = \begin{cases} false & \text{if } n = \mathbf{e} \\ \prod_{m \in succ(n)} \mathbf{NDNSAFE}_m & \text{otherwise} \end{cases}$$

⇝ Greatest fixed point solution: *NDnSafe* and *XDnSafe*

b) Up-Safety Analysis

$$\mathbf{NUPSAFE}_n = \begin{cases} false & \text{if } n = \mathbf{s} \\ \prod_{m \in pred(n)} \mathbf{XUPSAFE}_m & \text{otherwise} \end{cases}$$

$$\mathbf{XUPSAFE}_n = Transp_n \cdot (Comp_n + \mathbf{NUPSAFE}_n)$$

⇝ Greatest fixed point solution: *NUpSafe* and *XUpSafe*

2. Computation of Earliestness: (No data flow analysis!)

$$NEarliest_n \stackrel{\text{def}}{=} NDnSafe_n \cdot \begin{cases} true & \text{if } n = \mathbf{s} \\ \sum_{m \in pred(n)} \overline{XUpSafe_m + XDnSafe_m} & \text{otherwise} \end{cases}$$

$$XEarliest_n \stackrel{\text{def}}{=} XDnSafe_n \cdot \overline{Transp_n}$$

3. Insertion and Replacement Points of BEM$_\varphi$*:*

$$\text{BEM}_\varphi\text{-}NInsert_n \stackrel{\text{def}}{=} NEarliest_n$$

$$\text{BEM}_\varphi\text{-}XInsert_n \stackrel{\text{def}}{=} XEarliest_n$$

$$\text{BEM}_\varphi\text{-}Replace_n \stackrel{\text{def}}{=} Comp_n$$

Table 3.1. Computing BEM$_\varphi$

1. Perform steps 1) and 2) of Table 3.1.

2. Delayability Analysis:

$$\mathbf{NDELAYED}_n = \mathit{NEarliest}_n + \begin{cases} \mathit{false} & \mathit{if}\ \ n = \mathbf{s} \\ \prod_{m \in pred(n)} \mathbf{XDELAYED}_m & \mathit{otherwise} \end{cases}$$

$$\mathbf{XDELAYED}_n = \mathit{XEarliest}_n + \mathbf{NDELAYED}_n \cdot \overline{\mathit{Comp}_n}$$

$\rightsquigarrow$ Greatest fixed point solution: *NDelayed* and *XDelayed*

3. Computation of Latestness: (No data flow analysis!)

$$\mathit{N\text{-}Latest}_n \stackrel{\text{def}}{=} \mathit{NDelayed}_n \cdot \mathit{Comp}_n$$

$$\mathit{X\text{-}Latest}_n \stackrel{\text{def}}{=} \mathit{XDelayed}_n \cdot \sum_{m \in succ(n)} \overline{\mathit{NDelayed}_m}$$

4. Insertion and Replacement Points of $\mathtt{LEM}_\varphi$*:*

$$\mathtt{LEM}_\varphi\text{-}\mathit{NInsert}_n \stackrel{\text{def}}{=} \mathit{N\text{-}Latest}_n$$

$$\mathtt{LEM}_\varphi\text{-}\mathit{XInsert}_n \stackrel{\text{def}}{=} \mathit{X\text{-}Latest}_n$$

$$\mathtt{LEM}_\varphi\text{-}\mathit{Replace}_n \stackrel{\text{def}}{=} \mathit{Comp}_n$$

Table 3.2. Computing $\mathtt{LEM}_\varphi$

3.6 The Complexity

As presented in the prior section both the busy and the lazy single-expression approach to expression motion are based on unidirectional data flow analyses on the Boolean lattice. It is well-known that such equation systems can be solved efficiently by using an iterative workset algorithm [Hec77] whose workset can be updated sparsely on demand, i.e. only elements that actually changed their value are added to the workset. This is demonstrated in Algorithm 3.6.1 by using down-safety as a representative example.

Algorithm 3.6.1.

Input: An annotation of N with **NDNSAFE** and **XDNSAFE** being initialised as follows:

$$\mathbf{NDNSAFE}_n \stackrel{\text{def}}{=} \mathit{true}$$

$$\mathbf{XDNSAFE}_n \stackrel{\text{def}}{=} \begin{cases} \mathit{false} & \text{if } n = \mathbf{e} \\ \mathit{true} & \text{otherwise} \end{cases}$$

Output: The maximal solution to the Equation System in Table 3.1(1).

```
workset := N;
while workset ≠ ∅ do
    let n ∈ workset;
    workset := workset \ {n};
    NDNSAFE_n := Comp_n + XDNSAFE_n · Transp_n;
    if ¬NDNSAFE_n
      then
        forall m ∈ pred(n) do
          if XDNSAFE_m
            then
              XDNSAFE_m := false;
              workset := workset ∪ {m}
          fi
    fi
od
```

Since the **XDNSAFE**-value of nodes added to the workset is immediately set to false, each node is added at most once to the workset when processing the while-loop. On the other hand, each element from the workset can be processed in time proportional to the number of incident nodes. Thus we have the following result:

Theorem 3.6.1 (Complexity of $\mathtt{BEM}_\varphi$ and $\mathtt{LEM}_\varphi$). *Both $\mathtt{BEM}_\varphi$ and $\mathtt{LEM}_\varphi$ can be performed with run-time complexity of order $\mathcal{O}(|G|)$.*

4. Optimal Expression Motion: The Multiple-Expression View

In this chapter we demonstrate how the results of Chapter 3 can be profitably used for the development of algorithms that are able to cope with a set of program expressions simultaneously. The extension is almost straightforward if the universe of program expressions is *flat*, i. e. only contains expressions which are independent in terms of the subexpression relation. This, for instance, holds for intermediate level programs whose expressions are completely decomposed into three-address format. However, decomposing large expressions comes at the price of weakening the potential for expression motion, as such process introduces a bunch of new modification sites.[1]

Nonetheless, the assumption of a flat universe of expressions is fairly standard in expression motion since Morel's and Renvoise's seminal paper [MR79]: almost all relevant algorithms are based on the "separation paradigm" of Morel/Renvoise-like expression motion.

In this chapter we show how to go beyond this paradigm by examining expression motion with respect to arbitrary (structured) expression sets. Section 4.1 starts with a short introduction to the standard situation under a flat universe of expressions. Section 4.2 then introduces to the notion of expression motion for structured universes of expressions and proves computational optimality for the structured variants of busy and lazy expression motion. Section 4.3 first provides an adequate notion of lifetime optimality incorporating trade-offs between the lifetime ranges of composite expressions and their subexpressions, and then presents the graph theoretical foundation for the algorithms presented in Section 4.4 and 4.5. The latter section also contains the main result of the book: an efficient algorithm for computationally and lifetime optimal expression motion working on arbitrary structured universes of expressions.

4.1 Flat Expression Motion

Expression motion of single expressions as investigated in the previous section can directly be applied for the simultaneous treatment of all program

[1] Fortunately, even in the case of decomposed expressions the ideas developed in this chapter are applicable using assignment motion (cf. Section 7.4).

expressions from a *flat universe of expressions* Φ_{fl}, i.e. a set of expressions such that

$$\forall \varphi \in \Phi_{fl}.\ SubExpr^*_{\Phi_{fl}}(\varphi) = \{\varphi\}$$

Definition 4.1.1 (Flat Expression Motion). *Let* $\{\mathtt{EM}_\varphi \mid \varphi \in \Phi_{fl}\}$ *be a set of expression motions as introduced in Definition 3.1.1.*

1. *A* flat expression *motion with respect to* Φ_{fl} *is a program transformation that*
   a) *inserts initialisations at program points that are determined by the insert predicates of the individual transformations, i.e. for any* $\psi \in \Phi_{fl}$ *and* $\dot{n} \in \dot{N}$

   $$\mathtt{EM}_{\Phi_{fl}}\text{-}Insert^{\psi}_{\dot{n}} \overset{def}{\Leftrightarrow} \mathtt{EM}_{\psi}\text{-}Insert^{\psi}_{\dot{n}}$$

   b) *replaces the original occurrences of expression patterns that are determined by the replacement predicates of the individual transformations, i.e. for any* $\varphi \in \Phi_{fl}$ *and* $\dot{n} \in \dot{N}$

   $$\mathtt{EM}_{\Phi_{fl}}\text{-}Replace^{\varphi}_{\dot{n}} \overset{def}{\Leftrightarrow} \mathtt{EM}_{\psi}\text{-}Replace^{\varphi}_{\dot{n}}$$

2. *A flat expression motion* $\mathtt{EM}_{\Phi_{fl}}$ *is admissible, if and only if each component transformation* $\mathtt{EM}_\varphi$ *is admissible (in the sense of Definition 3.1.3).*

It should be particularly noted that multiple insertions at the same program point can be done in an arbitrary order.

4.1.1 Flat Busy and Lazy Expression Motion

The optimality criteria $\precsim^{\varphi}_{exp}$ and $\precsim^{\varphi}_{lt}$ of Section 3.2.1 and Section 3.3.1 can be naturally extended to Φ_{fl} yielding corresponding notions for $\precsim^{\Phi_{fl}}_{exp}$ and $\precsim^{\Phi_{fl}}_{lt}$, respectively:

- $\mathtt{EM}_{\Phi_{fl}} \precsim^{\Phi_{fl}}_{exp} \mathtt{EM}'_{\Phi_{fl}} \overset{def}{\Leftrightarrow} \forall \varphi \in \Phi_{fl}.\ \mathtt{EM}_\varphi \precsim^{\varphi}_{exp} \mathtt{EM}'_\varphi$
- $\mathtt{EM}_{\Phi_{fl}} \precsim^{\Phi_{fl}}_{lt} \mathtt{EM}'_{\Phi_{fl}} \overset{def}{\Leftrightarrow} \forall \varphi \in \Phi_{fl}.\ \mathtt{EM}_\varphi \precsim^{\varphi}_{lt} \mathtt{EM}'_\varphi$

Moreover, this also induces notions of computational and lifetime optimality, respectively. Denoting the flat versions of busy and lazy expression motion with respect to Φ_{fl} by $\mathtt{BEM}_{\Phi_{fl}}$ and $\mathtt{LEM}_{\Phi_{fl}}$, respectively, we have according to Theorem 3.2.1 and Theorem 3.3.1:

Theorem 4.1.1 (Flat Expression Motion Theorem).

1. $\mathtt{BEM}_{\Phi_{fl}}$ *is computationally optimal with respect to* Φ_{fl}.
2. $\mathtt{LEM}_{\Phi_{fl}}$ *is computationally and lifetime optimal with respect to* Φ_{fl}.

4.2 Structured Expression Motion

In this section we will go beyond the restrictive assumption on a flat universe of program expressions, i. e. we are now faced with universes containing composite expressions as well as their subexpressions. As we will see, this does not seriously influence the reasoning on computational optimality. In fact, computationally optimal expression motions can still be obtained quite easily by means of the individual transformations of Chapter 3. On the other hand, the situation changes significantly with respect to lifetime considerations. This observation did not enter the reasoning on the register pressure problem in expression motion papers [Bri92a]. Throughout the remainder of this chapter let us fix a *structured universe of expressions* Φ, i. e. a set of expressions with

$$\forall \psi \in \Phi,\ \varphi \in SubExpr(\psi).\ SubExpr^*_{\Phi}(\varphi) \neq \emptyset \Rightarrow \varphi \in \Phi \tag{4.1}$$

This condition excludes gaps in the immediate subexpression relation on Φ. In particular, it ensures that the minimal expressions in Φ^{min} are flat. It should be noted that Assumption (4.1) does not impose any restriction with respect to the usual application situation. Nonetheless, we could even do without this assumption, however, at the price of a highly technical presentation. Finally, we introduce two further notions. The (relative) *level* of an expression pattern $\psi \in \Phi$ is defined by

$$Lev_{\Phi}(\psi) \stackrel{\text{def}}{=} \begin{cases} 0 & \text{if } \psi \in \Phi^{min} \\ 1 + \max\limits_{\varphi \in SubExpr_{\Phi}(\psi)} Lev_{\Phi}(\varphi) & \text{if } \psi \in \Phi \setminus \Phi^{min} \end{cases}$$

Moreover, let Φ^i, $\Phi^{\leqslant i}$ and $\Phi^{<i}$ refer to the expression patterns of Φ with level i, levels lower or equal than i or levels strictly lower than i, respectively. Obviously, also $\Phi^{<i}$ and $\Phi^{\leqslant i}$ are structured sets of expressions, i. e. meet the condition of Assumption (4.1) with $\Phi^{<i}$ or $\Phi^{\leqslant i}$ in place of Φ, respectively.

For an expression ψ the maximal occurrences of subexpressions that are part of Φ are defined by

$$MaxSubExpr_{\Phi}(\psi) \stackrel{\text{def}}{=} \begin{cases} \{\psi\} & \text{if } \psi \in \Phi \\ \bigcup\limits_{\varphi \in SubExpr(\psi)} MaxSubExpr_{\Phi}(\varphi) & \text{otherwise} \end{cases}$$

Remark 4.2.1. Note that there might be both maximal and non-maximal occurrences of $\varphi \in MaxSubExpr_{\Phi}(\psi)$ with respect to a given expression ψ. For instance, for $\psi \stackrel{\text{def}}{=} (a+b)*((a+b)+c)$ and $\Phi \stackrel{\text{def}}{=} \{a+b, (a+b)+c\}$ we have $MaxSubExpr_{\Phi}(\psi) = \{a+b, (a+b)+c\}$. However, only the first occurrence of

$a+b$ in ψ is actually maximal as the second one is covered by the expression $(a+b)+c$. However, for a program expression under consideration the maximal occurrences can be marked as a by-product of the recursive definition.

4.2.1 Defining Structured Expression Motion

Essentially, expression motions with respect to Φ are still composed out of the individual transformations as introduced in Chapter 3. However, as an additional constraint, initialisations with respect to large expressions are required to be preceded by the initialisations belonging to their subexpressions, and replacements of large expressions at a program point must force the replacement of all their subexpressions. For both right-hand sides of initialisations as well as for replacements of original expressions we have to ensure that the largest subexpressions being available at the program point are actually replaced. More formally this reads as follows:

Definition 4.2.1 (Structured Expression Motion).

1. *A* structured expression motion $\mathtt{EM}_\Phi$ *with respect to* Φ *is a transformation composed out of a set of individual expression motion transformations* $\{\mathtt{EM}_\varphi \mid \varphi \in \Phi\}$ *satisfying the following constraint:*
   - $\forall \psi \in \Phi,\ \dot{n} \in \dot{N}.\ \mathtt{EM}_\psi\text{-}Insert_{\dot{n}}^{\psi} \Rightarrow \forall \varphi \in SubExpr_\Phi(\psi).\ \mathtt{EM}_\varphi\text{-}Correct_{\dot{n}}^{\varphi}$
   - $\forall \psi \in \Phi,\ \dot{n} \in \dot{N}.\ \mathtt{EM}_\psi\text{-}Replace_{\dot{n}}^{\psi} \Rightarrow \forall \varphi \in SubExpr_\Phi(\psi).\ \mathtt{EM}_\varphi\text{-}Replace_{\dot{n}}^{\varphi}$

   This induces insertions and replacements of the following kind:
   a) *The insertion points are determined by the insertion points of the individual transformations, i. e. for any* $\psi \in \Phi$ *and* $\dot{n} \in \dot{N}$ *we have:*
      - $\mathtt{EM}_\Phi\text{-}Insert_{\dot{n}}^{\psi} \overset{\text{def}}{\Leftrightarrow} \mathtt{EM}_\psi\text{-}Insert_{\dot{n}}^{\psi}$

      Insertions wrt. $\psi \in \Phi$ *are built according to the following rules:*
      i. *Initialisation statements are of the form* $\mathbf{h}_\psi := \psi'$*, where* ψ' *results from* ψ *by replacing every operand* $\varphi \in SubExpr_\Phi(\psi)$ *by* $\mathbf{h}_\varphi$*. If there is an initialisation of* $\mathbf{h}_\varphi$ *at the same program point then it has to precede the initialisation of* $\mathbf{h}_\psi$*.*
      ii. *Except for the ordering constraint imposed in (1(a)i) multiple insertions at a program point can be ordered arbitrarily.*
   b) *Replacements of* $\mathtt{EM}_\Phi$ *are restricted to maximal occurrences, i. e. for any* $\varphi \in \Phi$ *and* $\dot{n} \in \dot{N}$ *we have:*
      - $\mathtt{EM}_\Phi\text{-}Replace_{\dot{n}}^{\varphi} \overset{\text{def}}{\Leftrightarrow} \varphi \in MaxSubExpr_{\Phi_{\mathtt{Repl}}}(\varphi_{\dot{n}}^{\mathtt{RHS}})$,

      where $\varphi_{\dot{n}}^{\mathtt{RHS}}$ *addresses the right-hand side expression that belongs to* $\dot{n}$ *and* $\Phi_{\mathtt{Repl}} \overset{\text{def}}{=} \{\varphi' \in \Phi \mid \mathtt{EM}_{\varphi'}\text{-}Replace_{\dot{n}}^{\varphi'}\}$*. For an expression* φ *that satisfies* $\mathtt{EM}_\Phi\text{-}Replace_{\dot{n}}^{\varphi}$ *some original occurrences in* $\varphi_{\mathtt{RHS}}$ *are replaced by* $\mathbf{h}_\varphi$ *(see Remark 4.2.1 for details).*
2. *A structured expression motion* $\mathtt{EM}_\Phi$ *is* admissible, *if and only if every component transformation* $\mathtt{EM}_\varphi$ *is admissible (in the sense of Definition 3.1.3).*

Figure 4.1 shows an admissible expression motion with respect to the set of expressions $\{(a+b)+c, a+b\}$. Let us denote the set of admissible structured expression motions with respect to Φ by $\mathcal{AEM}_\Phi$.

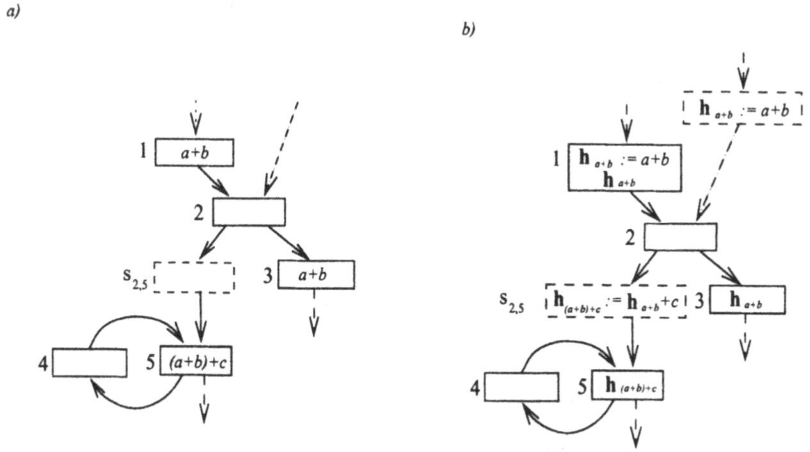

Fig. 4.1. Admissible structured expression motion with respect to the universe of expression $\Phi = \{a+b, (a+b)+c\}$

4.2.2 Computationally Optimal Structured Expression Motion

The preorder $\precsim^{\varphi}_{exp}$ on $\mathcal{AEM}_\varphi$ can be extended to a preorder $\precsim^{\Phi}_{exp}$ on $\mathcal{AEM}_\Phi$ in the same way as in Section 4.1:

– $\mathrm{EM}_\Phi \precsim^{\Phi}_{exp} \mathrm{EM}'_\Phi \overset{\mathrm{def}}{\Leftrightarrow} \forall \varphi \in \Phi.\ \mathrm{EM}_\varphi \precsim^{\varphi}_{exp} \mathrm{EM}'_\varphi$

This straightforward extension is feasible, since a structured expression motion results exactly in the same number of φ-computations on any path as its individual component for φ does. In fact, one can easily check that every φ-initialisation of EM_Φ corresponds to a φ-initialisation of EM_φ and vice versa. Similarly, every original computation of φ that is not replaced by EM_Φ is not replaced by EM_φ and vice versa. $\precsim^{\Phi}_{exp}$ also induces a corresponding notion of computational optimality. Let us denote the set of computationally optimal expression motions among $\mathcal{AEM}_\Phi$ by $\mathcal{COEM}_\Phi$.

Although the definition of computational optimality is particularly simple, it is not immediately obvious that $\mathcal{COEM}_\Phi$ is not empty. Fortunately, we can easily obtain a computationally optimal structured expression motion either by using busy expression motion or using lazy expression motion as individual components. This was also noticed by Drechsler and Stadel [DS93] who presented an adaption of our algorithm for lazy expression motion that deals with multiple expressions. Unfortunately, however, their presentation suggests that lifetime optimality carries over from the individual transformations, too. This, however, is based on a purely technical view of lifetime ranges that is not adequate. In section 4.2.3 we will discuss a reasonable notion of lifetime ranges, and present an algorithm that adequately deals with the lifetimes of multiple temporaries simultaneously. Before, however, let us first investigate the easier task of obtaining computational optimality and present the structured variants for both busy and lazy expression motion, respectively.

4.2.2.1 Structured Busy Expression Motion. All properties on the interdependencies between predicate values of large expressions and their subexpressions are based on the following trivial relationship among the local properties:

Lemma 4.2.1 (Structured Local Property Lemma).

1. $\forall \psi \in \Phi, \varphi \in SubExpr_\Phi(\psi),\ \dot{n} \in \dot{N}.\ Transp_{\dot{n}}^{\psi} \;\Rightarrow\; Transp_{\dot{n}}^{\varphi}$
2. $\forall \psi \in \Phi, \varphi \in SubExpr_\Phi(\psi),\ \dot{n} \in \dot{N}.\ Comp_{\dot{n}}^{\psi} \;\Rightarrow\; Comp_{\dot{n}}^{\varphi}$

A central property for combining the individual busy expression motion transformations in a structured way is that subexpressions are essentially more mobile with respect to hoistings than their superexpressions. In terms of the safety predicates this reads as:

Lemma 4.2.2 (Structured Safety Lemma).

1. $\forall \psi \in \Phi, \varphi \in SubExpr_\Phi(\psi),\ \dot{n} \in \dot{N}.\ UpSafe_{\dot{n}}^{\psi} \;\Rightarrow\; UpSafe_{\dot{n}}^{\varphi}$
2. $\forall \psi \in \Phi, \varphi \in SubExpr_\Phi(\psi),\ \dot{n} \in \dot{N}.\ DnSafe_{\dot{n}}^{\psi} \;\Rightarrow\; DnSafe_{\dot{n}}^{\varphi}$

Proof. The lemma trivially follows from the definition of up- and down-safety (cf. Definition 3.1.2) and the Lemma 4.2.1. □

For the upper borderline of the region of safe program points, the earliest program points, we additionally have:

Lemma 4.2.3 (Structured Earliestness Lemma).

$$\forall \psi \in \Phi, \varphi \in SubExpr_\Phi(\psi),\ \dot{n} \in \dot{N}.\ Earliest_{\dot{n}}^{\psi} \;\Rightarrow\; \texttt{BEM}_\Phi\text{-}Correct_{\dot{n}}^{\varphi}$$

Proof. We have

$$\begin{array}{rcl} & & Earliest_{\dot{n}}^{\psi} \\ [\text{Definition } Earliest] & \Rightarrow & Safe_{\dot{n}}^{\psi} \\ [\text{Lemma 3.1.1 \& 4.2.2}] & \Rightarrow & Safe_{\dot{n}}^{\varphi} \\ [\text{Lemma 3.2.1}] & \Rightarrow & \texttt{BEM}_\Phi\text{-}Correct_{\dot{n}}^{\varphi} \end{array}$$

□

Lemma 4.2.3 is sufficient to draw the conclusion that the individual busy expression motion transformations induce a structured expression motion in the sense of Definition 4.2.1. Moreover, admissibility and computational optimality of the individual transformations trivially carry over to the structured variant yielding:

Theorem 4.2.1 (Structured Busy Expression Motion Theorem). $\texttt{BEM}_\Phi$ *is*

1. *admissible, i. e.* $\texttt{BEM}_\Phi \in \mathcal{AEM}_\Phi$.
2. *computationally optimal with respect to* Φ, *i. e.* $\texttt{BEM}_\Phi \in \mathcal{COEM}_\Phi$.

4.2.2.2 Structured Lazy Expression Motion. The structured version of busy expression motion presented in the previous section evolved as the natural combination of its individual components. A dual optimal structured expression motion is induced by the combination of lazy component transformations. As mentioned the intuitive reason for the well-behavedness of $\texttt{BEM}_\Phi$ is the fact that large expressions are less mobile with respect to hoistings than their subexpressions. With regard to sinkings being based on the delayability predicate the situation becomes contrary, as now large expressions are more mobile than their subexpressions. Intuitively, this is because original occurrences of large expressions are blockades for all their subexpressions. A more formal argument is given in the forthcoming Lemma 4.2.5. Before, we shall investigate a result about correctness predicates of structured expression motions.

Lemma 4.2.4 (Structured Correctness Lemma).
Let $\texttt{EM}_\Phi \in \mathcal{AEM}_\Phi$, $\psi \in \Phi$, $\varphi \in \mathit{SubExpr}_\Phi(\psi)$ *and* $\dot{n} \in \dot{N}$. *Then*

$$\texttt{EM}_\Phi\text{-}\mathit{Correct}_{\dot{n}}^{\psi} \;\Rightarrow\; \texttt{EM}_\Phi\text{-}\mathit{Correct}_{\dot{n}}^{\varphi}$$

Proof.

$$\texttt{EM}_\psi\text{-}\mathit{Correct}_{\dot{n}}^{\psi}$$

[Definition $\texttt{EM}_\Phi$-*Correct*]

$$\Rightarrow\; \forall\, p \in \mathbf{P}[\dot{\mathbf{s}}, \dot{n}]\; \exists\, i \leqslant |p|.\; \texttt{EM}_\Phi\text{-}\mathit{Insert}_{p_i}^{\psi} \;\wedge\; \forall\, i \leqslant j < |p|.\; \mathit{Transp}_{p_j}^{\psi}$$

[Lemma 4.2.1(1)]

$$\Rightarrow\; \forall\, p \in \mathbf{P}[\dot{\mathbf{s}}, \dot{n}]\; \exists\, i \leqslant |p|.\; \texttt{EM}_\Phi\text{-}\mathit{Insert}_{p_i}^{\psi} \;\wedge\; \forall\, i \leqslant j < |p|.\; \mathit{Transp}_{p_j}^{\varphi}$$

[Definition 4.2.1(1)]

$$\Rightarrow\; \forall\, p \in \mathbf{P}[\dot{\mathbf{s}}, \dot{n}]\; \exists\, i \leqslant |p|.\; \texttt{EM}_\Phi\text{-}\mathit{Correct}_{p_i}^{\varphi} \;\wedge\; \forall\, i \leqslant j < |p|.\; \mathit{Transp}_{p_j}^{\varphi}$$

[Definition $\texttt{EM}_\Phi$-*Correct*]

$$\Rightarrow\; \forall\, p \in \mathbf{P}[\dot{\mathbf{s}}, \dot{n}]\; \exists\, j \leqslant |p|.\; \texttt{EM}_\Phi\text{-}\mathit{Insert}_{p_j}^{\varphi} \;\wedge\; \forall\, j \leqslant l < |p|.\; \mathit{Transp}_{p_l}^{\varphi}$$

[Definition $\texttt{EM}_\Phi$-*Correct*]

$$\Rightarrow\; \texttt{EM}_\Phi\text{-}\mathit{Correct}_{\dot{n}}^{\varphi}$$

□

Based on Lemma 4.2.4 we obtain the complement to Lemma 4.2.2.

Lemma 4.2.5 (Structured Delayability Lemma).
Let $\psi \in \Phi, \varphi \in SubExpr_\Phi(\psi)$ *and* $\dot{n} \in \dot{N}$. *Then*

1. $Delayed_{\dot{n}}^{\psi} \Rightarrow Delayed_{\dot{n}}^{\varphi} \vee \mathbf{LEM}_\Phi\text{-}Correct_{\dot{n}}^{\varphi}$
2. $Delayed_{\dot{n}}^{\varphi} \wedge DnSafe_{\dot{n}}^{\psi} \Rightarrow Delayed_{\dot{n}}^{\psi}$
3. $Delayed_{\dot{n}}^{\psi} \wedge \neg Earliest_{\dot{n}}^{\psi} \Rightarrow \neg Earliest_{\dot{n}}^{\varphi}$

Proof. Considering part (1) let us assume $\underbrace{\neg\mathbf{LEM}_\Phi\text{-}Correct_{\dot{n}}^{\varphi}}_{(\dagger)}$. Then

$$\begin{array}{rl} & Delayed_{\dot{n}}^{\psi} \\ [\text{Lemma 3.4.1(1)}] & \Rightarrow \; DnSafe_{\dot{n}}^{\psi} \\ [\text{Lemma 3.2.1}] & \Rightarrow \; \mathbf{BEM}_\Phi\text{-}Correct_{\dot{n}}^{\psi} \\ [\text{Lemma 4.2.4}] & \Rightarrow \; \mathbf{BEM}_\Phi\text{-}Correct_{\dot{n}}^{\varphi} \\ [\text{Assumption } (\dagger) \; \& \; \text{Lemma 3.4.1(2)}] & \Rightarrow \; Delayed_{\dot{n}}^{\varphi} \end{array}$$

For the proof of the second point we have

$$\begin{array}{ll} & DnSafe_{\dot{n}}^{\psi} \\ [\text{Def. } DnSafe \; \& \; Earliest] & \\ & \Rightarrow \; \forall\, p \in \mathbf{P}[\dot{\mathbf{s}}, \dot{n}] \; \exists\, i \leqslant |p|.\; Earliest_{p_i}^{\psi} \; \wedge \\ & \qquad\qquad \forall\, i \leqslant j < |p|.\; Transp_{p_j}^{\psi} \wedge DnSafe_{p_j}^{\psi} \\ [(4.2)] & \Rightarrow \; \forall\, p \in \mathbf{P}[\dot{\mathbf{s}}, \dot{n}] \; \exists\, i \leqslant |p|.\; Earliest_{p_i}^{\psi} \wedge \forall\, i \leqslant j < |p|.\; \neg Comp_{p_j}^{\psi} \\ [\text{Def. } Delayed] & \\ & \Rightarrow \; Delayed_{\dot{n}}^{\psi} \end{array}$$

There remains the proof of Implication (4.2). To this end let us assume a path $p \in \mathbf{P}[\dot{\mathbf{s}}, \dot{n}]$ and an index $i \leqslant |p|$ such that

$$Earliest_{p_i}^{\psi} \wedge \forall\, i \leqslant j < |p|.\; Transp_{p_j}^{\psi} \wedge DnSafe_{p_j}^{\psi}$$

Suppose there is an index $i \leqslant j < |p|$ such that $Comp_{p_j}^{\psi}$ holds. According to Lemma 4.2.1(2) this implies $Comp_{p_j}^{\varphi}$. Exploiting the other condition of the premise, namely that $Delayed_{\dot{n}}^{\varphi}$ holds, there must be an index l with $j < l \leqslant |p|$ satisfying $Earliest_{p_l}^{\varphi}$. By the definition of earliestness (see Definition 3.2.2 and Remark 3.2.1) this either implies $\neg Transp_{p_{l-1}}^{\varphi}$ or $\neg Safe_{p_{l-1}}^{\varphi}$. According to Lemma 4.2.1(1) the first case is in contradiction to the assumption $Transp_{p_{l-1}}^{\psi}$. Furthermore, according to Lemma 4.2.2 the second case would imply $\neg Safe_{p_{l-1}}^{\psi}$, which is in contradiction to the assumption $DnSafe_{p_j}^{\psi}$.

For the third part we have

$$\neg Earliest_{\dot n}^{\psi} \;\wedge\; Delayed_{\dot n}^{\psi}$$

[Definition *Delayed* & *Latest*]

$$\Rightarrow\;\; \forall\, \dot m \in pred(\dot n).\; Delayed_{\dot m}^{\psi} \;\wedge\; \neg Latest_{\dot m}^{\psi}$$

[Lemma 3.4.1(1) & Definition *Latest*]

$$\Rightarrow\;\; \forall\, \dot m \in pred(\dot n).\; DnSafe_{\dot m}^{\psi} \;\wedge\; \neg Comp_{\dot m}^{\psi}$$

[Lemma 4.2.1(2) & 4.2.2(2)]

$$\Rightarrow\;\; \forall\, \dot m \in pred(\dot n). DnSafe_{\dot m}^{\varphi} \;\wedge\; \neg Comp_{\dot m}^{\varphi}$$

[Lemma 3.2.1]

$$\Rightarrow\;\; \forall\, \dot m \in pred(\dot n).\; \mathtt{BEM}_{\Phi}\text{-}Correct_{\dot m}^{\varphi} \;\wedge\; DnSafe_{\dot m}^{\varphi} \;\wedge\; \neg Comp_{\dot m}^{\varphi}$$

[Definition *DnSafe*]

$$\Rightarrow\;\; \forall\, \dot m \in pred(\dot n).\; \mathtt{BEM}_{\Phi}\text{-}Correct_{\dot m}^{\varphi} \;\wedge\; Transp_{\dot m}^{\varphi}$$

[$\mathtt{BEM}_{\varphi} \in \mathcal{COEM}_{\varphi}$]

$$\Rightarrow\;\; \neg Earliest_{\dot n}^{\varphi}$$

□

Finally, as an application of Lemma 4.2.5 we get:

Lemma 4.2.6 (Structured Latestness Lemma).

$$\forall\, \psi \in \Phi, \varphi \in SubExpr_{\Phi}(\psi),\; \dot n \in \dot N.\; Latest_{\dot n}^{\psi} \;\Rightarrow\; \mathtt{LEM}_{\Phi}\text{-}Correct_{\dot n}^{\varphi}$$

Proof. By definition $Latest_{\dot n}^{\psi}$ implies

$$Delayed_{\dot n}^{\psi} \;\wedge\; (Comp_{\dot n}^{\psi} \;\vee\; \exists \dot m \in succ(\dot n).\; \neg Delayed_{\dot m}^{\psi})$$

We investigate both cases of the disjunction separately. First we have

$$\begin{array}{rll} & & Delayed_{\dot n}^{\psi} \;\wedge\; Comp_{\dot n}^{\psi} \\ \text{[Lemma 4.2.5(1)]} & \Rightarrow & (Delayed_{\dot n}^{\varphi} \;\vee\; \mathtt{LEM}_{\psi}\text{-}Correct_{\dot n}^{\varphi}) \;\wedge\; Comp_{\dot n}^{\psi} \\ \text{[Lemma 4.2.1(2)]} & \Rightarrow & (Delayed_{\dot n}^{\varphi} \;\vee\; \mathtt{LEM}_{\varphi}\text{-}Correct_{\dot n}^{\varphi}) \;\wedge\; Comp_{\dot n}^{\varphi} \\ \text{[Definition } Latest\text{]} & \Rightarrow & Latest_{\dot n}^{\varphi} \;\vee\; \mathtt{LEM}_{\varphi}\text{-}Correct_{\dot n}^{\varphi} \\ \text{[Definition } \mathtt{LEM}_{\Phi}\text{-}Correct\text{]} & \Rightarrow & \mathtt{LEM}_{\Phi}\text{-}Correct_{\dot n}^{\varphi} \end{array}$$

Otherwise, we may assume $\neg Comp_{\dot n}^{\psi}$ and argue as follows:

$$\begin{array}{rll} & & Delayed_{\dot n}^{\psi} \;\wedge\; \exists\, \dot m \in succ(\dot n).\; \neg Delayed_{\dot m}^{\psi} \\ \text{[Lemma 3.4.1(1)]} & \Rightarrow & DnSafe_{\dot n}^{\psi} \;\wedge\; \exists\, \dot m \in succ(\dot n).\; \neg Delayed_{\dot m}^{\psi} \\ \multicolumn{3}{l}{\text{[Definition } DnSafe \text{ \& Assumption } \neg Comp_{\dot n}^{\psi}\text{]}} \\ & \Rightarrow & \exists \dot m \in succ(\dot n).\; DnSafe_{\dot m}^{\psi} \;\wedge\; \neg Delayed_{\dot m}^{\psi} \\ \text{[Lemma 4.2.5(2)]} & \Rightarrow & \underbrace{\exists\, \dot m \in succ(\dot n).\; \neg Delayed_{\dot m}^{\varphi}}_{(\star)} \end{array}$$

As $Latest_n^{\psi}$ implies $Delayed_n^{\psi}$, Lemma 4.2.5(1) yields either $\texttt{LEM}_{\varphi}$-$Correct_n^{\varphi}$ or $Delayed_n^{\varphi}$. In the first case there is nothing to show, whereas in the other case Property (★) immediately yields $Latest_n^{\varphi}$, which particularly implies $\texttt{LEM}_{\varphi}$-$Correct_n^{\varphi}$, too. □

Lemma 4.2.6 is the reason that the individual lazy expression motion transformations can be combined to a structured variant in the sense of Definition 4.2.1. Moreover, as for $\texttt{BEM}_{\Phi}$ admissibility and computational optimality carry over directly from the individual transformations. Hence we obtain:

Theorem 4.2.2 (Structured Lazy Expression Motion Theorem). *$\texttt{LEM}_{\Phi}$ is*

1. *admissible, i. e. $\texttt{LEM}_{\Phi} \in \mathcal{AEM}_{\Phi}$*
2. *computationally optimal with respect to Φ, i. e. $\texttt{LEM}_{\Phi} \in \mathcal{COEM}_{\Phi}$.*

4.2.3 Lifetime Optimal Structured Expression Motion

Theorem 4.2.2 gives rise to the question, if $\texttt{LEM}_{\Phi}$ also preserves lifetime optimality of its component transformations. However, unlike $\precsim_{exp}^{\Phi}$ the preorder $\precsim_{lt}^{\Phi}$ cannot be composed straightforwardly out of the preorders being associated with the single expressions. Intuitively, the lack of compositionality is due to dependencies between lifetimes associated with large expressions and their subexpressions. The following section is devoted to this phenomenon.

4.2.3.1 Trade-Offs between the Lifetimes of Temporaries. To illustrate the problem let us consider the program in Figure 4.2.[2] The point of this example is that the structured extension to lazy expression motion would suggest to initialise the large term $a * b + c * d$ as well as its subterms $a * b$ and $c * d$ as late as possible. However, this is not a good choice in terms of the "overall" lifetimes of temporaries. Using this strategy two temporaries are necessary for keeping the values of the proper subterms $a * b$ and $c * d$. It should be noted that both operand expressions have to be evaluated prior to their original occurrences at node 1 (see Figure 4.2(b)). A better choice in terms of the overall lifetimes would be to initialise the large expression as early as possible. This way only the value of the large expression has to be stored in a temporary along the path from node 1 to node 2 as it is illustrated in Figure 4.2(c).

This example shows that we have to reconsider the notion of lifetimes of temporaries. The main difference in comparison to the flat approach is that now lifetimes not only may end at original computations, but may end at initialisation sites of a larger original expressions as well. In other words, the choice of a particular insertion point for a complex expression does not only affect

[2] For brevity we use $\mathbf{h}_1$, $\mathbf{h}_2$ and $\mathbf{h}_3$ instead of $\mathbf{h}_{a*b}$, $\mathbf{h}_{c*d}$ and $\mathbf{h}_{a*b+c*d}$, respectively.

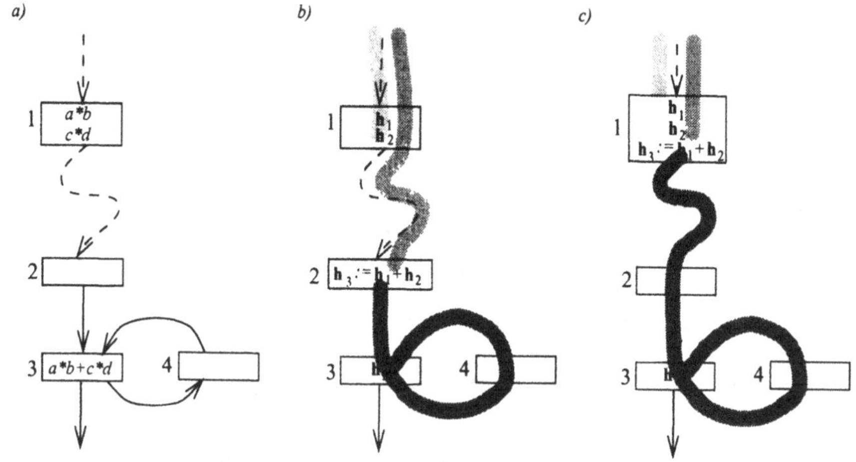

Fig. 4.2. Trade-offs between the lifetimes of temporaries

the lifetime of the associated temporary but may as well influence the lifetimes of the temporaries of its subexpressions To come to a reasonable notion of lifetimes in the case of structured expression motion let us first reconsider the notion of insertion-replacement paths as given in Section 3.3.1. For the reasons explained above we replace this notion by a notion of insertion-use paths.

$$\mathbf{IUP}(\mathtt{EM}_\Phi, \varphi) \stackrel{\text{def}}{=} \{\, p \in \mathbf{P} \mid |p| \geqslant 2 \wedge \underbrace{\mathtt{EM}_\Phi\text{-}Insert^{\varphi}_{p_1}}_{i)} \wedge \underbrace{Used^{\mathtt{EM}_\Phi}_{\varphi}\, p_{|p|}}_{ii)} \wedge \underbrace{\forall 1 < i \leqslant |p|.\ \neg \mathtt{EM}_\Phi\text{-}Insert^{\varphi}_{p_i}}_{iii)} \},$$

where the $Used^{\mathtt{EM}_\Phi}$ predicate reflects replacements of original computations as well as usages at initialisation points of larger expression patterns:

$$Used^{\mathtt{EM}_\Phi}_{\varphi}\, \dot{n} \;\Leftrightarrow\; \mathtt{EM}_\Phi\text{-}Replace^{\varphi}_{\dot{n}} \;\vee\; \exists\, \psi \in SupExpr_\Phi(\varphi).\ \mathtt{EM}_\Phi\text{-}Insert^{\psi}_{\dot{n}}$$

Like in Definition 3.3.1 the parts of the definition marked (i) and (ii) capture initialisations at node p_1 and usages at node $p_{|p|}$, respectively. The part indicated by (iii) establishes the correspondence between (i) and (ii). Moreover, the definition coincides with the former notion for maximal expressions in Φ. Hence

$$\forall\, \varphi \in \Phi^{max}.\ \mathbf{IUP}(\mathtt{EM}_\Phi, \varphi) \;=\; \mathbf{IRP}(\mathtt{EM}_\varphi, \varphi). \tag{4.3}$$

The usage of insertion-use paths instead of insertion-replacement paths is the only difference in a modified notion of lifetime ranges. Hence for $\mathtt{EM}_\Phi \in \mathcal{AEM}_\Phi$ the *structured lifetime range* with respect to $\varphi \in \Phi$ is defined by:

Definition 4.2.2 (Structured Lifetime Ranges).

$$SLtRg(\mathtt{EM}_\Phi,\varphi) \stackrel{\text{def}}{=} \bigcup_{p \,\in\, \mathbf{IUP}(\mathtt{EM}_\Phi,\varphi)} \{p_i \mid 1 \leqslant i < |p|\}$$

An important observation is that a program point being part of a structured lifetime range has a uniform history with respect to this lifetime range, i. e. the associated temporary is initialised on every program path leading to the program point. More formally, this reads as:

Lemma 4.2.7 (Lifetime Range Lemma). *Let* $\mathtt{EM}_\Phi \in \mathcal{AEM}_\Phi$. *Then*

$$\forall\, \varphi \in \Phi,\ \dot{n} \in \dot{N}.\ \dot{n} \in SLtRg(\mathtt{EM}_\Phi,\varphi) \Rightarrow \mathtt{EM}_\Phi\text{-}Correct^{\varphi}_{\dot{n}}$$

Proof. Let $\varphi \in SLtRg(\mathtt{EM}_\Phi,\varphi)$. Then Definition 4.2.2 ensures that there is an insertion-use path p with $|p| \geqslant 2$ such that

$$\underbrace{\mathtt{EM}_\Phi\text{-}Insert^{\varphi}_{p_1}}_{i)} \wedge \underbrace{Used^{\mathtt{EM}_\Phi}_{\varphi}\, p_{|p|}}_{ii)} \wedge \underbrace{1 < i \leqslant |p|.\ \neg \mathtt{EM}_\Phi\text{-}Insert^{\varphi}_{p_i}}_{iii)}$$

and there is an index $1 \leqslant k < |p|$ such that $p_k = \dot{n}$. Due to the initialisation conditions of structured expression motion Proposition (ii) ensures $\mathtt{EM}_\Phi\text{-}Correct^{\varphi}_{p_{|p|}}$. Using the absence of other insertions according to Condition (iii) we obviously have

$$\forall 1 \leqslant i \leqslant |p|.\ \mathtt{EM}_\Phi\text{-}Correct^{\varphi}_{p_i},$$

which particularly forces $\mathtt{EM}_\Phi\text{-}Correct^{\varphi}_{\dot{n}}$. □

4.2.3.2 Lifetime Optimality. Under the new notion of lifetime ranges it is obviously not possible to keep all lifetime ranges as small as possible. Our example in Figure 4.2 already showed that such an aim would indeed be too narrow, since the overall costs imposed by the usage of temporaries do not depend on the actual names[3] of lifetime ranges including a program point but rather on their number, which leads to a new notion of the lifetime-better preorder capturing their cumulated effects.

Definition 4.2.3 (Lifetime Optimality).

1. *An expression motion* $\mathtt{EM}_\Phi \in \mathcal{COEM}_\Phi$ *is* lifetime better *than an expression motion* $\mathtt{EM}'_\Phi \in \mathcal{COEM}_\Phi$*, if and only if for any* $\dot{n} \in \dot{N}$

$$|\{\varphi \in \Phi \mid \dot{n} \in SLtRg(\mathtt{EM}_\Phi,\varphi)\}| \leqslant |\{\varphi \in \Phi \mid \dot{n} \in SLtRg(\mathtt{EM}'_\Phi,\varphi)\}|$$

As before, we will use the notion $\mathtt{EM}'_\Phi \precsim^{\Phi}_{lt} \mathtt{EM}_\Phi$ *to refer to this situation.*

[3] That means the names of their associated expressions.

2. *An expression motion* $\mathtt{EM}_\Phi \in \mathcal{COEM}_\Phi$ *is* lifetime optimal *with respect to* Φ*, if and only if it is lifetime better than any other transformation in* $\mathcal{COEM}_\Phi$.

It should be noted that Lemma 4.2.7 ensures that the cumulation of lifetime ranges is adequate to model the usage of temporaries at a program point, as the temporaries are uniformly initialised on every program path that reaches the program point. For this reason the number of occupied temporaries at a program point does not depend on the particular history when reaching the program point.

As an immediate consequence of Definition 4.2.3 we have as a first result:

Lemma 4.2.8 (Lifetime Optimality Lemma). *Any lifetime optimal expression motion* $\mathtt{EM}_\Phi \in \mathcal{COEM}_\Phi$ *is lifetime better than both* $\mathtt{BEM}_\Phi$ *and* $\mathtt{LEM}_\Phi$.

4.2.3.3 Inductive Lifetime Optimality. In addition to the previous notion we also consider an alternative notion of lifetime optimality that is based on the special role of lazy expression motion in the flat approach. Here the fundamental observation is that the minimal expression patterns of Φ^{min} cannot participate in any profitable trade-offs with their subexpressions. Hence this suggests to determine their insertion points by means of the lazy expression motion strategy. Using the minimal expression patterns as the seed for initialisations with respect to more complex expression patterns leads to an inductive notion of lifetime optimality:

Definition 4.2.4 (Inductive Lifetime Optimality).
An expression motion $\mathtt{EM}_\Phi \in \mathcal{COEM}_\Phi$ *is* inductively lifetime optimal *with respect to* Φ*, if and only if it satisfies the following inductive characterisation:*

1. $\mathtt{EM}_{\Phi^0}$ *is lifetime optimal and*
2. $\forall i > 0,\ \mathtt{EM}'_\Phi \in \mathcal{COEM}_\Phi.\ \mathtt{EM}'_{\Phi^{<i}} = \mathtt{EM}_{\Phi^{<i}} \Rightarrow \mathtt{EM}'_{\Phi^{\leqslant i}} \precsim_{lt}^{\Phi^{\leqslant i}} \mathtt{EM}_{\Phi^{\leqslant i}}$

Essentially, the inductive notion differs from the full notion in its restricted field of view: it only aims at optimising the next local step from level $i-1$ towards level i. In fact, in general it leads to results that are strictly weaker than their fully lifetime optimal counterparts. On the other hand, a lifetime optimal program is not necessarily an inductively lifetime optimal one, too. Later in Section 4.5.2 we will discuss the limitations of inductive lifetime optimality in more details. Nonetheless, the reason that we are also considering this notion are twofold: first, the restricted notion leads to situations where trade-offs between lifetime ranges are much more evident. In fact, our algorithm that reaches full lifetime optimality would probably not have been found without the previous work on the inductive case. A second point that speaks for the inductive notion is the fact that a solution can be computed more efficiently in terms of computational complexity than one that meets the general condition (cf. Section 4.6).

Inductively lifetime optimality is only tailored towards improving lazy expression motion, while busy expression motion might do better by chance. Hence as a counterpart to Lemma 4.2.8 a simple induction proof shows:

Lemma 4.2.9 (Inductive Lifetime Optimality Lemma).
Any inductively lifetime optimal expression motion $\mathtt{EM}_\Phi \in \mathcal{COEM}_\Phi$ *is lifetime better than* $\mathtt{LEM}_\Phi$, *i. e.*

$$\mathtt{LEM}_\Phi \precsim_{lt}^{\Phi} \mathtt{EM}_\Phi$$

4.3 A Graph Theoretical View on Trade-Offs between Lifetimes

In this section we present the foundation for the development of our algorithms for lifetime optimal and inductively lifetime optimal expression motion. Reduced to its abstract kernel this leads to a graph theoretical problem that can be solved efficiently by using well-known matching techniques for bipartite graphs.

4.3.1 Motivation

As a motivation let us consider a restricted situation where, at a given program point, we are only faced with two kinds of expressions: elementary ones and composite ones whose operands are elementary. Let us further assume that the insertion points of elementary expressions are already determined in advance. Based upon this situation we are left to identify those composite expressions whose premature initialisation at the program point pays off and those elementary expressions whose associated temporaries can be released. Hence this trade-off situation is modelled by means of the following two sets:

- A set of *lower trade-off candidates*, i. e. a set of elementary expressions that are already initialised at the program point and that are used at most for the evaluation of large expressions that can be initialised there.
- A set of *upper trade-off candidates*, i. e. a set of large expressions whose corresponding temporaries can either be initialised immediately at this program point or optionally be postponed to later program points.

Essentially, the problem we are interested in is to find a subset of lower trade-off candidates whose set of neighbouring upper trade-off candidates is smaller in size. In this case it is profitable to terminate all the lifetime ranges associated with the chosen lower trade-off candidates at the price of starting lifetime ranges that are associated with the related upper trade-off candidates.

4.3.2 Tight Sets in Bipartite Graphs

The situation above is naturally modelled by means of a bipartite graph (cf. Section 2.1.1) with edges between lower and upper trade-off candidates reflecting the subexpression relation.

In the graph theoretical view the problem of finding a profitable trade-off between lower and upper trade-off candidates leads to the notion of tight sets [LP86], i. e. subsets of S that are covered by fewer vertices of T:

Definition 4.3.1 (S-Tight Sets).
Let $(S \uplus T, E)$ be a bipartite graph and $S' \subseteq S$.

1. *The value of the difference $|S'| - |neigh(S')|$ is called the S-*deficiency*, in symbols $defic_S(S')$, of S'.*
2. *If $defic_S(S') \geqslant 0$ then S' is called an S-*deficiency set.
3. *If S' is of maximum deficiency among all subsets of S, then it is called S-*tight.

For all notions the parameter S may be skipped, whenever S is understood from the context. Note that especially $\emptyset$ is a deficiency set.

4.3.3 An Efficient Decision Procedure

Let us first focus on our problem as a pure decision problem.

Problem 4.3.1 (Existence of a non-trivial S-deficiency set).
Instance: A bipartite graph $(T \uplus S, E)$.

Question: Does S possess a S-deficiency set $S' \neq \emptyset$?

Obviously, this problem is decidable, as the number of subsets is finite. The point of interest rather is, whether it can be answered effectively. At first glance a solution is not at all obvious. In fact, the straightforward approach would be to enumerate all subsets of S and then to check if their deficiency is non-negative. Since such a check is clearly in P, one might suspect that the problem is yet another member of the large class of NP-complete problems [GJ79] in the field of register allocation [CAC+81, Cha82, AJU77]. Fortunately, Problem 4.3.1 can be solved efficiently by employing some graph theoretical results on matchings in bipartite graphs.

4.3.3.1 Matchings in Bipartite Graphs.

Definition 4.3.2 (Matchings). *Let $(S \uplus T, E)$ be a bipartite graph.*

1. *A subset of independent edges $M \subseteq E$ is called a* matching*, i. e. for the edges of M we have: $\forall e_1, e_2 \in M.\ e_1 \cap e_2 = \emptyset$*
2. *A matching M is called a* maximum (cardinality) matching*, if and only if $|M|$ is maximal.*
3. *A matching M is* complete*, if and only if $|M| = \min\{|S|, |T|\}$.*

Figure 4.3 gives examples of maximum and complete matchings. Obviously, every complete matching is maximum. The converse does not necessarily hold as Figure 4.3(b) shows. Note that here as in following examples bold lines are chosen in order to emphasise edges belonging to the matching. Considering

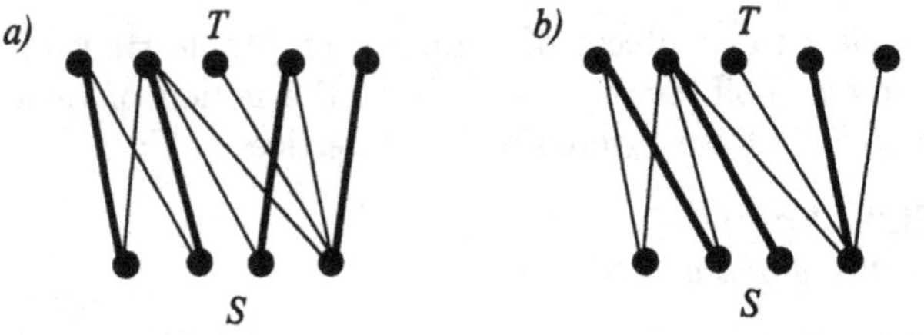

Fig. 4.3. a) A complete matching, b) A maximum yet non-complete matching

a matching M a vertex $v \in S \uplus T$ is is called *M-matched*, or simply *matched* if M is understood from the context, if $v \in e$ for some $e \in M$. A path that alternately contains edges in M and edges not in M is called an *alternating path*.

Obviously, Decision Problem 4.3.1 is trivial under the assumption that $|S| \geqslant |T|$, since we may simply choose $S' \stackrel{\text{def}}{=} S$. Therefore, let us assume that $|S| < |T|$. In this case the solution to problem 4.3.1 is due to a result of Hall [Hal35]:

Theorem 4.3.1 (P. Hall, 1935). *Let $(S \uplus T, E)$ be a bipartite graph with $|S| \leqslant |T|$. Then this graph has a complete matching, if and only if*

$$\forall\, S' \subseteq S.\ |neigh(S')| \geqslant |S'|.$$

Hall's Theorem is commonly associated with the *marriage problem*: given a set of girls S and a set of boys T, can all the girls can be married off to a candidate of their choice. Hall's Theorem gives a surprisingly simple answer to this question. A marriage arrangement can be found, if and only if every group of girls can choose among a set of candidates that is not smaller than the group itself.

Hall's Theorem also provides an immediate solution to a variation of Problem 4.3.1 where $\mathit{defic}(S') > 0$ is required in place of $\mathit{defic}(S') \geqslant 0$. This problem can be answered positively, if and only if no complete matching exists. On the other hand, Problem 4.3.1 can be efficiently reduced to the >-variation. This is achieved by testing the variant problem for any bipartite graph that results from removing a single vertex of T. This ensures that a subset with zero deficiency will have a positive deficiency in at least one of these graphs, while the deficiency of no subset can turn from negative to positive. Since a complete matching, i. e. one of size $|S|$, is particularly a maximum one, the problem finally reduces to the computation of an arbitrary maximal matching which has to be checked for its size. Fortunately, there are efficient algorithms to cope with this problem. The central idea of these algorithms is based on the characterisation of maximal matchings by means of augmenting paths.

Definition 4.3.3 (Augmenting Path). *Let $(S \uplus T, E)$ be a bipartite graph, and $M \subseteq E$ be a matching. An M-alternating path that starts and ends with an unmatched vertex is called an* augmenting path *with respect to M.*

The fundamental relationship between maximum matchings and augmenting paths is due to Berge [Ber57]:

Theorem 4.3.2 (Berge 1957). *Let $(S \uplus T, E)$ be a bipartite graph, and $M \subseteq E$ be a matching. M is maximum, if and only if there is no augmenting path with respect to M.*

This characterisation gives rise to an efficient procedure to determine maximum matchings. A standard algorithm successively enlarges a possibly empty initial matching by constructing augmenting paths in a breadth-first discipline. In this process for each depth an arbitrary augmenting path π is selected, supposed there is any. Then π is used to construct a larger matching M' from the current matching M in following way: the role of the edges of π is switched, i. e. the M-edges of π are removed from M' and conversely the non-M-edges of π are added to M'. This process is illustrated in Figure 4.4.

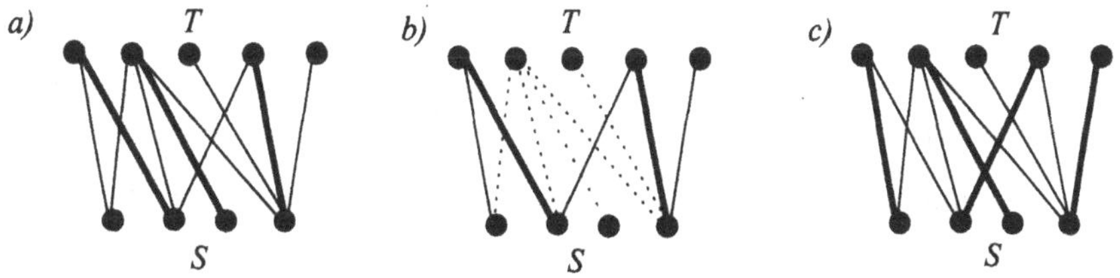

Fig. 4.4. a) A non-maximum matching M b) An augmenting path with respect to M c) The maximum matching induced by the augmenting path of b).

A more elaborated description of such an algorithm that runs with worst-case time complexity of order $\mathcal{O}(|V|\,|E|)$ for a bipartite graph (V, E) can be found in [AHU83]. Hopcroft and Karp [HK73] present a more sophisticated algorithm that slightly improves this bound towards $\mathcal{O}(|V|^{\frac{1}{2}}\,|E|)$.

4.3.4 Efficient Computation of Tight Sets

Unfortunately, the previous decision procedure is not constructive. However, we are actually interested in determining a subset with a maximum deficiency, that means a tight set.

Problem 4.3.2 (Finding a Tight Set).
Instance: A bipartite graph $(S \uplus T, E)$.
Goal: Find a tight set of S.

Fortunately, tight sets can be computed efficiently, too, by employing maximum matchings. Here we present two algorithms both suited for this purpose, one computing the largest and the other one the smallest tight set. Both algorithm are based on ideas used for determining the Gallai-Edmonds structure of a graph (cf. [LP86]). However, we give a much simpler formulation that is directly tailored for our application.

The algorithm computing the largest optimal solution successively removes vertices from an initial approximation S_M until a fixed point is reached:

Algorithm 4.3.1.

Input: Bipartite graph $G = (S \uplus T, E)$ and a maximum matching M
Output: The largest S-tight set $\mathcal{T}^{\top}(S) \subseteq S$

```
S_M := S;
R := {t ∈ T | t is unmatched};
WHILE R ≠ ∅ DO
    choose some x ∈ R;
    R := R \ {x};
    IF x ∈ S
       THEN S_M := S_M \ {x};
            R := R ∪ {y | {x,y} ∈ M}
       ELSE R := R ∪ neigh(x)
    FI
OD;
T^⊤(S) := S_M
```

The algorithm that computes the smallest solution proceeds contrary. It successively adds vertices of S to an initial approximation S_M until a fixed point is reached:

Algorithm 4.3.2.

Input: Bipartite graph $G = (S \uplus T, E)$ and a maximum matching M
Output: The smallest S-tight set $\mathcal{T}^{\perp}(S) \subseteq S$

```
S_M := ∅;
A := {s ∈ S | s is unmatched};
WHILE A ≠ ∅ DO
    choose some x ∈ A;
    A := A \ {x};
    IF x ∈ S
       THEN S_M := S_M ∪ {x};
            A := A ∪ neigh(x)
       ELSE A := A ∪ {y | {x,y} ∈ M}
    FI
OD;
T^⊥(S) := S_M
```

Both algorithms are perfectly suitable as the basic ingredient of an expression motion algorithm that exploits the optimal trade-off information. However, we have to decide for one strategy, since the globalisation presented in Section 4.4 requires consistency of the trade-off information. In other words, the solutions computed by Algorithm 4.3.1 and Algorithm 4.3.2 must not be mixed when computing tight sets within our overall algorithm. For the sake of presentation, we will choose Algorithm 4.3.1 from now on as the relevant trade-off algorithm. Let us therefore take a closer look at the function of this algorithm. Starting with an upper approximation of S_M those vertices that can be reached through an alternating path originating at an unmatched vertex of T are successively found and eliminated from S_M. Informatively, this process ensures that all removed S-vertices are matched, as otherwise this would establish an augmenting path in contradiction to the maximality of M. This is illustrated in Figure 4.5 where black circles indicate removed vertices, which means all vertices that have been added to R at least once.[4] Denoting the matching partner of a removed vertex $s \in S$ by $M(s)$, we can easily see that $neigh(\mathcal{T}^{\top}(S)) \cap M(S \setminus \mathcal{T}^{\top}(S)) = \emptyset$. Hence the subgraph induced by $S \setminus \mathcal{T}^{\top}(S)$ and $T \setminus neigh(\mathcal{T}^{\top}(S))$ is of negative deficiency and can be removed. Based on this idea, we can prove the main result of this section:

Theorem 4.3.3 (Tight Set Theorem). *For a bipartite graph $(S \uplus T, E)$ the set $\mathcal{T}^{\top}(S)$ constructed by Algorithm 4.3.1 is the largest S-tight set, i. e.*

1. *$\mathcal{T}^{\top}(S)$ contains any S-tight set and*
2. *$\mathcal{T}^{\top}(S)$ is tight itself.*

Proof of 1: Let S' be a tight set. Let us further denote the values of R and S_M after the i-th iteration by R^i and S_M^i, respectively. Then, by means of an induction on i, we are going to show:

$$S' \subseteq S_M^i$$

Induction Base: $i = 0$. In this case the inclusion $S' \subseteq S_M^0$ is trivial.
Induction Step: $i > 0$. Without loss of generality let $s \in S_M^{i-1} \cap R^{i-1}$ be the element that is removed from S_M in the i-th iteration step. Then we are going to show that $s \in S'$.

Due to the construction of R we may assume without loss of generality that s has a neighbour $t \in neigh(s)$ such that $\{s,t\} \notin M$ which has once added s to the workset. On the other hand, s must be matched. Otherwise, there would be an augmenting path between s and an initial vertex $t \in R^0$ by construction which would contradict to the maximality of M. Thus there is also a neighbour t' of s such that $\{s,t'\} \in M$.

[4] In fact, marking processed node the algorithm could be easily modified such that a vertex is added to R at most once.

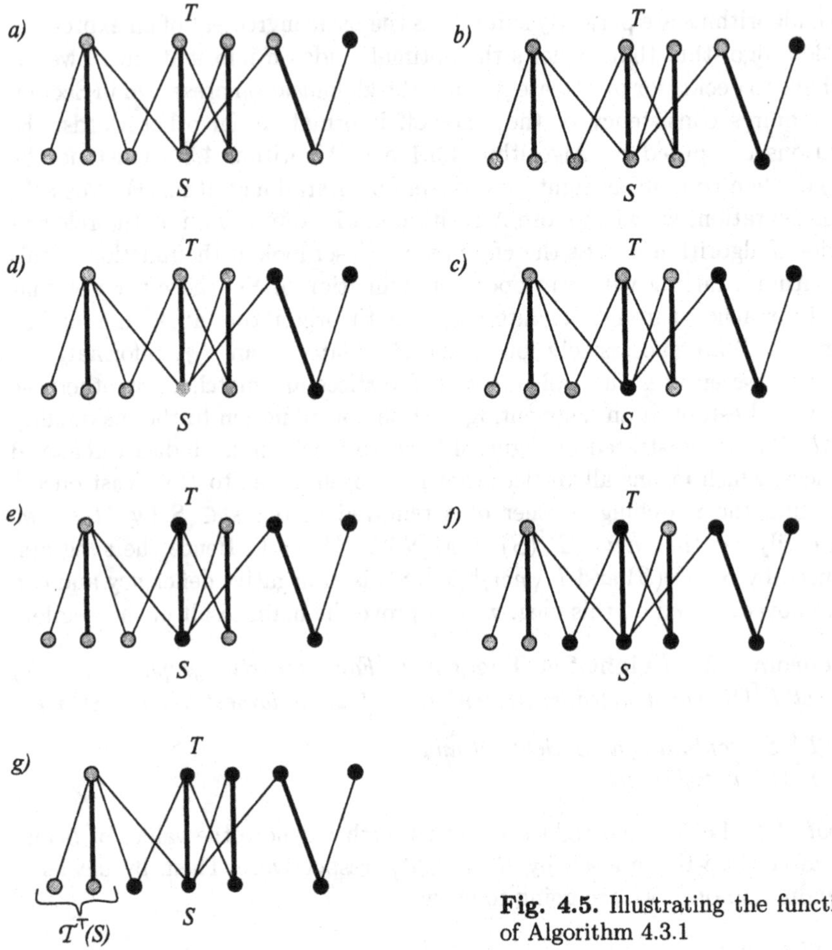

Fig. 4.5. Illustrating the function of Algorithm 4.3.1

Let us now define a set $\tilde{S}$ that contains all vertices in S' that are reachable from s via alternating paths starting with the matching edge $\{s, t'\}$. Immediately by construction we have:

i) $\tilde{S} \subseteq S'$

ii) $neigh(S' \setminus \tilde{S}) \cap neigh(\tilde{S}) = \emptyset$

iii) $|\tilde{S}| < |neigh(\tilde{S})|$

The idea behind this construction is sketched in Figure 4.6. Now it is left to show that $S' \setminus \tilde{S}$ has a greater deficiency than S', which is in contrast to the assumption that S' is tight. To this end we calculate

$$\begin{array}{rcl} & & |S' \setminus \tilde{S}| \; - \; |neigh(S' \setminus \tilde{S})| \\ \text{[Assumptions (i) \& (ii)]} & = & |S'| - |\tilde{S}| \; - \; (\; |neigh(S')| - |neigh(\tilde{S})| \;) \\ & = & |S'| - |neigh(S')| \; - \; (\; |\tilde{S}| - |neigh(\tilde{S})| \;) \\ \text{[Assumption (iii)]} & > & |S'| - |neigh(S')| + 1 \end{array}$$

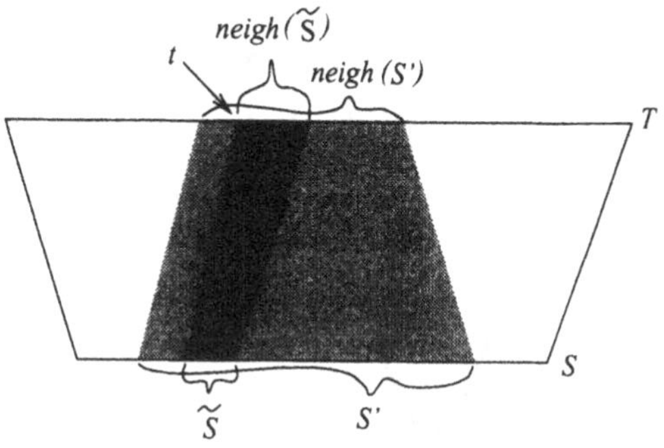

Fig. 4.6. Illustrating the construction of $\tilde{S}$

Proof of 2: Let us assume an arbitrary S-tight set S'. According to the first part we can assume that $S' \subseteq \mathcal{T}^{\top}(S)$ and thus also $neigh(S') \subseteq neigh(\mathcal{T}^{\top}(S))$. Since by construction every vertex in $neigh(\mathcal{T}^{\top}(S))$ is matched, particularly every $t \in neigh(\mathcal{T}^{\top}(S)) \setminus neigh(S')$ is matched by a unique adjacent vertex in $\mathcal{T}^{\top}(S) \setminus S'$. This situation is sketched in Figure 4.7.

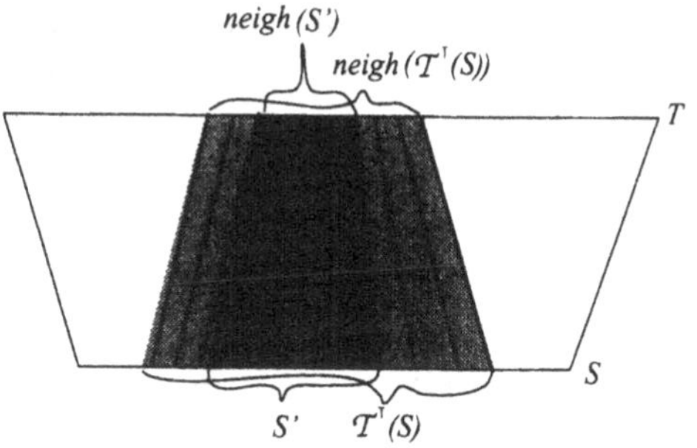

Fig. 4.7. Preservation of the deficiency of S' within $\mathcal{T}^{\top}(S)$

In particular, this guarantees:

$$|neigh(\mathcal{T}^{\top}(S)) \setminus neigh(S')| \leqslant |\mathcal{T}^{\top}(S) \setminus S'| \tag{4.4}$$

Thus we have:

$$\begin{aligned}
& |\mathcal{T}^{\top}(S)| - |neigh(\mathcal{T}^{\top}(S))| \\
[S' \subseteq \mathcal{T}^{\top}(S)] \quad = \quad & |S'| + |\mathcal{T}^{\top}(S) \setminus S'| - \\
& \qquad (\, |neigh(S')| + |neigh(\mathcal{T}^{\top}(S)) \setminus neigh(S')| \,) \\
= \quad & |S'| - |neigh(S')| + \\
& \qquad \underbrace{(\, |\mathcal{T}^{\top}(S) \setminus S'| - |neigh(\mathcal{T}^{\top}(S)) \setminus neigh(S')| \,)}_{\geqslant 0} \\
[\text{Inequation 4.4}] \quad \geqslant \quad & |S'| - |neigh(S')|
\end{aligned}$$

which means that the deficiency of $\mathcal{T}^{\top}(S)$ is no worse than the one of S'. □

Figure 4.8 gives some examples of tight sets as they are computed by means of Algorithm 4.3.1.

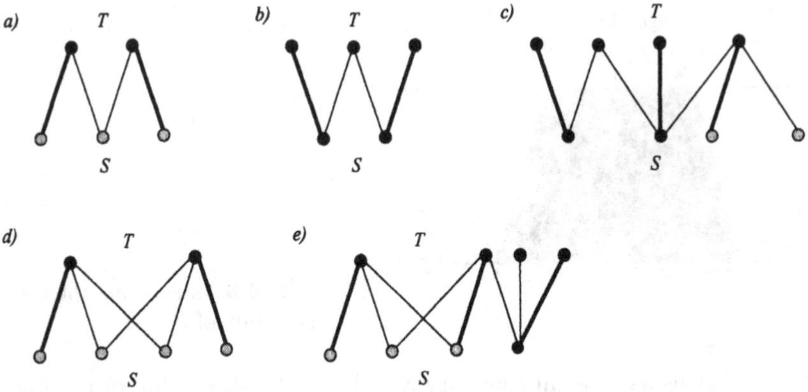

Fig. 4.8. Tight sets

We close this section by introducing a class of subsets that becomes important when we have to consider the relationship between bipartite graphs being associated with adjacent program points. Although these bipartite graphs usually do not coincide, some parts of the tight set at a program point $\dot{n}$ are preserved within the tight sets of its successor points. To this end we introduce:

Definition 4.3.4 (Irreducible Subsets).
Let $G \stackrel{\text{def}}{=} (S \uplus T, E)$ be a bipartite graph and $S' \subseteq S$.

1. *A pair $(\tilde{S}, \tilde{T})$ with $\tilde{S} \subseteq S'$ and $\tilde{T} \subseteq T$ is a* tightness defect *of S', if and only if the following three conditions are met:*
   a) $|\tilde{T}| > |\tilde{S}|$
   b) $neigh(\tilde{S}) \supseteq \tilde{T}$
   c) $neigh(S' \setminus \tilde{S}) \cap \tilde{T} = \emptyset$
2. *$S' \subseteq S$ is called* irreducible, *if and only if it has no tightness defects, otherwise it is called* reducible.

Obviously, an irreducible subset $S' \subseteq S$ is a deficiency set, too, as otherwise $(S', neigh(S'))$ itself would be a tightness defect. Actually, the criterion of being irreducible is much stronger. In particular, the absence of tightness defects means that there are no subsets of S' whose removal increases the deficiency (see Figure 4.9 for illustration).
Clearly, tight sets are irreducible. However, irreducible sets provide a more fine grain characterisation that is expressed in the following result.

Lemma 4.3.1 (Irreducible Subset Lemma).
Let $G \stackrel{\text{def}}{=} (S \uplus T, E)$ be a bipartite graph. Then we have:

1. *If $T' \subseteq neigh(\mathcal{T}^{\top}(S))$ then $neigh(T') \cap \mathcal{T}^{\top}(S)$ is an irreducible subset of S.*
2. *If $S' \subseteq S$ is an irreducible subset, then $S' \subseteq \mathcal{T}^{\top}(S)$.*

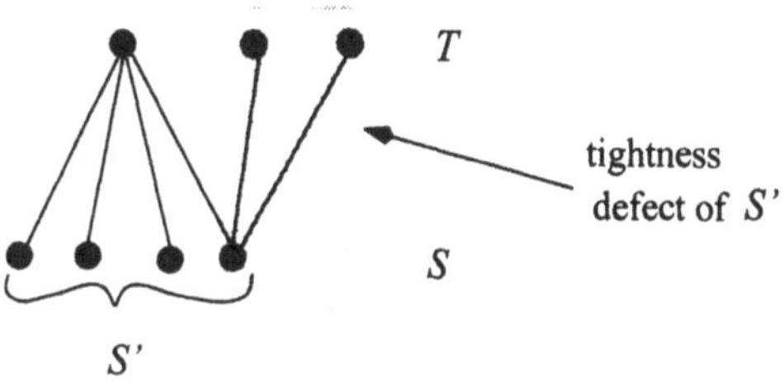

Fig. 4.9. Tightness defect of a set with positive deficiency

Proof. For the proof of Part (1) let us assume that $S' \stackrel{\text{def}}{=} neigh(T') \cap \mathcal{T}^{\top}(S)$ has a tightness defect $(\tilde{S}, \tilde{T})$ (see Figure 4.10(a) for illustration). As by construction $neigh(\mathcal{T}^{\top}(S) \setminus S') \cap T' = \emptyset$ this would enable to remove the vertices of $\tilde{S}$ from $\mathcal{T}^{\top}(S)$, while strictly improving the deficiency of $\mathcal{T}^{\top}(S)$, which is in contradiction to its tightness.

For the proof of Part (2) let us assume an irreducible subset $S' \subseteq S$ with $S' \not\subseteq \mathcal{T}^{\top}(S)$ (see Figure 4.10(b) for illustration). Let us consider $\tilde{S} \stackrel{\text{def}}{=} S' \setminus \mathcal{T}^{\top}(S)$ and $\tilde{T} \stackrel{\text{def}}{=} neigh(S') \setminus neigh(\mathcal{T}^{\top}(S))$. It is easy to see that $(\tilde{S}, \tilde{T})$ meets condition (b) and (c) of Definition 4.3.4(1). Hence condition (a) must be violated, which means $|\tilde{T}| \leqslant |\tilde{S}|$, since otherwise $(\tilde{S}, \tilde{T})$ would be a tightness defect of S', which is in contradiction to its irreducibility. Using this inequality we immediately get that $S' \cup \mathcal{T}^{\top}(S)$ is a subset of S whose deficiency is no worse than the one of $\mathcal{T}^{\top}(S)$ and that strictly comprises $\mathcal{T}^{\top}(S)$. This, however, is in contradiction to Theorem 4.3.3. Hence we have $S' \subseteq \mathcal{T}^{\top}(S)$ as desired. □

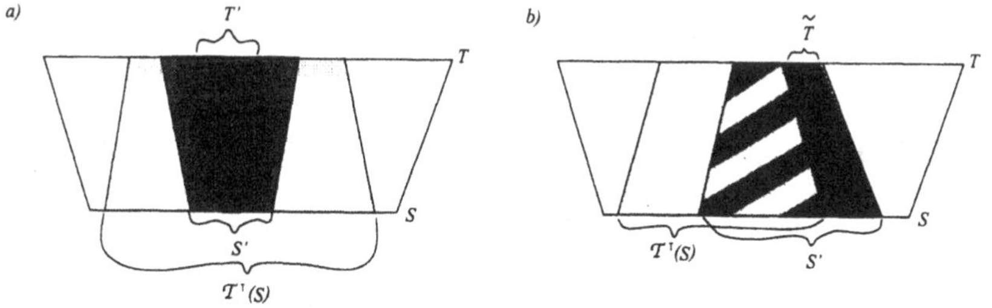

Fig. 4.10. a) Situation in Lemma 4.3.1(1) b) Situation in Lemma 4.3.1(2)

4.4 Levelwise Flexible Expression Motion

In this section the main results of Section 4.3 are utilised in order to construct the proposed algorithm for inductively lifetime optimal expression motion. We will call this transformation *Levelwise Flexible Expression Motion*, for short $\mathtt{LFEM}_\Phi$. The adjective *flexible* addresses the fact that its insertion points are no longer chosen according to a fixed strategy as in the case of

$\mathtt{BEM}_\Phi$ and $\mathtt{LEM}_\Phi$, but are rather determined flexibly somewhere between the earliest and the latest initialisation points incorporating trade-offs between the lifetime ranges of different temporaries. However, the method progresses in a *levelwise* fashion rather than to consider all expressions at once. We will discuss limitations of this approach in Section 4.5.2 which serves as a motivation for a fully fledged algorithm for expression motion not being limited in this way.

4.4.1 Defining $\mathtt{LFEM}_\Phi$

As $\mathtt{BEM}_\Phi$ and $\mathtt{LEM}_\Phi$ also the component transformations of $\mathtt{LFEM}_\Phi$ are such that original computations are always replaced. Hence we have for any $\varphi \in \Phi$ and $\dot{n} \in \dot{N}$:

$$\mathtt{LFEM}_\varphi\text{-}Replace_{\dot{n}}^{\varphi} \overset{\text{def}}{\Leftrightarrow} Comp_{\dot{n}}^{\varphi}$$

According to Definition 4.2.1 this ensures that actual replacements of the structured transformation with respect to Φ are restricted to maximal occurrences.

$$\mathtt{LFEM}_\Phi\text{-}Replace_{\dot{n}}^{\varphi} \overset{\text{def}}{\Leftrightarrow} \varphi \in MaxSubExpr_\Phi(\varphi_{\dot{n}}^{\mathtt{RHS}}),$$

where $\varphi_{\dot{n}}^{\mathtt{RHS}}$ addresses the right-hand side expression associated with $\dot{n}$.

Insertions of the transformation are determined by a process that refines delayability as defined in Definition 3.3.3 level by level starting with the minimal expression patterns, i. e. the 0-level expressions of Φ.[5]

I. The Induction Base: *expressions in* Φ^0

Minimal expression patterns are initialised according to the individual lazy expression motion transformations. Thus we have for any $\dot{n} \in \dot{N}$ and expression pattern $\varphi \in \Phi^0$

$$\mathtt{LFEM}_\varphi\text{-}Insert_{\dot{n}}^{\varphi} \overset{\text{def}}{\Leftrightarrow} \mathtt{LEM}_\varphi\text{-}Insert_{\dot{n}}^{\varphi}$$

II. The Induction Step: *expressions in* Φ^i, $i \geqslant 1$

The algorithm proceeds from level 1 to higher levels computing the optimal initialisation points for expressions of the level under consideration, while capturing profitable trade-offs between the current level and levels already processed. To this end, the local trade-off information which is determined by means of the techniques of Section 4.3 is globalised by

5 The idea to use our algorithm for lazy expression motion as the basis of a refinement process also led to an algorithm for lazy strength reduction [KRS93] that combines expression motion with strength reduction [ACK81, CK77, CP91, JD82a, JD82b, Dha89b, Dha89a].

adjustments of the central predicates involved in the definition of lazy expression motion.

II.a First Adjustment. For structured expression motion Definition 4.2.1 imposes a constraint on the order of initialisations. This constraint is reflected in a modification of the down-safety predicate. Now the range of down-safe program points is further restricted to program points where it can be granted that immediate subexpressions are initialised before :

$$A1\text{-}DnSafe_{\dot n}^{\psi} \overset{\text{def}}{\Leftrightarrow} DnSafe_{\dot n}^{\psi} \wedge \forall \varphi \in SubExpr_{\Phi}(\psi).\ \texttt{LFEM}_{\varphi}\text{-}Correct_{\dot n}^{\varphi}$$

This definition straightforwardly induces modified predicates for safety, earliestness, delayability and latestness, respectively, that are all marked by a preceding $A1$-, as for instance $A1$-*Delayed*.

II.b Second Adjustment. Our central concern, that is to capture trade-offs between lifetimes of temporaries, is now addressed by means of a further adjustment of the delayability property: delayability of i-level expressions is terminated at program points where their premature initialisation pays off in terms of the overall lifetimes of temporaries.

To this end we introduce two sets of *trade-off candidates* associated with every program point $\dot n$:

$\Theta_{\dot n}^{\mathrm{up}(i)}$, the set of *upper trade-off candidates* at $\dot n$, refers to expressions of level i whose initialisation is possible at $\dot n$ but can optionally be postponed to strictly later program points as well.

$$\boxed{\Theta_{\dot n}^{\mathrm{up}(i)} \overset{\text{def}}{=} \{\psi \in \Phi^i \mid A1\text{-}Delayed_{\dot n}^{\psi} \wedge \neg A1\text{-}Latest_{\dot n}^{\psi}\}}$$

$\Theta_{\dot n}^{\mathrm{dn}(i)}$, the set of *lower trade-off candidates* at $\dot n$, refers to expressions of level strictly lower than i whose associated lifetime-ranges may possibly be terminated at $\dot n$. This excludes expressions whose associated lifetime ranges have to survive $\dot n$ anyhow.

For a formal criterion we introduce a predicate $UsedLater[\tilde\Phi]$ that captures situations, where a lifetime range always has to survive the program point irrespective of the expression motion under consideration. The predicate is supplemented by a structured subset of expressions $\tilde\Phi \subseteq \Phi$ that fixes its scope:[6]

$$\begin{aligned} UsedLater_{\dot n}^{\varphi}[\tilde\Phi] \overset{\text{def}}{\Leftrightarrow}\ & \exists p \in \mathbf{P}[\dot n, \dot{\mathbf{e}}]\ \exists 1 < j \leqslant |p|. \\ & \Big(\texttt{LFEM}_{\tilde\Phi}\text{-}Replace_{p_j}^{\varphi} \vee \exists \psi \in SupExpr_{\tilde\Phi}(\varphi).\ A1\text{-}Earliest_{p_j}^{\psi}\Big) \wedge \\ & \qquad \forall 1 < k \leqslant j.\ \neg A1\text{-}Earliest_{p_k}^{\varphi} \end{aligned}$$

[6] For expressions of maximal level $UsedLater[\Phi]$ coincides with the complement of the *isolation* predicate in [KRS92, KRS94a], which was introduced in order to eliminate insertions that are only used immediately afterwards. In fact, in $\texttt{LFEM}_{\Phi}$ this step evolves as the natural add-on that results from exploiting *LUsedLater*-information also with respect to the maximum level.

Based upon this predicate the formal definition of $\Theta_{\dot{n}}^{\mathrm{dn}(i)}$ is:

$$\boxed{\Theta_{\dot{n}}^{\mathrm{dn}(i)} \stackrel{\mathrm{def}}{=} \{\varphi \in \Phi^{<i} \mid \neg \mathit{UsedLater}_{\dot{n}}^{\varphi}[\Phi^{\leqslant i}] \wedge \mathit{SupExpr}_{\Theta_{\dot{n}}^{\mathrm{up}(i)}}(\varphi) \neq \emptyset\}}$$

$\Theta_{\dot{n}}^{\mathrm{dn}(i)}$ and $\Theta_{\dot{n}}^{\mathrm{up}(i)}$ form the vertices of a bipartite graph whose edges are given by the immediate subexpression relation. Algorithm 4.3.1 is used in order to define a local predicate *LChange* capturing those computations whose premature initialisations are profitable with respect to the expressions of levels below:

$$\boxed{\mathit{LChange}_{\dot{n}}^{\varphi} \stackrel{\mathrm{def}}{\Leftrightarrow} \varphi \in \mathit{neigh}(\mathcal{T}^{\top}(\Theta_{\dot{n}}^{\mathrm{dn}(i)}))}$$

This new local predicate is taken into account for a second adjustment of delayability, where in addition delayability of an upper trade-off candidate is terminated as soon as a profitable change becomes possible.

$$\begin{aligned} \mathit{A2\text{-}Delayed}_{\dot{n}}^{\varphi} \stackrel{\mathrm{def}}{\Leftrightarrow} \ & \forall p \in \mathbf{P}[\dot{\mathbf{s}}, \dot{n}]\ \exists j \leqslant |p|.\ \mathit{A1\text{-}Earliest}_{p_j}^{\varphi} \wedge \\ & \forall j \leqslant k < |p|.\ \neg \mathit{Comp}_{p_k}^{\varphi} \wedge \neg \mathit{LChange}_{p_k}^{\varphi} \end{aligned}$$

The modified delayability predicate induces a corresponding adjusted predicate for latestness that is also marked by a subscript `Adj2`:

$$\begin{aligned} \mathit{A2\text{-}Latest}_{\dot{n}}^{\varphi} \stackrel{\mathrm{def}}{\Leftrightarrow} \ & \mathit{A2\text{-}Delayed}_{\dot{n}}^{\varphi} \wedge \\ & (\mathit{Comp}_{\dot{n}}^{\varphi} \vee \exists \dot{m} \in \mathit{succ}(\dot{n}).\ \neg \mathit{A2\text{-}Delayed}_{\dot{m}}^{\varphi}) \end{aligned}$$

II.c Initialisation Points: The results determined in step II.b) induce the insertion points for $\varphi \in \Phi^i$:

$$\mathtt{LFEM}_{\varphi}\text{-}\mathit{Insert}_{\dot{n}}^{\varphi} \stackrel{\mathrm{def}}{\Leftrightarrow} \mathit{A2\text{-}Latest}_{\dot{n}}^{\varphi}$$

4.4.2 Proving Admissibility

The proof of admissibility of $\mathtt{LFEM}_{\Phi}$ is quite straightforward, since the definition of the predicates is already tuned in a way that the conditions of Definition 4.2.1 are automatically met. We start by collecting some properties on adjusted delayability.

Lemma 4.4.1 (Delayability Lemma for $\mathtt{LFEM}_{\Phi}$).

1. $\forall \psi \in \Phi,\ \dot{n} \in \dot{N}.\ \mathit{A2\text{-}Delayed}_{\dot{n}}^{\psi} \Rightarrow \mathit{A1\text{-}Delayed}_{\dot{n}}^{\psi} \Rightarrow \mathit{Delayed}_{\dot{n}}^{\psi}$
2. $\forall \psi \in \Phi,\ \dot{n} \in \dot{N}.\ \mathit{A1\text{-}Delayed}_{\dot{n}}^{\psi} \Rightarrow \mathit{A1\text{-}DnSafe}_{\dot{n}}^{\psi} \Rightarrow \mathit{DnSafe}_{\dot{n}}^{\psi}$
3. $\forall \psi \in \Phi,\ \dot{n} \in \dot{N}.\ \mathit{A1\text{-}Delayed}_{\dot{n}}^{\psi} \Leftrightarrow \mathit{Delayed}_{\dot{n}}^{\psi} \wedge \mathit{A1\text{-}DnSafe}_{\dot{n}}^{\psi}$

Proof. Part (1) is directly due to the definitions of the different notions of delayability. The first implication of Part (2) can be proved along the lines of Lemma 3.4.1(1) by using the corresponding adjusted notions, whereas the second implication is immediate from the definition of $A1\text{-}DnSafe$. The $\Rightarrow$-direction of Part (3) is immediately implied by Part (1) and (2). Finally, the $\Leftarrow$-direction of Part (3) follows from a path-based argument:

$$
\begin{array}{ll}
 & Delayed_{\dot n}^{\psi} \\
\text{[Definition } Delayed\text{]} & \\
 & \Rightarrow \;\; \forall p \in \mathbf{P}[\dot{\mathbf{s}}, \dot n]\, \exists i \leqslant |p|.\; Earliest_{p_i}^{\psi} \;\wedge\; \forall i \leqslant k < |p|.\; \neg Comp_{p_k}^{\psi} \\
\text{[(4.5)]} & \Rightarrow \;\; \forall p \in \mathbf{P}[\dot{\mathbf{s}}, \dot n]\, \exists i \leqslant |p|.\; A1\text{-}Earliest_{p_i}^{\psi} \;\wedge\; \forall i \leqslant k < |p|.\; \neg Comp_{p_k}^{\psi} \\
\text{[Definition } A1\text{-}Delayed\text{]} & \\
 & \Rightarrow \;\; A1\text{-}Delayed_{\dot n}^{\psi}
\end{array}
$$

Implication (4.5) is justified, because the assumption $A1\text{-}DnSafe_{\dot n}^{\psi}$ ensures that there is a least index $i \leqslant j \leqslant |p|$ such that $A1\text{-}DnSafe_{p_k}^{\psi}$ holds for all $j \leqslant k \leqslant |p|$. For this j the condition $Earliest_{p_i}^{\psi}$ implies $A1\text{-}Earliest_{p_j}^{\psi}$. This is trivial if $i = j$, otherwise one can easily check that $\neg UpSafe_{p_k}^{\psi}$ is true for any $i \leqslant k < j$. □

Finally, for latestness as the limit points of delayability we have some strong characterisations:

Lemma 4.4.2 (Latestness Lemma for LFEM$_\Phi$).

1. $\forall \psi \in \Phi,\; \dot n \in \dot N.\; A1\text{-}Latest_{\dot n}^{\psi} \;\Rightarrow\; \texttt{LFEM}_{\Phi}\text{-}Correct_{\dot n}^{\psi}$
2. $\forall \psi \in \Phi,\; \dot n \in \dot N.\; Latest_{\dot n}^{\psi} \;\Rightarrow\; A1\text{-}DnSafe_{\dot n}^{\psi}$
3. $\forall \psi \in \Phi,\; \dot n \in \dot N.\; Latest_{\dot n}^{\psi} \;\Leftrightarrow\; A1\text{-}Latest_{\dot n}^{\psi}$

Proof. Considering Part (1) we use that $A1\text{-}Latest_{\dot n}^{\psi}$ together with Lemma 4.4.1(1) yields

$$Comp_{\dot n}^{\psi} \;\vee\; \exists \dot m \in succ(\dot n).\; \neg A2\text{-}Delayed_{\dot m}^{\psi}. \tag{4.6}$$

Then we have

$$
\begin{array}{ll}
 & A1\text{-}Latest_{\dot n}^{\psi} \\
\text{[Definition } A1\text{-}Latest\text{]} & \\
 & \Rightarrow \;\; A1\text{-}Delayed_{\dot n}^{\psi} \\
\text{[Definition } A1\text{-}Delayed\text{]} & \\
 & \Rightarrow \;\; \forall p \in \mathbf{P}[\dot{\mathbf{s}}, \dot n]\, \exists i \leqslant |p|.\; A1\text{-}Earliest_{p_i}^{\psi} \;\wedge\; \forall i \leqslant k < |p|.\; \neg Comp_{p_k}^{\psi} \\
\text{[Definition } A2\text{-}Delayed\text{]} & \\
 & \Rightarrow \;\; \forall p \in \mathbf{P}[\dot{\mathbf{s}}, \dot n]\, \exists i \leqslant |p|.\; A2\text{-}Delayed_{p_i}^{\psi} \;\wedge\; \forall i \leqslant k < |p|.\; \neg Comp_{p_k}^{\psi} \\
\text{[Assumption (4.6) \& Definition } A2\text{-}Delayed\text{]} & \\
 & \Rightarrow \;\; \forall p \in \mathbf{P}[\dot{\mathbf{s}}, \dot n]\, \exists i \leqslant |p|.\; A2\text{-}Latest_{p_i}^{\psi} \;\wedge\; \forall i \leqslant k < |p|.\; \neg Comp_{p_k}^{\psi}
\end{array}
$$

$$[(4.7)] \quad \Rightarrow \quad \forall p \in \mathbf{P}[\dot{s}, \dot{n}]\ \exists i \leqslant |p|.\ \textit{A2-Latest}^{\psi}_{p_i} \ \wedge\ \forall i \leqslant k < |p|.\ \textit{Transp}^{\psi}_{p_k}$$

[Definition LFEM$_\Phi$-*Correct*]

$$\Rightarrow \quad \text{LFEM}_\Phi\text{-}\textit{Correct}^{\psi}_{\dot{n}}$$

To prove Implication (4.7) let us assume an index k with $i \leqslant k < |p|$ such that $\textit{Transp}^{\psi}_{p_k}$ is violated. As $\textit{A2-Latest}^{\psi}_{p_i}$ implies $\textit{DnSafe}^{\psi}_{p_i}$ (cf. Lemma 4.4.1(1&2)) the definition of down-safety would mean that there is an index l with $i \leqslant l \leqslant k$ such that $\textit{Comp}^{\psi}_{p_l}$ is true in contradiction the premise of the implication.

Part (2) is proved together with the $\Rightarrow$-direction of Part (3) by means of an induction on the structure of ψ. For the induction base $\psi \in \Phi^0$ Part (2) is due to the following sequence of implications:

$$\textit{Latest}^{\psi}_{\dot{n}} \ \Rightarrow\ \textit{Delayed}^{\psi}_{\dot{n}} \ \Rightarrow\ \textit{DnSafe}^{\psi}_{\dot{n}} \ \Rightarrow\ \textit{A1-DnSafe}^{\psi}_{\dot{n}},$$

where the first implication is due to the Definition of $\textit{Latest}^{\psi}_{\dot{n}}$, the second one follows from Lemma 3.4.1(1) and the third one is a consequence of the fact that $\psi \in \Phi^0$ combined with the Definition of $\textit{A1-DnSafe}^{\psi}_{\dot{n}}$. Then Part (2) can already be used for the $\Rightarrow$-direction of Part (3):

$$\textit{Latest}^{\psi}_{\dot{n}}$$

[Definition *Latest*]

$$\Rightarrow \quad \textit{Delayed}_{\wedge}\ (\textit{Comp}^{\psi}_{\dot{n}} \ \vee\ \exists \dot{m} \in \textit{succ}(\dot{n}).\ \neg\textit{Delayed}^{\psi}_{\dot{m}})$$

[Part (2)]

$$\Rightarrow \quad \textit{Delayed}^{\psi}_{\dot{n}} \ \wedge\ \textit{A1-DnSafe}^{\psi}_{\dot{n}} \ \wedge \quad (\textit{Comp}^{\psi}_{\dot{n}} \ \vee\ \exists \dot{m} \in \textit{succ}(\dot{n}).\ \neg\textit{Delayed}^{\psi}_{\dot{m}})$$

[Lemma 4.4.1(1&3)]

$$\Rightarrow \quad \textit{A1-Delayed}^{\psi}_{\dot{n}} \ \wedge\ (\textit{Comp}^{\psi}_{\dot{n}} \ \vee\ \exists \dot{m} \in \textit{succ}(\dot{n}).\ \neg\textit{A1-Delayed}^{\psi}_{\dot{m}})$$

[Definition *A1-Latest*]

$$\Rightarrow \quad \textit{A1-Latest}^{\psi}_{\dot{n}}$$

For the induction step we shall consider $\psi \in \Phi^i$ $(i \geqslant 1)$ and prove the implication of Part (2) in first place:

$$\textit{Latest}^{\psi}_{\dot{n}}$$

[Definition *Latest* & Lemma 3.4.1(2) & LEM$_\Phi$ $\in \mathcal{AEM}_\Phi$]

$$\Rightarrow \quad \textit{DnSafe}^{\psi}_{\dot{n}} \ \wedge\ \forall \varphi \in \textit{SubExpr}_\Phi(\psi).\ \text{LEM}_\Phi\text{-}\textit{Correct}^{\varphi}_{\dot{n}}$$

[Definition LEM$_\Phi$-*Correct*]

$$\Rightarrow \quad \textit{DnSafe}^{\psi}_{\dot{n}} \ \wedge\ \forall \varphi \in \textit{SubExpr}_\Phi(\psi),\ p \in \mathbf{P}[\dot{s}, \dot{n}]\ \exists j \leqslant |p|. \quad \textit{Latest}^{\varphi}_{p_j} \ \wedge\ \forall j \leqslant k < |p|.\ \textit{Transp}^{\psi}_{p_k}$$

[Induction Hypothesis]

$$\Rightarrow \quad \mathit{DnSafe}_{\dot n}^{\psi} \ \wedge\ \forall\, \varphi \in \mathit{SubExpr}_{\Phi}(\psi),\ \ p \in \mathbf{P}[\dot{\mathbf{s}}, \dot n]\ \exists\, j \leqslant |p|.$$
$$A1\text{-}\mathit{Latest}_{p_j}^{\varphi} \ \wedge\ \forall\, j \leqslant k < |p|.\ \mathit{Transp}_{p_k}^{\psi}$$

[Part (1)]

$$\Rightarrow \quad \mathit{DnSafe}_{\dot n}^{\psi} \ \wedge\ \forall\, \varphi \in \mathit{SubExpr}_{\Phi}(\psi),\ \ p \in \mathbf{P}[\dot{\mathbf{s}}, \dot n]\ \exists\, j \leqslant |p|.$$
$$\mathtt{LFEM}_{\Phi}\text{-}\mathit{Correct}_{p_j}^{\varphi} \ \wedge\ \forall\, j \leqslant k < |p|.\ \mathit{Transp}_{p_k}^{\psi}$$

[Definition $\mathtt{LFEM}_{\Phi}$-*Correct*]

$$\Rightarrow \quad \mathit{DnSafe}_{\dot n}^{\psi} \ \wedge\ \forall\, \varphi \in \mathit{SubExpr}_{\Phi}(\psi).\ \mathtt{LFEM}_{\Phi}\text{-}\mathit{Correct}_{\dot n}^{\varphi}$$

[Definition *A*1-*DnSafe*]

$$\Rightarrow \quad A1\text{-}\mathit{DnSafe}_{\dot n}^{\psi}$$

The induction step of the $\Rightarrow$-direction of Part (3) can be done as in the induction base.

Finally, for proving of the $\Leftarrow$-direction of Part (3) let us assume $A1\text{-}\mathit{Latest}_{\dot n}^{\psi}$, which means by definition

$$A1\text{-}\mathit{Delayed}_{\dot n}^{\psi} \wedge (\mathit{Comp}_{\dot n}^{\psi} \vee \exists\, \dot m \in \mathit{succ}(\dot n).\ \neg A1\text{-}\mathit{Delayed}_{\dot m}^{\psi})$$

Using Lemma 4.4.1(3) this implies

$$A1\text{-}\mathit{Delayed}_{\dot n}^{\psi} \wedge (\mathit{Comp}_{\dot n}^{\psi} \vee \exists\, \dot m \in \mathit{succ}(\dot n).\ \neg \mathit{Delayed}_{\dot m}^{\psi} \vee \neg \mathit{DnSafe}_{\dot m}^{\psi})$$

At this point it is easy to see that the case $\neg \mathit{DnSafe}_{\dot m}^{\psi}$ is subsumed by $\mathit{Comp}_{\dot n}^{\psi}$. To this end we use Lemma 4.4.1(2), which delivers $\mathit{DnSafe}_{\dot n}^{\psi}$. By definition of *DnSafe* this in combination with $\neg \mathit{DnSafe}_{\dot m}^{\psi}$ implies $\mathit{Comp}_{\dot n}^{\psi}$. Therefore, we get

$$A1\text{-}\mathit{Delayed}_{\dot n}^{\psi} \wedge (\mathit{Comp}_{\dot n}^{\psi} \vee \exists\, \dot m \in \mathit{succ}(\dot n).\ \neg \mathit{Delayed}_{\dot m}^{\psi}),$$

which after a final application of Lemma 4.4.1(1) yields $\mathit{Latest}_{\dot n}^{\psi}$ as desired. □

These results suffice to show the admissibility of $\mathtt{LFEM}_{\Phi}$.

Theorem 4.4.1 (Transformation Theorem for $\mathtt{LFEM}_{\Phi}$). $\mathtt{LFEM}_{\Phi}$ *is*

1. *a structured expression motion in the sense of Definition 4.2.1 and*
2. *admissible, i. e.* $\mathtt{LFEM}_{\Phi} \in \mathcal{AEM}_{\Phi}$

Proof. For the first part one has to show that the initialisations of subexpressions are already available at their initialisation points, i. e.

i) $\forall \psi \in \Phi,\ \dot n \in \dot N.\ \mathtt{LFEM}_{\Phi}\text{-}\mathit{Insert}_{\dot n}^{\psi} \Rightarrow \forall\, \varphi \in \mathit{SubExpr}_{\Phi}(\psi).\ \mathtt{LFEM}_{\Phi}\text{-}\mathit{Correct}_{\dot n}^{\varphi}$.

For the second part, i.e. the admissibility of $\mathbf{LFEM}_\Phi$, it is sufficient to show

ii) $\forall \psi \in \Phi,\ \dot{n} \in \dot{N}.\ \mathbf{LFEM}_\Phi\text{-}Insert_{\dot{n}}^{\psi} \Rightarrow Safe_{\dot{n}}^{\psi}$

iii) $\forall \psi \in \Phi,\ \dot{n} \in \dot{N}.\ \mathbf{LFEM}_\Phi\text{-}Replace_{\dot{n}}^{\psi} \Rightarrow \mathbf{LFEM}_\Phi\text{-}Correct_{\dot{n}}^{\psi}$

Point i) and ii) can be proved simultaneously:

$$\begin{array}{rcl} & & \mathbf{LFEM}_\Phi\text{-}Insert_{\dot{n}}^{\psi} \\ [\text{Def. } \mathbf{LFEM}_\Phi\text{-}Insert] & \Rightarrow & A2\text{-}Delayed_{\dot{n}}^{\psi} \\ [\text{Lemma 4.4.1(1)}] & \Rightarrow & A1\text{-}Delayed_{\dot{n}}^{\psi} \\ [\text{Lemma 4.4.1(2)}] & \Rightarrow & A1\text{-}DnSafe_{\dot{n}}^{\psi} \\ [\text{Def. } A1\text{-}DnSafe] & \Rightarrow & DnSafe_{\dot{n}}^{\psi} \wedge \forall \varphi \in SubExpr_\Phi(\psi).\ \mathbf{LFEM}_\Phi\text{-}Correct_{\dot{n}}^{\varphi} \end{array}$$

Finally, let us consider point iii). Here we have:

$$\begin{array}{l} \quad \mathbf{LFEM}_\Phi\text{-}Replace_{\dot{n}}^{\psi} \\ [\text{Def. } \mathbf{LFEM}_\Phi \ \& \ \mathbf{LEM}_\Phi] \\ \quad \Leftrightarrow \ \mathbf{LEM}_\Phi\text{-}Replace_{\dot{n}}^{\psi} \\ [\mathbf{LEM}_\Phi \in \mathcal{AEM}_\Phi] \\ \quad \Rightarrow \ \mathbf{LEM}_\Phi\text{-}Correct_{\dot{n}}^{\psi} \\ [\text{Def. } \mathbf{LEM}_\Phi\text{-}Correct] \\ \quad \Rightarrow \ \forall p \in \mathbf{P}[\dot{s}, \dot{n}]\ \exists 1 \leqslant i \leqslant |p|.\ Latest_{p_i}^{\psi} \wedge \forall i \leqslant j < |p|.\ Transp_{p_j}^{\psi} \\ [\text{Lemma 4.4.2(1\&3)}] \\ \quad \Rightarrow \ \forall p \in \mathbf{P}[\dot{s}, \dot{n}]\ \exists 1 \leqslant i \leqslant |p|.\ \mathbf{LFEM}_\Phi\text{-}Correct_{p_i}^{\psi} \wedge \\ \qquad\qquad\qquad\qquad\qquad\qquad\qquad \forall i \leqslant j < |p|.\ Transp_{p_j}^{\psi} \\ [\text{Def. } \mathbf{LFEM}_\Phi\text{-}Correct] \\ \quad \Rightarrow \ \mathbf{LFEM}_\Phi\text{-}Correct_{\dot{n}}^{\psi} \end{array}$$

□

With the admissibility of $\mathbf{LFEM}_\Phi$ it is now possible to propose a result which complements the Structured Safety Lemma 4.2.2:

Lemma 4.4.3 (Structured Adjusted Safety Lemma).

$$\forall \psi \in \Phi,\ \varphi \in SubExpr_\Phi(\psi),\ \dot{n} \in \dot{N}.\ A1\text{-}DnSafe_{\dot{n}}^{\psi} \Rightarrow A1\text{-}DnSafe_{\dot{n}}^{\varphi}$$

Proof. Let $\psi \in \Phi$ with $A1\text{-}DnSafe_{\dot{n}}^{\psi}$ and $\varphi \in SubExpr_\Phi(\psi)$. According to the definition of *A1-DnSafe* and Lemma 4.2.2(2) we get $DnSafe_{\dot{n}}^{\varphi}$. Hence it is only left to show

$$\forall \bar{\varphi} \in SubExpr_\Phi(\varphi).\ \mathbf{LFEM}_\Phi\text{-}Correct_{\dot{n}}^{\bar{\varphi}} \tag{4.8}$$

To this end we shall use that $A1\text{-}DnSafe_{\dot{n}}^{\psi}$ implies $\mathbf{LFEM}_\Phi\text{-}Correct_{\dot{n}}^{\varphi}$ and then exploit that the admissibility of $\mathbf{LFEM}_\Phi$ allows to apply Lemma 4.2.4 in order to obtain Property (4.8) as desired. □

4.4.3 Proving Computational Optimality

Central for the computational optimality of $\mathtt{LFEM}_\Phi$ is the following characterisation on the behaviour of the adjusted predicates on intervals between earliest and latest program points (see Figure 4.11 for illustration). Since the lemma is used for an induction proof of computational optimality, the individual transformations belonging to the subexpressions of the expression under consideration are assumed to be computationally optimal.

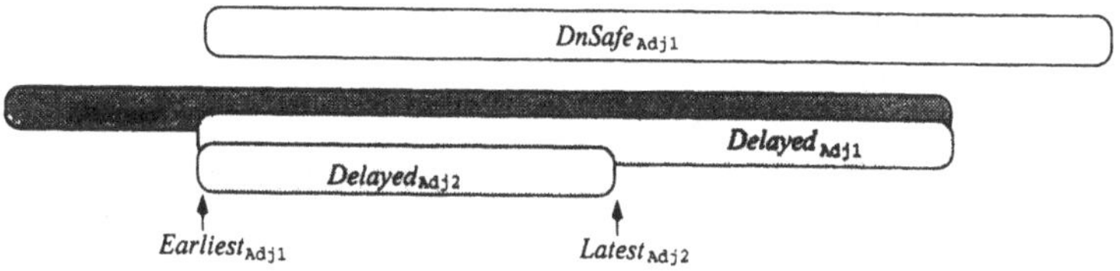

Fig. 4.11. Situation in Lemma 4.4.4

Lemma 4.4.4 (Adjustment Lemma for $\mathtt{LFEM}_\Phi$).
Let $\psi \in \Phi$ such that (IH) $\mathtt{LFEM}_\varphi$ is computationally optimal for any $\varphi \in SubExpr_\Phi(\psi)$. Moreover, let p be an interval of program points between the earliest and latest program point (cf. Lemma 3.4.2(2)), i. e. a path with (A1) $Earliest^\psi_{p_1}$, (A2) $Latest^\psi_{p_{|p|}}$ and (A3) $\forall 1 \leqslant k < |p|.\ Delayed^\psi_{p_k} \wedge \neg Latest^\psi_{p_k}$. Then there are indices $1 \leqslant i \leqslant j \leqslant |p|$ such that:

1. $\forall 1 \leqslant k \leqslant |p|.\ A1\text{-}Earliest^\psi_{p_k} \ \Leftrightarrow\ (i = k)$
2. $\forall 1 \leqslant k \leqslant |p|.\ A1\text{-}Delayed^\psi_{p_k} \ \Leftrightarrow\ (i \leqslant k)$
3. $\forall 1 \leqslant k \leqslant |p|.\ A2\text{-}Delayed^\psi_{p_k} \ \Leftrightarrow\ (i \leqslant k \leqslant j)$
4. $\forall 1 \leqslant k \leqslant |p|.\ A2\text{-}Latest^\psi_{p_k} \ \Leftrightarrow\ (j = k)$

Proof. First let us collect some properties on the path p under consideration:

$$\forall 1 \leqslant k < |p|.\ \neg Comp^\psi_{p_k} \tag{4.9a}$$

$$\forall 1 \leqslant k \leqslant |p|.\ DnSafe^\psi_{p_k} \tag{4.9b}$$

$$\forall 1 \leqslant k \leqslant |p|.\ \neg UpSafe^\psi_{p_k} \tag{4.9c}$$

$$\forall 1 \leqslant k < |p|.\ Transp^\psi_{p_k} \tag{4.9d}$$

Point (4.9a) is an immediate consequence of Assumptions (A2) and (A3) using the definitions of delayability and latestness. Moreover, according to Lemma 4.4.1(2) Assumptions (A2) and (A3) also imply Property (4.9b). The earliestness of p_1 together with Property (4.9a) induces Property (4.9c). For the proof of Property (4.9d) let us assume an index $k < |p|$ with $\neg Transp^\psi_{p_k}$. As, according to Property (4.9a), also $\neg Comp^\psi_{p_k}$ holds, we obtain $\neg DnSafe^\psi_{p_k}$ in contradiction to Property (4.9b). Now we shall in turn deal with the proofs of Point (1) to (4):

Proof of 1: Let us choose i as the smallest index that satisfies $A1\text{-}DnSafe^{\psi}_{p_i}$. Such an index exists, since Assumption (A2) combined with Lemma 4.4.2(2) ensures $A1\text{-}DnSafe^{\psi}_{p_{|p|}}$. With this choice $A1\text{-}Earliest^{\psi}_{p_i}$ is implied by Assumption (A1) if $i=1$, otherwise it follows from Property (4.9c). To show also the uniqueness of i, i. e. the forward-implication of Point (1), it is sufficient to show

$$\forall\, k \geqslant i.\ A1\text{-}DnSafe^{\psi}_{p_k} \tag{4.10}$$

For $i \leqslant k < |p|$ we have

$$
\begin{array}{ll}
 & A1\text{-}DnSafe^{\psi}_{p_k} \\
\text{[Definition } A1\text{-}DnSafe] & \\
\Leftrightarrow & DnSafe^{\psi}_{p_k} \wedge \forall\, \varphi \in SubExpr_{\Phi}(\psi).\ \mathtt{LFEM}_{\Phi}\text{-}Correct^{\varphi}_{p_k} \\
\text{[Property (4.9b)]} & \\
\Rightarrow & DnSafe^{\psi}_{p_{k+1}} \wedge \forall\, \varphi \in SubExpr_{\Phi}(\psi).\ \mathtt{LFEM}_{\Phi}\text{-}Correct^{\varphi}_{p_k} \\
\text{[(4.11)]}\ \Rightarrow & DnSafe^{\psi}_{p_{k+1}} \wedge \forall\, \varphi \in SubExpr_{\Phi}(\psi).\ \mathtt{LFEM}_{\Phi}\text{-}Correct^{\psi}_{p_{k+1}} \\
\text{[Definition } A1\text{-}DnSafe] & \\
\Rightarrow & A1\text{-}DnSafe^{\psi}_{p_{k+1}}
\end{array}
$$

For Implication (4.11) let us assume $\varphi \in SubExpr_{\Phi}(\psi)$ with $\mathtt{LFEM}_{\Phi}\text{-}Correct^{\varphi}_{p_k}$. Now we are going to show that also $\mathtt{LFEM}_{\Phi}\text{-}Correct^{\varphi}_{p_{k+1}}$ must hold. As Assumption (A3) ensures $Delayed^{\psi}_{p_{k+1}}$, Lemma 4.2.5(1) yields

$$\underbrace{Delayed^{\varphi}_{p_{k+1}} \wedge \neg Latest^{\varphi}_{p_{k+1}}}_{i)} \vee \underbrace{\mathtt{LEM}_{\Phi}\text{-}Correct^{\varphi}_{p_{k+1}}}_{ii)}$$

In the case of (i) we argue with Lemma 3.4.2(2) and Remark 3.4.1 which are applicable, since, by (IH), $\mathtt{LFEM}_{\varphi}$ is assumed to be computationally optimal. These results then establish that $\mathtt{LFEM}_{\Phi}\text{-}Correct^{\varphi}_{p_k}$ carries over to p_{k+1} yielding $\mathtt{LFEM}_{\Phi}\text{-}Correct^{\varphi}_{p_{k+1}}$.

Considering (ii) we can argue similarly. Here we succeed using Corollary 3.4.1, which allows to conclude $\mathtt{LFEM}_{\Phi}\text{-}Correct^{\varphi}_{p_{k+1}}$ from $\mathtt{LEM}_{\Phi}\text{-}Correct^{\varphi}_{p_{k+1}}$. Again this requires to exploit Assumption (IH).

Proof of 2: For indices $k < i$ we have $\neg A1\text{-}DnSafe^{\psi}_{p_k}$ by construction, which forces also $\neg A1\text{-}Delayed^{\psi}_{p_k}$ according to Lemma 4.4.1(2). On the other hand for $k \geqslant i$ we have using Point (4.10) as well as Assumption (A2) and (A3):

$$\forall\, k \geqslant i.\ Delayed^{\psi}_{p_k} \wedge A1\text{-}DnSafe^{\psi}_{p_k},$$

which according to Lemma 4.4.1 means $\forall\, k \geqslant i.\ A1\text{-}Delayed^{\psi}_{p_k}$.

Proof of 3: Let us choose index j as the largest index in the range $\{i, \dots, |p|\}$ such that the backward-implication of Part (3) is valid, i. e. $\forall i \leqslant k \leqslant j.\ \textit{A2-Delayed}^{\psi}_{p_k}$. Note that at least $\textit{A2-Delayed}^{\psi}_{p_i}$ holds, and thus the existence of such an index j can be ensured. For the forward-implication it is left to prove that

$$\underbrace{\forall 1 \leqslant k < i.\ \neg \textit{A2-Delayed}^{\psi}_{p_k}}_{i)} \ \wedge \ \underbrace{\forall j < k \leqslant |p|.\ \neg \textit{A2-Delayed}^{\psi}_{p_k}}_{ii)}$$

First, the fact that Part (2) ensures $\forall 1 \leqslant k < i.\ \neg \textit{A1-Delayed}^{\psi}_{p_k}$ also grants (i) using Lemma 4.4.1(1). For the proof of (ii) we shall assume without loss of generality that $j < |p|$. Then $\neg \textit{A2-Delayed}^{\psi}_{p_{j+1}}$ is satisfied by definition of j, and for $j < k < |p|$ the following inductive argument applies:

$$\begin{aligned} \neg \textit{A2-Delayed}^{\psi}_{p_k} &\Rightarrow \neg \textit{A2-Delayed}^{\psi}_{p_{k+1}} \vee \textit{A1-Earliest}^{\psi}_{p_{k+1}} \\ &\Rightarrow \neg \textit{A2-Delayed}^{\psi}_{p_{k+1}}, \end{aligned}$$

where the first implication is a trivial consequence of the path characterisation of *A2-Delayed* (*A2-Delayed* can only be triggered at program points satisfying the *A1-Earliest*-predicate) and the second one is a consequence of Part (1) which ensures $\neg \textit{A1-Earliest}^{\psi}_{p_{k+1}}$. Finally, Part (3) immediately implies Point (4), if $j < |p|$. Otherwise, Part (4) can be concluded from $\textit{A1-Latest}^{\psi}_{p_{|p|}}$. □

Lemma 4.4.4 can be applied levelwise establishing the computational optimality of the individual $\texttt{LFEM}_{\varphi}$-transformations for any $\varphi \in \Phi$. This directly carries over to $\texttt{LFEM}_{\Phi}$ yielding:

Theorem 4.4.2 (Computational Optimality Theorem for $\texttt{LFEM}_{\Phi}$). *$\texttt{LFEM}_{\Phi}$ is computationally optimal, i. e. $\texttt{LFEM}_{\Phi} \in \mathcal{COEM}_{\Phi}$.*

We close Section 4.4.3 by providing two further results that crucially depend on the computational optimality of $\texttt{LFEM}_{\Phi}$. In addition to Lemma 4.4.4 that can be understood as the counterpart of Lemma 3.4.2(2) also the first part of Lemma 3.4.2 that states that computationally optimal transformations must place their insertions inside of intervals of delayable program points has its equivalent in the first part of the following lemma. Moreover, the second part expresses the fact that subexpressions must be available over the whole range of adjusted delayability. Note that this part has some similarities to Lemma 4.2.5(3).

Lemma 4.4.5 (Insertion Lemma for $\texttt{LFEM}_{\Phi}$). *Let $\texttt{EM}_{\Phi} \in \mathcal{COEM}_{\Phi}$ such that $\texttt{EM}_{\Phi^{<i}} = \texttt{LFEM}_{\Phi^{<i}}$, $\psi \in \Phi^{\leqslant i}$ and $\dot{n} \in \dot{N}$. Then we have:*

1. $\texttt{EM}_{\Phi^{\leqslant i}}\textit{-Insert}^{\psi}_{\dot{n}} \Rightarrow \textit{A1-Delayed}^{\psi}_{\dot{n}}$
2. $\textit{A1-Earliest}^{\psi}_{\dot{n}} \vee \neg \textit{A1-Delayed}^{\psi}_{\dot{n}} \Rightarrow \forall \varphi \in \textit{SubExpr}_{\Phi}(\psi).\ \neg \texttt{EM}_{\Phi}\textit{-Insert}^{\varphi}_{\dot{n}}$

Proof. The proof of Part (1) is trivial for $\varphi \in \Phi^{<i}$. Hence let us assume $\varphi \in \Phi^i$. Then the requirements on structured expression motion (cf. Definition 4.2.1) ensure that subexpressions of ψ are available at $\dot{n}$, i. e.

$$\forall \varphi \in \mathit{SubExpr}_\Phi(\psi).\ \mathbf{EM}_\Phi\text{-}\mathit{Correct}^\varphi_{\dot{n}}$$

Using our assumption on $\mathbf{EM}_\Phi$ we have

$$\forall \varphi \in \mathit{SubExpr}_\Phi(\psi).\ \mathbf{LFEM}_\Phi\text{-}\mathit{Correct}^\varphi_{\dot{n}} \tag{4.12}$$

According to Lemma 3.4.2(1), which is applicable due to the computational optimality of $\mathbf{LFEM}_\Phi$, we further have $\mathit{Delayed}^\psi_{\dot{n}}$, which due to Lemma 3.4.1(1) implies $\mathit{DnSafe}^\psi_{\dot{n}}$. This together with Property (4.12) yields $\mathit{A1\text{-}DnSafe}^\psi_{\dot{n}}$. Hence Lemma 4.4.1(3) finally establishes $\mathit{A1\text{-}Delayed}^\psi_{\dot{n}}$.

For the proof of Part (2) let $\varphi \in \mathit{SubExpr}_\Phi(\psi)$. Then

$$\neg \mathit{A1\text{-}Earliest}^\psi_{\dot{n}} \wedge \mathit{A1\text{-}Delayed}^\psi_{\dot{n}}$$

[Definition *A1-Delayed* & *A1-Latest*]

$$\Rightarrow\ \forall \dot{m} \in \mathit{pred}(\dot{n}).\ \mathit{A1\text{-}Delayed}^\psi_{\dot{m}} \wedge \neg \mathit{A1\text{-}Latest}^\psi_{\dot{m}}$$

[Lemma 4.4.1(2) & Definition *A1-Latest*]

$$\Rightarrow\ \forall \dot{m} \in \mathit{pred}(\dot{n}).\ \mathit{A1\text{-}DnSafe}^\psi_{\dot{m}} \wedge \neg \mathit{Comp}^\psi_{\dot{m}}$$

[Definition *A1-DnSafe*]

$$\Rightarrow\ \forall \dot{m} \in \mathit{pred}(\dot{n}).\ \mathbf{LFEM}_\Phi\text{-}\mathit{Correct}^\varphi_{\dot{m}} \wedge \mathit{DnSafe}^\psi_{\dot{m}} \wedge \neg \mathit{Comp}^\psi_{\dot{m}}$$

[Definition *DnSafe*]

$$\Rightarrow\ \forall \dot{m} \in \mathit{pred}(\dot{n}).\ \mathbf{LFEM}_\Phi\text{-}\mathit{Correct}^\varphi_{\dot{m}} \wedge \mathit{Transp}^\psi_{\dot{m}}$$

[Lemma 4.2.1(1)]

$$\Rightarrow\ \forall \dot{m} \in \mathit{pred}(\dot{n}).\ \mathbf{LFEM}_\Phi\text{-}\mathit{Correct}^\varphi_{\dot{m}} \wedge \mathit{Transp}^\varphi_{\dot{m}}$$

[$\mathbf{EM}_{\Phi^{<i}} = \mathbf{LFEM}_{\Phi^{<i}}$]

$$\Rightarrow\ \forall \dot{m} \in \mathit{pred}(\dot{n}).\ \mathbf{EM}_\Phi\text{-}\mathit{Correct}^\varphi_{\dot{m}} \wedge \mathit{Transp}^\varphi_{\dot{m}}$$

[$\mathbf{EM}_\Phi \in \mathcal{COEM}_\Phi$]

$$\Rightarrow\ \neg \mathbf{EM}_{\Phi^i}\text{-}\mathit{Insert}^\varphi_{\dot{m}}$$

□

4.4.4 Proving Inductive Lifetime Optimality

The proof of inductive lifetime optimality for $\mathbf{LFEM}_\Phi$ is more challenging. We start this section by proving some basic properties of the *LUsedLater* predicate. We have:

Lemma 4.4.6 (*LUsedLater*-Lemma).
Let $\mathbf{EM}_\Phi \in \mathcal{COEM}_\Phi$ such that $\mathbf{EM}_{\Phi^{<i}} = \mathbf{LFEM}_{\Phi^{<i}}$ and $\dot{n} \in \dot{N}$. Then

1. $\forall\, \psi \in \Phi^i.\ \mathit{A1\text{-}DnSafe}^{\psi}_{\dot n} \wedge \mathit{Transp}^{\psi}_{\dot n} \;\Rightarrow\; \mathit{UsedLater}^{\psi}_{\dot n}[\Phi^{\leqslant i}]$
2. a) $\forall\, \varphi \in \Phi.\ \mathtt{EM}_{\Phi}\text{-}\mathit{Correct}^{\varphi}_{\dot n} \wedge \mathit{UsedLater}^{\varphi}_{\dot n}[\Phi^{\leqslant i}] \Rightarrow\ \dot n \in \mathit{SLtRg}(\mathtt{EM}_{\Phi^{\leqslant i}}, \varphi)$
   b) $\forall\, \psi \in \Phi^i.\ \dot n \in \mathit{SLtRg}(\mathtt{EM}_{\Phi^{\leqslant i}}, \psi) \Rightarrow \mathtt{EM}_{\Phi}\text{-}\mathit{Correct}^{\psi}_{\dot n} \wedge \mathit{UsedLater}^{\psi}_{\dot n}[\Phi^{\leqslant i}]$

Proof. Considering Part (1) let us assume $\psi \in \Phi^i$ such that

$$\mathit{A1\text{-}DnSafe}^{\psi}_{\dot n} \wedge \mathit{Transp}^{\psi}_{\dot n}$$

holds. According to the definition of *A1-DnSafe* this means that there is a path $p \in \mathbf{P}[\dot n, \dot{\mathbf{e}}]$ and an index $1 < j \leqslant |p|$ such that:

$$\mathit{Comp}^{\psi}_{p_j} \wedge \forall\, 1 \leqslant k < j.\ \mathit{A1\text{-}DnSafe}^{\psi}_{p_k} \wedge \mathit{Transp}^{\psi}_{p_k}$$

Using the fact that ψ is maximal in $\Phi^{\leqslant i}$ and the definition of *A1-Earliest* this particularly implies:

$$\mathtt{LFEM}_{\Phi^{\leqslant i}}\text{-}\mathit{Replace}^{\psi}_{p_j} \wedge \forall\, 1 \leqslant k < j.\ \neg \mathit{A1\text{-}Earliest}^{\psi}_{p_k},$$

which means $\mathit{UsedLater}^{\psi}_{\dot n}[\Phi^{\leqslant i}]$ as desired.

For Part (2a) we first note that the definition of $\mathtt{EM}_{\Phi}$-*Correct* ensures that there is a path $q \in \mathbf{P}[\dot{\mathbf{s}}, \dot n]$ and an index $j \leqslant |p|$ such that

$$\mathtt{EM}_{\Phi^{\leqslant i}}\text{-}\mathit{Insert}^{\varphi}_{q_j} \wedge \forall\, j < k \leqslant |p|.\ \neg \mathtt{EM}_{\Phi^{\leqslant i}}\text{-}\mathit{Insert}^{\varphi}_{q_k} \tag{4.13}$$

On the other hand, due to condition $\mathit{UsedLater}^{\varphi}_{\dot n}[\Phi^{\leqslant i}]$ that there is a path $\bar q \in \mathbf{P}[\dot n, \dot{\mathbf{e}}]$ and an index $1 < j \leqslant |\bar q|$ such that

$$\begin{aligned}(\exists\, \psi \in \mathit{SupExpr}_{\Phi^i}(\varphi).\ \mathit{A1\text{-}Earliest}^{\psi}_{\bar q_j} \vee \mathtt{LFEM}_{\Phi^{\leqslant i}}\text{-}\mathit{Replace}^{\varphi}_{\bar q_j}) \wedge \\ \forall\, 1 < k \leqslant j.\ \neg \mathit{A1\text{-}Earliest}^{\varphi}_{\bar q_k}\end{aligned} \tag{4.14}$$

Let us first investigate the case, where $\mathtt{LFEM}_{\Phi^{\leqslant i}}\text{-}\mathit{Replace}^{\varphi}_{\bar q_j}$ holds. Thus we have:

$$\underbrace{\mathtt{LFEM}_{\Phi^{\leqslant i}}\text{-}\mathit{Replace}^{\varphi}_{\bar q_j}}_{i)} \wedge \underbrace{\forall\, 1 < k \leqslant j.\ \neg \mathit{A1\text{-}Earliest}^{\varphi}_{\bar q_k}}_{ii)} \tag{4.15}$$

Now we are going to prove:

$$\forall\, 1 < k \leqslant j.\ \neg \mathtt{EM}_{\Phi^{\leqslant i}}\text{-}\mathit{Insert}^{\varphi}_{\bar q_k}$$

Suppose there is an index $1 < k \leqslant j$ with $\mathtt{EM}_{\Phi^{\leqslant i}}\text{-}\mathit{Insert}^{\varphi}_{\bar q_k}$. Then Lemma 4.4.5(1) ensures that $\bar q_k$ is preceded on every path from $\dot{\mathbf{s}}$ to $\bar q_k$ by a program point satisfying *A1-Earliest*. Using Condition (ii) this point must precede $\dot n$ yielding

$$\forall\, 1 < l \leqslant k.\ \mathit{A1\text{-}Delayed}^{\varphi}_{\bar q_l} \wedge \neg \mathit{A1\text{-}Latest}^{\varphi}_{\bar q_l}$$

Due to the fact that $\mathtt{EM}_{\Phi^{\leqslant i}}\text{-}Correct^{\varphi}_{\dot{n}}$ holds this, however, would mean that $\mathtt{EM}_{\Phi}$ has two φ-insertions on an interval of delayable program points, which is in contradiction to Lemma 3.4.2(2). Similarly, the previous argument also ensures that Condition (i) implies $\mathtt{EM}_{\Phi^{\leqslant i}}\text{-}Replace^{\varphi}_{p_j}$, since otherwise $\mathtt{EM}_{\Phi^{\leqslant i}}$ would again have two computations of φ on an interval of delayable program points contradicting Lemma 3.4.2(2). Hence Condition (4.15) can be transformed to

$$\underbrace{\mathtt{EM}_{\Phi^{\leqslant i}}\text{-}Replace^{\varphi}_{\bar{q}_j}}_{i)} \;\wedge\; \underbrace{\forall\, 1 < k \leqslant j.\ \neg \mathtt{EM}_{\Phi^{\leqslant i}}\text{-}Insert^{\varphi}_{\bar{q}_k}}_{ii)} \tag{4.16}$$

Investigating the other alternative of Condition (4.14) the assumption on $\mathtt{EM}_{\Phi}$ delivers:

$$\begin{array}{l} \underbrace{\exists\, \psi \in SupExpr_{\Phi^i}(\varphi).\ A1\text{-}Earliest^{\psi}_{\bar{q}_j}}_{iii)} \;\wedge \\ \underbrace{\forall\, 1 < k \leqslant j.\ \neg \mathtt{EM}_{\Phi^{\leqslant i}}\text{-}Insert^{\varphi}_{\bar{q}_k}}_{iv)} \end{array} \tag{4.17}$$

Using Lemma 4.4.5(1) Condition (iii) further ensures that there is an index $l \geqslant j$ such that $\mathtt{EM}_{\Phi^{\leqslant i}}\text{-}Insert^{\psi}_{\bar{q}_l}$ holds and such that

$$\forall\, j < k \leqslant l.\ A1\text{-}Delayed^{\psi}_{\bar{q}_k} \wedge \neg A1\text{-}Earliest^{\psi}_{\bar{q}_k}$$

Due to Lemma 4.4.5(2) this finally excludes an φ-insertion of $\mathtt{EM}_{\Phi}$ between $\bar{q}_{j+1}$ and $\bar{q}_l$. Hence we finally get

$$\exists\, \psi \in SupExpr_{\Phi^i}(\varphi).\ \mathtt{EM}_{\Phi^{\leqslant i}}\text{-}Insert^{\psi}_{\bar{q}_l} \;\wedge\; \forall\, 1 < k \leqslant l.\ \neg \mathtt{EM}_{\Phi^{\leqslant i}}\text{-}Insert^{\varphi}_{\bar{q}_k} \tag{4.18}$$

Putting together the "upward-situation " of Condition (4.13) and the "downward-situation" of Condition (4.16) or Condition (4.18), respectively, we obtain a path p with $|p| \geqslant 2$ and:

i) $\mathtt{EM}_{\Phi^{\leqslant i}}\text{-}Insert^{\varphi}_{p_1}$
ii) $\exists\, \psi \in SupExpr_{\Phi^i}(\varphi).\ \mathtt{EM}_{\Phi^{\leqslant i}}\text{-}Insert^{\varphi}_{p_{|p|}} \vee \mathtt{LFEM}_{\Phi^{\leqslant i}}\text{-}Replace^{\varphi}_{p_{|p|}}$
iii) $\forall\, 1 < k \leqslant |p|.\ \neg \mathtt{EM}_{\Phi^{\leqslant i}}\text{-}Insert^{\varphi}_{p_k}$

This, however, means $\dot{n} \in SLtRg(\mathtt{EM}_{\Phi^{\leqslant i}}, \varphi)$.

Investigating Part (2b) Lemma 4.2.7 delivers $\mathtt{EM}_{\Phi}\text{-}Correct^{\psi}_{\dot{n}}$. On the other hand, $UsedLater^{\psi}_{\dot{n}}[\Phi^{\leqslant i}]$ is immediate from the maximality of ψ, which requires that the lifetime range reaches an original replacement site of ψ. □

We continue with some useful properties on trade-off candidates:

Lemma 4.4.7 (Trade-off Candidate Lemma for $\mathtt{LFEM}_\Phi$).

1. $\forall\, \dot{n} \in \dot{N},\ \dot{m} \in \mathit{pred}(\mathit{succ}(\dot{n})).\ \Theta^{\mathrm{up}(i)}_{\dot{n}} = \Theta^{\mathrm{up}(i)}_{\dot{m}}$
2. a) $\forall\, \dot{n} \in \dot{N},\ \psi \in \Theta^{\mathrm{up}(i)}_{\dot{n}}.\ \mathit{UsedLater}^{\psi}_{\dot{n}}[\Phi^{\leqslant i}]$
   b) $\forall\, \dot{n} \in \dot{N},\ \varphi \in \Theta^{\mathrm{dn}(i)}_{\dot{n}}.\ \mathit{UsedLater}^{\varphi}_{\dot{n}}[\Phi^{< i}]$
3. $\forall\, \dot{n} \in \dot{N},\ \varphi \in \Theta^{\mathrm{dn}(i)}_{\dot{n}}.\ \mathtt{LFEM}_{\Phi^{\leqslant i}}\text{-}\mathit{Correct}^{\varphi}_{\dot{n}}$
4. a) $\forall\, \dot{n} \in \dot{N},\ \psi \in \Theta^{\mathrm{up}(i)}_{\dot{n}},\ \dot{n}_s \in \mathit{succ}(\dot{n}).\ \neg \mathit{A1\text{-}Earliest}^{\psi}_{\dot{n}_s}$
   b) $\forall\, \dot{n} \in \dot{N},\ \varphi \in \Theta^{\mathrm{dn}(i)}_{\dot{n}},\ \dot{n}_s \in \mathit{succ}(\dot{n}).\ \neg \mathit{A1\text{-}Earliest}^{\varphi}_{\dot{n}_s}$

Proof. Considering Part (1) let $\psi \in \Theta^{\mathrm{up}(i)}_{\dot{n}}$. If $\dot{n}$ is an entry point of a node there is nothing to show since $\mathit{pred}(\mathit{succ}(\dot{n})) = \{\dot{n}\}$. Similarly, if $|\mathit{succ}(\dot{n})| \geqslant 2$ then Control Flow Lemma 2.2.1(2) ensures $\mathit{pred}(\mathit{succ}(\dot{n})) = \{\dot{n}\}$. Therefore, we may assume:

$$\mathit{succ}(\dot{n}) = \{\dot{n}_s\} \tag{4.19}$$

Then we have:

$$\psi \in \Theta^{\mathrm{up}(i)}_{\dot{n}}$$

[Definition $\Theta^{\mathrm{up}(i)}_{\dot{n}}$]

$$\Rightarrow\ \mathit{A1\text{-}Delayed}^{\psi}_{\dot{n}} \wedge \neg \mathit{A1\text{-}Latest}^{\psi}_{\dot{n}}$$

[Definition *A1-Latest* & Lemma 4.4.4]

$$\Rightarrow\ \mathit{A1\text{-}Delayed}^{\psi}_{\dot{n}_s} \wedge \neg \mathit{A1\text{-}Earliest}^{\psi}_{\dot{n}_s}$$

[Definition *A1-Delayed* & *A1-Latest*]

$$\Rightarrow\ \mathit{A1\text{-}Delayed}^{\psi}_{\dot{n}_s} \wedge \forall\, \dot{m} \in \mathit{pred}(\dot{n}_s).\ \mathit{A1\text{-}Delayed}^{\psi}_{\dot{m}} \wedge \neg \mathit{A1\text{-}Latest}^{\psi}_{\dot{m}}$$

[Assumption $\mathit{pred}(\mathit{succ}(\dot{n})) = \{\dot{n}\}$]

$$\Rightarrow\ \forall\, \dot{m} \in \mathit{pred}(\mathit{succ}(\dot{n})).\ \mathit{A1\text{-}Delayed}^{\psi}_{\dot{m}} \wedge \neg \mathit{A1\text{-}Latest}^{\psi}_{\dot{m}}$$

[Definition $\Theta^{\mathrm{up}(i)}_{\dot{m}}$]

$$\Rightarrow\ \forall\, \dot{m} \in \mathit{pred}(\mathit{succ}(\dot{n})).\ \psi \in \Theta^{\mathrm{up}(i)}_{\dot{m}}$$

Symmetric arguments prove the equality of all $\Theta^{\mathrm{up}(i)}_{\dot{m}}$ for $\dot{m} \in \mathit{pred}(\mathit{succ}(\dot{n}))$.

Investigating Part (2a) we have:

$$\psi \in \Theta^{\mathrm{up}(i)}_{\dot{n}}$$

$$[\text{Definition } \Theta^{\mathrm{up}(i)}_{\dot{n}}] \ \Rightarrow\ \mathit{A1\text{-}Delayed}^{\psi}_{\dot{n}} \wedge \neg \mathit{A1\text{-}Latest}^{\psi}_{\dot{n}}$$

$$[\text{Definition } \mathit{A1\text{-}Latest}] \ \Rightarrow\ \mathit{A1\text{-}Delayed}^{\psi}_{\dot{n}} \wedge \neg \mathit{Comp}^{\psi}_{\dot{n}}$$

$$\begin{array}{rcl}
\text{[Lemma 4.4.1(2)]} & \Rightarrow & \mathit{A1\text{-}DnSafe}_{\dot n}^{\psi} \wedge \neg \mathit{Comp}_{\dot n}^{\psi} \\
\text{[Definition } \mathit{A1\text{-}DnSafe}\text{]} & \Rightarrow & \mathit{A1\text{-}DnSafe}_{\dot n}^{\psi} \wedge \mathit{Transp}_{\dot n}^{\psi} \\
\text{[Lemma 4.4.6(1)]} & \Rightarrow & \mathit{UsedLater}_{\dot n}^{\psi}[\Phi^{\leqslant i}]
\end{array}$$

For the proof of Part (2b) we may use parts of the proof of Part (2a):

$$\begin{array}{rcl}
 & & \varphi \in \Theta_{\dot n}^{\mathbf{dn}(i)} \\
\text{[Definition } \Theta_{\dot n}^{\mathbf{dn}(i)}\text{]} & \Rightarrow & \exists\, \psi \in \mathit{neigh}(\varphi).\ \Theta_{\dot n}^{\mathbf{up}(i)} \\
\text{[Proof Part (2a)]} & \Rightarrow & \exists\, \psi \in \mathit{neigh}(\varphi).\ \mathit{A1\text{-}DnSafe}_{\dot n}^{\psi} \wedge \mathit{Transp}_{\dot n}^{\psi} \\
\text{[Lemma 4.2.1(1) \& 4.4.3]} & \Rightarrow & \exists\, \psi \in \mathit{neigh}(\varphi).\ \mathit{A1\text{-}DnSafe}_{\dot n}^{\varphi} \wedge \mathit{Transp}_{\dot n}^{\varphi} \\
\text{[Lemma 4.4.6(1)]} & \Rightarrow & \mathit{UsedLater}_{\dot n}^{\varphi}[\Phi^{<i}]
\end{array}$$

For the proof of Part (3) let $\varphi \in \Theta_{\dot n}^{\mathbf{dn}(i)}$. Obviously, then there is an expression $\psi \in \mathit{neigh}(\varphi)$ that gives rise to the following argumentation:

$$\begin{array}{rcl}
 & & \psi \in \Theta_{\dot n}^{\mathbf{up}(i)} \\
\text{[Definition } \Theta_{\dot n}^{\mathbf{up}(i)}\text{]} & \Rightarrow & \mathit{A1\text{-}Delayed}_{\dot n}^{\psi} \\
\text{[Lemma 4.4.1(2)]} & \Rightarrow & \mathit{A1\text{-}DnSafe}_{\dot n}^{\psi} \\
\text{[Definition } \mathit{A1\text{-}DnSafe}\text{]} & \Rightarrow & \mathbf{LFEM}_{\Phi^{\leqslant i}}\text{-}\mathit{Correct}_{\dot n}^{\varphi}
\end{array}$$

Investigating the proof of Part (4a) we have for $\dot n_s \in \mathit{succ}(\dot n)$:

$$\begin{array}{rcl}
 & & \psi \in \Theta_{\dot n}^{\mathbf{up}(i)} \\
\text{[Part (1)]} & \Rightarrow & \forall\, \dot m \in \mathit{pred}(\dot n_s).\ \psi \in \Theta_{\dot m}^{\mathbf{up}(i)} \\
\text{[Proof Part (2a)]} & \Rightarrow & \forall\, \dot m \in \mathit{pred}(\dot n_s).\ \mathit{A1\text{-}DnSafe}_{\dot m}^{\psi} \wedge \mathit{Transp}_{\dot m}^{\psi} \\
\text{[Definition } \mathit{A1\text{-}Earliest}\text{]} & \Rightarrow & \neg \mathit{A1\text{-}Earliest}_{\dot n_s}^{\psi}
\end{array}$$

Finally, Part (4b) can rely on the proof of Part (4a):

$$\begin{array}{rcl}
 & & \varphi \in \Theta_{\dot n}^{\mathbf{dn}(i)} \\
\text{[Definition } \Theta_{\dot n}^{\mathbf{dn}(i)}\text{]} & \Rightarrow & \exists\, \psi \in \mathit{neigh}(\varphi).\ \Theta_{\dot n}^{\mathbf{up}(i)} \\
\text{[Proof Part (4a)]} & \Rightarrow & \\
 & & \exists\, \psi \in \mathit{neigh}(\varphi)\ \forall\, \dot m \in \mathit{pred}(\dot n_s).\ \mathit{A1\text{-}DnSafe}_{\dot m}^{\psi} \wedge \mathit{Transp}_{\dot m}^{\psi} \\
\text{[Lem. 4.2.1(1) \& 4.4.3]} & \Rightarrow & \forall\, \dot m \in \mathit{pred}(\dot n_s).\ \mathit{A1\text{-}DnSafe}_{\dot m}^{\varphi} \wedge \mathit{Transp}_{\dot m}^{\varphi} \\
\text{[Definition } \mathit{A1\text{-}Earliest}\text{]} & \Rightarrow & \neg \mathit{A1\text{-}Earliest}_{\dot n_s}^{\varphi}
\end{array}$$

□

The following lemma has a key role in the whole proof of inductive lifetime optimality, as it ensures that the local trade-off information given by the *LChange* predicate is perfectly conform with its globalisation given in terms of the second adjustment of delayability. This means, a premature initialisation that is found to be profitable at one program point remains profitable (from a local point of view) within the whole delayability range. Besides being important for the proof of inductive lifetime optimality, this property also simplifies the implementation, since the adjustment of delayability can be computed by a trivial local refinement step (cf. Section 4.4.5). Finally, however, we should note that the result relies on Lemma 4.4.7(1) and therefore crucially depends on the absence of critical edges.

Lemma 4.4.8 (Trade-off Lemma for LFEM_Φ).

$$\forall \dot{n} \in \dot{N},\ \psi \in \Theta_{\dot{n}}^{\mathtt{up}(i)}.\ LChange_{\dot{n}}^{\psi} \Leftrightarrow \forall \dot{m} \in succ(\dot{n}).\ \neg A2\text{-}Delayed_{\dot{m}}^{\psi}$$

Proof. The $\Rightarrow$-direction is almost trivial, as it is a direct consequence of the definition of *A2-Delayed* and Lemma 4.4.7(4a). In contrast, the proof of the $\Leftarrow$-direction is more intricate. Therefore, let us consider a program point $\dot{m} \in succ(\dot{n})$ with $\neg A2\text{-}Delayed_{\dot{m}}^{\psi}$.[7] Since $\psi \in \Theta_{\dot{n}}^{\mathtt{up}(i)}$ there is a path $p \in \mathbf{P}[\dot{\mathbf{s}}, \dot{m}]$ on which *A2-Delayed* is terminated by the *LChange* predicate, i. e. there is an index $j < |p|$ such that the following two properties are satisfied:

$$LChange_{p_j}^{\psi} \tag{4.20a}$$

$$\forall j \leqslant k < |p|.\ A1\text{-}Delayed_{p_k}^{\psi} \wedge \neg A1\text{-}Latest_{p_k}^{\psi} \tag{4.20b}$$

Now we are going to show that the *LChange* predicate stays true after position j, i. e.

$$\forall j \leqslant k < |p|.\ LChange_{p_k}^{\psi}$$

This is proved by means of an induction on $k - j$.

Induction Base: $k - j = 0$.

Trivial due to Assumption (4.20a).

Induction Step: $k - j > 0,\ k < |p|$.

Here we aim at constructing an irreducible subset $S \subseteq \Theta_k^{\mathtt{dn}(i)}$ such that $\psi \in neigh_k(S)$.[8] In this case $\psi \in neigh_k(\mathcal{T}^{\top}(\Theta_k^{\mathtt{dn}(i)}))$ follows from Lemma 4.3.1(2), which is a synonym for $LChange_{p_k}^{\psi}$.

Let us consider the following sets of expressions:

$$\begin{aligned} T &\stackrel{\text{def}}{=} neigh_{k-1}(\mathcal{T}^{\top}(\Theta_{k-1}^{\mathtt{dn}(i)})) \cap \Theta_k^{\mathtt{up}(i)} \\ S &\stackrel{\text{def}}{=} neigh_{k-1}(T) \cap \mathcal{T}^{\top}(\Theta_{k-1}^{\mathtt{dn}(i)}) \end{aligned}$$

---

[7] Note that $\psi \in \Theta_{\dot{n}}^{\mathtt{up}(i)}$ particularly excludes that $\dot{n} = \dot{\mathbf{e}}$, which guarantees the existence of such a successor.

[8] For the sake of simplicity we write of $\Theta_k^{\mathtt{dn}(i)}$ and $\Theta_k^{\mathtt{up}(i)}$ in place of $\Theta_{p_k}^{\mathtt{dn}(i)}$ and $\Theta_{p_k}^{\mathtt{up}(i)}$, respectively. Vertices of the bipartite graphs involved are identified with their associated expressions. In order to make the underlying bipartite graph explicit we use an indexed notation $neigh_{k-1}$ and $neigh_k$, respectively.

Then we are going to show that S defines an irreducible subset of $\Theta_k^{\mathrm{dn}(i)}$. To this end we first prove:

A) $S \subseteq \Theta_k^{\mathrm{dn}(i)}$

B) $neigh_k(S) \subseteq \Theta_{k-1}^{\mathrm{up}(i)}$.

Starting with the proof of A) let $\varphi \in S$. Since $SupExpr_{\Theta_k^{\mathrm{up}(i)}}(\varphi) \neq \emptyset$ is ensured by construction, it is sufficient to show

$$\neg\, UsedLater_{p_k}^{\varphi}[\Phi^{\leqslant i}].$$

Exploiting that $\varphi \in \Theta_{k-1}^{\mathrm{dn}(i)}$ holds we obtain $\neg\, UsedLater_{p_{k-1}}^{\varphi}[\Phi^{\leqslant i}]$. By the definition of $UsedLater_{p_{k-1}}^{\varphi}[\Phi^{\leqslant i}]$ the proof of $\neg\, UsedLater_{p_k}^{\varphi}[\Phi^{\leqslant i}]$ can be accomplished by showing that $\neg A1\text{-}Earliest_{p_k}^{\varphi}$ holds. This, however, is a trivial consequence of the definition of S that grants $\varphi \in \Theta_{k-1}^{\mathrm{dn}(i)}$ and Lemma 4.4.7(4b).

For the proof of B) let $\varphi \in S$ and $\tilde{\psi} \in neigh_k(\varphi)$. First we show

$$\neg A1\text{-}Earliest_{p_k}^{\tilde{\psi}} \tag{4.21}$$

Like in the proof of Inclusion (A) we have $\neg A1\text{-}Earliest_{p_k}^{\varphi}$, which in turn also forces $\neg A1\text{-}Earliest_{p_k}^{\tilde{\psi}}$, since otherwise $UsedLater_{p_{k-1}}^{\varphi}[\Phi^{\leqslant i}]$ would be valid in contradiction to $\varphi \in \Theta_{k-1}^{\mathrm{dn}(i)}$. Then we have:

$$\begin{array}{rcl} & & \tilde{\psi} \in \Theta_k^{\mathrm{up}(i)} \\ [\text{Definition } \Theta_k^{\mathrm{up}(i)}] & \Rightarrow & A1\text{-}Delayed_{p_k}^{\tilde{\psi}} \\ [\text{Property (4.21)}] & \Rightarrow & A1\text{-}Delayed_{p_k}^{\tilde{\psi}} \wedge \neg A1\text{-}Earliest_{p_k}^{\tilde{\psi}} \\ [\text{Defs. } Delayed \;\&\; Latest] & \Rightarrow & A1\text{-}Delayed_{p_{k-1}}^{\tilde{\psi}} \wedge \neg A1\text{-}Latest_{p_{k-1}}^{\tilde{\psi}} \\ [\text{Definition } \Theta_{k-1}^{\mathrm{up}(i)}] & \Rightarrow & \tilde{\psi} \in \Theta_{k-1}^{\mathrm{up}(i)} \end{array}$$

Based on Condition (A) we may investigate properties of S when considered at program point p_k:

C) $neigh_k(S) \supseteq T$

D) S is an irreducible subset of $\Theta_k^{\mathrm{dn}(i)}$

Starting with the proof of (C), the definitions of S and T obviously imply $neigh_{k-1}(S) \supseteq T$. Since $S \subseteq \Theta_k^{\mathrm{dn}(i)}$ (according to (A)) and $T \subseteq \Theta_k^{\mathrm{up}(i)}$ (by definition) this carries over to program point p_k yielding $neigh_k(S) \supseteq T$.

For the proof of (D) Lemma 4.3.1(1) and the definition of S deliver

D') S is an irreducible subset of $\Theta_{k-1}^{\mathrm{dn}(i)}$

Because (B) implies that a tightness defect of S at p_k would also be a tightness defect of S at p_{k-1}, (D) is then an obvious consequence of (D').

We finish the proof by showing:

E) $\psi \in neigh_k(\mathcal{T}^{\top}(\Theta_k^{\mathtt{up}(i)}))$

Using the induction hypothesis we have $LChange^{\psi}_{p_{k-1}}$, which stands as a synonym for $\psi \in neigh_{k-1}(\mathcal{T}^{\top}(\Theta_{k-1}^{\mathtt{dn}(i)}))$. Moreover, Assumption (4.20b) delivers $\psi \in \Theta_k^{\mathtt{up}(i)}$. Together we have $\psi \in T$. Using (D) and Lemma 4.3.1(2) we obtain $S \subseteq \mathcal{T}^{\top}(\Theta_k^{\mathtt{dn}(i)})$. Thus using Condition (C) this also implies $neigh_k(\mathcal{T}^{\top}(\Theta_k^{\mathtt{dn}(i)})) \supseteq T$, which finally yields $LChange^{\psi}_{p_k}$ as desired. □

Analysing the proof of Lemma 4.4.8 we recognise:

Remark 4.4.1. Lemma 4.4.8 can alternatively be formulated with existential in place of universal quantification, i. e.

$$\forall \psi \in \Theta_{\dot{n}}^{\mathtt{up}(i)}.\ LChange^{\psi}_{\dot{n}} \Leftrightarrow \exists \dot{m} \in succ(\dot{n}).\ \neg A2\text{-}Delayed^{\psi}_{\dot{m}}$$

Before we are going to state the proposed lifetime optimality result we shall investigate some important properties on lifetime ranges. In particular, the following lemma is devoted to results expressing lifetime ranges in terms of upper and lower trade-off candidates. Whereas the first part refers to an arbitrary computationally optimal expression motion, the second part addresses the special situation under $\mathtt{LFEM}_{\Phi}$, where Trade-off Lemma 4.4.8 can be employed in order to yield a particularly simple characterisation.

Lemma 4.4.9 (Lifetime Range Lemma for $\mathtt{LFEM}_{\Phi}$).
Let $\mathtt{EM}_{\Phi} \in \mathcal{COEM}_{\Phi}$ such that $\mathtt{EM}_{\Phi^{<i}} = \mathtt{LFEM}_{\Phi^{<i}}$ and $\dot{n} \in \dot{N}$. Then we have:

1. $\forall \varphi \in \Theta_{\dot{n}}^{\mathtt{dn}(i)}.\ \dot{n} \in SLtRg(\mathtt{EM}_{\Phi^{\leqslant i}}, \varphi) \Leftrightarrow \exists \psi \in neigh(\varphi).\ \neg\mathtt{EM}_{\Phi^{\leqslant i}}\text{-}Correct^{\psi}_{\dot{n}}$
2. a) $\forall \psi \in \Theta_{\dot{n}}^{\mathtt{up}(i)}.\ \dot{n} \in SLtRg(\mathtt{LFEM}_{\Phi^{\leqslant i}}, \psi) \Leftrightarrow LChange^{\psi}_{\dot{n}}$
   b) $\forall \varphi \in \Theta_{\dot{n}}^{\mathtt{dn}(i)}.\ \dot{n} \in SLtRg(\mathtt{LFEM}_{\Phi^{\leqslant i}}, \varphi) \Leftrightarrow \varphi \notin \mathcal{T}^{\top}(\Theta_{\dot{n}}^{\mathtt{dn}(i)})$

Proof of 1: Starting with the $\Rightarrow$-direction let us assume $\varphi \in \Theta_{\dot{n}}^{\mathtt{dn}(i)}$ such that $\dot{n} \in SLtRg(\mathtt{EM}_{\Phi^{\leqslant i}}, \varphi)$. As $\varphi \in \Theta_{\dot{n}}^{\mathtt{dn}(i)}$ implies $\neg\, UsedLater^{\varphi}_{\dot{n}}[\Phi^{\leqslant i}]$ we can exclude a strictly later original replacement of φ. Thus the definition of $SLtRg(\mathtt{EM}_{\Phi^{\leqslant i}}, \varphi)$ yields that there is an expression $\psi \in SupExpr_{\Phi^i}(\varphi)$ such that φ is used for the initialisation of this superexpression. That means there is a path $p \in \mathbf{P}[\dot{n}, \dot{\mathbf{e}}]$ and an index $1 < j \leqslant |p|$ with

$$\mathtt{EM}_{\Phi}\text{-}Insert^{\psi}_{p_j} \wedge \forall 1 < k \leqslant j.\ \neg\mathtt{EM}_{\Phi}\text{-}Insert^{\varphi}_{p_k}$$

Using the general assumption for $\mathbf{EM}_\Phi$ this can be rewritten as

$$\mathbf{EM}_\Phi\text{-}Insert^{\psi}_{p_j} \wedge \forall\, 1 < k \leqslant j.\ \neg\mathbf{LFEM}_\Phi\text{-}Insert^{\varphi}_{p_k} \tag{4.22}$$

Now we are going to show that this also implies

$$\mathbf{EM}_\Phi\text{-}Insert^{\psi}_{p_j} \wedge \forall\, 1 < k \leqslant j.\ \neg A1\text{-}Earliest^{\varphi}_{p_k} \tag{4.23}$$

Suppose, there would be an index $1 < k \leqslant j$ such that $A1\text{-}Earliest^{\varphi}_{p_k}$ holds. Then Lemma 4.2.5(3) implies that *A1-Delayed* for φ is terminated at least at p_{j+1}. Hence according to Lemma 4.4.4 $\mathbf{LFEM}_\Phi$ must have a φ-insertion on $\langle p_k, \dots, p_j \rangle$ in contradiction to Property (4.22).

Furthermore, using Lemma 4.4.5(1) we have $A1\text{-}Delayed^{\psi}_{p_j}$. According to the definition of the *A1-Delayed* predicate program point p_j must be preceded on every path from $\dot{\mathbf{s}}$ to p_j by a program point that satisfies *A1-Earliest*. Suppose, such a position would be situated on the path $\langle p_1, \dots, p_j \rangle$ strictly behind $\dot{n}$, i.e. there is an index $1 < k \leqslant j$ such that $A1\text{-}Earliest^{\psi}_{p_k}$ holds. Then this together with Property (4.23) delivers

$$A1\text{-}Earliest^{\psi}_{p_k} \wedge \forall\, 1 < l \leqslant k.\ \neg A1\text{-}Earliest^{\varphi}_{p_l},$$

which therefore means $UsedLater^{\varphi}_{\dot{n}}[\Phi^{\leqslant i}]$ in contradiction to the assumption $\varphi \in \Theta^{\mathrm{dn}(i)}_{\dot{n}}$. Hence we have

$$\forall\, 1 \leqslant k < j.\ A1\text{-}Delayed^{\psi}_{p_k} \wedge \neg A1\text{-}Latest^{\psi}_{p_k}$$

In particular, this means $\psi \in \Theta^{\mathrm{up}(i)}_{\dot{n}}$ and thus $\psi \in neigh(\varphi)$. On the other hand, we also have $\neg\mathbf{EM}_\Phi\text{-}Correct^{\psi}_{\dot{n}}$, as otherwise $\mathbf{EM}_\Phi$ would have two ψ-insertions on an interval of delayable program points in contradiction to Lemma 3.4.2(2).

For the proof of the $\Leftarrow$-direction we shall use Lemma 3.4.2(2) which yields that the assumption $\neg\mathbf{EM}_\Phi\text{-}Correct^{\psi}_{\dot{n}}$ together with $Delayed^{\psi}_{\dot{n}}$ implies that there is a path $p \in \mathbf{P}[\dot{n}, \dot{\mathbf{e}}]$ and an index $1 < j \leqslant |p|$ with

$$\mathbf{EM}_\Phi\text{-}Insert^{\psi}_{p_j} \wedge \forall\, 1 \leqslant k < j.\ Delayed^{\psi}_{p_k} \wedge \neg Latest^{\psi}_{p_k}$$

Since $\psi \in \Theta^{\mathrm{up}(i)}_{\dot{n}}$ and following Lemma 4.4.4 this can be strengthened towards

$$\mathbf{EM}_\Phi\text{-}Insert^{\psi}_{p_j} \wedge \forall\, 1 \leqslant k < j.\ A1\text{-}Delayed^{\psi}_{p_k} \wedge \neg A1\text{-}Latest^{\psi}_{p_k} \tag{4.24}$$

This almost establishes the desired result $\dot{n} \in SLtRg(\mathbf{EM}_{\Phi^{\leqslant i}}, \varphi)$: $\mathbf{EM}_\Phi\text{-}Correct^{\varphi}_{\dot{n}}$ holds by Lemma 4.4.7(3) and in addition p_j of Property (4.24) defines a potential use-site of $\mathbf{h}_\varphi$. In order to ensure that p_j is indeed a use-site of $\mathbf{h}_\varphi$ it is left to prove that $\mathbf{EM}_\Phi$ has no other φ-insertions in between $\dot{n}$ and p_j, i.e.

$$\forall\, 1 < k \leqslant j.\ \neg\mathbf{EM}_\Phi\text{-}Insert^{\varphi}_{p_k} \tag{4.25}$$

To this end Property (4.24) gives us

$$1 < k \leqslant j.\ \mathit{A1\text{-}Delayed}^{\psi}_{p_k} \wedge \neg \mathit{A1\text{-}Earliest}^{\psi}_{p_k},$$

which directly implies Property (4.25) according to Lemma 4.4.5(2).

Proof of 2a: We are first going to show

$$\forall\, \psi \in \Theta^{\mathrm{up}(i)}_{\dot{n}}.\ \mathtt{LFEM}_{\Phi}\text{-}\mathit{Correct}^{\psi}_{\dot{n}} \;\Leftrightarrow\; \mathit{LChange}^{\psi}_{\dot{n}}. \tag{4.26}$$

We start by proving the contrapositive of the $\Rightarrow$-direction, which is the more interesting one as it uses the non-trivial direction of the Trade-off Lemma 4.4.8.

$$\begin{array}{rcl} & & \neg \mathit{LChange}^{\psi}_{\dot{n}} \\ \text{[Lemma 4.4.8]} & \Rightarrow & \exists\, \dot{m} \in \mathit{succ}(\dot{n}).\ \mathit{A2\text{-}Delayed}^{\psi}_{\dot{m}} \\ \text{[Lemma 4.4.7(4a)]} & \Rightarrow & \exists\, \dot{m} \in \mathit{succ}(\dot{n}).\ \mathit{A2\text{-}Delayed}^{\psi}_{\dot{m}} \wedge \neg \mathit{A1\text{-}Earliest}^{\psi}_{\dot{m}} \\ \text{[Def. } \mathit{A2\text{-}Delayed}] & \Rightarrow & \mathit{A2\text{-}Delayed}^{\psi}_{\dot{n}} \\ \text{[Lemma 4.4.4]} & \Rightarrow & \neg \mathtt{LFEM}_{\Phi}\text{-}\mathit{Correct}^{\psi}_{\dot{n}} \end{array}$$

For the $\Leftarrow$-direction we have

$$\begin{array}{rcl} & & \mathit{LChange}^{\psi}_{\dot{n}} \\ [\psi \in \Theta^{\mathrm{up}(i)}_{\dot{n}}] & \Rightarrow & \mathit{LChange}^{\psi}_{\dot{n}} \wedge \mathit{A1\text{-}Delayed}^{\psi}_{\dot{n}} \wedge \neg \mathit{A1\text{-}Latest}^{\psi}_{\dot{n}} \\ \text{[Lemma 4.4.8]} & \Rightarrow & \\ \multicolumn{3}{l}{\forall\, \dot{m} \in \mathit{succ}(\dot{n}).\ \neg \mathit{A2\text{-}Delayed}^{\psi}_{\dot{m}} \wedge \mathit{A1\text{-}Delayed}^{\psi}_{\dot{n}} \wedge \neg \mathit{A1\text{-}Latest}^{\psi}_{\dot{n}}} \\ \text{[Lemma 4.4.4]} & \Rightarrow & \mathtt{LFEM}_{\Phi}\text{-}\mathit{Correct}^{\psi}_{\dot{n}} \end{array}$$

It is immediate from Lemma 4.2.7 that the $\Rightarrow$-direction of Proposition (4.26) already implies the $\Rightarrow$-direction of Part (2a). For the $\Leftarrow$-direction we shall exploit that Lemma 4.4.7(2a) delivers $\mathit{UsedLater}^{\psi}_{\dot{n}}[\Phi^{\leqslant i}]$. Hence this and the $\Leftarrow$-direction of Proposition (4.26) yield

$$\mathtt{LFEM}_{\Phi}\text{-}\mathit{Correct}^{\psi}_{\dot{n}} \wedge \mathit{UsedLater}^{\psi}_{\dot{n}}[\Phi^{\leqslant i}],$$

which according to Lemma 4.4.6(2a) implies $\dot{n} \in \mathit{SLtRg}(\mathtt{LFEM}_{\Phi^{\leqslant i}}, \psi)$.

Proof of 2b: Here we succeed by using the results of the previous parts:

$$\begin{array}{rcl} & & \varphi \in \mathcal{T}^{\top}(\Theta^{\mathrm{dn}(i)}_{\dot{n}}) \\ \text{[Definition } \mathit{LChange}] & \Leftrightarrow & \forall\, \psi \in \mathit{neigh}(\varphi).\ \mathit{LChange}^{\psi}_{\dot{n}} \\ \text{[Proposition (4.26)]} & \Leftrightarrow & \forall\, \psi \in \mathit{neigh}(\varphi).\ \mathtt{LFEM}_{\Phi^{\leqslant i}}\text{-}\mathit{Correct}^{\psi}_{\dot{n}} \\ \text{[Part (1)]} & \Leftrightarrow & \dot{n} \notin \mathit{SLtRg}(\mathtt{LFEM}_{\Phi^{\leqslant i}}, \varphi) \end{array}$$

□

Remark 4.4.2. The assumption of the first part of Lemma 4.4.2, $\varphi \in \Theta_{\dot n}^{\mathrm{dn}(i)}$, can be weakened. Analysing the proof we actually only need the requirement $\neg\, UsedLater_{\dot n}^{\varphi}[\Phi^{\leqslant i}]$. Hence we have for $\mathtt{EM}_\Phi \in \mathcal{COEM}_\Phi$ with $\mathtt{EM}_{\Phi^{<i}} = \mathtt{LFEM}_{\Phi^{<i}}$, $\dot n \in \dot N$ and $\varphi \in \Phi$:

$$\neg\, UsedLater_{\dot n}^{\varphi}[\Phi^{\leqslant i}] \;\Rightarrow\; (\dot n \in SLtRg(\mathtt{EM}_{\Phi^{\leqslant i}}, \varphi) \;\Leftrightarrow\; \exists\, \psi \in SupExpr_{\Theta_{\dot n}^{\mathrm{up}(i)}}(\varphi).\ \neg \mathtt{EM}_{\Phi^{\leqslant i}}\text{-}Correct_{\dot n}^{\psi})$$

With all these results we are finally able to prove the proposed result on inductive lifetime optimality:

Theorem 4.4.3 (Lifetime Optimality Theorem for $\mathtt{LFEM}_\Phi$).
$\mathtt{LFEM}_\Phi$ *is inductively lifetime optimal.*

Proof. The proof has to consider two cases according to the definition of inductive lifetime optimality (cf. Definition 4.2.4).

<u>$i=0$:</u> In this case lifetime optimality is guaranteed by the lifetime optimality of $\mathtt{LEM}_\Phi$, which is applied to the 0-level expressions.

<u>$i>0$:</u> Let us consider a structured expression motion $\mathtt{EM}_\Phi \in \mathcal{COEM}_\Phi$ such that

$$\mathtt{EM}_{\Phi^{<i}} \;=\; \mathtt{LFEM}_{\Phi^{<i}} \tag{4.27}$$

In order to prove $\mathtt{EM}_{\Phi^{\leqslant i}} \precsim_{lt}^{\Phi^{\leqslant i}} \mathtt{LFEM}_{\Phi^{\leqslant i}}$ we have to show for every $\dot n \in \dot N$ the inequation:

$$|\{\varphi \in \Phi^{\leqslant i} \mid \dot n \in SLtRg(\mathtt{LFEM}_{\Phi^{\leqslant i}}, \varphi)\}| \;\leqslant\; |\{\varphi \in \Phi^{\leqslant i} \mid \dot n \in SLtRg(\mathtt{EM}_{\Phi^{\leqslant i}}, \varphi)\}| \tag{4.28}$$

To keep the notation simple let us fix $\dot n \in \dot N$ and introduce an abbreviation scheme $\Lambda_{\mathtt{TR}}^{\mathrm{rg}}$ for the set of expressions in Φ^{rg} being involved in a lifetime range at $\dot n$ with respect to an expression motion $\mathtt{TR}$. For instance, $\Lambda_{\mathtt{EM}_{\Phi^{\leqslant i}}}^{i}$ stands for those expressions in Φ^i whose associated lifetime ranges with respect to $\mathtt{EM}_{\Phi^{\leqslant i}}$ cover $\dot n$, i. e.

$$\Lambda_{\mathtt{EM}_{\Phi^{\leqslant i}}}^{i} = \{\varphi \in \Phi^i \mid \dot n \in SLtRg(\mathtt{EM}_{\Phi^{\leqslant i}}, \varphi)\}$$

With this notion Proposition (4.28) reads as: $|\Lambda_{\mathtt{LFEM}_{\Phi^{\leqslant i}}}^{\leqslant i}| \leqslant |\Lambda_{\mathtt{EM}_{\Phi^{\leqslant i}}}^{\leqslant i}|$

Starting point of the proof is a decomposition of lifetime ranges:

$$\Lambda_{\mathtt{EM}_{\Phi^{\leqslant i}}}^{\leqslant i} \;=\; \Lambda_{\mathtt{EM}_{\Phi^{\leqslant i}}}^{i} \uplus \Lambda_{\mathtt{EM}_{\Phi^{<i}}}^{<i} \setminus \underbrace{(\Lambda_{\mathtt{EM}_{\Phi^{<i}}}^{<i} \setminus \Lambda_{\mathtt{EM}_{\Phi^{\leqslant i}}}^{<i})}_{\Lambda_{\mathtt{EM}_{\Phi^{<i}}}^{<i,\mathrm{rm}}} \tag{4.29a}$$

$$\Lambda^{\leqslant i}_{\mathtt{LFEM}_{\Phi\leqslant i}} = \Lambda^{i}_{\mathtt{LFEM}_{\Phi\leqslant i}} \uplus \Lambda^{<i}_{\mathtt{LFEM}_{\Phi<i}} \setminus \underbrace{(\Lambda^{<i}_{\mathtt{LFEM}_{\Phi<i}} \setminus \Lambda^{<i}_{\mathtt{LFEM}_{\Phi\leqslant i}})}_{\Lambda^{<i,\mathtt{rm}}_{\mathtt{LFEM}_{\Phi<i}}} \qquad (4.29b)$$

$\Lambda^{i}_{\mathtt{EM}_{\Phi\leqslant i}}$ and $\Lambda^{i}_{\mathtt{LFEM}_{\Phi\leqslant i}}$ characterise "new" lifetime ranges due to i-level computations. While $\Lambda^{<i}_{\mathtt{EM}_{\Phi<i}}$ and $\Lambda^{<i}_{\mathtt{LFEM}_{\Phi<i}}$ refer to the "old" lifetime ranges of expressions with levels lower than i, i. e. the lifetime ranges as they appear from the point of view when considering the transformations being restricted to the universe $\Phi^{<i}$, some of these lifetime ranges are obsolete due to trade-offs with i-level lifetime ranges, which is captured by means of the sets $\Lambda^{<i,\mathtt{rm}}_{\mathtt{EM}_{\Phi<i}}$ and $\Lambda^{<i,\mathtt{rm}}_{\mathtt{LFEM}_{\Phi<i}}$, respectively.

For these sets we collect a number of properties that are mainly based on the results on lifetime ranges given by Lemma 4.2.7, Lemma 4.4.6 and Lemma 4.4.9:

$$\Lambda^{i}_{\mathtt{EM}_{\Phi\leqslant i}} \setminus \Theta^{\mathtt{up}(i)}_{\dot{n}} = \Lambda^{i}_{\mathtt{LFEM}_{\Phi\leqslant i}} \setminus \Theta^{\mathtt{up}(i)}_{\dot{n}} \qquad (4.30a)$$

$$\Lambda^{<i,\mathtt{rm}}_{\mathtt{EM}_{\Phi<i}} \setminus \Theta^{\mathtt{dn}(i)}_{\dot{n}} = \Lambda^{<i,\mathtt{rm}}_{\mathtt{LFEM}_{\Phi<i}} \setminus \Theta^{\mathtt{dn}(i)}_{\dot{n}} \qquad (4.30b)$$

$$neigh(\Lambda^{<i,\mathtt{rm}}_{\mathtt{EM}_{\Phi<i}} \cap \Theta^{\mathtt{dn}(i)}_{\dot{n}}) \subseteq \Lambda^{i}_{\mathtt{EM}_{\Phi\leqslant i}} \cap \Theta^{\mathtt{up}(i)}_{\dot{n}} \qquad (4.30c)$$

$$\Lambda^{<i,\mathtt{rm}}_{\mathtt{LFEM}_{\Phi<i}} \cap \Theta^{\mathtt{dn}(i)}_{\dot{n}} = \Theta^{\mathtt{dn}(i)}_{\dot{n}} \setminus \Lambda^{<i}_{\mathtt{LFEM}_{\Phi\leqslant i}} \qquad (4.30d)$$

Starting with Equation (4.30a) let $\psi \in \Lambda^{i}_{\mathtt{EM}_{\Phi\leqslant i}} \setminus \Theta^{\mathtt{up}(i)}_{\dot{n}}$. Then the definiton of $\Lambda^{i}_{\mathtt{EM}_{\Phi\leqslant i}}$ delivers $\dot{n} \in SLtRg(\mathtt{EM}_{\Phi^{\leqslant i}}, \psi)$. According to Lemma 4.4.6(2b) this implies both $\mathtt{EM}_{\Phi^{\leqslant i}}\text{-}Correct^{\psi}_{\dot{n}}$ and $UsedLater^{\psi}_{\dot{n}}[\Phi^{\leqslant i}]$. Using Lemma 4.4.5(1) and Lemma 4.4.4 together with $\psi \notin \Theta^{\mathtt{up}(i)}_{\dot{n}}$ the condition $\mathtt{EM}_{\Phi^{\leqslant i}}\text{-}Correct^{\psi}_{\dot{n}}$ implies $\mathtt{LEM}_{\Phi^{\leqslant i}}\text{-}Correct^{\psi}_{\dot{n}}$. The other way round we have $\mathtt{LFEM}_{\Phi^{\leqslant i}}\text{-}Correct^{\psi}_{\dot{n}}$ by Corollary 3.4.1, and Lemma 4.4.6(2a) finally delivers $\dot{n} \in SLtRg(\mathtt{LFEM}_{\Phi^{\leqslant i}}, \psi)$. The $\supseteq$-inclusion is by a symmetric argument.

For the proof of Equation (4.30b) we argue as follows

$$\begin{array}{rcl} & & \Lambda^{<i,\mathtt{rm}}_{\mathtt{EM}_{\Phi<i}} \setminus \Theta^{\mathtt{dn}(i)}_{\dot{n}} \\ [\dagger] & = & \{\varphi \in \Lambda^{<i}_{\mathtt{EM}_{\Phi<i}} \mid \neg\, UsedLater^{\varphi}_{\dot{n}}[\Phi^{\leqslant i}] \wedge SupExpr_{\Theta^{\mathtt{up}(i)}_{\dot{n}}}(\varphi) = \emptyset\} \\ [(4.27)] & = & \{\varphi \in \Lambda^{<i}_{\mathtt{LFEM}_{\Phi<i}} \mid \neg\, UsedLater^{\varphi}_{\dot{n}}[\Phi^{\leqslant i}] \wedge SupExpr_{\Theta^{\mathtt{up}(i)}_{\dot{n}}}(\varphi) = \emptyset\} \\ [\ddagger] & = & \Lambda^{<i,\mathtt{rm}}_{\mathtt{LFEM}_{\Phi<i}} \setminus \Theta^{\mathtt{dn}(i)}_{\dot{n}} \end{array}$$

Considering Equation (†) let us first take a look at the $\subseteq$-inclusion, where we have

$$\begin{array}{rcl} & & \varphi \in \Lambda^{<i,\mathtt{rm}}_{\mathtt{EM}_{\Phi<i}} \\ [\text{Definition } \Lambda^{<i,\mathtt{rm}}_{\mathtt{EM}_{\Phi<i}}] & \Rightarrow & \varphi \in \Lambda^{<i}_{\mathtt{EM}_{\Phi<i}} \setminus \Lambda^{<i}_{\mathtt{EM}_{\Phi\leqslant i}} \\ [\text{Def. } \Lambda^{<i}_{\mathtt{EM}_{\Phi<i}} \;\&\; \Lambda^{<i}_{\mathtt{EM}_{\Phi\leqslant i}}] & \Rightarrow & \dot{n} \in SLtRg(\mathtt{EM}_{\Phi^{<i}}, \varphi) \wedge \dot{n} \notin SLtRg(\mathtt{EM}_{\Phi^{\leqslant i}}, \varphi) \end{array}$$

$$\begin{array}{lll} \text{[Lemma 4.2.7]} & \Rightarrow & \text{EM}_\Phi\text{-}\mathit{Correct}_{\dot n}^{\varphi} \wedge \dot n \notin \mathit{SLtRg}(\text{EM}_{\Phi^{\leqslant i}}, \varphi) \\ \text{[Lemma 4.4.6(2a)]} & \Rightarrow & \neg\, \mathit{UsedLater}_{\dot n}^{\varphi}[\Phi^{\leqslant i}] \end{array}$$

This together with the definition of $\Theta_{\dot n}^{\mathrm{dn}(i)}$ also immediately excludes that φ has a superexpression in $\Theta_{\dot n}^{\mathrm{up}(i)}$.

For the $\supseteq$-inclusion of (†) we may directly argue with Lemma 4.4.9(1) in its variant as stated in Remark 4.4.2. Finally, for Equation (‡) the same reasoning as for Equation (†) applies.

For Inclusion (4.30c) let us consider $\varphi \in \Lambda_{\mathrm{EM}_{\Phi^{<i}}}^{<i,\mathrm{rm}} \cap \Theta_{\dot n}^{\mathrm{dn}(i)}$ and $\psi \in \mathit{neigh}(\varphi)$. The fact that $\varphi \notin \Lambda_{\mathrm{EM}_{\Phi^{\leqslant i}}}^{<i}$ grants that Lemma 4.4.9(1) becomes applicable yielding EM_Φ-$\mathit{Correct}_{\dot n}^{\psi}$. Due to Lemma 4.4.7(2a) we have in addition $\mathit{UsedLater}_{\dot n}^{\psi}[\Phi^{\leqslant i}]$. Putting both results together Lemma 4.4.6(2a) delivers $\dot n \in \mathit{SLtRg}(\mathrm{EM}_{\Phi^{\leqslant i}}, \psi)$ as desired.

Finally, the $\subseteq$-inclusion of Equation (4.30d) is trivial, while for the $\supseteq$-inclusion Lemma 4.4.7(2b,3) yields

$$\mathrm{EM}_\Phi\text{-}\mathit{Correct}_{\dot n}^{\varphi} \;\wedge\; \mathit{UsedLater}_{\dot n}^{\varphi}[\Phi^{<i}],$$

which by Lemma 4.4.6(2a) means $\varphi \in \Lambda_{\mathrm{LFEM}_{\Phi^{<i}}}^{<i}$.

The key properties, however, are the ones that close the gap between optimal trade-offs and lifetime ranges. Here Lemma 4.4.9(2) gives us:

$$\Lambda_{\mathrm{LFEM}_{\Phi^{\leqslant i}}}^{i} \cap \Theta_{\dot n}^{\mathrm{up}(i)} = \mathit{neigh}(\mathcal{T}^{\top}(\Theta_{\dot n}^{\mathrm{dn}(i)})) \tag{4.31a}$$

$$\Theta_{\dot n}^{\mathrm{dn}(i)} \setminus \Lambda_{\mathrm{LFEM}_{\Phi^{\leqslant i}}}^{<i} = \mathcal{T}^{\top}(\Theta_{\dot n}^{\mathrm{dn}(i)}) \tag{4.31b}$$

Now we may calculate:

$$\begin{array}{ll} & |\Lambda_{\mathrm{EM}_{\Phi^{\leqslant i}}}^{\leqslant i}| \\ \multicolumn{2}{l}{\text{[Equation (4.29a)]}} \\ = & |\Lambda_{\mathrm{EM}_{\Phi^{<i}}}^{<i}| + |\Lambda_{\mathrm{EM}_{\Phi^{\leqslant i}}}^{i}| - |\Lambda_{\mathrm{EM}_{\Phi^{<i}}}^{<i,\mathrm{rm}}| \\ \multicolumn{2}{l}{\text{[Splitting of } \Lambda_{\mathrm{EM}_{\Phi^{\leqslant i}}}^{i} \text{ and } \Lambda_{\mathrm{EM}_{\Phi^{<i}}}^{<i,\mathrm{rm}}]} \\ = & |\Lambda_{\mathrm{EM}_{\Phi^{<i}}}^{<i}| + |\Lambda_{\mathrm{EM}_{\Phi^{\leqslant i}}}^{i} \setminus \Theta_{\dot n}^{\mathrm{up}(i)}| + |\Lambda_{\mathrm{EM}_{\Phi^{\leqslant i}}}^{i} \cap \Theta_{\dot n}^{\mathrm{up}(i)}| \\ & \qquad - (|\Lambda_{\mathrm{EM}_{\Phi^{<i}}}^{<i,\mathrm{rm}} \setminus \Theta_{\dot n}^{\mathrm{dn}(i)}| + |\Lambda_{\mathrm{EM}_{\Phi^{<i}}}^{<i,\mathrm{rm}} \cap \Theta_{\dot n}^{\mathrm{dn}(i)}|) \\ \multicolumn{2}{l}{\text{[Equations (4.27) \& (4.30a) \& (4.30b)]}} \\ = & |\Lambda_{\mathrm{LFEM}_{\Phi^{<i}}}^{<i}| + |\Lambda_{\mathrm{LFEM}_{\Phi^{\leqslant i}}}^{i} \setminus \Theta_{\dot n}^{\mathrm{up}(i)}| + |\Lambda_{\mathrm{EM}_{\Phi^{\leqslant i}}}^{i} \cap \Theta_{\dot n}^{\mathrm{up}(i)}| \\ & \qquad - (|\Lambda_{\mathrm{LFEM}_{\Phi^{<i}}}^{<i,\mathrm{rm}} \setminus \Theta_{\dot n}^{\mathrm{dn}(i)}| + |\Lambda_{\mathrm{EM}_{\Phi^{<i}}}^{<i,\mathrm{rm}} \cap \Theta_{\dot n}^{\mathrm{dn}(i)}|) \\ \multicolumn{2}{l}{\text{[Rearranging terms]}} \\ = & |\Lambda_{\mathrm{LFEM}_{\Phi^{<i}}}^{<i}| + |\Lambda_{\mathrm{LFEM}_{\Phi^{\leqslant i}}}^{i} \setminus \Theta_{\dot n}^{\mathrm{up}(i)}| - |\Lambda_{\mathrm{LFEM}_{\Phi^{<i}}}^{<i,\mathrm{rm}} \setminus \Theta_{\dot n}^{\mathrm{dn}(i)}| \\ & \qquad - (|\Lambda_{\mathrm{EM}_{\Phi^{<i}}}^{<i,\mathrm{rm}} \cap \Theta_{\dot n}^{\mathrm{dn}(i)}| - |\Lambda_{\mathrm{EM}_{\Phi^{\leqslant i}}}^{i} \cap \Theta_{\dot n}^{\mathrm{up}(i)}|) \end{array}$$

[Inclusion (4.30c)]

$$\geqslant \quad |\Lambda^{<i}_{\mathtt{LFEM}_{\Phi<i}}| + |\Lambda^{i}_{\mathtt{LFEM}_{\Phi\leqslant i}} \setminus \Theta^{\mathtt{up}(i)}_{\dot{n}}| - |\Lambda^{<i,\mathtt{rm}}_{\mathtt{LFEM}_{\Phi<i}} \setminus \Theta^{\mathtt{dn}(i)}_{\dot{n}}| \\ - (|\Lambda^{<i,\mathtt{rm}}_{\mathtt{EM}_{\Phi<i}} \cap \Theta^{\mathtt{dn}(i)}_{\dot{n}}| - |neigh(\Lambda^{<i,\mathtt{rm}}_{\mathtt{EM}_{\Phi<i}} \cap \Theta^{\mathtt{dn}(i)}_{\dot{n}})|)$$

[Theorem 4.3.3]

$$\geqslant \quad |\Lambda^{<i}_{\mathtt{LFEM}_{\Phi<i}}| + |\Lambda^{i}_{\mathtt{LFEM}_{\Phi\leqslant i}} \setminus \Theta^{\mathtt{up}(i)}_{\dot{n}}| - |\Lambda^{<i,\mathtt{rm}}_{\mathtt{LFEM}_{\Phi<i}} \setminus \Theta^{\mathtt{dn}(i)}_{\dot{n}}| \\ - (|\mathcal{T}^{\top}(\Theta^{\mathtt{dn}(i)}_{\dot{n}})| - |neigh(\mathcal{T}^{\top}(\Theta^{\mathtt{dn}(i)}_{\dot{n}}))|)$$

[Equations (4.31a,b)]

$$= \quad |\Lambda^{<i}_{\mathtt{LFEM}_{\Phi<i}}| + |\Lambda^{i}_{\mathtt{LFEM}_{\Phi\leqslant i}} \setminus \Theta^{\mathtt{up}(i)}_{\dot{n}}| - |\Lambda^{<i,\mathtt{rm}}_{\mathtt{LFEM}_{\Phi<i}} \setminus \Theta^{\mathtt{dn}(i)}_{\dot{n}}| \\ -(|\Theta^{\mathtt{dn}(i)}_{\dot{n}} \setminus \Lambda^{<i}_{\mathtt{LFEM}_{\Phi\leqslant i}}| - |\Lambda^{i}_{\mathtt{LFEM}_{\Phi\leqslant i}} \cap \Theta^{\mathtt{up}(i)}_{\dot{n}}|)$$

[Equation (4.30d)]

$$= \quad |\Lambda^{<i}_{\mathtt{LFEM}_{\Phi<i}}| + |\Lambda^{i}_{\mathtt{LFEM}_{\Phi\leqslant i}} \setminus \Theta^{\mathtt{up}(i)}_{\dot{n}}| - |\Lambda^{<i,\mathtt{rm}}_{\mathtt{LFEM}_{\Phi<i}} \setminus \Theta^{\mathtt{dn}(i)}_{\dot{n}}| \\ - (|\Lambda^{<i,\mathtt{rm}}_{\mathtt{LFEM}_{\Phi<i}} \cap \Theta^{\mathtt{dn}(i)}_{\dot{n}}| - |\Lambda^{i}_{\mathtt{LFEM}_{\Phi\leqslant i}} \cap \Theta^{\mathtt{up}(i)}_{\dot{n}}|)$$

[Merging of $\Lambda^{i}_{\mathtt{LFEM}_{\Phi\leqslant i}}$ and $\Lambda^{<i,\mathtt{rm}}_{\mathtt{LFEM}_{\Phi<i}}$]

$$= \quad |\Lambda^{<i}_{\mathtt{LFEM}_{\Phi<i}}| + |\Lambda^{i}_{\mathtt{LFEM}_{\Phi\leqslant i}}| - |\Lambda^{<i,\mathtt{rm}}_{\mathtt{LFEM}_{\Phi<i}}|$$

[Equation (4.29b)]

$$= \quad |\Lambda^{\leqslant i}_{\mathtt{LFEM}_{\Phi\leqslant i}}|$$

□

4.4.5 Computing $\mathtt{LFEM}_\Phi$

As in Section 3.5, where the equation systems for individual busy and lazy expression motion were given, this section aims at providing a brief algorithmically oriented summary of the steps of $\mathtt{LFEM}_\Phi$.

Table 4.1 gives an overview of the general structure of the algorithm. In fact, the algorithm is essentially a refinement approach, i. e. all the analyses that are associated with $\mathtt{LEM}_\Phi$ are computed just as before. Each of the two adjustment steps only requires one additional data flow analysis that is triggered levelwise.

The detailed steps that are associated with the first and the second refinement step are summarised in Table 4.2 and 4.3, respectively. It should be noted that both delayability adjustments in Table 4.2(4) and Table 4.3(3) use the alternative characterisations given in Lemma 4.4.1(3) and Lemma 4.4.8, respectively. Finally, the practical implementation (as opposed to the theoretically oriented presentation earlier) only requires trade-off information that is restricted to exit points of nodes. This is due to the fact that a profitable trade-off whose origin is at the entry of a node remains profitable also at the exit (cf. Lemma 4.4.8).

1. Replacement Points ($\psi \in \Phi$):

$\mathtt{LFEM}_{\Phi}$-$\mathit{Replace}_n^{\psi} \stackrel{\text{def}}{=} \psi \in \mathit{MaxSubExpr}_{\Phi}(\varphi_n^{\mathrm{RHS}})$ where φ_n^{RHS} is RHS expression at n

2. Relevant Global Analyses ($\psi \in \Phi$):

Computation of all relevant global predicates of $\mathtt{LEM}_{\Phi}$ according to Table 3.1 and Table 3.2:
- $\mathit{NDnSafe}_n^{\psi}$, $\mathit{XDnSafe}_n^{\psi}$, $\mathit{NUpSafe}_n^{\psi}$, $\mathit{XUpSafe}_n^{\psi}$
- $\mathit{NDelayed}_n^{\psi}$, $\mathit{XDelayed}_n^{\psi}$

3. Insertion Points wrt. Φ^0 ($\psi \in \Phi^0$):

- $\mathtt{LFEM}_{\Phi}$-$\mathit{NInsert}_n^{\psi} \stackrel{\text{def}}{=} \mathit{N\text{-}Latest}_n^{\psi}$
- $\mathtt{LFEM}_{\Phi}$-$\mathit{XInsert}_n^{\psi} \stackrel{\text{def}}{=} \mathit{X\text{-}Latest}_n^{\psi}$

4. Insertion Points wrt. Φ^i ($i > 0$):

For each level $i > 0$ in increasing order do

a) Perform the first adjustment as described in Table 4.2.
b) Perform the second adjustment as described in Table 4.3.
c) Determine the insertion points ($\psi \in \Phi^i$):
  - $\mathtt{LFEM}_{\Phi}$-$\mathit{NInsert}_n^{\psi} \stackrel{\text{def}}{=} \mathit{A2\text{-}NLatest}_n^{\psi}$
  - $\mathtt{LFEM}_{\Phi}$-$\mathit{XInsert}_n^{\psi} \stackrel{\text{def}}{=} \mathit{A2\text{-}XLatest}_n^{\psi}$

Table 4.1. Skeleton of the $\mathtt{LFEM}_{\Phi}$-algorithm

4.5 Fully Flexible Expression Motion

Although $\mathtt{LFEM}_{\Phi}$ is a major step forwards in capturing trade-offs between lifetimes of temporaries, we have to be aware of the fact that the inductive notion of lifetime optimality (cf. Definition 4.2.4) is weaker than the "full" notion of lifetime optimality (cf. Definition 4.2.3). In this section we will present, how even full lifetime optimality can be reached efficiently. In contrast to the inductively progressing $\mathtt{LFEM}_{\Phi}$, where bipartite graphs are natural to model the relation between the expressions of the actual and lower levels, the general problem can be expressed more adequately in terms of expression DAGs. Fortunately, the situation which seems to be more complex at first glance can be reduced to the bipartite case.

In fact, this way the algorithm for the computation of tight sets of a bipartite graph still provides the algorithmic kernel of the full method. The section is organised as follows. First we give a classification of expressions at a program point that are relevant for the general trade-off problem. After discussing limitations of $\mathtt{LFEM}_{\Phi}$ we introduce a more general view of profitable trade-offs between the lifetimes of temporaries and show how to reduce the

1. Correctness Analysis ($\varphi \in SubExpr_\Phi(\Phi^i)$):

$$\mathbf{NCORRECT}^\varphi_n \;=\; \texttt{LFEM}_\Phi\text{-}NInsert^\varphi_n + \begin{cases} false & \text{if } n = \mathbf{s} \\ \prod_{m \in pred(n)} \mathbf{XCORRECT}^\varphi_m & \text{otherwise} \end{cases}$$

$$\mathbf{XCORRECT}^\varphi_n \;=\; \texttt{LFEM}_\Phi\text{-}XInsert^\varphi_n + Transp^\varphi_n \cdot \mathbf{NCORRECT}^\varphi_n$$

$\leadsto$ Greatest fixed point solution: $\texttt{LFEM}_{\Phi^{<i}}\text{-}NCorrect$ and $\texttt{LFEM}_{\Phi^{<i}}\text{-}XCorrect$

2. Adjusting Down-Safety ($\psi \in \Phi^i$, *No data flow analysis!*)

$$A\text{-}NDnSafe^\psi_n \;\stackrel{\text{def}}{=}\; NDnSafe^\psi_n \cdot \prod_{\varphi \in SubExpr_\Phi(\psi)} \texttt{LFEM}_{\Phi^{<i}}\text{-}NCorrect^\varphi_n$$

$$A\text{-}XDnSafe^\psi_n \;\stackrel{\text{def}}{=}\; XDnSafe^\psi_n \cdot \prod_{\varphi \in SubExpr_\Phi(\psi)} \texttt{LFEM}_{\Phi^{<i}}\text{-}XCorrect^\varphi_n$$

3. Computation of Earliestness: ($\psi \in \Phi^i$, *No data flow analysis!*)

$$A1\text{-}NEarliest^\psi_n \;\stackrel{\text{def}}{=}\; A\text{-}NDnSafe^\psi_n \cdot \begin{cases} true & \text{if } n = \mathbf{s} \\ \sum_{m \in pred(n)} \overline{XUpSafe^\psi_m + A\text{-}XDnSafe^\psi_m} & \text{otherwise} \end{cases}$$

$$A1\text{-}XEarliest^\psi_n \;\stackrel{\text{def}}{=}\; A\text{-}XDnSafe^\psi_n \cdot \overline{Transp^\psi_n}$$

Table 4.2. (Part 1) Computing the first adjustment of $\texttt{LFEM}_\Phi$ with respect to level $i > 0$

general situation to the well-known problem of computing tight sets of bipartite graphs. A condensed presentation of the results of this section can be found in [Rüt98b].

4.5.1 A Classification of Expressions

Among the expressions of Φ we distinguish between four categories of expressions with respect to a program point $\dot{n}$. These four classes evolve from two dissections made on the set of expressions: the first dissection separates *used-later expressions* from *release candidates*, where the former ones are those whose associated temporaries are definitely used at a later program point and the latter ones are those whose temporaries can possibly be released.

4. Adjusting Delayability ($\psi \in \Phi^i$, No data flow analysis!)

$$A1\text{-}NDelayed_n^{\psi} \stackrel{\text{def}}{=} A\text{-}NDnSafe_n^{\psi} \cdot NDelayed_n^{\psi}$$

$$A1\text{-}XDelayed_n^{\psi} \stackrel{\text{def}}{=} A\text{-}XDnSafe_n^{\psi} \cdot XDelayed_n^{\psi}$$

5. Adjusting Latestness: ($\psi \in \Phi^i$, No data flow analysis!)

$$A1\text{-}NLatest_n^{\psi} \stackrel{\text{def}}{=} A1\text{-}NDelayed_n^{\psi} \cdot Comp_n^{\psi}$$

$$A1\text{-}XLatest_n^{\psi} \stackrel{\text{def}}{=} A1\text{-}XDelayed_n^{\psi} \cdot \sum_{m \in succ(n)} \overline{A1\text{-}NDelayed_m^{\psi}}$$

Table 4.2. (Part 2) Computing the first adjustment of $\mathtt{LFEM}_\Phi$ with respect to level $i > 0$

The second combination, *register expressions* vs. *initialisation candidates*, models, whether the associated temporaries are definitely initialised before or if we can choose between the options to initialise the temporary now or later.

In order to give a formal definition of these classes we have to modify the used-later predicate of Section 4.4.1 (see page 61). As we now no longer proceed levelwise, the variant of the predicate considered here can be determined at once for all expressions and can be completely founded on $\mathtt{BEM}_\Phi$.

$$\begin{aligned} UsedLater_{\dot n}^{\varphi} \stackrel{\text{def}}{\Leftrightarrow}\ & \exists p \in \mathbf{P}[\dot n, \dot{\mathbf{e}}]\ \exists 1 < j \leqslant |p|. \\ & \left(\mathtt{BEM}_\Phi\text{-}Replace_{p_j}^{\varphi} \vee \exists \psi \in SupExpr_\Phi(\varphi).\ Earliest_{p_j}^{\psi}\right) \wedge \\ & \qquad \forall 1 < k \leqslant j.\ \neg Earliest_{p_k}^{\varphi} \end{aligned}$$

Now the formal criteria for the proposed classification are given below, together with graphical attributes that are assigned to each class of expressions. These attributes are used in order to label the vertices of an expression DAG that presents the subexpression relation among the classified expressions at a program point. Shaded symbols are used for register expressions, while unshaded ones stand for initialisation candidates. Moreover, expressions whose associated temporaries are definitely used later are represented by a square, while release candidates are represented by a circle. Thus the formal classification for an expression $\varphi \in \Phi$ and a program point $\dot n \in \dot N$ is:

Register expression & Used-later expression:
  Formal condition: $\mathtt{LEM}_\Phi\text{-}Correct_{\dot n}^{\varphi} \wedge UsedLater_{\dot n}^{\varphi}$
  Attribute: ■

Register expression & Release Candidate:
  Formal condition: $\texttt{LEM}_\Phi\text{-}Correct_{\dot{n}}^{\varphi} \wedge \neg\, UsedLater_{\dot{n}}^{\varphi}$
  Attribute: ●
Initialisation candidate & Used-later expression:
  Formal condition: $Delayed_{\dot{n}}^{\varphi} \wedge \neg Latest_{\dot{n}}^{\varphi} \wedge UsedLater_{\dot{n}}^{\varphi}$
  Attribute: □
Initialisation candidate & Release Candidate:
  Formal condition: $Delayed_{\dot{n}}^{\varphi} \wedge \neg Latest_{\dot{n}}^{\varphi} \wedge \neg\, UsedLater_{\dot{n}}^{\varphi}$
  Attribute: ○

Note that in contrast to the inductive approach the used-later predicate as well as the correctness predicate can be determined completely in advance. It should also be noted that the used-later predicate is based on $\texttt{BEM}_\Phi$, while the correctness predicate is based on $\texttt{LEM}_\Phi$. This way the transformation can exploit information about the full universe Φ, which particularly makes the new approach sensitive to superexpressions of any level. Using the computational optimality of $\texttt{LEM}_\Phi$ it is easy to see that the formal conditions for register expressions and initialisation candidates are mutually exclusive. Therefore, the classification of an expression is uniquely determined. Figure 4.12 shows a labelled expression DAG[9] associated with the exit of node 2, where expressions of all four kinds can be observed.

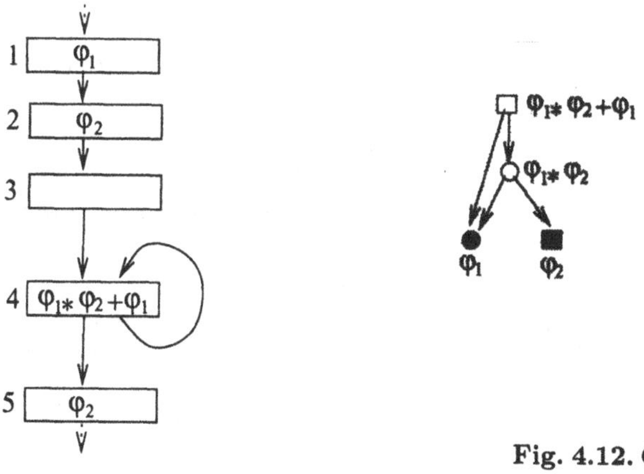

Fig. 4.12. Classification of expressions

Obviously, φ_1 and φ_2 are register expressions, since their latest initialisation points precede the exit of node 2. The only initialisation relying on $\mathbf{h}_{\varphi_1}$ is the one associated with the composite expression $\varphi_1 * \varphi_2$ which may be placed already at the exit of node 2. Hence φ_1 is a release candidate. On the other hand, $\mathbf{h}_{\varphi_2}$ has a strictly later use at node 5, where an original occurrence of φ_2 has to be replaced, which makes φ_2 a used-later expression. Complementary, both initialisations associated with $\varphi_1 * \varphi_2$ and with $\varphi_1 *$

[9] A formal definition is given in Section 4.5.3.

$\varphi_2+\varphi_1$ are initialisation candidates as their corresponding initialisations can be delayed across the exit of node 2. However, only an initialisation with respect to $\varphi_1*\varphi_2+\varphi_1$ must be used strictly later at node 4, while its earliest initialisation point at the exit of node 2 makes $\varphi_1*\varphi_2$ a release candidate.

4.5.2 Limitations of Inductive Lifetime Optimality

Before we are going to give a precise notion on general trade-offs between lifetimes of temporaries, we briefly discuss the limitations of the inductive notion of lifetime optimality as this helps to elucidate the additional power of the general approach.

The most striking deficiency of $\mathtt{LFEM}_\Phi$ as a method that only aims at inductive lifetime optimality is its missing up-sensitivity, i.e. it only captures trade-offs between the current level and levels already processed, but cannot recognise "future opportunities" of higher levels. Figure 4.13(a) shows a labelled expression DAG as it could possibly be associated with a program point $\dot{n}$. The point of this example is that we can get rid of three lifetimes associated with the 0-level expressions at the cost of introducing one initialisation with respect to the unique large expression of level 3. All initialisations associated with expressions of levels 1 and 2 only induce local lifetimes of their associated temporaries. $\mathtt{LFEM}_\Phi$, however, would not recognise this opportunity, as the trade-off balance of three 0-level lifetimes against four 1-level lifetimes is negative.[10]

A special case of this effect shows up for the expressions of level 0, which by the levelwise approach were assumed to be placed best by means of lazy expression motion, because no trade-offs with expressions of lower levels can be exploited. However, even this can be suboptimal as depicted in Figure 4.13(b). In this figure the two operand expressions of type ● can be traded against the expression of type □, since the operand of type ○ only causes a local lifetime. However, the inductive approach treats the expressions of level 0 uniquely by means of lazy expression motion. Thus trade-offs between level 1 and 0 are only considered, if level 0 solely consists of operands of type ●.

4.5.3 General Trade-Offs

Labelled Expression DAGs With the previous classification of expressions the general trade-off situation between the lifetimes of temporaries can be expressed quite naturally in terms of conditions on expression DAGs. Formally, the *labelled expression DAG* associated with a program point $\dot{n}$ is a triple $D_{\dot{n}} = (\Theta_{\dot{n}}, E_{\dot{n}}, \ell_{\dot{n}})$, where $\Theta_{\dot{n}}$ is the subset of expressions in Φ

[10] Note, however, that as soon as one of the initialisations associated with a 1-level expression gets forced to be placed in a (mediate) successor of $\dot{n}$, all other initialisations would be enabled, because there are no non-profitable intermediate trade-offs anymore.

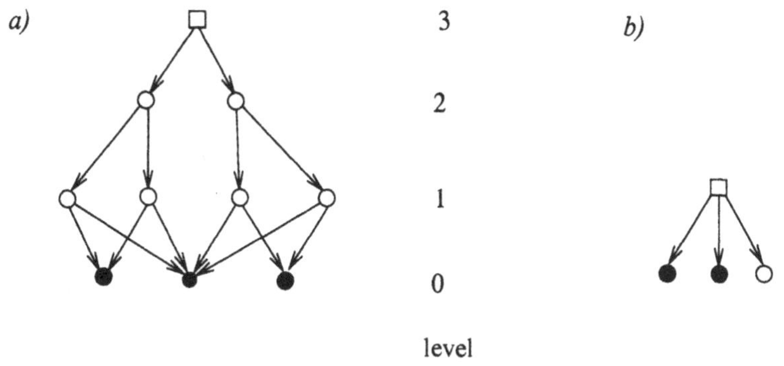

Fig. 4.13. Limitations of inductive lifetime optimality a) Missed trade-off due to intermediate degradation b) Missed trade-off due to non-register-expression as 0-level operand

that can be classified according to one of the four criteria of Section 4.5.1, $\ell_{\dot{n}} : \Theta_{\dot{n}} \rightarrow \{\bullet, \blacksquare, \circ, \square\}$ is the corresponding labelling of the vertices in $\Theta_{\dot{n}}$ and $E_{\dot{n}} \subseteq \Theta_{\dot{n}} \times \Theta_{\dot{n}}$ is the set of directed edges defined by:

$$(\psi, \varphi) \in E_{\dot{n}} \overset{\text{def}}{\Leftrightarrow}.\ \ell_{\dot{n}}(\psi) \in \{\circ, \square\} \ \wedge\ \varphi \in \mathit{SubExpr}_{\Theta_{\dot{n}}}(\psi)$$

Because subexpression relations among register expressions are irrelevant, $E_{\dot{n}}$ can be considered as the relevant part of the (immediate) subexpression relation. This view is particularly justified, since the first point of the following lemma ensures completeness.

Lemma 4.5.1 (Expression DAG Lemma).
Let $D_{\dot{n}} = (\Theta_{\dot{n}}, E_{\dot{n}}, \ell_{\dot{n}})$ the labelled expression DAG with respect to $\dot{n} \in \dot{N}$. Then we have the following properties:

1. $\forall \psi \in \Theta_{\dot{n}}.\ \ell_{\dot{n}}(\psi) \in \{\circ, \square\} \ \Rightarrow\ \forall \varphi \in \mathit{SubExpr}_{\Phi}(\psi).\ \varphi \in \Theta_{\dot{n}}$
2. $\forall \varphi \in \Theta_{\dot{n}}.\ \ell_{\dot{n}}(\varphi) \in \{\circ, \square\} \ \Rightarrow\ \forall \psi \in \mathit{SupExpr}_{\Theta_{\dot{n}}}(\varphi).\ \ell_{\dot{n}}(\psi) \in \{\circ, \square\}$
3. $\forall \varphi \in \Theta_{\dot{n}}.\ \ell_{\dot{n}}(\varphi) \in \{\bullet, \blacksquare\} \ \Rightarrow$ *φ is a leaf node of $D_{\dot{n}}$*

Proof. Part (1) is just a reformulation of Lemma 4.2.5(1). For the proof of Part (2) let us assume $\psi \in \mathit{SupExpr}_{\Theta_{\dot{n}}}(\varphi)$ such that $\ell_{\dot{n}}(\psi) \in \{\bullet, \blacksquare\}$. This means that $\mathtt{LEM}_{\Phi}\text{-}\mathit{Correct}_{\dot{n}}^{\psi}$ holds. According to Lemma 4.2.6 this induces $\mathtt{LEM}_{\Phi}\text{-}\mathit{Correct}_{\dot{n}}^{\varphi}$, too, which, however, would mean that $\ell_{\dot{n}}(\varphi) \in \{\bullet, \blacksquare\}$ in contradiction to the assumption. Finally, Part (3) is immediate from the construction of $E_{\dot{n}}$. □

Optimal Trade-Offs in Labelled Expression DAGs Now the trade-off problem for a given labelled expression DAG $D_{\dot{n}} = (\Theta_{\dot{n}}, E_{\dot{n}}, \ell_{\dot{n}})$ can be formulated. To this end let us first consider a formalisation of profitable trade-offs between register expressions and initialisation candidates:

Definition 4.5.1 (Trade-off Pair). $(\Xi^{re}_{\dot n}, \Xi^{ic}_{\dot n})$ *with* $\Xi^{re}_{\dot n}, \Xi^{ic}_{\dot n} \subseteq \Theta_{\dot n}$ *is a* trade-off pair *at* $\dot n$, *if and only if the following conditions are satisfied:*

1. $\Xi^{re}_{\dot n}$ *is a set of register expressions, i. e. :* $\forall \varphi \in \Xi^{re}_{\dot n}.\ \ell_{\dot n}(\varphi) \in \{\bullet, \blacksquare\}$
2. $\Xi^{ic}_{\dot n}$ *is a set of initialisation candidates, i. e. :* $\forall \psi \in \Xi^{ic}_{\dot n}.\ \ell_{\dot n}(\psi) \in \{\circ, \square\}$
3. $\Xi^{re}_{\dot n}$ *is covered by* $\Xi^{ic}_{\dot n}$, *i. e. :* $\forall \varphi \in \Xi^{re}_{\dot n},\ \psi \in pred_{D_{\dot n}}(\varphi).\ \psi \in \Xi^{ic}_{\dot n}$
4. $\Xi^{ic}_{\dot n}$ *is well-structured (cf. Definition 4.2.1), i. e. :*[11]
$$\forall \psi \in \Xi^{ic}_{\dot n}\ \forall \varphi \in succ_{D_{\dot n}}(\psi).\ \ell_{\dot n}(\varphi) \in \{\circ, \square\} \Rightarrow \varphi \in \Xi^{ic}_{\dot n}$$

Informatively, $\Xi^{re}_{\dot n}$ defines a set of register expressions whose registers can (partly) be released at the costs of introducing new lifetime ranges associated with the initialisation of large expressions in $\Xi^{ic}_{\dot n}$. To be more specific we define the *relevant register expressions* among a set of expressions $\tilde\Phi$ by:

$$\forall \tilde\Phi \subseteq \Theta_{\dot n}.\ \mathcal{R}^{re}_{\dot n}(\tilde\Phi) \stackrel{\text{def}}{=} \{\varphi \in \tilde\Phi \mid \ell_{\dot n}(\varphi) = \bullet\ \}$$

and the *relevant initialisation candidates* among a set of expressions $\tilde\Phi$ by:

$$\forall \tilde\Phi \subseteq \Theta_{\dot n}.\ \mathcal{R}^{ic}_{\dot n}(\tilde\Phi) \stackrel{\text{def}}{=} \{\varphi \in \Xi^{ic}_{\dot n} \mid \ell_n(\varphi) = \square\ \vee \\ \exists \psi \in SupExpr_{\Theta_{\dot n}}(\varphi).\ \psi \notin \Xi^{ic}_{\dot n}\}$$

With these notions the difference $|\mathcal{R}^{re}_{\dot n}(\Xi^{re}_{\dot n})| - |\mathcal{R}^{ic}_{\dot n}(\Xi^{ic}_{\dot n})|$ defines the *gain* of the trade-off pair $(\Xi^{re}_{\dot n}, \Xi^{ic}_{\dot n})$. This is motivated by the fact that expressions in $\mathcal{R}^{re}_{\dot n}(\Xi^{re}_{\dot n})$ are actually setting free an occupied symbolic register, since Condition (3) of Definition 4.5.1 ensures that all their superexpressions are properly initialised, while those in $\mathcal{R}^{ic}_{\dot n}(\Xi^{ic}_{\dot n})$ start up a new lifetime range at $\dot n$, which is based on the fact that initialisations of temporaries belonging to expressions of type $\square$ always induce a lifetime range that comprises $\dot n$. On the other hand, an initialisation of a temporary that belongs to an expression of type $\circ$ has a local lifetime range, if and only if all its superexpressions are initialised at $\dot n$ as well.

Hence our optimisation problem is:

Problem 4.5.1 (Determining an Optimal Trade-off Pair).

Instance: A labelled expression DAG $D_{\dot n} = (\Theta_{\dot n}, E_{\dot n}, \ell_{\dot n})$.

Goal: Find an optimal trade-off pair $(\Xi^{re}_{\dot n}, \Xi^{ic}_{\dot n})$, i. e. one with maximal gain.

The notion is illustrated by means of Figure 4.14(a), which shows a labelled expression DAG with respect to a program point $\dot n$. Figure 4.14(b) shows the optimal trade-off pair that is given by $(\{1,2,4,5\}, \{6,7,8,9,10,12,13\})$. Actually, it is even the only trade-off pair that achieves a positive gain in this example. The relevant part of $\Xi^{ic}_{\dot n}$ is $\mathcal{R}^{ic}_{\dot n}(\Xi^{ic}_{\dot n}) = \{8, 12, 13\}$. It is worth noting

[11] This condition is necessary in order to ensure that subexpressions are always computed before the expression itself, which is a basic requirement of structured expression motion (cf.Definition 4.2.1).

that the vertex 8 is of type ○. Nonetheless, its initialisation is more profitable than initialisations with respect to its superexpressions, since this would force to include two additional relevant initialisation candidates, namely vertex 11 and 3. The vertices 6, 7, 9 and 10 do not impose costs, since they only represent internal calculations.

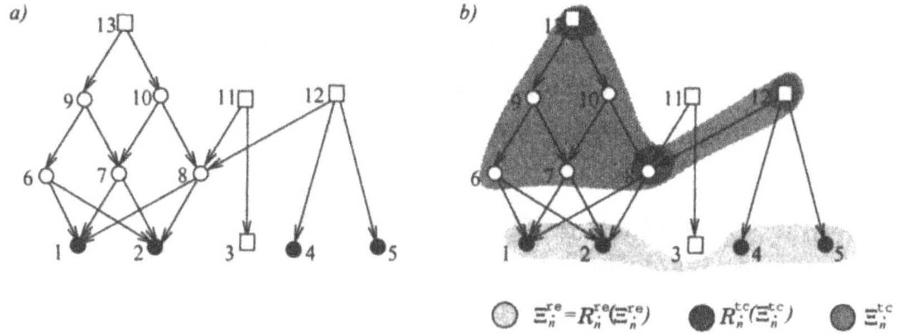

Fig. 4.14. a) A labelled expression DAG b) An optimal trade-off pair

Reduction to Bipartite Graphs At first glance Problem 4.5.1 appears to be harder than the problem of finding tight sets of bipartite graphs (cf. Problem 4.3.2). However, the conditions imposed on the structure of labelled expression DAGs and trade-off pairs allow to reduce labelled expression DAGs to bipartite graphs in a way that the optimisation problem can be solved by means of the matching based technique of Algorithm 4.3.1.

Algorithm 4.5.1.
Input: Labelled expression DAG $D_{\dot{n}} = (\Theta_{\dot{n}}, E_{\dot{n}}, \ell_{\dot{n}})$.
Output: Induced bipartite graph $B_{\dot{n}} = (\Theta^{\mathrm{dn}}_{\dot{n}} \uplus \Theta^{\mathrm{up}}_{\dot{n}}, E^B_{\dot{n}})$.

1. Set $\Theta^{\mathrm{dn}}_{\dot{n}} \stackrel{\mathrm{def}}{=} \{\varphi \in \Theta_{\dot{n}} \mid \ell_{\dot{n}}(\varphi) \in \{\bullet, \circ\}\}$ and $\Theta^{\mathrm{up}}_{\dot{n}} \stackrel{\mathrm{def}}{=} \{\varphi \in \Theta_{\dot{n}} \mid \ell_{\dot{n}}(\varphi) \in \{\circ, \square\}\}$. For expressions φ belonging to both $\Theta^{\mathrm{dn}}_{\dot{n}}$ and $\Theta^{\mathrm{up}}_{\dot{n}}$ we assume that distinct copies are created in order to keep $\Theta^{\mathrm{dn}}_{\dot{n}}$ and $\Theta^{\mathrm{up}}_{\dot{n}}$ disjoint.
2. Set $E^B_{\dot{n}} \stackrel{\mathrm{def}}{=} \{\{\varphi, \psi\} \mid \varphi \in \Theta^{\mathrm{dn}}_{\dot{n}} \wedge \psi \in \Theta^{\mathrm{up}}_{\dot{n}} \wedge \psi \in \mathit{succ}^*_{D_n}(\mathit{pred}_{D_n}(\varphi))\}$

Essentially, the algorithm puts release candidates into the partition $\Theta^{\mathrm{dn}}_{\dot{n}}$ and initialisation candidates into $\Theta^{\mathrm{up}}_{\dot{n}}$. In particular, it is worth noting that $\Theta_{\dot{n}}$-vertices of type ○ are common to both levels. Informatively, this ensures that non-relevant initialisation candidates in $\Theta^{\mathrm{up}}_{\dot{n}}$ can be compensated by corresponding release candidates in $\Theta^{\mathrm{dn}}_{\dot{n}}$.

Some edges of $E^B_{\dot{n}}$ are directly induced by corresponding edges of $E_{\dot{n}}$. However, in order to project the internal structure of $D_{\dot{n}}$ onto the two levels of $B_{\dot{n}}$ an edge $\{\varphi, \psi\}$ with $\psi \in \Theta^{\mathrm{up}}_{\dot{n}}$ additionally induces corresponding edges between φ and the $\Theta^{\mathrm{up}}_{\dot{n}}$-elements in the successor-closure of ψ.

Remark 4.5.1. Obviously, $\Theta_{\dot n}^{dn}$ and $\Theta_{\dot n}^{up}$ can be written as:

$$\begin{aligned}\Theta_{\dot n}^{dn} &= \{\varphi \in \Phi \mid \neg\mathit{UsedLater}_{\dot n}^{\varphi}\}\\ \Theta_{\dot n}^{up} &= \{\varphi \in \Phi \mid \mathit{Delayed}_{\dot n}^{\varphi} \wedge \neg\mathit{Latest}_{\dot n}^{\varphi}\}\end{aligned}$$

This formulations are almost completely along the lines of the definition of $\Theta_{\dot n}^{dn(i)}$ and $\Theta_{\dot n}^{up(i)}$ on page 61, which makes it quite easy to carry over major parts of the reasoning on trade-off candidates to the new situation. Parts where differences become essential, however, are elaborated in full details.

The central result emphasising the role of the reduction of Algorithm 4.5.1 is:

Theorem 4.5.1 (Reduction Theorem). *Let $D_{\dot n} = (\Theta_{\dot n}, E_{\dot n}, \ell_{\dot n})$ be a labelled expression DAG associated with $\dot n \in \dot N$ and let $B = (\Theta_{\dot n}^{dn} \uplus \Theta_{\dot n}^{up}, E_{\dot n}^{B})$ be the corresponding bipartite graph (computed by means of Algorithm 4.5.1). Then we have:*

1. *If $(\Xi_{\dot n}^{re}, \Xi_{\dot n}^{ic})$ is an optimal trade-off pair of $D_{\dot n}$, then the subset of $\Theta_{\dot n}^{dn}$ defined by $\mathcal{R}_{\dot n}^{re}(\Xi_{\dot n}^{re}) \uplus (\Xi_{\dot n}^{ic} \setminus \mathcal{R}_{\dot n}^{ic}(\Xi_{\dot n}^{ic}))$ is a tight set. In particular, its deficiency*[12] *is equal to the gain of $(\Xi_{\dot n}^{re}, \Xi_{\dot n}^{ic})$.*
2. *If $\Theta_{\dot n}^{opt} \subseteq \Theta_{\dot n}^{dn}$ is a tight set, then $(\mathcal{R}_{\dot n}^{re}(\Theta_{\dot n}^{opt}), \mathit{neigh}(\Theta_{\dot n}^{opt}))$ is a trade-off pair of $D_{\dot n}$, whose gain coincides with the deficiency of $\Theta_{\dot n}^{opt}$.*

Proof. It is sufficient to show:

A) For every trade-off pair $(\Xi_{\dot n}^{re}, \Xi_{\dot n}^{ic})$ the set $\mathcal{R}_{\dot n}^{re}(\Xi_{\dot n}^{re}) \uplus (\Xi_{\dot n}^{ic} \setminus \mathcal{R}_{\dot n}^{ic}(\Xi_{\dot n}^{ic}))$ defines a subset of $\Theta_{\dot n}^{dn}$ that has a better or the same deficiency as the gain of $(\Xi_{\dot n}^{re}, \Xi_{\dot n}^{ic})$.

B) Every subset $\Theta_{\dot n}^{opt} \subseteq \Theta_{\dot n}^{dn}$ induces a trade-off pair $(\mathcal{R}_{\dot n}^{re}(\Theta_{\dot n}^{opt}), \mathit{neigh}(\Theta_{\dot n}^{opt}))$ whose gain is at least as good as the deficiency of $\Theta_{\dot n}^{opt}$.

Let us start with the proof of (A). With $\Theta_{\dot n}^{opt} \stackrel{def}{=} \mathcal{R}_{\dot n}^{re}(\Xi_{\dot n}^{re}) \uplus (\Xi_{\dot n}^{ic} \setminus \mathcal{R}_{\dot n}^{ic}(\Xi_{\dot n}^{ic}))$ we first have

$$\mathit{neigh}(\Theta_{\dot n}^{opt}) \subseteq \Xi_{\dot n}^{ic} \tag{4.32}$$

To show this inclusion we shall first exploit that Definition 4.5.1(3) ensures that $\mathit{pred}_{D_{\dot n}}(\varphi) \subseteq \Xi_{\dot n}^{ic}$, if φ is a register expression in $\mathcal{R}_{\dot n}^{re}(\Xi_{\dot n}^{re})$, while the definition of relevancy yields the same, if φ is an irrelevant vertex in $\Xi_{\dot n}^{ic} \setminus \mathcal{R}_{\dot n}^{ic}(\Xi_{\dot n}^{ic})$. Finally, Definition 4.5.1(4) even grants for the successor-closure $\mathit{succ}_{D_{\dot n}}^{*}(\mathit{pred}_{D_{\dot n}}(\varphi)) \cap \Theta_{\dot n}^{up} \subseteq \Xi_{\dot n}^{ic}$. Hence according to the construction of $E_{\dot n}^{B}$ Inclusion (4.32) is satisfied. Now we can finish the proof of (A) by calculating:

$$\begin{aligned} & |\Theta_{\dot n}^{opt}| - |\mathit{neigh}(\Theta_{\dot n}^{opt})|\\ [\text{Def. } \Theta_{\dot n}^{opt} \text{ \& Inclusion (4.32)}] \quad \geqslant\ & |\mathcal{R}_{\dot n}^{re}(\Xi_{\dot n}^{re}) \uplus (\Xi_{\dot n}^{ic} \setminus \mathcal{R}_{\dot n}^{ic}(\Xi_{\dot n}^{ic})| - |\Xi_{\dot n}^{ic}|\end{aligned}$$

[12] Recall that the deficiency of a subset $\Psi \subseteq \Theta_{\dot n}^{dn}$ is defined as $|\Psi| - |\mathit{neigh}(\Psi)|$.

$$\begin{aligned}[\mathcal{R}^{\mathtt{ic}}_{\dot n}(\Xi^{\mathtt{ic}}_{\dot n}) \subseteq \Xi^{\mathtt{ic}}_{\dot n}] \quad &= \quad |\mathcal{R}^{\mathtt{re}}_{\dot n}(\Xi^{\mathtt{re}}_{\dot n})| + |\Xi^{\mathtt{ic}}_{\dot n}| - |\mathcal{R}^{\mathtt{ic}}_{\dot n}(\Xi^{\mathtt{ic}}_{\dot n})| - |\Xi^{\mathtt{ic}}_{\dot n}| \\ &= \quad |\mathcal{R}^{\mathtt{re}}_{\dot n}(\Xi^{\mathtt{re}}_{\dot n})| - |\mathcal{R}^{\mathtt{ic}}_{\dot n}(\Xi^{\mathtt{ic}}_{\dot n})|\end{aligned}$$

For the proof of (B) let us set $\Xi^{\mathtt{re}}_{\dot n} \stackrel{\mathrm{def}}{=} \mathcal{R}^{\mathtt{re}}_{\dot n}(\Theta^{\mathtt{opt}}_{\dot n})$ and $\Xi^{\mathtt{ic}}_{\dot n} \stackrel{\mathrm{def}}{=} neigh(\Theta^{\mathtt{opt}}_{\dot n})$. It is easy to check that $(\Xi^{\mathtt{re}}_{\dot n}, \Xi^{\mathtt{ic}}_{\dot n})$ is a trade-off pair, i. e. fulfils the four requirements of Definition 4.5.1. Point (1) and (2) hold trivially and Point (3) is immediate by construction. Point (4), however, is again due to the successor-closure that is employed in the Definition of $E^{B}_{\dot n}$.

As we have $neigh(\varphi) \subseteq \Xi^{\mathtt{ic}}_{\dot n}$ for each $\varphi \in \Theta^{\mathtt{opt}}_{\dot n}$ this particularly means $SupExpr_{\Theta_{\dot n}}(\varphi) \subseteq \Xi^{\mathtt{ic}}_{\dot n}$ for each $\varphi \in \Xi^{\mathtt{re}}_{\dot n}$. Hence according to the definition of relevant initialisation candidates we get by the fact that all $\varphi \in \Theta^{\mathtt{opt}}_{\dot n} \setminus \Xi^{\mathtt{re}}_{\dot n}$ are of type O: $\forall \varphi \in \Theta^{\mathtt{opt}}_{\dot n} \setminus \Xi^{\mathtt{re}}_{\dot n}.\ \varphi \notin \mathcal{R}^{\mathtt{ic}}_{\dot n}(\Xi^{\mathtt{ic}}_{\dot n})$. In particular, this induces the following inclusion:

$$\mathcal{R}^{\mathtt{ic}}_{\dot n}(\Xi^{\mathtt{ic}}_{\dot n}) \ \subseteq\ \Xi^{\mathtt{ic}}_{\dot n} \setminus (\Theta^{\mathtt{opt}}_{\dot n} \setminus \Xi^{\mathtt{re}}_{\dot n}) \tag{4.33}$$

Now we can calculate:

$$\begin{aligned} & & & |\mathcal{R}^{\mathtt{re}}_{\dot n}(\Xi^{\mathtt{re}}_{\dot n})| - |\mathcal{R}^{\mathtt{ic}}_{\dot n}(\Xi^{\mathtt{ic}}_{\dot n})| \\ [\text{Definition } \Xi^{\mathtt{re}}_{\dot n}] & & = \quad & |\Xi^{\mathtt{re}}_{\dot n}| - |\mathcal{R}^{\mathtt{ic}}_{\dot n}(\Xi^{\mathtt{ic}}_{\dot n})| \\ [\text{Inclusion (4.33)}] & & \geqslant \quad & |\Xi^{\mathtt{re}}_{\dot n}| - |\Xi^{\mathtt{ic}}_{\dot n} \setminus (\Theta^{\mathtt{opt}}_{\dot n} \setminus \Xi^{\mathtt{re}}_{\dot n})| \\ [\Theta^{\mathtt{opt}}_{\dot n} \setminus \Xi^{\mathtt{re}}_{\dot n} \subseteq \Xi^{\mathtt{ic}}_{\dot n} \ \&\ \Xi^{\mathtt{re}}_{\dot n} \subseteq \Theta^{\mathtt{opt}}_{\dot n})] & & = \quad & |\Xi^{\mathtt{re}}_{\dot n}| - (|\Xi^{\mathtt{ic}}_{\dot n}| - (|\Theta^{\mathtt{opt}}_{\dot n}| - |\Xi^{\mathtt{re}}_{\dot n}|))| \\ [\text{Definition } \Xi^{\mathtt{ic}}_{\dot n}] & & = \quad & |\Theta^{\mathtt{opt}}_{\dot n}| - |neigh(\Theta^{\mathtt{opt}}_{\dot n})| \qquad \square \end{aligned}$$

We illustrate the message of this theorem by means of the example of Figure 4.14. Figure 4.15 shows the corresponding bipartite graph together with its unique tight set $\{1, 2, 4, 5, 6, 7, 9, 10\}$. Note that the number of edges is quite large due to the closure operation applied in Algorithm 4.5.1. The irrelevant $\Xi^{\mathtt{ic}}_{\dot n}$-vertices of Figure 4.14, namely $\{6, 7, 9, 10\}$, are now reflected by vertices that are common to both levels. Informatively, this way the costs imposed by irrelevant upper trade-off candidates are compensated by corresponding lower trade-off candidates, which can be considered pseudo-operands.

4.5.4 Defining FFEM$_{\Phi}$

As for the counterpart LFEM$_{\Phi}$ the trade-offs by themselves only cope with the local situation at a given program point $\dot n$. However, they can be employed for a global algorithm that now determines fully lifetime optimal computation points of expressions somewhere in between their earliest and their latest initialisation points. We again succeed with a globalisation that is particularly easy to implement, as the local trade-off information can be directly fed into an adjustment of the delayability predicate. Actually, the refinement process is even simpler than the one used for the definition of LFEM$_{\Phi}$. This is due

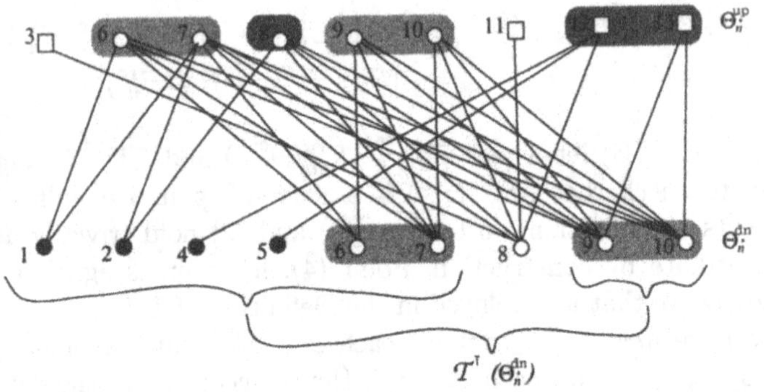

Fig. 4.15. The bipartite graph corresponding to Figure 4.14 with largest tight subset

to the fact that now there is no need for a first adjustment, which in the definition of $\texttt{LFEM}_\Phi$ was necessary in order to ensure that large expressions are initialised only at those program points where all their subexpressions are already initialised before. Now this condition is automatically fulfilled, as Part (4) of Definition 4.5.1 ensures that the premature initialisation of a large trade-off candidate always forces the prior initialisation of its subexpressions, too.

The Transformation The key for the definition of *Fully Flexible Expression Motion* ($\texttt{FFEM}_\Phi$) is a refinement of the delay predicate, which takes into account opportunities for profitable trade-offs. The local trade-off information at a program point $\dot{n}$ give rise to a predicate $Change_{\dot{n}}^{\varphi}$ indicating, if φ should be initialised prematurely due to a profitable trade-off between lifetimes of temporaries. Formally, it is defined similarly to its counterpart on page 62

$$\boxed{Change_{\dot{n}}^{\varphi} \overset{\text{def}}{\Leftrightarrow} \varphi \in neigh(\mathcal{T}^{\top}(\Theta_{\dot{n}}^{\text{dn}})),}$$

where now $\Theta_{\dot{n}}^{\text{dn}}$ refers to the underlying bipartite graph at $\dot{n}$ computed by means of Algorithm 4.5.1. Then we have

$$\begin{aligned} A\text{-}Delayed_{\dot{n}}^{\varphi} \overset{\text{def}}{\Leftrightarrow}\ & \forall p \in \mathbf{P}[\dot{\mathbf{s}}, \dot{n}]\ \exists 1 \leqslant i \leqslant |p|.\ Earliest_{p_i}^{\varphi} \wedge \\ & \forall i \leqslant j < |p|.\ \neg Comp_{p_j}^{\varphi} \wedge \neg Change_{p_j}^{\varphi} \end{aligned}$$

Again the adjusted delayability predicate induces a corresponding predicate for latestness $A\text{-}Latest_{\dot{n}}^{\varphi}$, which finally determines the insertion points of $\texttt{FFEM}_\Phi$. Thus we have for any $\varphi \in \Phi$ and $\dot{n} \in \dot{N}$:

$$\texttt{FFEM}_\Phi\text{-}Replace_{\dot{n}}^{\varphi} \overset{\text{def}}{\Leftrightarrow} \varphi \in MaxSubExpr_\Phi(\varphi_{\dot{n}}^{\text{RHS}}),$$

where $\varphi_{\dot{n}}^{\text{RHS}}$ refers to the right-hand side expression associated with $\dot{n}$, and

$$\texttt{FFEM}_\Phi\text{-}Insert_{\dot{n}}^{\varphi} \overset{\text{def}}{\Leftrightarrow} A\text{-}Latest_{\dot{n}}^{\varphi}.$$

Similar to LFEM$_\Phi$ also FFEM$_\Phi$ has to be proved of being admissible, computationally optimal and finally now also lifetime optimal. Fortunately, most parts of the proofs of Section 4.4 carry over quite easily to the new situation. For this reason we will only point to the corresponding proofs, whenever the reasoning is straightforward to adapt.

4.5.5 Proving Admissibility

Surprisingly, here the situation is simpler than it was for LFEM$_\Phi$. In particular, we get along without all of the results dealing with properties of the first adjustment. On the other hand, this part of LFEM$_\Phi$ automatically forced the subexpression criterion of structured expression motion. In contrast, the argumentation for FFEM$_\Phi$ is not as straightforward. We briefly summarise the main results that are necessary in order to establish admissibility of FFEM$_\Phi$.

As counterparts to Lemma 4.4.1(1) and Lemma 4.4.2(1&2) we have:

Lemma 4.5.2 (Delayability Lemma for FFEM$_\Phi$).

$$\forall \psi \in \Phi,\ \dot{n} \in \dot{N}.\ \textit{A-Delayed}_{\dot{n}}^{\psi} \ \Rightarrow\ \textit{Delayed}_{\dot{n}}^{\psi}$$

Lemma 4.5.3 (Latestness Lemma for FFEM$_\Phi$).

1. $\forall \psi \in \Phi,\ \dot{n} \in \dot{N}.\ \textit{Latest}_{\dot{n}}^{\psi} \ \Rightarrow\ \texttt{FFEM}_\Phi\textit{-Correct}_{\dot{n}}^{\psi}$
2. $\forall \psi \in \Phi,\ \dot{n} \in \dot{N}.\ \textit{Latest}_{\dot{n}}^{\psi} \ \Rightarrow\ \forall \varphi \in \textit{SubExpr}_\Phi(\psi).\ \texttt{FFEM}_\Phi\textit{-Correct}_{\dot{n}}^{\varphi}$

Both lemmas are proved straightforwardly along the lines of the corresponding versions for LFEM$_\Phi$.

Moreover, in analogy to LFEM$_\Phi$ the central characterisation of trade-offs, Trade-off Lemma 4.4.8, has an almost identical counterpart in terms of Lemma 4.5.4(1). Compared to LFEM$_\Phi$, however, we use this result at an earlier stage, as it helps to keep the reasoning on adjusted delayability local. In addition, Trade-off Lemma 4.5.4 is now supplemented by a second part, which can be considered as a completion of the Structured Local Property Lemma 4.2.1.[13]

Lemma 4.5.4 (Trade-off Lemma for FFEM$_\Phi$).

1. $\forall \dot{n} \in \dot{N},\ \psi \in \Theta_{\dot{n}}^{\mathrm{up}}.\ \textit{Change}_{\dot{n}}^{\psi} \ \Leftrightarrow\ \forall \dot{m} \in \textit{succ}(\dot{n}).\ \neg \textit{A-Delayed}_{\dot{m}}^{\psi}$
   $\phantom{\forall \dot{n} \in \dot{N},\ \psi \in \Theta_{\dot{n}}^{\mathrm{up}}.\ \textit{Change}_{\dot{n}}^{\psi}} \ \Leftrightarrow\ \exists \dot{m} \in \textit{succ}(\dot{n}).\ \neg \textit{A-Delayed}_{\dot{m}}^{\psi}$
2. $\forall \dot{n} \in \dot{N},\ \psi \in \Theta_{\dot{n}}^{\mathrm{up}}.\ \textit{Change}_{\dot{n}}^{\psi} \ \Rightarrow\ \forall \varphi \in \textit{SubExpr}_{\Theta_{\dot{n}}^{\mathrm{up}}}(\psi).\ \textit{Change}_{\dot{n}}^{\varphi}$

---

[13] Since the trade-off information can be computed completely in advance, the *Change* predicate can be considered the third local property besides *Transp* and *Comp*. From this point of view the second part of the Trade-off Lemma is perfectly compatible with Lemma 4.2.1.

The second part is immediately due to Theorem 4.5.1(2), which grants that the expressions satisfying the *Change* predicate are exactly the initialisation candidates of the corresponding trade-off pair, together with Definition 4.5.1(4) ensuring that initialisation candidates are closed with respect to the subexpression relation.

Part (1) can be proved almost exactly as Lemma 4.4.8, since the characterisation of the upper and lower trade-off candidates as given in Remark 4.5.1 allows to use the same reasoning, where now $\Theta_{\dot{n}}^{\mathrm{dn}}$ and $\Theta_{\dot{n}}^{\mathrm{up}}$ take the role of $\Theta_{\dot{n}}^{\mathrm{dn}(i)}$ and $\Theta_{\dot{n}}^{\mathrm{up}(i)}$, respectively. For the second equivalence, i. e. the equivalence of existential and universal quantification, see Remark 4.4.1. Furthermore, we shall be aware that the proof of this point also requires to adapt a version of Lemma 4.4.7 (now restricted to parts (1) and (4)), which now reads as:

Lemma 4.5.5 (Trade-off Candidate Lemma for FFEM$_\Phi$).

1. $\forall \dot{n} \in \dot{N},\ \dot{m} \in pred(succ(\dot{n})).\ \Theta_{\dot{n}}^{\mathrm{up}} = \Theta_{\dot{m}}^{\mathrm{up}}$

2. *a)* $\forall \dot{n} \in \dot{N},\ \ \psi \in \Theta_{\dot{n}}^{\mathrm{up}},\ \dot{n}_s \in succ(\dot{n}).\ \neg Earliest_{\dot{n}_s}^{\psi}$

b) $\forall \dot{n} \in \dot{N},\ \ \varphi \in neigh(\Theta_{\dot{n}}^{\mathrm{up}}),\ \dot{n}_s \in succ(\dot{n}).\ \neg Earliest_{\dot{n}_s}^{\varphi}$

Again the proofs of Lemma 4.4.7 carry over straightforwardly by leaving out all the parts being involved with a special reasoning on the first adjustment. However, we have to be careful with the proof of Part (1), since the proof of Lemma 4.4.7(1) uses Lemma 4.4.4, a result whose counterpart is not available yet. Fortunately, here we succeed without such an argument. For $succ(\dot{n}) = \{\dot{n}_s\}$ we have:

$$\psi \in \Theta_{\dot{n}}^{\mathrm{up}}$$

[Definition $\Theta_{\dot{n}}^{\mathrm{up}}$]

$$\Rightarrow\ Delayed_{\dot{n}}^{\psi} \wedge \neg Latest_{\dot{n}}^{\psi}$$

[Definition *Latest* & Lemma 3.4.2(2)]

$$\Rightarrow\ Delayed_{\dot{n}_s}^{\psi} \wedge \neg Earliest_{\dot{n}_s}^{\psi}$$

[Definition *Delayed* & *Latest*]

$$\Rightarrow\ Delayed_{\dot{n}_s}^{\psi} \wedge \forall \dot{m} \in pred(\dot{n}_s).\ Delayed_{\dot{m}}^{\psi} \wedge \neg Latest_{\dot{m}}^{\psi}$$

[$succ(\dot{n}) = \{\dot{n}_s\}$]

$$\Rightarrow\ \forall \dot{m} \in pred(succ(\dot{n})).\ Delayed_{\dot{m}}^{\psi} \wedge \neg Latest_{\dot{m}}^{\psi}$$

[Definition $\Theta_{\dot{m}}^{\mathrm{up}}$]

$$\Rightarrow\ \forall \dot{m} \in pred(succ(\dot{n})).\ \psi \in \Theta_{\dot{m}}^{\mathrm{up}}$$

□

As the equivalent to Theorem 4.4.1 we finally get:

Theorem 4.5.2 (Transformation Theorem for FFEM$_\Phi$). FFEM$_\Phi$ *is*

1. *a structured expression motion transformation in the sense of Definition 4.2.1 and*
2. *admissible, i. e.* FFEM$_\Phi$ $\in \mathcal{AEM}_\Phi$

Proof. In contrast to $\mathtt{LFEM}_\Phi$ the first point is not as obvious. We have to show

i) $\forall \dot{n} \in \dot{N},\ \psi \in \Phi.\ \mathtt{FFEM}_\Phi\text{-}\mathit{Insert}_{\dot{n}}^{\psi} \Rightarrow \forall \varphi \in \mathit{SubExpr}_\Phi(\psi).\ \mathtt{FFEM}_\Phi\text{-}\mathit{Correct}_{\dot{n}}^{\varphi}.$

Let us assume $\mathtt{FFEM}_\Phi\text{-}\mathit{Insert}_{\dot{n}}^{\psi}$ and $\varphi \in \mathit{SubExpr}_\Phi(\psi)$. Immediately by the according definitions we obtain the following trivial sequence of implications

$$\mathtt{FFEM}_\Phi\text{-}\mathit{Insert}_{\dot{n}}^{\psi} \Rightarrow \mathit{A\text{-}Latest}_{\dot{n}}^{\psi} \Rightarrow \mathit{A\text{-}Delayed}_{\dot{n}}^{\psi} \Rightarrow \mathit{Delayed}_{\dot{n}}^{\psi} \tag{4.34}$$

Using Lemma 4.2.5(1) we then obtain $\underbrace{\mathit{Delayed}_{\dot{n}}^{\varphi}}_{a)} \vee \underbrace{\mathtt{LEM}_\Phi\text{-}\mathit{Correct}_{\dot{n}}^{\varphi}}_{b)}$

In the case of (b) we easily conclude $\mathtt{FFEM}_\Phi\text{-}\mathit{Correct}_{\dot{n}}^{\varphi}$ from applying Lemma 4.5.3(1) to the path characterization of $\mathtt{LEM}_\Phi\text{-}\mathit{Correct}_{\dot{n}}^{\varphi}$. Thus we are left with (a). The case when $\neg \mathit{A\text{-}Delayed}_{\dot{n}}^{\varphi}$ holds is also subsumed by (b), as in this case the path characterizations of *Delayed* and *A-Delayed* deliver

$$\mathit{Delayed}_{\dot{n}}^{\varphi} \wedge \neg \mathit{A\text{-}Delayed}_{\dot{n}}^{\varphi} \Rightarrow \mathtt{LEM}_\Phi\text{-}\mathit{Correct}_{\dot{n}}^{\varphi}.$$

A formal proof of this implication would be almost the same as the one of Part (1) of Lemma 4.5.3. Similarly, Lemma 4.5.3(1) directly grants that the situation when $\mathit{Latest}_{\dot{n}}^{\varphi}$ holds is also covered by (b). Thus we are left with a situation, where (a) reduces to

$$\mathit{A\text{-}Delayed}_{\dot{n}}^{\varphi}$$

Now we are going to show that $\mathit{A\text{-}Latest}_{\dot{n}}^{\varphi}$ holds, which trivially implies

$$\mathtt{LEM}_\Phi\text{-}\mathit{Correct}_{\dot{n}}^{\varphi}$$

To this end we use the fact that $\mathit{A\text{-}Latest}_{\dot{n}}^{\psi}$ implies:

$$\underbrace{\mathit{Comp}_{\dot{n}}^{\psi}}_{c)} \vee \underbrace{\exists\, \dot{m} \in \mathit{succ}(\dot{n}).\ \neg \mathit{A\text{-}Delayed}_{\dot{n}}^{\psi}}_{d)}$$

Lemma 4.2.1(2) delivers that $\mathit{Comp}_{\dot{n}}^{\varphi}$ follows from (c), which immediately establishes the desired result $\mathit{A\text{-}Latest}_{\dot{n}}^{\varphi}$. So let us investigate the remaining case (d). Due to Lemma 4.2.6 we may assume $\neg \mathit{Latest}_{\dot{n}}^{\psi}$, as otherwise again (b) would become true. This, however, means $\psi \in \Theta_{\dot{n}}^{\mathrm{up}}$, which allows to apply Lemma 4.5.4(1) yielding $\mathit{Change}_{\dot{n}}^{\psi}$. According to Lemma 4.5.4(2) this induces $\mathit{Change}_{\dot{n}}^{\varphi}$. Applying Lemma 4.5.4(1) once more we finally get $\mathit{A\text{-}Latest}_{\dot{n}}^{\varphi}$ as desired.

In order to prove the second part of the lemma we have to show that initialisations are safe and replacements are correct, i. e.

ii) $\forall \psi \in \Phi,\ \dot{n} \in \dot{N}.\ \texttt{FFEM}_{\Phi}\text{-}Insert_{\dot{n}}^{\psi} \Rightarrow Safe_{\dot{n}}^{\psi}$
iii) $\forall \psi \in \Phi,\ \dot{n} \in \dot{N}.\ \texttt{FFEM}_{\Phi}\text{-}Replace_{\dot{n}}^{\psi} \Rightarrow \texttt{FFEM}_{\Phi}\text{-}Correct_{\dot{n}}^{\psi}$.

Starting with Point (ii), Sequence (4.34) ensures that $\texttt{FFEM}_{\Phi}\text{-}Insert_{\dot{n}}^{\psi}$ implies $Delayed_{\dot{n}}^{\psi}$. From Lemma 3.4.1(1) we then get $DnSafe_{\dot{n}}^{\psi}$ as desired. Finally, the proof of (iii) is based on the fact that $\texttt{FFEM}_{\Phi}\text{-}Replace_{\dot{n}}^{\psi}$ implies $Comp_{\dot{n}}^{\psi}$, which delivers $\texttt{LEM}_{\Phi}\text{-}Correct_{\dot{n}}^{\psi}$. Again (see proof of (b) above) Lemma 4.5.3(1) also forces $\texttt{FFEM}_{\Phi}\text{-}Correct_{\dot{n}}^{\psi}$. □

4.5.6 Proving Computational Optimality

The proof of computational optimality is also straightforward along the lines of the corresponding proof for $\texttt{LFEM}_{\Phi}$. As the counterpart of Lemma 4.4.4 we get:

Lemma 4.5.6 (Adjustment Lemma for $\texttt{FFEM}_{\Phi}$). *Let $\psi \in \Phi$ and $p \in \mathbf{P}$ an interval of program points between the earliest and latest program point (cf. Lemma 3.4.2(2)), i. e. (A1) $Earliest_{p_1}^{\psi}$, (A2) $Latest_{p_{|p|}}^{\psi}$ and (A3) $\forall 1 \leqslant k < |p|.\ Delayed_{p_k}^{\psi} \wedge \neg Latest_{p_k}^{\psi}$. Then there is an index $1 \leqslant i \leqslant |p|$ such that:*

1. $\forall 1 \leqslant k \leqslant |p|.\ A\text{-}Delayed_{p_k}^{\psi} \Leftrightarrow (1 \leqslant k \leqslant i)$
2. $\forall 1 \leqslant k \leqslant |p|.\ A\text{-}Latest_{p_k}^{\psi} \Leftrightarrow (i = k)$

This directly gives rise to the following result:

Theorem 4.5.3 (Computational Optimality Theorem for $\texttt{FFEM}_{\Phi}$). *$\texttt{FFEM}_{\Phi}$ is computationally optimal, i. e. $\texttt{FFEM}_{\Phi} \in \mathcal{COEM}_{\Phi}$.*

4.5.7 Proving Lifetime Optimality

Like for the reasoning on inductive lifetime optimality it is necessary to collect a number of results concerned with lifetime ranges. Fortunately, all these results are quite close to their counterparts in Section 4.4. Starting with the counterpart to Lemma 4.4.6 we have:[14]

Lemma 4.5.7 (*UsedLater*-Lemma). *Let $\texttt{EM}_{\Phi} \in \mathcal{COEM}_{\Phi}$ and $\dot{n} \in \dot{N}$. Then*

1. $\forall\ \psi \in \Phi^{max}.\ DnSafe_{\dot{n}}^{\psi} \wedge Transp_{\dot{n}}^{\psi} \Rightarrow UsedLater_{\dot{n}}^{\psi}$
2. $\forall\ \varphi \in \Phi.\ \texttt{EM}_{\Phi}\text{-}Correct_{\dot{n}}^{\varphi} \wedge UsedLater_{\dot{n}}^{\varphi} \Rightarrow \dot{n} \in SLtRg(\texttt{EM}_{\Phi}, \varphi)$

As for $\texttt{LFEM}_{\Phi}$ the key for establishing lifetime-optimality lies in a lemma that captures the relationship between lifetime ranges of upper and lower trade-off candidates. Along the lines of Lemma 4.4.9 we have:

[14] Note that we do not need a counterpart of Lemma 4.4.6(2b).

Lemma 4.5.8 (Lifetime Range Lemma for $\mathtt{FFEM}_\Phi$).
Let $\mathtt{EM}_\Phi \in \mathcal{COEM}_\Phi$ and $\dot{n} \in \dot{N}$. Then

1. $\forall\, \varphi \in \Theta^{dn}_{\dot{n}}.\ \dot{n} \in SLtRg(\mathtt{EM}_\Phi, \varphi) \Leftrightarrow$
$$\mathtt{EM}_\Phi\text{-}Correct^{\varphi}_{\dot{n}} \wedge \exists\, \psi \in pred_{D_{\dot{n}}}(\varphi).\ \neg \mathtt{EM}_\Phi\text{-}Correct^{\psi}_{\dot{n}}$$
2. a) $\forall\, \psi \in \Theta^{up}_{\dot{n}} \setminus \Theta^{dn}_{\dot{n}}.\ \dot{n} \in SLtRg(\mathtt{FFEM}_\Phi, \psi) \Leftrightarrow Change^{\psi}_{\dot{n}}$
   b) $\forall\, \varphi \in \Theta^{dn}_{\dot{n}} \setminus \Theta^{up}_{\dot{n}}.\ \dot{n} \in SLtRg(\mathtt{FFEM}_\Phi, \varphi) \Leftrightarrow \varphi \notin \mathcal{T}^{\top}(\Theta^{dn}_{\dot{n}})$
   c) $\forall\, \varphi \in \Theta^{dn}_{\dot{n}} \cap \Theta^{up}_{\dot{n}}.\ \dot{n} \in SLtRg(\mathtt{FFEM}_\Phi, \varphi) \Leftrightarrow$
$$\varphi \in neigh(\mathcal{T}^{\top}(\Theta^{dn}_{\dot{n}})) \setminus \mathcal{T}^{\top}(\Theta^{dn}_{\dot{n}})$$

Part (1) is almost identical to its counterpart Lemma 4.4.9(1). The only difference is that now the right-hand side of the equivalence has to require correctness with respect to φ. This is for the reason that - as opposed to the levelwise approach - lower trade-off candidates may violate the correctness predicate. In fact, a straightforward adaption of Lemma 4.4.9(1) would not be true either, since under the new situation we might be faced with expressions of type O, whose lifetime ranges at $\dot{n}$ are only local.

The second part of the lemma slightly differs from Lemma 4.4.9(2). The most striking difference is that the characterisation is divided into three parts rather than two. Again this is due to the fact that expressions of type O may only be associated with local lifetime ranges, which requires a separate reasoning in this case.

Due to the important role that this lemma has for the proof of lifetime optimality we will elaborate its proof in full details, even though some parts are similar to the arguments given in the proof of Lemma 4.4.9.

Proof of 1: Starting with the $\Rightarrow$-direction let us assume $\varphi \in \Theta^{dn}_{\dot{n}}$ such that $\dot{n} \in SLtRg(\mathtt{EM}_\Phi, \varphi)$. First, according to Lemma 4.2.7 this immediately implies $\mathtt{EM}_\Phi\text{-}Correct^{\varphi}_{\dot{n}}$. On the other hand, we have $\neg UsedLater^{\varphi}_{\dot{n}}$ and thus can exclude a strictly later original replacement of φ. Hence the definition of $SLtRg(\mathtt{EM}_\Phi, \varphi)$ yields that there is an expression $\psi \in SupExpr_{\Phi^i}(\varphi)$ such that φ is used for the initialisation of this superexpression. That means there is a path $p \in \mathbf{P}[\dot{n}, \dot{\mathbf{e}}]$ and an index $1 < j \leqslant |p|$ with

$$\mathtt{EM}_\Phi\text{-}Insert^{\psi}_{p_j} \wedge \forall\, 1 < k \leqslant j.\ \neg \mathtt{EM}_\Phi\text{-}Insert^{\varphi}_{p_k} \tag{4.35}$$

First, we are going to show

$$1 < k \leqslant j.\ \neg Earliest^{\varphi}_{p_k} \tag{4.36}$$

Suppose there would be an index $1 < k \leqslant j$ such that $Earliest^{\varphi}_{p_k}$ is true. Using that $\mathtt{EM}_\Phi$ is a structured expression motion especially means $\mathtt{EM}_\Phi\text{-}Correct^{\varphi}_{p_j}$. Hence according to Lemma 3.4.2(2) this would imply an index $k \leqslant l \leqslant j$ with $\mathtt{EM}_\Phi\text{-}Insert^{\varphi}_{p_l}$ in contradiction to the assumption in (4.35).

Furthermore, due to Lemma 3.4.2(2) $\mathbf{EM}_\Phi$-$\mathit{Insert}^\psi_{p_j}$ implies that program point p_j must be preceded on every program path from $\dot{\mathbf{s}}$ to p_j by a program point that satisfies *Earliest*. Suppose, such a position would be on the path $\langle p_1, \ldots, p_j \rangle$ strictly behind $\dot{n}$, i.e. there is an index $1 < k \leqslant j$ such that $\mathit{Earliest}^\psi_{p_k}$ holds. Then this together with Property (4.36) delivers

$$\mathit{Earliest}^\psi_{p_k} \ \wedge\ \forall 1 < l \leqslant k.\ \neg \mathit{Earliest}^\varphi_{p_l},$$

which therefore means $\mathit{UsedLater}^\varphi_{\dot{n}}$ in contradiction to the assumption $\varphi \in \Theta^{\mathrm{dn}}_{\dot{n}}$. Hence we have

$$\forall 1 \leqslant k < j.\ \mathit{Delayed}^\psi_{p_k} \ \wedge\ \neg \mathit{Latest}^\psi_{p_k}$$

In particular, this means $\psi \in \Theta^{\mathrm{up}}_{\dot{n}}$ and thus $\psi \in \mathit{pred}_{D_{\dot{n}}}(\varphi)$. On the other hand, we also have $\neg\mathbf{EM}_\Phi$-$\mathit{Correct}^\psi_{\dot{n}}$, as otherwise $\mathbf{EM}_\Phi$ would have two ψ-insertions on an interval of delayable program points in contradiction to Lemma 3.4.2(2).

For the proof of the $\Leftarrow$-direction we shall use Lemma 3.4.2(2) which yields that the assumption $\neg\mathbf{EM}_\Phi$-$\mathit{Correct}^\psi_{\dot{n}}$ together with $\mathit{Delayed}^\psi_{\dot{n}}$ implies that there is a path $p \in \mathbf{P}[\dot{n}, \dot{\mathbf{e}}]$ and an index $1 < j \leqslant |p|$ with:

$$\mathbf{EM}_\Phi\text{-}\mathit{Insert}^\psi_{p_j} \ \wedge\ \forall 1 \leqslant k < j.\ \mathit{Delayed}^\psi_{p_k} \ \wedge\ \neg \mathit{Latest}^\psi_{p_k} \tag{4.37}$$

This almost establishes the desired result $\dot{n} \in \mathit{SLtRg}(\mathbf{EM}_\Phi, \varphi)$: $\mathbf{EM}_\Phi$-$\mathit{Correct}^\varphi_{\dot{n}}$ holds by assumption and in addition p_j defines a potential use-site of $\mathbf{h}_\varphi$. In order to ensure that p_j is actually a use-site of $\mathbf{h}_\varphi$ we are left with the proof that $\mathbf{EM}_\Phi$ has no other φ-insertions in between $\dot{n}$ and p_j, i.e.

$$\forall 1 < k \leqslant j.\ \neg\mathbf{EM}_\Phi\text{-}\mathit{Insert}^\varphi_{p_k} \tag{4.38}$$

To this end, let us assume an index $1 < k \leqslant j$ with $\mathbf{EM}_\Phi$-$\mathit{Insert}^\varphi_{p_k}$. Due to our assumption $\mathbf{EM}_\Phi$-$\mathit{Correct}^\varphi_{\dot{n}}$ then Lemma 3.4.2(2) implies that there must be an index $1 < l \leqslant k$ such that $\mathit{Earliest}^\varphi_{p_l}$ holds. This, however, is in contradiction to Lemma 4.2.5(3) which is applicable, since Property (4.37) forces $\mathit{Delayed}^\psi_{p_l} \ \wedge\ \neg\mathit{Earliest}^\psi_{p_l}$.

Proof of 2: Investigating the proof of Part (2a) we start by providing two auxiliary properties. First we have for upper trade-off candidates:

$$\forall\, \psi \in \Theta^{\mathrm{up}}_{\dot{n}}.\ \mathbf{FFEM}_\Phi\text{-}\mathit{Correct}^\psi_{\dot{n}} \ \Leftrightarrow\ \mathit{Change}^\psi_{\dot{n}} \tag{4.39}$$

Starting with the contrapositive of the $\Rightarrow$-direction we have

$$\begin{array}{rcl} & & \neg Change_{\dot{n}}^{\psi} \\ [\text{Lemma 4.5.4}] & \Rightarrow & \forall\, \dot{m} \in succ(\dot{n}).\ A\text{-}Delayed_{\dot{m}}^{\psi} \\ [\text{Lemma 4.5.5(2a)}] & \Rightarrow & \forall\, \dot{m} \in succ(\dot{n}).\ A\text{-}Delayed_{\dot{m}}^{\psi} \wedge \neg Earliest_{\dot{m}}^{\psi} \\ [\text{Definition } A\text{-}Delayed] & \Rightarrow & A\text{-}Delayed_{\dot{n}}^{\psi} \wedge \neg A\text{-}Latest_{\dot{n}}^{\psi} \\ [\text{Lemma 4.5.6}] & \Rightarrow & \neg \texttt{FFEM}_{\Phi}\text{-}Correct_{\dot{n}}^{\psi} \end{array}$$

The $\Leftarrow$-direction is similar:

$$\begin{array}{rcl} & & Change_{\dot{n}}^{\psi} \\ [\psi \in \Theta_{\dot{n}}^{\text{up}}] & \Rightarrow & Change_{\dot{n}}^{\psi} \wedge Delayed_{\dot{n}}^{\psi} \wedge \neg Latest_{\dot{n}}^{\psi} \\ [\text{Lemma 4.5.4}] & \Rightarrow & \\ \multicolumn{3}{c}{\forall\, \dot{m} \in succ(\dot{n}).\ \neg A\text{-}Delayed_{\dot{m}}^{\psi} \wedge Delayed_{\dot{n}}^{\psi} \wedge \neg Latest_{\dot{n}}^{\psi}} \\ [\text{Lemma 4.5.6}] & \Rightarrow & \texttt{FFEM}_{\Phi}\text{-}Correct_{\dot{n}}^{\psi} \end{array}$$

The second auxiliary property addresses the lower trade-off candidates:

$$\forall\, \varphi \in \Theta_{\dot{n}}^{\text{dn}}.\ \varphi \in \mathcal{T}^{\top}(\Theta_{\dot{n}}^{\text{dn}}) \Leftrightarrow \forall\, \psi \in pred_{D_n}(\varphi).\ \texttt{FFEM}_{\Phi}\text{-}Correct_{\dot{n}}^{\psi} \qquad (4.40)$$

Here we have

$$\begin{array}{rcl} & & \varphi \in \mathcal{T}^{\top}(\Theta_{\dot{n}}^{\text{dn}}) \\ [\text{Def. } Change] & \Leftrightarrow & \forall\, \psi \in neigh(\varphi).\ Change_{\dot{n}}^{\psi} \\ [\text{Prop. (4.39)}] & \Leftrightarrow & \forall\, \psi \in neigh(\varphi).\ \texttt{FFEM}_{\Phi}\text{-}Correct_{\dot{n}}^{\psi} \\ [(\dagger)] & \Leftrightarrow & \forall\, \psi \in pred_{D_n}(\varphi).\ \texttt{FFEM}_{\Phi}\text{-}Correct_{\dot{n}}^{\psi} \end{array}$$

The equivalence marked (†) requires a short explanation. Whereas the forward-implication is obvious, for the backward-direction let us assume an expression $\psi \in pred_{D_n}(\varphi)$ such that $\texttt{FFEM}_{\Phi}\text{-}Correct_{\dot{n}}^{\psi}$ holds. Due to Theorem 4.5.2 Lemma 4.2.4 becomes applicable yielding $\texttt{FFEM}_{\Phi}\text{-}Correct_{\dot{n}}^{\varphi'}$ for all $\varphi' \in SubExpr_{\Phi}^{*}(\psi)$. Hence due to the definition of edges in the associated bipartite graph (cf. Algorithm 4.5.1) this ensure that $\texttt{FFEM}_{\Phi}\text{-}Correct_{\dot{n}}^{\psi}$ even holds for $\psi \in neigh(\varphi)$.

Now we can turn to the proofs of Part (2a) to (2c). The $\Rightarrow$-direction of Part (2a) is a direct consequence of the forward-implication of Proposition (4.39) together with Lemma 4.2.7. For the $\Leftarrow$-direction we can exploit that $\psi \in \Theta_{\dot{n}}^{\text{up}} \backslash \Theta_{\dot{n}}^{\text{dn}}$ delivers $UsedLater_{\dot{n}}^{\psi}$. This together with the backward-direction of Proposition (4.39) implies

$$\texttt{FFEM}_{\Phi}\text{-}Correct_{\dot{n}}^{\psi} \wedge UsedLater_{\dot{n}}^{\psi},$$

which according to Lemma 4.5.7(2) yields $\dot{n} \in SLtRg(\texttt{FFEM}_{\Phi}, \psi)$.

For Part (2b) we have

$$\begin{array}{rcl} & & \varphi \in \mathcal{T}^{\top}(\Theta_{\dot n}^{\mathrm{dn}}) \\ \text{[Proposition (4.40)]} & \Leftrightarrow & \forall \psi \in pred_{D_n}(\varphi).\ \mathtt{FFEM}_{\Phi}\text{-}Correct_{\dot n}^{\psi} \\ \text{[Part (1) with } \varphi \in \Theta_{\dot n}^{\mathrm{dn}} \setminus \Theta_{\dot n}^{\mathrm{up}}] & \Leftrightarrow & \dot n \in SLtRg(\mathtt{FFEM}_{\Phi}, \varphi) \end{array}$$

Finally, let us investigate the new point (2c) whose proof is also quite simple using the Propositions (4.39) and (4.40):

$$\begin{array}{rcl} & & \varphi \in neigh(\mathcal{T}^{\top}(\Theta_{\dot n}^{\mathrm{dn}})) \setminus \mathcal{T}^{\top}(\Theta_{\dot n}^{\mathrm{dn}}) \\ \text{[Def. } LChange] & \Leftrightarrow & Change_{\dot n}^{\varphi} \wedge \varphi \notin \mathcal{T}^{\top}(\Theta_{\dot n}^{\mathrm{dn}}) \\ \text{[Prop. (4.39 \& 4.40)]} & \Leftrightarrow & \mathtt{FFEM}_{\Phi}\text{-}Correct_{\dot n}^{\varphi} \wedge \\ & & \qquad \exists \psi \in pred_{D_n}(\varphi).\ \neg \mathtt{FFEM}_{\Phi}\text{-}Correct_{\dot n}^{\psi} \\ \text{[Part (1)]} & \Leftrightarrow & \dot n \in SLtRg(\mathtt{FFEM}_{\Phi}, \varphi) \end{array}$$

□

Now we finally succeed in proving the main result:

Theorem 4.5.4 (Lifetime Optimality Theorem for $\mathtt{FFEM}_{\Phi}$).
$\mathtt{FFEM}_{\Phi}$ is lifetime optimal.

Proof. Let us consider a structured expression motion $\mathtt{EM}_{\Phi} \in \mathcal{COEM}_{\Phi}$. In order to prove $\mathtt{EM}_{\Phi} \precsim_{lt}^{\Phi} \mathtt{FFEM}_{\Phi}$ we have to show for every $\dot n \in \dot N$ the inequation:

$$|\{\varphi \in \Phi \mid \dot n \in SLtRg(\mathtt{FFEM}_{\Phi}, \varphi)\}| \leqslant \\ |\{\varphi \in \Phi \mid \dot n \in SLtRg(\mathtt{EM}_{\Phi}, \varphi)\}| \tag{4.41}$$

For the sake of a simple notation let us fix $\dot n \in \dot N$ and introduce the following abbreviations:

$$\begin{array}{rcl} \Lambda_{\mathtt{EM}_{\Phi}} & \stackrel{\mathrm{def}}{=} & \{\varphi \in \Phi | \dot n \in SLtRg(\mathtt{EM}_{\Phi}, \varphi)\} \\ \Lambda_{\mathtt{FFEM}_{\Phi}} & \stackrel{\mathrm{def}}{=} & \{\varphi \in \Phi | \dot n \in SLtRg(\mathtt{FFEM}_{\Phi}, \varphi)\}. \end{array}$$

Furthermore, for both sets the subsets of expressions of type $\{\blacksquare, \square, \bullet, \circ\}$ are indicated by a corresponding superscript out of $\{\blacksquare, \square, \bullet, \circ\}$, e.g., $\Lambda_{\mathtt{EM}_{\Phi}}^{\blacksquare} \stackrel{\mathrm{def}}{=} \{\varphi \in \Lambda_{\mathtt{EM}_{\Phi}} | \ell_{\dot n}(\varphi) = \blacksquare\}$. Before we turn to the estimation on the number of lifetime ranges at $\dot n$ we shall collect some elementary properties. We start with propositions characterising lifetime ranges being out of the scope of trade-offs: for instance, expressions not in $\Theta_{\dot n}$ do not contribute to lifetime ranges at $\dot n$ at all and lifetime ranges of expressions of type $\blacksquare$ are independent from the expression motion under consideration:

$$\Lambda_{\mathtt{EM}_{\Phi}} \subseteq \Theta_{\dot n} \tag{4.42a}$$

$$\Lambda_{\mathtt{FFEM}_{\Phi}} \subseteq \Theta_{\dot n} \tag{4.42b}$$

$$\Lambda_{\mathtt{EM}_{\Phi}}^{\blacksquare} = \Lambda_{\mathtt{FFEM}_{\Phi}}^{\blacksquare} \tag{4.42c}$$

Starting with Inclusion (4.42a) let us assume $\varphi \in \Lambda_{\mathtt{EM}_\Phi}$. According to Lemma 4.2.7 this implies $\mathtt{EM}_\Phi\text{-}Correct_{\dot{n}}^{\varphi}$, which due to Lemma 3.4.1(2) means either $\mathtt{LEM}_\Phi\text{-}Correct_{\dot{n}}^{\varphi}$ or $Delayed_{\dot{n}}^{\varphi}$. As $Latest_{\dot{n}}^{\varphi}$ is subsumed by $\mathtt{LEM}_\Phi\text{-}Correct_{\dot{n}}^{\varphi}$, this can be even strengthened towards

$$\mathtt{LEM}_\Phi\text{-}Correct_{\dot{n}}^{\varphi} \;\vee\; (Delayed_{\dot{n}}^{\varphi} \wedge \neg Latest_{\dot{n}}^{\varphi}),$$

which by definition is equal to $\varphi \in \Theta_{\dot{n}}$. Inclusion (4.42b) follows from an analogous argument. For the proof of Equation (4.42c) let us assume $\varphi \in \Lambda_{\mathtt{EM}_\Phi}^{\blacksquare}$. By definition this means $\mathtt{LEM}_\Phi\text{-}Correct_{\dot{n}}^{\varphi}$ and $UsedLater_{\dot{n}}^{\varphi}$. As $\mathtt{LEM}_\Phi\text{-}Correct_{\dot{n}}^{\varphi}$ implies $\mathtt{FFEM}_\Phi\text{-}Correct_{\dot{n}}^{\varphi}$ (cf. Lemma 4.5.6) we obtain using Lemma 4.5.7(2) that $\varphi \in \Lambda_{\mathtt{FFEM}_\Phi}^{\blacksquare}$. The inclusion $\Lambda_{\mathtt{FFEM}_\Phi}^{\blacksquare} \subseteq \Lambda_{\mathtt{EM}_\Phi}^{\blacksquare}$ follows in a symmetric way.

The central ingredients of the proof, however, are some propositions that close the gap between lifetime ranges and trade-off pairs. With

$$\Xi_{\dot{n}}^{\mathtt{re}} \stackrel{\mathtt{def}}{=} \Theta_{\dot{n}}^{\mathtt{dn}} \setminus (\Theta_{\dot{n}}^{\mathtt{up}} \cup \Lambda_{\mathtt{EM}_\Phi}^{\bullet})$$

and

$$\Xi_{\dot{n}}^{\mathtt{ic}} \stackrel{\mathtt{def}}{=} \{\varphi \in \Theta_{\dot{n}} \mid \exists \psi \in \Lambda_{\mathtt{EM}_\Phi}^{\bigcirc} \cup \Lambda_{\mathtt{EM}_\Phi}^{\square}.\ \varphi \in succ_{D_{\dot{n}}}^{*}(\psi)\}$$

these propositions read as:

$$(\Xi_{\dot{n}}^{\mathtt{re}}, \Xi_{\dot{n}}^{\mathtt{ic}}) \quad \text{is a trade-off pair in} \quad D_{\dot{n}} \tag{4.43a}$$

$$\mathcal{R}_{\dot{n}}^{\mathtt{re}}(\Xi_{\dot{n}}^{\mathtt{re}}) \;=\; \Xi_{\dot{n}}^{\mathtt{re}} \;=\; \Theta_{\dot{n}}^{\mathtt{dn}} \setminus (\Theta_{\dot{n}}^{\mathtt{up}} \;\cup\; \Lambda_{\mathtt{EM}_\Phi}^{\bullet}) \tag{4.43b}$$

$$\mathcal{R}_{\dot{n}}^{\mathtt{ic}}(\Xi_{\dot{n}}^{\mathtt{ic}}) \;\subseteq\; \Lambda_{\mathtt{EM}_\Phi}^{\bigcirc} \;\uplus\; \Lambda_{\mathtt{EM}_\Phi}^{\square} \tag{4.43c}$$

Considering Proposition (4.43a) conditions (1), (2) and (4) of Definition 4.5.1 are trivially satisfied. For the remaining Point (3) we have to show that a register expression $\varphi \in \Xi_{\dot{n}}^{\mathtt{re}}$ is covered by $\Xi_{\dot{n}}^{\mathtt{ic}}$. Let $\psi \in pred_{D_{\dot{n}}}(\varphi)$. According to the definition of $\Xi_{\dot{n}}^{\mathtt{re}}$ Lemma 4.5.8(1) becomes applicable yielding $\mathtt{EM}_\Phi\text{-}Correct_{\dot{n}}^{\psi}$. In the case that ψ is of type □ Lemma 4.4.6(2) then yields $\psi \in \Lambda_{\mathtt{EM}_\Phi}^{\square}$. Otherwise, if ψ is of type ○ we either have $\psi \in \Lambda_{\mathtt{EM}_\Phi}^{\bigcirc}$, in which case we are done, or $\psi \notin \Lambda_{\mathtt{EM}_\Phi}^{\bigcirc}$, which establishes the same situation as before with ψ taking the role of φ. For the reason that expressions of maximum level in $\Theta_{\dot{n}}^{\mathtt{up}}$ satisfy property *UsedLater* (by Lemma 4.4.6(1)) we eventually succeed in showing $\psi \in succ_{D_{\dot{n}}}^{*}(\psi')$ for some $\psi' \in \Lambda_{\mathtt{EM}_\Phi}^{\bigcirc} \cup \Lambda_{\mathtt{EM}_\Phi}^{\square}$.

Because $\Theta_{\dot{n}}^{\mathtt{dn}} \setminus \Theta_{\dot{n}}^{\mathtt{up}}$ only contains expressions of type $\Lambda_{\mathtt{FFEM}_\Phi}^{\bullet}$, Equation (4.43b) is trivial.

For Inclusion (4.43c) let us assume $\varphi \in \mathcal{R}_{\dot{n}}^{\mathtt{ic}}(\Xi_{\dot{n}}^{\mathtt{ic}})$ and show that $\varphi \in \Lambda_{\mathtt{EM}_\Phi}^{\bigcirc} \uplus \Lambda_{\mathtt{EM}_\Phi}^{\square}$. In the case that φ is of type □ we have by definition

$$\text{LEM}_\Phi\text{-}Correct^{\varphi}_{\dot n} \wedge UsedLater^{\varphi}_{\dot n},$$

which by Corollary 3.4.1 implies

$$\text{EM}_\Phi\text{-}Correct^{\varphi}_{\dot n} \wedge UsedLater^{\varphi}_{\dot n}$$

Hence by using Lemma 4.5.7(2) we succeed in showing $\varphi \in \Lambda^{\square}_{\text{EM}_\Phi}$. In the remaining case that φ is of type $\bigcirc$ let us assume that $\varphi \notin \Lambda^{\bigcirc}_{\text{EM}_\Phi}$. In this case the same argument as in the proof of Property (4.43a) delivers that all predecessors in $pred_{D_n}(\varphi)$ are part of $\Xi^{\text{ic}}_{\dot n}$, too, which would be in contradiction to the relevancy of φ. Hence we obtain $\varphi \in \Lambda^{\bigcirc}_{\text{EM}_\Phi}$ as desired.

Then we finally obtain the following sequence of inequations:

$$|\Lambda_{\text{EM}_\Phi}|$$

[Equation 4.42(a)]

$$= \quad |\Lambda_{\text{EM}_\Phi} \cap \Theta_{\dot n}|$$

[Splitting $\Lambda_{\text{EM}_\Phi} \cap \Theta_{\dot n}$]

$$= \quad |\Lambda^{\bullet}_{\text{EM}_\Phi}| + |\Lambda^{\bigcirc}_{\text{EM}_\Phi}| + |\Lambda^{\square}_{\text{EM}_\Phi}| + |\Lambda^{\blacksquare}_{\text{EM}_\Phi}|$$

[Equation 4.42(c)]

$$= \quad |\Lambda^{\bullet}_{\text{EM}_\Phi}| + |\Lambda^{\bigcirc}_{\text{EM}_\Phi}| + |\Lambda^{\square}_{\text{EM}_\Phi}| + |\Lambda^{\blacksquare}_{\text{FFEM}_\Phi}|$$

$$= \quad |\Theta^{\text{dn}}_{\dot n} \setminus \Theta^{\text{up}}_{\dot n}| - ((|\Theta^{\text{dn}}_{\dot n} \setminus \Theta^{\text{up}}_{\dot n}| - |\Lambda^{\bullet}_{\text{EM}_\Phi}|) - (|\Lambda^{\bigcirc}_{\text{EM}_\Phi}| + |\Lambda^{\square}_{\text{EM}_\Phi}|)) + |\Lambda^{\blacksquare}_{\text{FFEM}_\Phi}|$$

[$\Lambda^{\bullet}_{\text{EM}_\Phi} \subseteq \Theta^{\text{dn}}_{\dot n} \setminus \Theta^{\text{up}}_{\dot n}$, $\Lambda^{\bigcirc}_{\text{EM}_\Phi} \cap \Lambda^{\square}_{\text{EM}_\Phi} = \emptyset$]

$$= \quad |\Theta^{\text{dn}}_{\dot n} \setminus \Theta^{\text{up}}_{\dot n}| - ((|\Theta^{\text{dn}}_{\dot n} \setminus (\Theta^{\text{up}}_{\dot n} \cup \Lambda^{\bullet}_{\text{EM}_\Phi})|) - (|\Lambda^{\bigcirc}_{\text{EM}_\Phi} \uplus \Lambda^{\square}_{\text{EM}_\Phi}|)) + |\Lambda^{\blacksquare}_{\text{FFEM}_\Phi}|$$

[Equation 4.43(b) & Inclusion 4.43(c)]

$$\geqslant \quad |\Theta^{\text{dn}}_{\dot n} \setminus \Theta^{\text{up}}_{\dot n}| - (|\mathcal{R}^{\text{re}}_{\dot n}(\Xi^{\text{re}}_{\dot n})| - |\mathcal{R}^{\text{ic}}_{\dot n}(\Xi^{\text{ic}}_{\dot n})|) + |\Lambda^{\blacksquare}_{\text{FFEM}_\Phi}|$$

[Proposition 4.43(a) & Theorem 4.5.1 & Theorem 4.3.3]

$$\geqslant \quad |\Theta^{\text{dn}}_{\dot n} \setminus \Theta^{\text{up}}_{\dot n}| - (|\mathcal{T}^{\top}(\Theta^{\text{dn}}_{\dot n})| - |neigh(\mathcal{T}^{\top}(\Theta^{\text{dn}}_{\dot n}))|) + |\Lambda^{\blacksquare}_{\text{FFEM}_\Phi}|$$

[Decomposing $\mathcal{T}^{\top}(\Theta^{\text{dn}}_{\dot n})$ & $neigh(\mathcal{T}^{\top}(\Theta^{\text{dn}}_{\dot n}))$]

$$\begin{aligned} = \quad & |\Theta^{\text{dn}}_{\dot n} \setminus \Theta^{\text{up}}_{\dot n}| - (|\mathcal{T}^{\top}(\Theta^{\text{dn}}_{\dot n}) \setminus \Theta^{\text{up}}_{\dot n}| + |\mathcal{T}^{\top}(\Theta^{\text{dn}}_{\dot n}) \cap \Theta^{\text{up}}_{\dot n}| - \\ & |neigh(\mathcal{T}^{\top}(\Theta^{\text{dn}}_{\dot n})) \cap \Theta^{\text{dn}}_{\dot n}| - |neigh(\mathcal{T}^{\top}(\Theta^{\text{dn}}_{\dot n})) \setminus \Theta^{\text{dn}}_{\dot n}|) + |\Lambda^{\blacksquare}_{\text{FFEM}_\Phi}| \end{aligned}$$

[Combining $\mathcal{T}^{\top}(\Theta^{\text{dn}}_{\dot n}) \cap \Theta^{\text{up}}_{\dot n}$ & $neigh(\mathcal{T}^{\top}(\Theta^{\text{dn}}_{\dot n})) \cap \Theta^{\text{dn}}_{\dot n}$]

$$\begin{aligned} = \quad & |\Theta^{\text{dn}}_{\dot n} \setminus \Theta^{\text{up}}_{\dot n}| - |\mathcal{T}^{\top}(\Theta^{\text{dn}}_{\dot n}) \setminus \Theta^{\text{up}}_{\dot n}| + \\ & |(neigh(\mathcal{T}^{\top}(\Theta^{\text{dn}}_{\dot n})) \setminus \mathcal{T}^{\top}(\Theta^{\text{dn}}_{\dot n})) \cap \Theta^{\text{dn}}_{\dot n} \cap \Theta^{\text{up}}_{\dot n}| + \\ & |neigh(\mathcal{T}^{\top}(\Theta^{\text{dn}}_{\dot n})) \setminus \Theta^{\text{dn}}_{\dot n}| + |\Lambda^{\blacksquare}_{\text{FFEM}_\Phi}| \end{aligned}$$

[Lemma 4.5.8(2a,b,c)]

$$= \quad |\Theta^{\text{dn}}_{\dot n} \setminus \Theta^{\text{up}}_{\dot n}| - |\Theta^{\text{dn}}_{\dot n} \setminus (\Theta^{\text{up}}_{\dot n} \cup \Lambda^{\bullet}_{\text{FFEM}_\Phi})| + |\Lambda^{\bigcirc}_{\text{FFEM}_\Phi}| + |\Lambda^{\square}_{\text{FFEM}_\Phi}| + |\Lambda^{\blacksquare}_{\text{FFEM}_\Phi}|$$

$$= \quad |\Theta^{\text{dn}}_{\dot n} \setminus \Theta^{\text{up}}_{\dot n}| - |(\Theta^{\text{dn}}_{\dot n} \setminus \Theta^{\text{up}}_{\dot n}) \setminus \Lambda^{\bullet}_{\text{FFEM}_\Phi}| + |\Lambda^{\bigcirc}_{\text{FFEM}_\Phi}| + |\Lambda^{\square}_{\text{FFEM}_\Phi}| + |\Lambda^{\blacksquare}_{\text{FFEM}_\Phi}|$$

$[\Lambda^{\bullet}_{\mathtt{FFEM}_\Phi} \subseteq \Theta^{\mathrm{dn}}_{\dot{n}} \setminus \Theta^{\mathrm{up}}_{\dot{n}}]$

$$= \quad |\Theta^{\mathrm{dn}}_{\dot{n}} \setminus \Theta^{\mathrm{up}}_{\dot{n}}| - (|\Theta^{\mathrm{dn}}_{\dot{n}} \setminus \Theta^{\mathrm{up}}_{\dot{n}}| - |\Lambda^{\bullet}_{\mathtt{FFEM}_\Phi}|) + |\Lambda^{\circ}_{\mathtt{FFEM}_\Phi}| + |\Lambda^{\square}_{\mathtt{FFEM}_\Phi}| + |\Lambda^{\blacksquare}_{\mathtt{FFEM}_\Phi}|$$

$$= \quad |\Lambda^{\bullet}_{\mathtt{FFEM}_\Phi}| + |\Lambda^{\circ}_{\mathtt{FFEM}_\Phi}| + |\Lambda^{\square}_{\mathtt{FFEM}_\Phi}| + |\Lambda^{\blacksquare}_{\mathtt{FFEM}_\Phi}|$$

[Combining $\Lambda_{\mathtt{FFEM}_\Phi} \cap \Theta_{\dot{n}}$]

$$= \quad |\Lambda_{\mathtt{FFEM}_\Phi} \cap \Theta_{\dot{n}}|$$

[Equation 4.42(b)]

$$= \quad |\Lambda_{\mathtt{FFEM}_\Phi}| \qquad \square$$

4.5.8 Computing $\mathtt{FFEM}_\Phi$

Like in the section on $\mathtt{LFEM}_\Phi$ we will complete this section with the presentation of the algorithmically oriented summary of the steps of $\mathtt{FFEM}_\Phi$.

Table 4.4 gives a survey on the general structure of the algorithm. Again the algorithm is a refinement approach which is based on the original analyses belonging to $\mathtt{BEM}_\Phi$ and $\mathtt{LEM}_\Phi$. However, the absence of a counterpart to the first adjustment step of $\mathtt{LFEM}_\Phi$ and the general kind of trade-offs (as opposed to the levelwise approach) makes the description of $\mathtt{FFEM}_\Phi$ significantly simpler. In fact, essentially $\mathtt{LEM}_\Phi$ has only to be supplemented by a preprocess for computing the new local *Change*-property, which requires only one additional data flow analysis that can even be done in a bit-vector fashion.

1. Used-Later Analysis ($\varphi \in SubExpr_{\Phi}(\Phi^i)$):

$$\mathbf{NUSEDLAT}_{\dot n}^{\varphi} = \overline{A1\text{-}XEarliest_{\dot n}^{\varphi}} \cdot \Big(\sum_{\psi \in SupExpr_{\Phi^i}(\varphi)} A1\text{-}XEarliest_{\dot n}^{\psi} + \mathbf{XUSEDLAT}_{\dot n}^{\varphi} \Big)$$

$$\mathbf{XUSEDLAT}_{\dot n}^{\varphi} = \sum_{m \in succ(n)} \overline{A1\text{-}NEarliest_{m}^{\varphi}} \cdot \Big(\mathbf{LFEM}_{\Phi}\text{-}Replace_{m}^{\varphi} + \sum_{\psi \in SupExpr_{\Phi^i}(\varphi)} A1\text{-}NEarliest_{m}^{\psi} + \sum_{\psi \in SupExpr_{\Phi^{>i}}(\varphi)} Comp_{m}^{\psi} + \mathbf{NUSEDLAT}_{m}^{\varphi} \Big)$$

$\rightsquigarrow$ Least fixed point solution: $NUsedLater[\Phi^{\leqslant i}]$ and $XUsedLater[\Phi^{\leqslant i}]$

2. Computation of $\Theta_{\dot n}^{dn(i)}$, $\Theta_{\dot n}^{up(i)}$ *for exit point* $\dot n$ *of* n

a) Determine $\Theta_{\dot n}^{dn(i)}$ by means of point 1).
b) Determine $\Theta_{\dot n}^{up(i)}$ by means of point 4) & 5) of Table 4.2.

3. Computation of $\mathcal{T}^{\top}(\Theta_{\dot n}^{dn(i)})$

Determine $\mathcal{T}^{\top}(\Theta_{\dot n}^{dn(i)})$ by means of Algorithm 4.3.1.
$\rightsquigarrow$ $LChange_{n}^{\psi} \stackrel{\text{def}}{=} \psi \in neigh(\mathcal{T}^{\top}(\Theta_{\dot n}^{dn(i)}))$

4. Adjusting Delayability ($\psi \in \Phi^i$, *No data flow analysis! Compute Compute* $A2\text{-}NDelayed_{\dot n}^{\psi}$ *before* $A2\text{-}XDelayed_{\dot n}^{\psi}$)

$$A2\text{-}NDelayed_{n}^{\psi} \stackrel{\text{def}}{=} \prod_{m \in pred(n)} A1\text{-}XDelayed_{n}^{\psi} \cdot \overline{LChange_{n}^{\psi}}$$

$$A2\text{-}XDelayed_{n}^{\psi} \stackrel{\text{def}}{=} A2\text{-}NDelayed_{n}^{\psi} \cdot \overline{Comp_{n}^{\psi}}$$

5. Adjusting Latestness: ($\psi \in \Phi^i$, *No data flow analysis!*)

$$A2\text{-}NLatest_{n}^{\psi} \stackrel{\text{def}}{=} A2\text{-}NDelayed_{n}^{\psi} \cdot Comp_{n}^{\psi}$$

$$A2\text{-}XLatest_{n}^{\psi} \stackrel{\text{def}}{=} A2\text{-}XDelayed_{n}^{\psi} \cdot \sum_{m \in succ(n)} \overline{A2\text{-}NDelayed_{m}^{\psi}}$$

Table 4.3. Computing the second adjustment of $\mathbf{LFEM}_{\Phi}$ with respect to level $i > 0$

1. Replacement Points ($\varphi \in \Phi$):

$$\mathbf{FFEM}_{\Phi}\text{-}Replace^{\varphi}_{n} \stackrel{\text{def}}{=} \psi \in MaxSubExpr_{\Phi}(\varphi^{\text{RHS}}_{\dot{n}})$$

where $\varphi^{\text{RHS}}_{\dot{n}}$ is RHS expression at n

2. Relevant Global Analyses ($\varphi \in \Phi$):

Computation of all relevant global predicates of $\mathbf{LEM}_{\Phi}$ according to Table 3.1 and Table 3.2:

- $NDnSafe^{\varphi}_{n}$, $XDnSafe^{\varphi}_{n}$, $NUpSafe^{\varphi}_{n}$, $XUpSafe^{\varphi}_{n}$, $NEarliest^{\varphi}_{n}$, $XEarliest^{\varphi}_{n}$
- $NDelayed^{\varphi}_{n}$, $XDelayed^{\varphi}_{n}$, $N\text{-}Latest^{\varphi}_{n}$, $X\text{-}Latest^{\varphi}_{n}$

3. Adjustment of Delayability:

Adjust the delayability predicate as described in Table 4.5.

4. Insertion Points ($\varphi \in \Phi$):

Determine the insertion points by:

$$\mathbf{FFEM}_{\Phi}\text{-}NInsert^{\varphi}_{n} \stackrel{\text{def}}{=} A\text{-}NLatest^{\varphi}_{n}$$
$$\mathbf{FFEM}_{\Phi}\text{-}XInsert^{\varphi}_{n} \stackrel{\text{def}}{=} A\text{-}XLatest^{\varphi}_{n}$$

Table 4.4. Skeleton of the $\mathbf{FFEM}_{\Phi}$-algorithm

1. Used-Later Analysis ($\varphi \in \Phi$):

$$\mathbf{NUSEDLAT}_n^{\varphi} = \overline{XEarliest_n^{\varphi}} \cdot \Big(\sum_{\psi \in SupExpr_{\Phi}(\varphi)} XEarliest_n^{\psi} + \mathbf{XUSEDLAT}_n^{\varphi} \Big)$$

$$\mathbf{XUSEDLAT}_n^{\varphi} = \sum_{m \in succ(n)} \overline{NEarliest_m^{\varphi}} \cdot \Big(\mathbf{FFEM}_{\Phi}\text{-}Replace_m^{\varphi} + \sum_{\psi \in SupExpr_{\Phi}(\varphi)} NEarliest_m^{\psi} + \mathbf{NUSEDLAT}_m^{\varphi} \Big)$$

$\rightsquigarrow$ Least fixed point solution: *NUsedLater* and *XUsedLater*

2. Computation of $\Theta_{\dot{n}}^{dn}$, $\Theta_{\dot{n}}^{up}$ for exit point $\dot{n}$ of n

a) Determine $\Theta_{\dot{n}}^{up}$ by means of Point 2) of Table 4.4.
b) Determine $\Theta_{\dot{n}}^{dn}$ by means of Point 1).
c) Determine edges $E_{\dot{n}}^{B}$ between $\Theta_{\dot{n}}^{dn}$ and $\Theta_{\dot{n}}^{up}$:

$$\forall \varphi \in \Theta_{\dot{n}}^{dn},\ \psi \in \Theta_{\dot{n}}^{up}.\ \{\varphi, \psi\} \in E_{\dot{n}}^{B} \Leftrightarrow \psi \in SubExpr^{*}_{\Theta_{\dot{n}}^{dn}}(SupExpr_{\Theta_{\dot{n}}^{up}}(\varphi))$$

3. Computation of $\mathcal{T}^{\top}(\Theta_{\dot{n}}^{dn})$

Determine $\mathcal{T}^{\top}(\Theta_{\dot{n}}^{dn})$ by means of Algorithm 4.3.1.
$\rightsquigarrow$ $Change_n^{\varphi} \overset{def}{=} \varphi \in neigh(\mathcal{T}^{\top}(\Theta_{\dot{n}}^{dn}))$

4. Adjusting Delayability ($\varphi \in \Phi$, No data flow analysis! Compute $A\text{-}NDelayed_n^{\varphi}$ before $A\text{-}XDelayed_n^{\varphi}$)

$$A\text{-}NDelayed_n^{\varphi} \overset{def}{=} \prod_{m \in pred(n)} XDelayed_n^{\varphi} \cdot \overline{Change_n^{\varphi}}$$

$$A\text{-}XDelayed_n^{\varphi} \overset{def}{=} A\text{-}NDelayed_n^{\varphi} \cdot \overline{Comp_n^{\varphi}}$$

5. Adjusting Latestness: ($\varphi \in \Phi$, No data flow analysis!)

$$A\text{-}NLatest_n^{\varphi} \overset{def}{=} A\text{-}NDelayed_n^{\varphi} \cdot Comp_n^{\varphi}$$

$$A\text{-}XLatest_n^{\varphi} \overset{def}{=} A\text{-}XDelayed_n^{\varphi} \cdot \sum_{m \in succ(n)} \overline{A\text{-}NDelayed_m^{\varphi}}$$

Table 4.5. Computing the adjustment step of $\mathbf{FFEM}_{\Phi}$

4.6 The Complexity

In this section we will discuss the complexity of the multiple-expression motion approaches presented in this chapter. In particular, we will see that $\mathtt{LFEM}_\Phi$ and $\mathtt{FFEM}_\Phi$ only impose moderate additional costs.

4.6.1 The Complexity of $\mathtt{BEM}_\Phi$ and $\mathtt{LEM}_\Phi$

The complexity of $\mathtt{BEM}_\Phi$ and $\mathtt{LEM}_\Phi$ can be obtained straightforwardly by applying Theorem 3.6.1 of Section 3.6. Hence:

Theorem 4.6.1 (Complexity of $\mathtt{BEM}_\Phi$ and $\mathtt{LEM}_\Phi$). $\mathtt{BEM}_\Phi$ *and* $\mathtt{LEM}_\Phi$ *can be performed with run-time complexity of order* $\mathcal{O}(|G|\,|\Phi|)$ *for both flat and structured sets of expressions* Φ.

4.6.2 The Complexity of $\mathtt{LFEM}_\Phi$

Let us now investigate the worst-case time complexity of $\mathtt{LFEM}_\Phi$. Obviously, the "old" global data flow analyses addressed in Table 4.1(3) can be solved in order $\mathcal{O}(|G|\,|\Phi|)$ as before. The same also applies to the refinement steps mentioned in Table 4.2(4 & 5) and Table 4.3(4 & 5) and the new global correctness analysis of Table 4.2(1).

The refinement step of Table 4.2(2) and the new global used-later analysis of Table 4.3(1), however, refer to expressions of both $\Theta_{\dot{n}}^{\mathrm{dn}(i)}$ and $\Theta_{\dot{n}}^{\mathrm{up}(i)}$ for a level i under consideration. However, it is easy to see that both steps are of order $\mathcal{O}(|\Theta_{\dot{n}}^{\mathrm{dn}(i)}|\,|\Theta_{\dot{n}}^{\mathrm{up}(i)}|)$ for each level i and exit point $\dot{n}$. Summarised over all levels and nodes of the flow graph this amounts to[15]

$$\mathcal{O}(\sum_{\dot{n}\in\dot{N}}\sum_{i\geqslant 0}|\Theta_{\dot{n}}^{\mathrm{dn}(i)}|\,|\Theta_{\dot{n}}^{\mathrm{up}(i)}|) \leqslant \mathcal{O}(|G|\,|\Phi|\sum_{i\geqslant 0}|\Theta_{\dot{n}}^{\mathrm{up}(i)}|) \leqslant \mathcal{O}(|G|\,|\Phi|^2)$$

If arities of operators are assumed to be bound by a constant, then the estimation for each level reduces to $\mathcal{O}(|\Theta_{\dot{n}}^{\mathrm{up}(i)}|)$, which results in $\mathcal{O}(|G|\,|\Phi|)$ for the complete analysis.

Finally, we have to examine the costs of step (3) of Table 4.3, which computes the local trade-off information at a node. As mentioned on page 53 the computational complexity for determining a maximal matching of a bipartite graph (V,E) is of order $\mathcal{O}(|V|^{\frac{1}{2}}\,|E|)$. Algorithm 4.3.1 which computes the largest tight set of a bipartite graph $(S \uplus T, E)$ is subsumed by this estimation, since under the assumption that a maximal matching is already computed in advance the algorithm terminates within a bound of order $\mathcal{O}(|E|)$. This is due to the fact that processing a vertex in R at most requires

[15] Note that $\sum_{i\geqslant 0}|\Theta_{\dot{n}}^{\mathrm{up}(i)}| \leqslant |\Phi|$.

to inspect all its neighbouring vertices.[16] Hence for each level i and each exit point $\dot{n}$ Step (3) of Table 4.3 takes time of order

$$\mathcal{O}((|\Theta_{\dot{n}}^{\mathtt{dn}(i)}| + |\Theta_{\dot{n}}^{\mathtt{up}(i)}|)^{\frac{1}{2}} \, |\Theta_{\dot{n}}^{\mathtt{dn}(i)}| \, |\Theta_{\dot{n}}^{\mathtt{up}(i)}|)$$

Summarising this result over all levels and nodes of the flow graph the overall computational complexity of step (3) of Table 4.3 is[15]

$$\begin{aligned}
&\mathcal{O}(\sum_{\dot{n}\in\dot{N}} \sum_{i\geqslant 0} (|\Theta_{\dot{n}}^{\mathtt{dn}(i)}| + |\Theta_{\dot{n}}^{\mathtt{up}(i)}|)^{\frac{1}{2}} \, |\Theta_{\dot{n}}^{\mathtt{dn}(i)}| \, |\Theta_{\dot{n}}^{\mathtt{up}(i)}|) \\
&\leqslant \mathcal{O}(|G| \sum_{i\geqslant 0} (|\Theta_{\dot{n}}^{\mathtt{dn}(i)}|^{\frac{3}{2}} \, |\Theta_{\dot{n}}^{\mathtt{up}(i)}| + |\Theta_{\dot{n}}^{\mathtt{up}(i)}|^{\frac{3}{2}} \, |\Theta_{\dot{n}}^{\mathtt{dn}(i)}|)) \\
&\leqslant \mathcal{O}(|G| \, (|\Phi|^{\frac{3}{2}} \sum_{i\geqslant 0} |\Theta_{\dot{n}}^{\mathtt{up}(i)}| + |\Phi| \sum_{i\geqslant 0} |\Theta_{\dot{n}}^{\mathtt{up}(i)}|^{\frac{3}{2}})) \\
&\leqslant \mathcal{O}(|G| \, (|\Phi|^{\frac{5}{2}} + |\Phi| | \sum_{i\geqslant 0} \Theta_{\dot{n}}^{\mathtt{up}(i)}|^{\frac{3}{2}})) \\
&\leqslant \mathcal{O}(|G| \, |\Phi|^{\frac{5}{2}})
\end{aligned}$$

In the case that the arities of operators are bound by a constant this estimation can be improved towards $\mathcal{O}(|G| \, |\Phi|^{\frac{3}{2}})$, as the levelwise estimation could be reduced towards $\mathcal{O}((|\Theta_{\dot{n}}^{\mathtt{dn}(i)}| + |\Theta_{\dot{n}}^{\mathtt{up}(i)}|) \, |\Theta_{\dot{n}}^{\mathtt{up}(i)}|)$, which is a consequence of the fact that the number of edges between $\Theta_{\dot{n}}^{\mathtt{dn}(i)}$ and $\Theta_{\dot{n}}^{\mathtt{up}(i)}$ are of order $\mathcal{O}(|\Theta_{\dot{n}}^{\mathtt{up}(i)}|)$. Summing up, we have the following result:

Theorem 4.6.2 (Complexity of $\mathtt{LFEM}_\Phi$).

1. $\mathtt{LFEM}_\Phi$ *can be performed with run-time complexity of order* $\mathcal{O}(|G| \, |\Phi|^{\frac{5}{2}})$ *for any structured set of expressions* Φ.
2. $\mathtt{LFEM}_\Phi$ *can be performed with run-time complexity of order* $\mathcal{O}(|G| \, |\Phi|^{\frac{3}{2}})$ *for a structured set of expressions* Φ*, where arities of operators are bound by a constant.*

4.6.3 The Complexity of $\mathtt{FFEM}_\Phi$

For the worst-case complexity of $\mathtt{FFEM}_\Phi$ a similar argumentation as for $\mathtt{LFEM}_\Phi$ applies. Again the overall complexity is subsumed by the complexity for the computation of the local trade-off information, i. e. Step (3) of Table 4.5. Here, the only significant difference is that we cannot exploit boundedness of operator arities anymore, since the construction of edges between $\Theta_{\dot{n}}^{\mathtt{dn}}$ and $\Theta_{\dot{n}}^{\mathtt{up}}$ in Table 4.5(2c) introduces additional edges reflecting also mediate subexpression relations. Thus we obtain:

[16] Marking processed vertices one can easily achieve to include a vertex at most once in D.

Theorem 4.6.3 (Complexity of the $\mathtt{FFEM}_\Phi$).
$\mathtt{FFEM}_\Phi$ can be performed with run-time complexity of order $\mathcal{O}(|G|\,|\Phi|^{\frac{5}{2}})$ for any structured set of expressions Φ.

4.6.4 Bit-Vector Complexity of $\mathtt{BEM}_\Phi$, $\mathtt{LEM}_\Phi$, $\mathtt{LFEM}_\Phi$ and $\mathtt{FFEM}_\Phi$

Besides this pure complexity estimations a serious amount of research has been put into the development of techniques that are tuned for the simultaneous treatment of all entities under consideration. These techniques that are known as *bit-vector* techniques are based on the paradigm that a whole bit-vector operation is considered as an elementary step. This assumption is caused by the fact that bit-vector operations can be implemented reasonably fast for moderately sized bit-vectors on most machines. Therefore, the intent of bit-vector algorithms is to exploit the structure of the flow graph in a way that the complexity for solving a problem for all objects simultaneously is almost the same as the complexity for solving the problem for one particular object (under the assumption of elementary bit-vector operations). In fact, a number of algorithms exist whose complexities are almost linear in the number of nodes of the flow graph. The superlinear behaviour is only reflected by a factor which in most cases can be considered reasonably small in practice. In details the most important techniques are:

- *Iterative techniques* like that of Kam an Ullman [KU76, KU77] whose run-time complexity is of order $\mathcal{O}(|G|\,\mathtt{d})$, where $\mathtt{d}$, the *depth* of the flow graph, is determined by the maximum number of back edges that can occur on an acyclic program path.
- *Node listing techniques* like that of Kennedy [Ken75], whose complexity is shown in [AU75] to be of order $\mathcal{O}(|G|\,\log(|G|))$ for reducible control flow [Hec77].
- *Elimination techniques* as summarised in the survey paper of Ryder and Paull [RP88] reaching also the bound of $\mathcal{O}(|G|\,\log(|G|))$ for reducible control flow.[17]
- *Path compression algorithms* like that of Tarjan [Tar79, Tar81b, Tar81a] yielding the famous $\mathcal{O}(|G|\,\alpha(|G|))$-bound for irreducible control flow, where α is a function that grows slower than the functional inverse of Ackermann's function.

In particular, even in the case of unrestricted control flow we have according to [KU76, KU77]:

Theorem 4.6.4 (Bit-Vector Complexity of $\mathtt{BEM}_\Phi$ and $\mathtt{LEM}_\Phi$).
Both $\mathtt{BEM}_\Phi$ and $\mathtt{LEM}_\Phi$ can be computed by means of global data flow analyses that stabilise within $\mathtt{d}+1$ round robin iterations.[18]

[17] For arbitrary control flow some of these show up a pathological exponential behaviour.

[18] With the nodes of the flow graphs sorted topologically according to the postorder or reverse postorder.

Unfortunately, neither $\mathtt{LFEM}_\Phi$ nor $\mathtt{FFEM}_\Phi$ can take full advantage of bit-vector analyses, since the trade-off algorithms are beyond the scope of bit-vector operations. However, from a pragmatical point of view, most of the analyses of $\mathtt{LFEM}_\Phi$ and even all of the analyses of $\mathtt{FFEM}_\Phi$ can be handled with bit-vector techniques. In fact, as mentioned $\mathtt{FFEM}_\Phi$ only differs from $\mathtt{LEM}_\Phi$ by the non-bit-vector postprocess computing local trade-offs and adjusting predicates. Therefore, an efficient implementation can take advantage of the available bit-vector potential as well as possible.

The results of this section are summarised in Table 4.6. This table gives a good impression, how the computational complexity of different techniques is reflected in the order of the second parameter, which may vary from almost constant in the bit-vector case up to order $2\frac{1}{2}$ for the flexible approaches.

	pure complexity arities of operators		bit-vector complexity
	bound	unbound	
$\mathtt{BEM}_\Phi$, $\mathtt{LEM}_\Phi$	$\mathcal{O}(\lvert G\rvert\,\lvert\Phi\rvert)$	$\mathcal{O}(\lvert G\rvert\,\lvert\Phi\rvert)$	$\mathcal{O}(\lvert G\rvert\,\mathtt{d})$
$\mathtt{LFEM}_\Phi$	$\mathcal{O}(\lvert G\rvert\,\lvert\Phi\rvert^{\frac{3}{2}})$	$\mathcal{O}(\lvert G\rvert\,\lvert\Phi\rvert^{\frac{5}{2}})$	/
$\mathtt{FFEM}_\Phi$	$\mathcal{O}(\lvert G\rvert\,\lvert\Phi\rvert^{\frac{5}{2}})$	$\mathcal{O}(\lvert G\rvert\,\lvert\Phi\rvert^{\frac{5}{2}})$	/

Table 4.6. Worst case time complexities of expression motion: A classification

5. Expression Motion in the Presence of Critical Edges

It is well-known since Morel's and Renvoise's [MR79] pioneering work that critical edges may cause serious problems for expression motion:

- First, the lack of suitable placement points usually leads to suboptimal results, i. e. results that are strictly worse in terms of the number of computations than competitive results that could be obtained in a flow graph after splitting critical edges. Figure 2.2 of Chapter 2 gives an illustration of this phenomenon.
- Second, the equation system of Morel and Renvoise uses bidirectional data flow analyses. In fact, the bidirectionality of their algorithm became model in the field of bit-vector based expression motion (cf. [Cho83, Dha88, Dha89b, Dha91, DK93, DRZ92, DS88, JD82a, JD82b, Mor84, MR81, Sor89]). Bidirectional algorithms, however, are in general conceptually and computationally more complex than unidirectional ones. In particular, critical edges prevent the application of fast unidirectional bit-vector methods, which in the case of reducible control are almost linear in the program size (cf. Section 4.6.4). In contrast, the best known estimations for bidirectional bit-vector analyses are of order $O(|G|^2)$ (cf. [Dha91, DK93, DP93]).

In this chapter we are going to provide a systematic approach to expression motion in the presence of critical edges. To this end, we investigate the impact of the presence of critical edges for both the single-expression view and the multiple-expression view. Whereas the "classical" deficiencies as sketched above all address the single-expression view, the multiple-expression case has not been previously explored. Surprisingly, we found that the difficulties arising in the latter case are more serious than the "classical" ones.

5.1 The Single-Expression View

In this section we are going to examine the impact of critical edges on definitions and algorithms presented in Chapter 3 for the single-expression view of expression motion. To this end, we are first going to provide a fresh and conceptually clean view on the phenomena causing the need for bidirectional analyses. Afterwards, we will show how to avoid bidirectionality completely by enriching the flow graph by (virtual) shortcut edges.

Throughout this section we adapt the definition and notions of Chapter 3. Moreover, like in Chapter 3 the presentation is developed for a fixed flow graph G that is now assumed to be part of $\mathfrak{FG}_{\text{Crit}}$ and a fixed expression pattern φ.

5.1.1 Computational Optimal Expression Motion

As opposed to flow graphs without critical edges there are usually no computationally optimal expression motions operating on $\mathfrak{FG}_{\text{Crit}}$. In fact, Figure 5.1 shows two admissible, but $\precsim_{exp}^{a+b}$-incomparable expression motions that cannot be improved any further. The first one is simply given by the identy transformation of the program in Figure 5.1(a), the result of the second one is displayed in Figure 5.1(b). Each of the resulting programs has exactly one computation on the path that is emphasized in the dark shade of grey, while having two computations on the path being emphasized in the light shade of grey, respectively. Thus there is no computationally optimal expression motion with respect to the original program in Figure 5.1(a).

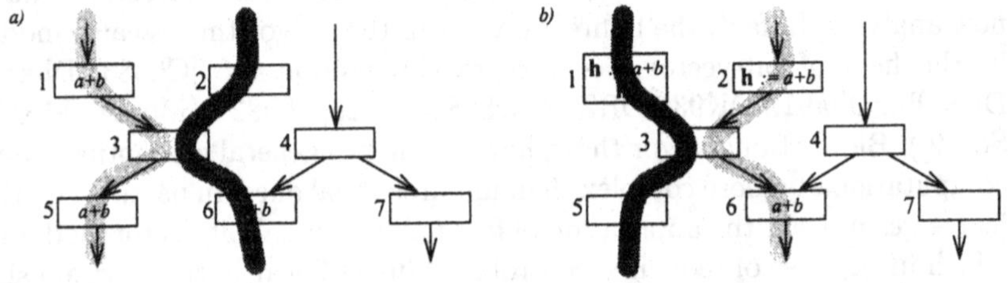

Fig. 5.1. Incomparable admissible program transformations

However, in the example above the solution of Figure 5.1(b) should be excluded as a reasonable expression motion, since this transformation would require to increase the number of computations on some program path. Essentially, this is caused by the fact that the initialisation at node 2 is not used on the program path through node 3 and 6. To this end, we restrict ourselves to expression motions that are *profitable*, i. e. that introduce initializations only when they are actually needed on every program path originating at the initialisation site. This particularly ensures that such a transformation is computationally better than the identity transformation.

Definition 5.1.1 (Profitability). $\text{EM}_\varphi \in \mathcal{AEM}_\varphi$ *is* profitable *if and only if every intialization is used on every program path leading to the end node, i. e.*

$$\text{EM}_\varphi\text{-}Insert_{\dot{n}} \Leftrightarrow \forall p \in \mathbf{P}[\dot{n}, \dot{\mathbf{e}}]\ \exists i \leqslant |p|.\ \text{EM}_\varphi\text{-}Replace_{p_i}\ \wedge \\ \forall 1 < j \leqslant i.\ \neg\text{EM}_\varphi\text{-}Insert_{p_j}$$

Let us denote the set of profitable expression motions in $\mathcal{AEM}_\varphi$ by $\mathcal{PAEM}_\varphi$. Obviously, profitability is guaranteed for computationally optimal expression motions out of $\mathcal{COEM}_\varphi$. Hence this condition does not impose a further restriction for flow graphs without critical edges, where computationally optimal expression motions are granted to exist. In the presence of critical edges, however, the restriction to $\mathcal{PAEM}_\varphi$ is necessary in order to yield computationally optimal results at all. Then we may use almost the same definition for computational optimality as in Chapter 3 (cf. Definition 3.2.1) in order to define $\mathcal{COEM}_\varphi^{\mathtt{Crit}}$, the set of computationally optimal expression motions operating on $\mathfrak{FG}_{\mathtt{Crit}}$. As mentioned, the only essential divergence is that the underlying universe now is $\mathcal{PAEM}_\varphi$ instead of $\mathcal{AEM}_\varphi$.

5.1.2 Busy Expression Motion

Unfortunately, busy expression motion as presented in Section 3.2 cannot be adapted to flow graphs with critical edges, since it may not define a profitable expression motion. Even worse, a naive adaption may even cause a program degradation as illustrated in Figure 5.2. In this slight modification of Figure 5.1 the marked range of down-safe program points depicted in Figure 5.2(a) would yield earliest initialization points at nodes 1 and 5 leading to the program displayed in Figure 5.2(b). This, however, introduces an additional computation on the path leading through node 1 and 5, while no path at all is strictly improved.

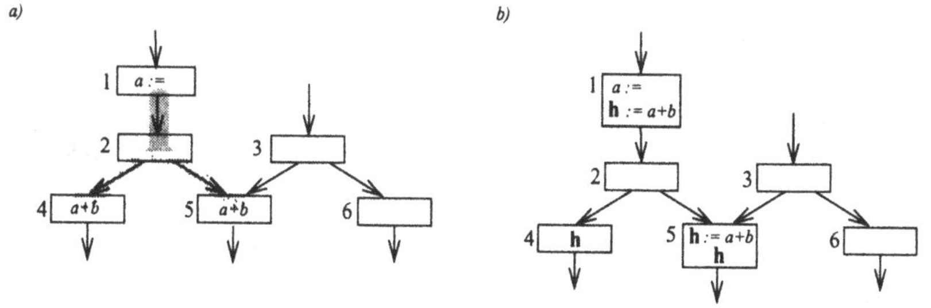

Fig. 5.2. Program degradation through a naive adaption of busy expression motion

The key for a reasonable definition of busy expression motion on flow graphs with critical edges is to impose a homogeneity requirement on down-safety that ensures that the information propagates either to all or to none of its predecessors, which grants that earliest program points become a proper upper borderline of the region of safe program points. In fact, in the absence of critical edges down-safety has the following homogeneity property:

$$\forall \dot{n} \in \dot{N}.\ DnSafe_{\dot{n}} \Rightarrow (\forall \dot{m} \in pred(\dot{n}).\ Safe_{\dot{m}}) \vee (\forall \dot{m} \in pred(\dot{n}).\ \neg DnSafe_{\dot{m}})$$

Note that the first term of the disjunction uses safety rather than down-safety, since propagation of down-safety to predecessors that are up-safe anyhow is not necessary.[1] Now this property has to be forced explicitly. For instance in Figure 5.2(a) the entry of node 5 as well as the exit of node 2 are down-safe, while the exit of node 3 is not. Therefore, let us consider the following notion of *homogeneous safety*:

Definition 5.1.2 (Homogeneous Down-Safety). *A predicate HDnSafe on the program points of $\dot{N}$ is a* homogeneous down-safety predicate, *if and only if for any $\dot{n} \in \dot{N}$*

1. HDnSafe is conform with down-safety:

$$HDnSafe_{\dot{n}} \Rightarrow Comp_{\dot{n}} \vee ((\dot{n} \neq \dot{\mathbf{e}}) \wedge Transp_{\dot{n}} \wedge \forall\, \dot{m} \in succ(\dot{n}).\ HDnSafe_{\dot{m}})$$

2. HDnSafe is homogeneous:

$$HDnSafe_{\dot{n}} \Rightarrow (\forall\, \dot{m} \in pred(\dot{n}).\ HDnSafe_{\dot{m}} \vee UpSafe_{\dot{m}}) \vee (\forall\, \dot{m} \in pred(\dot{n}).\ \neg HDnSafe_{\dot{m}})$$

Obviously, homogeneous down-safety predicates are closed under "union".[2] Thus there exists a unique largest homogeneous down-safety predicate denoted by *Hom-DnSafe*, which gives rise to a homogeneous version of safety, too:

$$\forall\, \dot{n} \in \dot{N}.\ Hom\text{-}Safe_{\dot{n}} \overset{\text{def}}{=} Hom\text{-}DnSafe_{\dot{n}} \vee UpSafe_{\dot{n}}$$

Earliest program points are then defined along the lines of Definition 3.2.2.

Definition 5.1.3 (Homogeneous Earliestness). *For any $\dot{n} \in \dot{N}$*

$$Hom\text{-}Earliest_{\dot{n}} \overset{\text{def}}{=} Hom\text{-}DnSafe_{\dot{n}} \wedge ((\dot{n} = \dot{\mathbf{s}}) \vee \exists\, \dot{m} \in pred(\dot{n}).\ \neg Transp_{\dot{m}} \vee \neg Hom\text{-}Safe_{\dot{m}})$$

Then busy expression motion for flow graphs with critical edges ($\mathtt{CBEM}_\varphi$) is defined as follows:

- Insert initialisation statements $\mathbf{h}_\varphi := \varphi$ at every program point $\dot{n}$ satisfying *Hom-Earliest*.
- Replace every original occurrence of φ by $\mathbf{h}_\varphi$.

As an equivalent to Theorem 3.2.1 we obtain:

Theorem 5.1.1 (Optimality Theorem for $\mathtt{CBEM}_\varphi$).
$\mathtt{CBEM}_\varphi$ is computationally optimal within $\mathcal{PAEM}_\varphi$, i. e. $\mathtt{CBEM}_\varphi \in \mathcal{COEM}_\varphi^{\mathtt{Crit}}$.

[1] In the absence of critical edges this makes no difference to requiring $\forall\, \dot{m} \in pred(\dot{n}).\ DnSafe_{\dot{m}}$.

[2] This means the predicate defined by the pointwise conjunction of the predicate values.

5.1.3 Lazy Expression Motion

Similar to the situation in Section 5.1.2 also the relevant analyses of $\texttt{LEM}_\varphi$ as defined in Chapter 3 cannot naively be adapted to flow graphs with critical edges. This even holds, if the appropriate busy expression motion, that is $\texttt{CBEM}_\varphi$, is assumed as the basis for the delay process, which shall be illustrated by means of the example in Figure 5.3. Figure 5.3(a) already shows the result of $\texttt{CBEM}_{a+b}$. A naive adaption of lazy expression motion would determine delayable program points as emphasized in the figure. Thus initializations at latest program points would yield a program as displayed in Figure 5.3(b). Note, however, that this transformation increases the number of computations of $a+b$ on the path $\langle 1,3,5,8,\dots\rangle$ compared to $\texttt{CBEM}_{a+b}$.

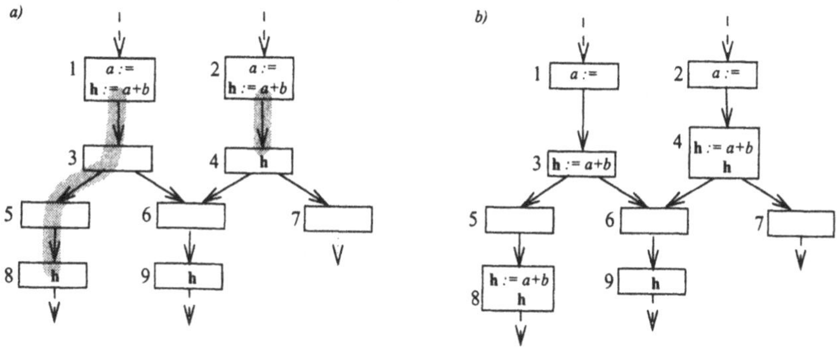

Fig. 5.3. Program degradation through a naive adaption of lazy expression motion

Again the reason for this behaviour lies in a homogeneity defect, but now with respect to delayability. In fact, for flow graphs without critical edges we have

$$Delayed_{\dot n} \;\Rightarrow\; (\forall\, \dot m \in succ(\dot n).\ Delayed_{\dot m}) \;\vee\; (\forall\, \dot m \in succ(\dot n).\ \neg Delayed_{\dot m})$$

This property may now be violated due to the presence of critical edges. For instance, in Figure 5.3(a) both the exit of node 3 and the entry of node 5 satisfy delayability, whereas the entry of node 6 does not. Hence this homogeneity property has to be forced explicitly in order to obtain a reasonable adaption of lazy expression motion to $\mathfrak{FG}_{\texttt{Crit}}$. Therefore, let us consider the following notion of *homogeneous delayability*.

Definition 5.1.4 (Homogeneous Delayability). *A predicate HDelayed on $\dot N$ is a* homogeneous delayability *predicate, if and only if for any $\dot n \in \dot N$*

1. *HDelayed is conform with delayability:*

$$HDelayed_{\dot n} \;\Rightarrow\; Hom\text{-}Earliest_{\dot n} \;\vee$$
$$((\dot n \neq \dot{\mathbf{s}}) \;\wedge\; \forall\, \dot m \in pred(\dot n).\ HDelayed_{\dot m} \wedge \neg Comp_{\dot m})$$

2. HDelayed is homogeneous:

$$\begin{aligned} HDelayed_{\dot{n}} \;\Rightarrow\; & (\forall\, \dot{m} \in succ(\dot{n}).\; HDelayed_{\dot{m}}) \;\vee \\ & (\forall\, \dot{m} \in succ(\dot{n}).\; \neg HDelayed_{\dot{m}}) \end{aligned}$$

Obviously, homogeneous delayability predicates are closed under "union". Thus there exists a unique largest homogeneous delayability predicate that shall be denoted by *Hom-Delayed*. This gives rise to a new notion of latestness defined along the lines of Definition 3.3.4:

Definition 5.1.5 (Homogeneous Latestness). *For every* $\dot{n} \in \dot{N}$

$$\begin{aligned} \textit{Hom-Latest}_{\dot{n}} \;\overset{def}{\Leftrightarrow}\; & \textit{Hom-Delayed}_{\dot{n}} \;\wedge \\ & (Comp_{\dot{n}} \;\vee\; \exists\, \dot{m} \in succ(\dot{n}).\; \neg \textit{Hom-Delayed}_{\dot{m}}) \end{aligned}$$

Then lazy expression motion for flow graphs with critical edges ($\mathtt{CLEM}_\varphi$) is defined as follows:

- Insert initialisation statements $\mathbf{h}_\varphi := \varphi$ at every program point $\dot{n}$ satisfying *Hom-Latest*.
- Replace every original occurrence of φ by $\mathbf{h}_\varphi$.

Using the same definition for lifetime optimality as in Chapter 3 (cf. Definition 3.3.1) we succeed in proving lifetime optimality along the lines of Theorem 3.3.1.

Theorem 5.1.2 ($\mathtt{CLEM}_\varphi$-Theorem).
$\mathtt{CLEM}_\varphi$ *is lifetime optimal within the universe* $\mathcal{COEM}_\varphi^{\mathtt{Crit}}$.

5.1.4 Computing $\mathtt{CBEM}_\varphi$ and $\mathtt{CLEM}_\varphi$

In this section we are going to present how busy and lazy expression motion can actually be computed for flow graphs with critical edges. In fact, the analyses that are presented are the first proposals for computationally and lifetime optimal expression motion in the presence of critical edges. As an achievement of our systematic approach to critical edges we even succeed in giving two alternative approaches: (1) A classical approach via bidirectional analyses and (2) a new non-standard approach that transforms the problem into a unidirectional form.

5.1.4.1 The Classical Approach: Bidirectional Analyses. As in Section 3.5 the analyses associated with busy and lazy expression motion are summarized in form of two tabulars. The most significant differences with respect to their counterparts in Table 3.1 and Table 3.2 are:

1. Safety Analyses:

a) Up-Safety Analysis $\rightsquigarrow$ See Figure 3.1

b) Homogeneous Down-Safety Analysis (with respect to Up-Safety)

$$\mathbf{NDNSAFE}_n = Comp_n + Transp_n \cdot \mathbf{XDNSAFE}_n$$

$$\mathbf{XDNSAFE}_n = \begin{cases} false & \text{if } n = \mathbf{e} \\ \prod_{m \in succ(n)} \mathbf{NDNSAFE}_m \cdot \prod_{n' \in pred(m)} \mathbf{XDNSAFE}_{n'} + XUpSafe_{n'} & \text{otherwise} \end{cases}$$

$\rightsquigarrow$ Greatest fixed point solution: *Hom-NDnSafe* and *Hom-XDnSafe*

2. Computation of Homogeneous Earliestness: (No data flow analysis!)

$$Hom\text{-}NEarliest_n \stackrel{\text{def}}{=} Hom\text{-}NSafe_n \cdot \begin{cases} false & \text{if } n = \mathbf{s} \\ \prod_{m \in pred(n)} \overline{XUpSafe_m + Hom\text{-}XDnSafe_m} & \text{otherwise} \end{cases}$$

$$Hom\text{-}XEarliest_n \stackrel{\text{def}}{=} Hom\text{-}XSafe_n \cdot \overline{Transp_n}$$

3. Insertion and Replacement Points of the CBEM$_\varphi$*-Transformation:*

$$\texttt{CBEM}_\varphi\text{-}NInsert_n \stackrel{\text{def}}{=} Hom\text{-}NEarliest_n$$

$$\texttt{CBEM}_\varphi\text{-}XInsert_n \stackrel{\text{def}}{=} Hom\text{-}XEarliest_n$$

$$\texttt{CBEM}_\varphi\text{-}Replace_n \stackrel{\text{def}}{=} Comp_n$$

Table 5.1. Computing CBEM$_\varphi$: The bidirectional approach

- Homogeneity of safety and delayability is forced explicitly by the usage of bidirectional equations, i. e. equations whose right-hand side values depend on information of both predecessors and successors.
- Homogeneous down-safety depends on up-safety. To this end the safety analyses have to be performed sequentially.[3]

[3] A similar phenomenon shows up for semantic expression motion, even in the absence of critical edges [KRS96a].

1. Perform steps 1) and 2) of Table 3.1.

2. Delayability Analysis:

$$\mathbf{NDELAYED}_n = \textit{Hom-NEarliest}_n + \begin{cases} \textit{false} & \textit{if } n = \mathbf{s} \\ \prod_{m \in pred(n)} \mathbf{XDELAYED}_m \cdot \prod_{n' \in succ(m)} \mathbf{NDELAYED}_{n'} & \textit{otherwise} \end{cases}$$

$$\mathbf{XDELAYED}_n = \textit{Hom-XEarliest}_n + \mathbf{NDELAYED}_n \cdot \overline{\textit{Comp}_n}$$

⇝ Greatest fixed point solution: *Hom-NDelayed* and *Hom-XDelayed*

3. Computation of Latestness: (No data flow analysis!)

$$\textit{Hom-NLatest}_n \stackrel{\text{def}}{=} \textit{Hom-NDelayed}_n \cdot \textit{Comp}_n$$

$$\textit{Hom-XLatest}_n \stackrel{\text{def}}{=} \textit{Hom-XDelayed}_n \cdot \sum_{m \in succ(n)} \overline{\textit{Hom-NDelayed}_m}$$

4. Insertion and Replacement Points of the $\mathtt{CLEM}_\varphi$*-Transformation:*

$$\mathtt{CLEM}_\varphi\textit{-NInsert}_n \stackrel{\text{def}}{=} \textit{Hom-NLatest}_n$$

$$\mathtt{CLEM}_\varphi\textit{-XInsert}_n \stackrel{\text{def}}{=} \textit{Hom-XLatest}_n$$

$$\mathtt{CLEM}_\varphi\textit{-Replace}_n \stackrel{\text{def}}{=} \textit{Comp}_n$$

Table 5.2. Computing $\mathtt{CLEM}_\varphi$: The bidirectional approach

However, in contrast to competing bidirectional data flow analyses proposed for expression motion [Cho83, Dha88, Dha89b, Dha91, DK93, DRZ92, DS88, JD82a, JD82b, Mor84, MR81, Sor89] the approach presented here succeeds in carrying over the main advantages of the non-critical versions of Chapter 3:

- The hierarchical construction of lazy expression motion on the basis of busy expression motion yields a clean separation between the primary optimisation goal, the elimination of partially redundant expressions, and lifetime considerations.
- The approach is still structurally significantly simpler than for instance, the original proposal of Morel and Renvoise [MR79]. In fact, the conceptual view of bidirectionality as an instrument to establish homogeneity leads to a well-understood and sparse usage of this feature. The latter aspect

particularly helps to avoid equations with unnecessarily intricate mutual dependencies.[4]

5.1.4.2 The Alternative Approach: Unidirectional Analyses. An important observation with respect to the bidirectional equation systems occurring in Table 5.2 is that information at a node can be influenced by information that flows along "zig-zag paths" of critical edges.[5] This gives rise to the idea to incorporate such zig-zag paths directly into the data flow analysis by introducing (virtual) shortcut edges between the origin and the destination of such paths. This is illustrated in Figure 5.4(a) which shows a fragment of a program that contains a nest of critical edges being emphasised by thick lines.[6] Figure 5.4(b) shows the set of zig-zag successors of node 1 and the associated set of (virtual) shortcut edges.

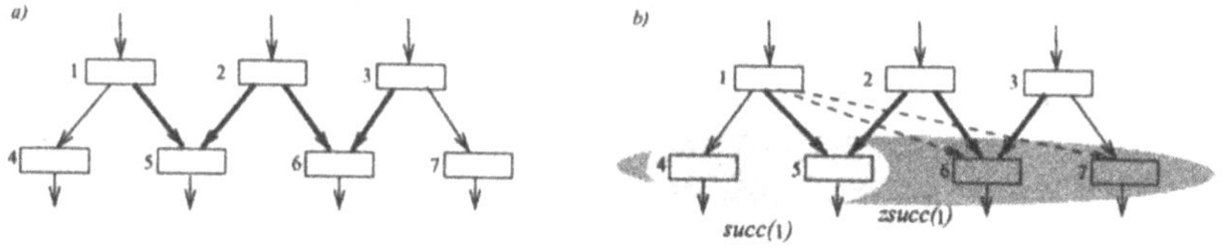

Fig. 5.4. (a) Program fragment with a nest of critical edges (b) Zig-zag successors and virtual shortcut edges of node **1**

Formally, zig-zag predecessors $zpred(n)$ and zig-zag successors $zsucc(n)$ of a node $n \in N$ are defined as the smallest set of nodes satisfying

1. a) $pred(n) \subseteq zpred(n)$
   b) $\forall\, m \in zpred(n).\ pred(succ(m)) \subseteq zpred(n)$
2. a) $succ(n) \subseteq zsucc(n)$
   b) $\forall m \in zsucc(n).\ succ(pred(m)) \subseteq zsucc(n)$

Although the above characterisation of zig-zag predecessors perfectly fits for the treatment of a bidirectional equation system like the one of delayability in Table 5.2, the notion of zig-zag successors cannot immediately be used for the transformation of the bidirectional equation system for safety in Table 5.1, since this equation system incorporates also information on up-safety. However, we can easily overcome this drawback by parameterising the definitions of zig-zag predecessors and zig-zag successors by a set of nodes $M \subseteq N$ which models program points that terminate the construction of the zig-zag sets. Hence the parameterised notions of zig-zag predecessors $zpred_M(n)$ and

[4] Note that for instance in [Dha88, Dha91, DK93] equations requiring minimal and maximal fixpoint solutions are mixed in a way such that subtle difficulties in the treatment of loops show up (*hoisting through the loop effect*) which prevent these algorithms from reaching lifetime optimality.

[5] Path means here an underlying undirected path, i. e. one where the orientation of edges is ignored.

[6] Such patterns are expected to be rare in real life programs.

zig-zag successors $zsucc_M(n)$ with respect to a node n and a set of nodes $M \subseteq N$, respectively, are defined as the smallest set of nodes satisfying

1. a) $pred(n) \subseteq zpred_M(n)$
   b) $\forall\, m \in zpred_M(n).\ pred(succ(m) \setminus M) \subseteq zpred_M(n)$
2. a) $succ(n) \subseteq zsucc_M(n)$
   b) $\forall m \in zsucc_M(n).\ succ(pred(m) \setminus M) \subseteq zsucc_M(n)$

Based upon this notion the analyses of Table 5.1 and Table 5.2 can be reformulated in a way that the equations have unidirectional character (see Table 5.3 and Table 5.4), however, strictly speaking on the flow graph that is enlarged by (virtual) shortcut edges. Nonetheless, we will see in Section 5.2.3 that this procedure significantly improves on the bit-vector complexity compared to the counterpart based on bidirectional bit-vector analyses. In particular, this algorithm renders the first estimation that isolates the extra costs imposed by critical edges by means of a factor that is a structural property of the flow graph under consideration.

5.1.5 The Complexity

The well-known fact that bidirectional analyses in expression motion are computationally more complex than unidirectional analyses [Dha88, DK93, KD94, DP93] does not show up unless structural properties of the flow graph come into play due to the consideration of bit-vector steps. As a consequence, in the single-expression view critical edges do not add to the complexity, a fact that has first been noticed by Khedker and Dhamdhere [KD94] and more recently by Masticola et al. [MMR95]. Essentially, this is because the fixed point algorithms for bidirectional equation systems are only slightly more complicated than their unidirectional counterparts which is reflected in a more general update mechanism for the current node that is chosen from the workset: here predecessors as well as successors have to be updated and possibly added to the workset. For instance, Algorithm 5.1.1 in Table 5.5 shows the fixed point computation for down-safety as defined by the bidirectional equation system of Table 5.2(1b) which only differs from Algorithm 3.6.1 by the extended environment for updates of the workset. In fact, as the counterpart to Theorem 3.6.1 we have:

Theorem 5.1.3 (Complexity of $\mathtt{CBEM}_\varphi$ and $\mathtt{CLEM}_\varphi$). $\mathtt{CBEM}_\varphi$ *and* $\mathtt{CLEM}_\varphi$ *can both be performed with run-time complexity of order* $\mathcal{O}(|G|)$.

[7] The auxiliary predicate is used to witness the **XSAFE**-values of the predecessor nodes: It is set to true if and only if all predecessors satisfy **XDNSAFE**.

1. *Safety Analyses:*

   a) *Up-Safety Analysis* $\rightsquigarrow$ See Figure 3.1

   b) *Homogeneous Safety Analysis (with respect to Up-Safety)*
   Set $\mathtt{XUS} \stackrel{\text{def}}{=} \{m \in N \mid XUpSafe_m\}$.

$$\mathbf{NDNSAFE}_n = Comp_n + Transp_n \cdot \mathbf{XDNSAFE}_n$$

$$\mathbf{XSAFE}_n = + \begin{cases} false & \textit{if } n = \mathbf{e} \\ \prod_{m \in zsucc_{\mathtt{XUS}}(n)} \mathbf{NDNSAFE}_m & \textit{otherwise} \end{cases}$$

$\rightsquigarrow$ Greatest fixed point solution: *Hom-NDnSafe* and *Hom-XDnSafe*

2. *Computation of Homogeneous Earliestness: (No data flow analysis!)*

$$Hom\text{-}NEarliest_n \stackrel{\text{def}}{=} Hom\text{-}NSafe_n \cdot \begin{cases} false & \text{if } n = \mathbf{s} \\ \prod_{m \in pred(n)} \overline{XUpSafe_m + Hom\text{-}XDnSafe_m} & \text{otherwise} \end{cases}$$

$$Hom\text{-}XEarliest_n \stackrel{\text{def}}{=} Hom\text{-}XSafe_n \cdot \overline{Transp_n}$$

3. *Insertion and Replacement Points of the* $\mathtt{CBEM}_\varphi$*-Transformation:*

$$\mathtt{CBEM}_\varphi\text{-}NInsert_n \stackrel{\text{def}}{=} Hom\text{-}NEarliest_n$$

$$\mathtt{CBEM}_\varphi\text{-}XInsert_n \stackrel{\text{def}}{=} Hom\text{-}XEarliest_n$$

$$\mathtt{CBEM}_\varphi\text{-}Replace_n \stackrel{\text{def}}{=} Comp_n$$

Table 5.3. Computing $\mathtt{CBEM}_\varphi$: The unidirectional variant

1. Perform steps 1) and 2) of Table 3.1.

2. Delayability Analysis:

$$\mathbf{NDELAYED}_n = \mathit{Hom\text{-}NEarliest}_n + \begin{cases} \mathit{false} & \text{if } n = \mathbf{s} \\ \prod_{m \in zpred(n)} \mathbf{XDELAYED}_m & \text{otherwise} \end{cases}$$

$$\mathbf{XDELAYED}_n = \mathit{Hom\text{-}XEarliest}_n + \mathbf{NDELAYED}_n \cdot \overline{\mathit{Comp}_n}$$

⤳ Greatest fixed point solution: *Hom-NDelayed* and *Hom-XDelayed*

3. Computation of Latestness: (No data flow analysis!)

$$\mathit{Hom\text{-}NLatest}_n \stackrel{\text{def}}{=} \mathit{Hom\text{-}NDelayed}_n \cdot \mathit{Comp}_n$$

$$\mathit{Hom\text{-}XLatest}_n \stackrel{\text{def}}{=} \mathit{Hom\text{-}XDelayed}_n \cdot \sum_{m \in succ(n)} \overline{\mathit{Hom\text{-}NDelayed}_m}$$

4. Insertion and Replacement Points of the $\mathtt{CLEM}_\varphi$*-Transformation:*

$$\mathtt{CLEM}_\varphi\text{-}\mathit{NInsert}_n \stackrel{\text{def}}{=} \mathit{Hom\text{-}NLatest}_n$$

$$\mathtt{CLEM}_\varphi\text{-}\mathit{XInsert}_n \stackrel{\text{def}}{=} \mathit{Hom\text{-}XLatest}_n$$

$$\mathtt{CLEM}_\varphi\text{-}\mathit{Replace}_n \stackrel{\text{def}}{=} \mathit{Comp}_n$$

Table 5.4. Computing $\mathtt{CLEM}_\varphi$: The unidirectional variant

Algorithm 5.1.1.

Input: Annotation of N with predicates **NDNSAFE** and **XDNSAFE** and an auxiliary predicate **PRED-XSAFE** being initialized as follows:[7]

$$\mathbf{NSAFE}_n \;=\; \mathbf{PRED\text{-}XSAFE}_n \stackrel{\text{def}}{=} \mathit{true}$$

$$\mathbf{XSAFE}_n \stackrel{\text{def}}{=} \begin{cases} \mathit{false} & \text{if } n = \mathbf{e} \\ \mathit{true} & \text{otherwise} \end{cases}$$

Output: Maximal solution to the Equation System of Table 5.1(1b).

```
workset := N;
while workset ≠ ∅ do
    let n ∈ workset;
    workset := workset \ {n};
    if ¬XSAFE_n)
       then { Update Successor Nodes }
          forall m ∈ succ(n) do
             if PRED-XSAFE_m
                then
                   PRED-XSAFE_m := false;
                   workset := workset ∪ {m}
             fi
          od
    fi;
    if NSAFE_n
       then { Local Semantics }
          NSAFE_n := NUpSafe_m + Comp_n + XSAFE_n · Transp_n;
    fi;
    if ¬NSAFE_n ∧ PRED-XSAFE_n
       then { Update Predecessor Nodes }
          forall m ∈ pred(n) do
             if XSAFE_m ∧ ¬XUpSafe_m
                then
                   XSAFE_m := false;
                   workset := workset ∪ {m}
             fi
          od
    fi
od
```

Table 5.5. Bidirectional computation of safety

5.2 The Multiple-Expression View

In this section we focus on important aspects that are touched when combining the components of Section 5.1 to a transformation that deals with multiple expressions of a flat or structured universe of expressions. It will turn out that computational optimality is not influenced by such a combination. In contrast, we have to give up on a reasonable notion of lifetime optimality, since the presence of critical edges is a serious source for conflicts when globalising the local information on profitable lifetime trade-offs. In fact, this disappointing result is new and gives stronger evidence for the importance of splitting critical edges than the extensively discussed problems arising from slow convergence of bidirectional data flow analyses which are even diminished in the light of the new unidirectional alternatives presented in Table 5.3 and Table 5.4.

5.2.1 Flat Expression Motion

As in Chapter 4 it is trivial to extend the single-expression algorithms of the previous section towards algorithms that cope with all expressions of a flat universe of expressions $\Phi_{\mathtt{fl}}$ simultaneously.

5.2.2 Structured Expression Motion

5.2.2.1 Computational Optimal Expression Motion. Like under the situation for flow graphs without critical edges busy and lazy expression motion can easily be shown to be computationally optimal. This is due to the fact that the essential structural properties on safety and delayability carry over to the homogeneous versions of the predicates. Hence complementary to Lemma 4.2.2 and Lemma 4.2.5 we have:

Lemma 5.2.1 (Structured Homogeneous Safety Lemma).

$$\forall \psi \in \Phi, \varphi \in \mathit{SubExpr}_{\Phi}(\psi),\ \dot{n} \in \dot{N}.\ \mathit{Hom\text{-}DnSafe}_{\dot{n}}^{\psi} \Rightarrow \mathit{Hom\text{-}DnSafe}_{\dot{n}}^{\varphi}$$

Lemma 5.2.2 (Structured Homogeneous Delayability Lemma).
Let $\psi \in \Phi, \varphi \in \mathit{SubExpr}_{\Phi}(\psi)$ and $\dot{n} \in \dot{N}$. Then

1. $\mathit{Hom\text{-}Delayed}_{\dot{n}}^{\psi} \Rightarrow \mathit{Hom\text{-}Delayed}_{\dot{n}}^{\varphi} \vee \mathtt{CLEM}_{\Phi}\text{-}\mathit{Correct}_{\dot{n}}^{\varphi}$
2. $\mathit{Hom\text{-}Delayed}_{\dot{n}}^{\varphi} \wedge \mathit{Hom\text{-}DnSafe}_{\dot{n}}^{\psi} \Rightarrow \mathit{Hom\text{-}Delayed}_{\dot{n}}^{\psi}$
3. $\mathit{Hom\text{-}Delayed}_{\dot{n}}^{\psi} \wedge \neg \mathit{Hom\text{-}Earliest}_{\dot{n}}^{\psi} \Rightarrow \neg \mathit{Hom\text{-}Earliest}_{\dot{n}}^{\varphi}$

Then along the lines of Theorem 4.2.1 and Theorem 4.2.2 we may show the following result.

Theorem 5.2.1 (Homogeneous BEM and LEM Theorem).
Both $\mathtt{CBEM}_\Phi$ *and* $\mathtt{CLEM}_\Phi$ *are*

1. *admissible, i. e.* $\mathtt{CBEM}_\Phi, \mathtt{CLEM}_\Phi \in \mathcal{AEM}_\Phi$
2. *profitable, i. e.* $\mathtt{CBEM}_\Phi, \mathtt{CLEM}_\Phi \in \mathcal{PAEM}_\Phi$
3. *computationally optimal, i. e.* $\mathtt{CBEM}_\Phi, \mathtt{CLEM}_\Phi \in \mathcal{COEM}_\Phi^{\mathtt{Crit}}$

At this point, however, it should be mentioned that the component transformations have to be chosen carefully in order to yield a structured expression motion at all. Drechsler and Stadel [DS88], for instance, observed that the original proposal of Morel and Renvoise [MR79] is not suitable as a basis for an algorithm that operates on structured sets of expressions, since their equation system allows pathological cases where subexpressions cannot be hoisted in front of their superexpressions.

5.2.2.2 Structured Lifetimes in the Presence of Critical Edges. Unfortunately, the most serious drawback of critical edges comes into play when lifetimes of temporaries are taken into account. In fact, as opposed to the situation in Chapter 4 in general neither lifetime optimal nor inductively lifetime optimal results exist anymore. This is illustrated by means of Figure 5.5. The point of this example is that the subexpressions φ_1 and φ_2 are forced to be initialised on the path $\langle 1, 3, 5, 7, \ldots \rangle$, but not on the path $\langle 2, 4, 5, 7, \ldots \rangle$.

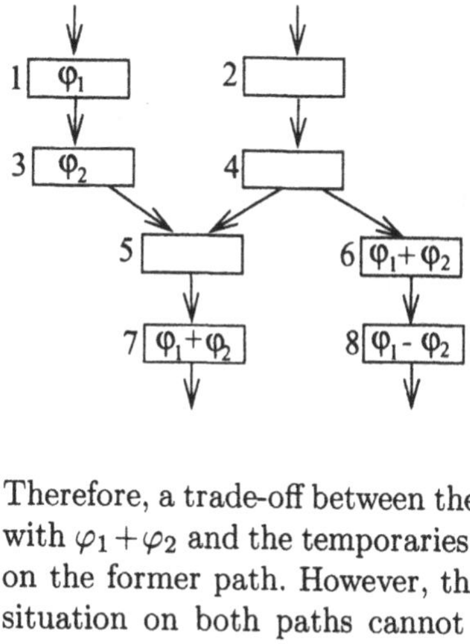

Fig. 5.5. Problems with trade-offs of lifetimes and critical edges

Therefore, a trade-off between the lifetime ranges of the temporary associated with $\varphi_1 + \varphi_2$ and the temporaries associated with φ_1 and φ_2 is only profitable on the former path. However, the critical edge $(4, 5)$ is responsible that the situation on both paths cannot properly be decoupled. As a consequence there are two alternatives for the initialisation of the temporary associated with $\varphi_1 + \varphi_2$ that are not comparable in terms of the lifetime better order as introduced in Definition 4.2.3. Figure 5.6(a) shows an early initialisation of $\mathbf{h}_3$ at node 3 that reduces the number of lifetime ranges at the exit of this node to one. However, this also forces an initialisation of $\mathbf{h}_3$ at node 4, which increases the number of lifetime ranges at the exit of this node to three.[8]

[8] Note that the values of the subexpressions have to be kept for the initialisation of $\mathbf{h}_4$ which cannot be done before the entry of node **6**.

On the other hand, Figure 5.6(b) shows the situation if $\mathbf{h}_3$ is initialised at node 5. Though in this case the profitable trade-off between lifetime ranges at node **3** is missed, this solution requires exactly two lifetime ranges at the exits of node 3 and 4, respectively. Hence the result is actually incomparable to the transformation of Figure 5.6(a).

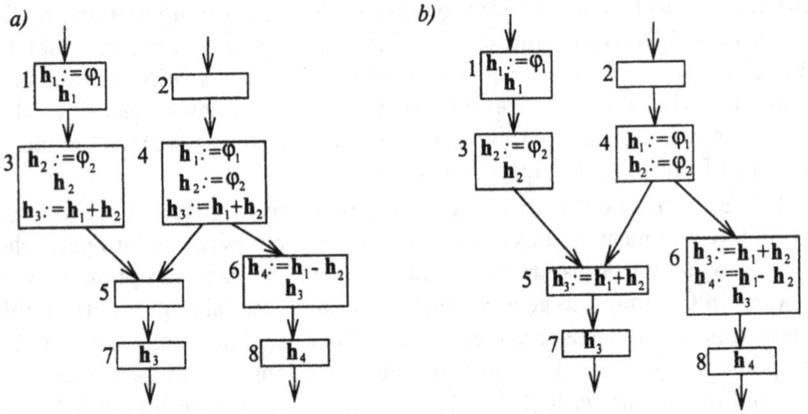

Fig. 5.6. Incomparable lifetime minimal expression motions

Finally, this example provides the opportunity to elucidate the advantage of edge splitting by investigating the situation, where in the example of Figure 5.5 the critical edge would be split by inserting a synthetic node. Then the lifetime optimal solution of Section 4.5 could exploit its full power by using profitable lifetime trade-offs as early as possible. This is shown in Figure 5.7. In fact, since conflicts are now completely resolved the number of lifetime ranges being active at the exits of node 3 and 4 is one and two, respectively, which strictly improves upon both results of Figure 5.6.

5.2.3 The Complexity

Due to the difficulties arising with lifetime considerations we only consider the multiple-expression versions of $\texttt{CBEM}_\Phi$ and $\texttt{CLEM}_\Phi$. As in Chapter 4 there is no difference in the complexity between the flat and structured versions. Obviously, from a pure point of view[9] a consequence of Theorem 5.1.3 is:

Theorem 5.2.2 (Complexity of $\texttt{CBEM}_\Phi$ and $\texttt{CLEM}_\Phi$). $\texttt{CBEM}_\Phi$ *and* $\texttt{CLEM}_\Phi$ *can be performed with run-time complexity of order* $\mathcal{O}(|G|\,|\Phi|)$ *for both a flat or a structured universe of expressions.*

[9] That means, without an assumption of elementary bit-vector operations.

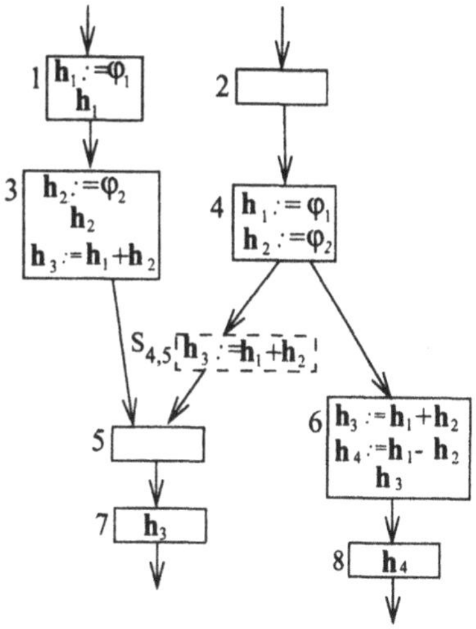

Fig. 5.7. Lifetime optimal expression motion after splitting of the critical edge

More interesting, however, is the question of the bit-vector complexities of the algorithms under consideration. Here, the well-known deficiency of the usage of bidirectional analyses shows up.

5.2.3.1 The Bidirectional Variants. In contrast to their unidirectional counterparts, which are reported to stabilize within a number of bit-vector steps that is almost linear in the size of the program (cp. Theorem 4.6.4) no corresponding result is available for bidirectional analyses. Recently, Dhamdhere and Khedker [DK93, KD94] came up with an estimation on bidirectonal data flow analyses given in terms of the *width* of a flow graph.

Theorem 5.2.3 (Complexity of bidirectional $\mathtt{CBEM}_\Phi$ and $\mathtt{CLEM}_\Phi$). *The (partly) bidirectional equation systems for* $\mathtt{CBEM}_\Phi$ *and* $\mathtt{CLEM}_\Phi$ *of Table 5.1 and Table 5.2 can be solved with* $\mathtt{w}+1$ *round robin iterations, where the* width $\mathtt{w}$ *denotes the number of non-conform edge traversals on an information flow path.*[10]

Note, however, the width of a flow graph is not a structural property of a flow graph, but varies with the bit-vector problem under consideration. In particular, it is larger for bidirectional problems than for unidirectional ones, and in the worst case it is linear in the size of the flow graph. Even worse, for the bidirectional equation systems used in expression motion, like ours in Table 5.1(1b) and Table 5.2(2), the width indeed usually grows linearly with the program size. This is even true for acyclic programs. We shall discuss this behaviour by means of our forwards directed bidirectional equation

[10] Informatively, an information flow path is a sequence of backwards or forwards directed edges along which a change of information can be propagated. A forward traversal along a forward edge or a backward traversal along a backward edge are conform with a round robin method proceeding (forwards) in reverse postorder. The other two kind of traversals are non-conform. Complemental notions apply to round robin iterations proceeding in postorder.

system for delayability (cp. Table 5.2(2)). To this end we are considering the program fragment sketched in Figure 5.8. This program fragment is an information flow path for delayability where the non-conform edge traversals are emphasized by a grey circle.

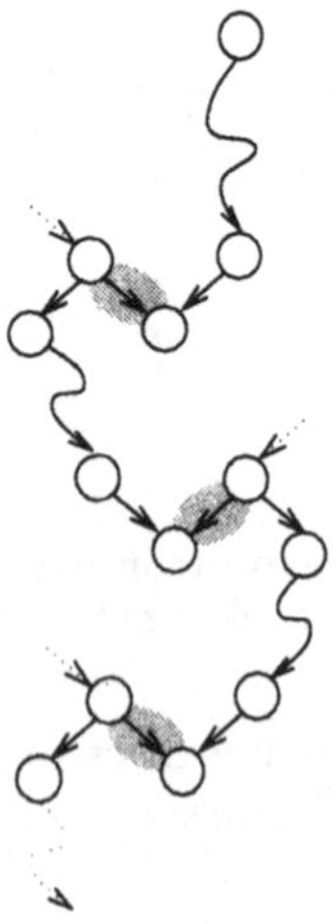

Fig. 5.8. Width of a flow graph: information flow path with non-conform edge traversals

Hence the width of a flow graph with such a fragment linearly depends on the "length" of the fragment. It should be noted that such programs are by no means pathological and thus the linear growth of the width is not unlikely for real life programs. In fact, the large width in this case is actually reflected in a poor behaviour of a round robin iteration schedule. Figure 5.9(a) shows how delayability information slowly propagates along this "path" being stopped in each iteration at a non-conform (critical) edge.[11]

5.2.3.2 The Unidirectional Variants. The drawbacks of bidirectional bit-vector analyses being presented in the previous section can be avoided by using the unidirectional variants of Table 5.3 and Table 5.4. Considering again the path of Figure 5.8 the unidirectional variant can take advantage of the shortcut edges yielding stabilization after the very first iteration as displayed in Figure 5.9(b). In general, we have the following result.

Theorem 5.2.4 (Complexity of unidirectional $\mathtt{CBEM}_\Phi$ and $\mathtt{CLEM}_\Phi$). *The unidirectional variants of* $\mathtt{CBEM}_\Phi$ *and* $\mathtt{CLEM}_\Phi$ *of Table 5.3 and Table 5.4 can be solved with* $\mathrm{d}'+1$ *round robin iterations, where* d' *denotes the depth (cp. Section 4.6.4) of the flow graph after adding virtual shortcut edges.*

As mentioned, for real life programs we do not expect pathological nests of critical edges as in Figure 5.4. For this reason both the additional setup-costs

[11] Shaded circles indicate the flow of informations along the "path". Actually, this means the propagation of the Boolean value "*false*", as the equation system in Table 5.2(2) computes the largest solution.

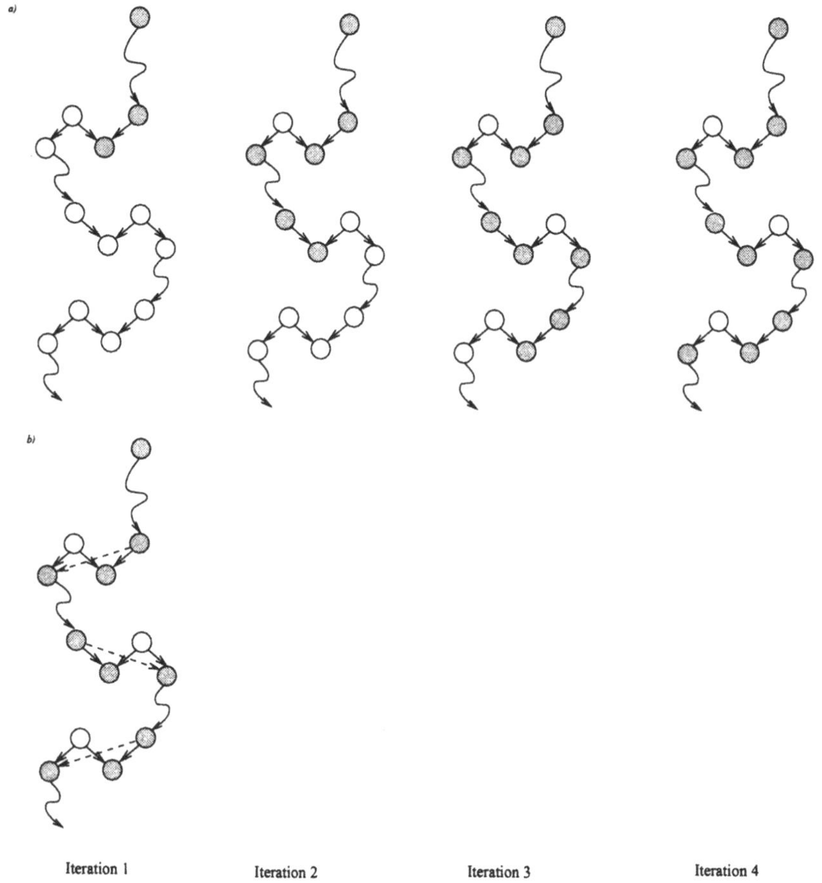

Fig. 5.9. (a) Slow convergence due to bidirectional data flow analysis (b) Fast convergence with unidirectional data flow analysis using shortcut edges

for determining zig-zag predecessors and zig-zag successors at a node as well as the growth of the parameter d′ in comparison to d can be expected to be bound by a small constant. However, in [Rüt98a] we further investigate a hybrid iteration strategy that does not actually add shortcut edges but rather intermixes a round robin schedule on the original flow graph with zig-zag propagation of information along critical edges.

Part II

Assignment Motion

Overview

Assignment Motion

Assignment motion is a technique that complements expression motion as presented in the first part of this monograph by incorporating the movement of left-hand side variables of assignments as well. Although such an extension may seem straightforward at first glance, the movement of left-hand sides of assignments has serious consequences that are subject of this part. In contrast to expression motion which has thoroughly been studied in program optimisation [Cho83, Dha83, Dha88, Dha89b, Dha91, DS88, DS93, JD82a, JD82b, Mor84, MR79, MR81, Sor89] the work on assignment motion based algorithms is quite limited. Rosen, Wegman and Zadeck [RWZ88] mention IBM's PL.8-compiler [AH82] for an iterated application of partial redundancy elimination. However, they neither give details on this extensions nor a first-hand reference. The only explicit description of an extension of partial redundancy elimination towards assignments is given by Dhamdhere [Dha91]. However, his proposal does not recognise the full potential that lies in such an extension. This part of the book provides a systematic approach to the phenomena associated with program transformations based upon assignment motion.

Second Order Effects

The most striking phenomenon of assignment motion based transformations are their *second order effects* [RWZ88, DRZ92]: one transformation may provide opportunities for others. As a consequence, assignment motion based transformations usually do not stabilise after their first application. However, the impact of second order effects is twofold: on one side, the optimisation potential increases significantly, as even few first order opportunities may cause numerous second order opportunities. On the other hand, we are faced with the problem that exhausting the optimisation potential completely, requires to iterate the component transformations involved. This gives raises issues on the *confluence* and *complexity* of the process, which will be of major concern in this part.

Assignment Hoisting and Assignment Sinking

For expression motion the direction of code movement is determined by definition, since initialisation sites have to precede their corresponding use sites. Hence expression motion stands as a synonym for expression hoisting. In contrast, assignment motion is not restricted in this way. Both alternatives, the hoisting and sinking of assignments, are reasonable directions of code movement. This symmetry was inspiration to develop an algorithm for *partial dead code elimination* [KRS94b] which complements partial redundancy elimination. While partial redundancy elimination hoists expressions to places where they become redundant with respect to others, partial dead code elimination rests on the idea to sink assignments to places where they become entirely dead. Alternatively, this transformation can even be further strengthened by eliminating *faint assignments* [HDT87, GMW81] rather then dead ones only.

On the other hand, assignment hoisting can be employed equally well in order to eliminate partially redundant assignments. More interesting, however, is the function of assignment hoisting as a catalyst for enhancing the potential of expression motion, which we demonstrated in an algorithm for the *uniform elimination of partially redundant expressions and assignments* [KRS95]. Here this approach will be further improved adapting the techniques for minimising lifetime range of Chapter 4.

A Uniform Framework

Common to assignment motion based program transformations is the fact that they combine a set of admissible assignment motions with a set of corresponding eliminations. Formalising this situation, we present a uniform framework for assignment motion based program transformations that is applicable in all practically relevant situations. In this setting we provide simple criteria that grant confluence and fast convergence of the exhaustive application of elementary transformations.

Structure of the Part

In Chapter 6 we give an overview on the most relevant applications in the field of assignment motion. In particular, we address the main applications of assignment motion: *partial dead (faint) code elimination* and the *uniform elimination of assignments and expressions.* Afterwards, Chapter 7 presents our general framework for assignment motion based transformations. In symmetry to the first part, the final Chapter 8 is again devoted to issues caused by the presence of critical edges.

Conventions

As in the first part of the book we mainly consider flow graphs whose nodes are elementary statements. However, sometimes we switch to the basic block representation. This is for the reason that the basic blocks of a program are structurally invariant during a sequence of transformation steps, whereas the positions of elementary statements may significantly change. Throughout this part we assume a fixed flow graph G which is assumed to be element of $\mathfrak{FG}$ in Chapter 6 and Chapter 7 and to be element of $\mathfrak{FG}_{\mathrm{Crit}}$ in Chapter 8.

6. Program Transformations Based on Assignment Motion

After introducing the central notion of the second part, assignment motion, we sketch the main applications for assignment motion based program transformations: the elimination of *partially dead (faint) assignments* (cf. [KRS94b]), the elimination of *partially redundant assignments* and the uniform elimination of *partially redundant assignments and expressions* (cf. [KRS95]). It should be noted that the reasoning on properties of these transformations is postponed to Section 7, where a uniform framework for assignment motion based program transformations is presented.

6.1 Assignment Motion

In this section we first introduce the notion of assignment motion as a counterpart to expression motion (cf. Definition 3.1.1). In contradistinction to expression motion, however, (admissible) assignment motion only aims at the pure movement and does not permit any program improvement on its own. Moreover, assignment motion becomes important for both the forward- and backward-direction.

Definition 6.1.1 (Assignment Motion). *For $\alpha \in \mathcal{AP}(G)$ we define:*

1. *an* assignment sinking *with respect to α is a program transformation that*
   a) *eliminates some original occurrences of α and*
   b) *inserts some instances of α at program points following an elimination point.*[1]
2. *an* assignment hoisting *with respect to α is a program transformation that*
   a) *eliminates some original occurrences of α and*
   b) *inserts some instances of α at program points preceding an elimination point.*[1]

The fact that G' results from G by an assignment sinking with respect to $\alpha \in \mathcal{AP}(G)$ shall be expressed by the notion $G \overset{as}{\longmapsto}_{\alpha} G'$. Accordingly, for

[1] That means, program points which follow (precede) the elimination point on some program path. Note that this condition is quite liberal, but will be further constrained when considering admissible code motion (cf. Definition 6.1.2).

assignment hoistings the notion $G \stackrel{ah}{\longmapsto}_\alpha G'$ is used. For convenience, for a given assignment motion like $\mathtt{AS}_\alpha \equiv G \stackrel{as}{\longmapsto}_\alpha G'$ a function-like notation $\mathtt{AS}_\alpha(G)$ is used in order to refer to the program G'.[2]

An assignment motion can completely be characterised by means of its insertion points and its elimination points. For instance, for an assignment sinking $\mathtt{AS}_\alpha$ and $\dot{n} \in \dot{N}$ we have:

$\mathtt{AS}_\alpha$-$Insert^\alpha_{\dot{n}}$: an instance of α is inserted at $\dot{n}$.

$\mathtt{AS}_\alpha$-$Remove^\alpha_{\dot{n}}$: an original occurrence of α is removed from $\dot{n}$.[3]

Local Predicates

For every node $n \in N$ that and every assignment pattern $\overbrace{x := \varphi}^{\alpha} \in \mathcal{AP}(G)$ a number of local predicates is defined. To this end, let us further assume that n is associated with an instruction pattern β_n with right-hand side expression $\beta_n^{\mathtt{rhs}}$ and left-hand side variable $\beta_n^{\mathtt{lhs}}$.[4]

$LhsMod^\alpha_n$: n modifies the left-hand side variable of α, i. e. $\beta_n^{\mathtt{lhs}} = x$

$RhsMod^\alpha_n$: n modifies the right-hand side expression of α, i. e. $\beta_n^{\mathtt{lhs}} \in SubExpr^*(\varphi)$

$AssMod^\alpha_n$: n modifies an operand of α, i. e. $LhsMod^\alpha_n \vee RhsMod^\alpha_n$

$LhsUsed^\alpha_n$: n uses the left-hand side variable of α, i. e. $x \in SubExpr^*(\beta_n^{\mathtt{rhs}})$

$AssOcc^\alpha_n$: the assignmnent pattern α occurs at n, i. e. $\beta_n = \alpha$

$Blocked^\alpha_n$: n *blocks* the movement of α, since the ordering of both instructions must not be changed, i. e. $AssMod^\alpha_n \vee LhsUsed^\alpha_n$

All local predicates are naturally extended to program points: entry properties are directly inherited from the properties of the associated nodes, while exit properties are uniquely set to *false*.

6.1.1 Admissibility

As for expression motion we have to impose additional constraints for assignment motion in order to grant that the semantics of the argument program

[2] This is in accordance with the view of $\mathtt{AS}_\alpha$ as a function from $\mathfrak{FG}$ to $\mathfrak{FG}$ defined by:

$$\forall G'' \in \mathfrak{FG}.\ \mathtt{AS}_\alpha(G'') \stackrel{\mathrm{def}}{=} \begin{cases} G' & \text{if } G'' = G \\ G'' & \text{otherwise} \end{cases}$$

[3] More precisely, $\dot{n}$ is the entry point of a node n where the occurrence is removed.

[4] In the case that the right-hand side expression does not exist, e.g., if $\beta = skip$, or that there is no left-hand side variable, e.g., if $\beta = out(\ldots)$, we assume that the special value $\perp$ is assigned to $\beta_n^{\mathtt{rhs}}$ and $\beta_n^{\mathtt{lhs}}$, respectively.

is preserved. However, we cannot naively adopt the same constraints as in expression motion. The requirement that no new expression patterns are inserted on a program path, for instance, would be far to liberal when generalised to assignments, since the insertion of an assignment like $x := x + 1$ is usually not sound, even on program paths containing an instance of this assignment pattern. Hence a reasonable notion of admissibility has to be much more restrictive than the one for expression motion: we require that the ordering among blocking instructions is entirely preserved. In other words, code motion must not violate a data dependency or anti-dependency in the original program.

Definition 6.1.2 (Admissible Assignment Motion).

1. *An assignment sinking* $\mathtt{AS}_\alpha \equiv G \overset{as}{\longmapsto}_\alpha G'$ *is* admissible *iff:*
   a) *the removed original assignment patterns of* α *are* substituted, *i. e. for each* $\dot n \in \dot N$ *(see Figure 6.1 for illustration)*

   $$\mathtt{AS}_\alpha\text{-}Remove_{\dot n}^\alpha \Rightarrow \mathtt{AS}_\alpha\text{-}Subst_{\dot n}^\alpha,$$

   $$\text{where } \mathtt{AS}_\alpha\text{-}Subst_{\dot n}^\alpha \overset{def}{\Leftrightarrow} \forall p \in \mathbf{P}[\dot n, \dot{\mathbf{e}}]\ \dot\exists 1 \leqslant i \leqslant |p|.\ \mathtt{AS}_\alpha\text{-}Insert_{p_i}^\alpha \wedge \forall 1 < j < i.\ \neg Blocked_{p_j}^\alpha$$

   b) *the inserted instances of* α *are* justified, *i. e. for each* $\dot n \in \dot N$ *(see Figure 6.2 for illustration)*

   $$\mathtt{AS}_\alpha\text{-}Insert_{\dot n}^\alpha \Rightarrow \mathtt{AS}_\alpha\text{-}Just_{\dot n}^\alpha,$$

   $$\text{where } \mathtt{AS}_\alpha\text{-}Just_{\dot n}^\alpha \overset{def}{\Leftrightarrow} \forall p \in \mathbf{P}[\dot{\mathbf{s}}, \dot n]\ \exists 1 \leqslant i < |p|.\ \mathtt{AS}_\alpha\text{-}Remove_{p_i}^\alpha \wedge \forall i < j < |p|.\ \neg Blocked_{p_j}^\alpha$$

2. *The admissibility of an assignment hoisting is defined analogously.*

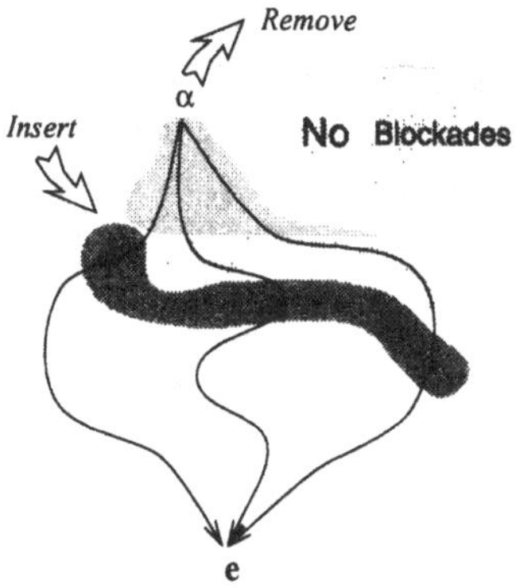

Fig. 6.1. Substitution of removed assignments

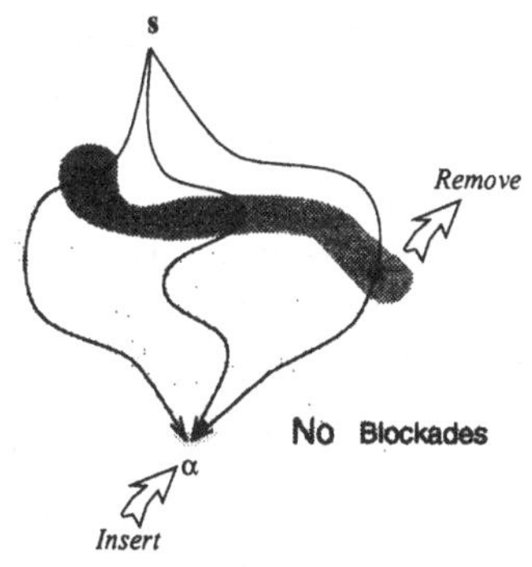

Fig. 6.2. Justification of inserted assignments

In essence, admissible assignment motions are pure repositionings of code that do not permit any program improvements on their own. Actually, on every program path from **s** to **e** there is a one-to-one correspondence between the replaced original occurrences and the inserted ones: on the one hand, there is a unique insertion belonging to each replaced original occurrence, which is forced by the usage of the $\dot{\exists}$-quantifier in the definition of the predicate $\mathtt{AS}_\alpha$-*Subst*, on the other hand the complemental predicate $\mathtt{AS}_\alpha$-*Just* also ensures that each insertion is at most justified through a unique removal on this path.[5] The set of all admissible assignment sinkings and the set of all admissible assignment hoistings with respect to α is denoted by $\mathcal{AAS}_\alpha$ and $\mathcal{AAH}_\alpha$, respectively.

6.2 Partial Dead Code Elimination

As an application of assignment sinking we present the *elimination of partially dead assignments*, or for short *partial dead code elimination*, as introduced in [KRS94b].

6.2.1 Motivation

Dead code elimination [Hec77, W.78, Kou77] is a technique for improving the efficiency of a program by avoiding unnecessary assignments to variables at run-time. Usually, an assignment is considered unnecessary, if it is *totally* dead, i. e. if the content of its left-hand side variable is not used in the remainder of the program. *Partially* dead assignments as the one in node **1** of Figure 6.3(a), which is dead on the left branch but alive on the right one, are out of the scope of (classical) dead code elimination.

In [KRS94b] we presented a technique for *partial dead code elimination* where assignments are sunk to places at which they become entirely dead and can be eliminated. The basic idea is illustrated in Figure 6.3. The point here is that the assignment to x at node **1** is only used on the right branch, since x is redefined at node **2**. After sinking the assignment to x from node **1** to node **3** and to the entry of node **2**, it becomes dead in the latter case and can be eliminated. Hence the point of partial dead code elimination is to sink partially dead assignments as far as possible in the direction of the control flow, while maintaining the program semantics. This way, statements are placed in an as specific context as possible, which maximises the potential of dead code elimination. Therefore, our approach in [KRS94b] is essentially dual to partial redundancy elimination as considered in the first part of this book, where expressions are hoisted against the control flow as far as possible, in order to make their effects as universal as possible. It should be noted that our approach was the first one that observed this duality. However,

[5] Note that in the case of two preceding removals the latter one would be a blockade for the former one.

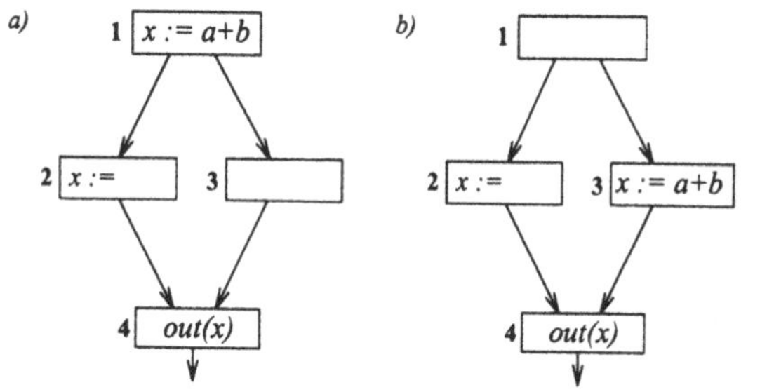

Fig. 6.3. Partial dead code elimination

independently from our algorithm two other approaches came up addressing the elimination of partially dead code.

Feigen et al. [FKCX94] developed an algorithm that builds more complex entities for movement whenever the elementary statements are blocked. In contrast to the usual code motion algorithms this particularly may modify the branching structure of the program under consideration. However, their algorithm is not capable of moving statements out of loops or even across loops. Furthermore, movements are restricted to one-to-one movements, i. e. code fragments are removed at one place in order to be implanted exactly at one other place, where the fragment is alive. Later Bodík and Gupta [BG97] developed a more systematic structure-modifying technique for partial dead code elimination based on the predication of instructions which, however, is of exponential run-time complexity when applied exhaustively.

Finally, Briggs and Cooper proposed an algorithm [BC94] that employs instruction sinking for the reassociation of expressions. As a by-product some partially dead assignments can be removed. However, in contrast to our algorithm their strategy of instruction sinking can significantly impair certain program executions, since instructions can be moved into loops in a way which cannot be "repaired" by a subsequent partial redundancy elimination.

6.2.2 Defining Partial Dead Code Elimination

Formally, partial dead code elimination ($\mathcal{PDCE}$) stands for any sequence of elementary transformations of the following type:

- admissible assignment sinkings and
- eliminations of dead assignments.

Whereas admissible assignment sinkings are already introduced (cf. Definition 6.1.2(1)), the elimination transformations need to be defined.

Definition 6.2.1 (Dead Assignment Elimination).

1. *An occurrence of an assignment pattern* $\alpha \equiv x := \varphi$ *is* dead *at* $n \in N$*, if on every path from* n *to* $\mathbf{e}$ *a usage of* x *is is always preceded by a redefinition of* x*. Formally, this is expressed by the following predicate:*

$$Dead_n^\alpha \overset{def}{\Leftrightarrow}$$
$$\forall p \in \mathbf{P}[n, \mathbf{e}],\ 1 < i \leqslant |p|.\ LhsUsed_{p_i}^\alpha \Rightarrow \exists 1 < j < i.\ LhsMod_{p_j}^\alpha$$

2. *A* dead assignment elimination *with respect to $\alpha \in \mathcal{AP}(G)$ is a program transformation that eliminates some dead original occurrences of α in the argument program.*

The set of all dead assignment eliminations with respect to α is denoted by $\mathcal{DAE}_\alpha$. As for assignment motions (cf. Definition 6.1.1) we use the notion $G \overset{dae}{\longmapsto}_\alpha G'$ to express that G' results from G by applying a dead assignment elimination with respect to α. Moreover, for a given dead assignment elimination $\mathtt{DAE}_\alpha \equiv G \overset{dae}{\longmapsto}_\alpha G'$ the term $\mathtt{DAE}_\alpha(G)$ refers to the program G' that results from the particular transformation.

6.2.3 Second Order Effects in Partial Dead Code Elimination

As already mentioned, the effect of partial dead code elimination is based on the mutual interactions of assignment sinkings and dead assignment eliminations. Each of these transformation types may expose opportunities for the other one. Such effects are commonly known as *second order effects* [RWZ88, DRZ92] in program optimisation. Since second order effects are of major importance for assignment motion based program transformations, we will use $\mathcal{PDCE}$ as a representative for a systematic classification of all possible effects.

Motion-Elimination Effects These are the effects of primary interest: an assignment is moved until it can be eliminated by a dead assignment elimination. Reconsider the motivating example of Figure 6.3 for illustration.

Motion-Motion Effects These are effects where the movement of one assignment may provide opportunities for other assignments to move. This can happen for various reasons, e.g., if the assignment that is moved first is a use site or redefinition site for the other one, or if it modifies an operand of the other's right-hand side expression. The latter case is illustrated in Figure 6.4(a).

Without the previous movement of the assignment at node **2** the assignment at node **1** can move at most to the entry of node **2**, since a further movement would deliver a different value for the right-hand side computation. However, if we anticipate the movement of the assignment at node **2** then it can be sunk to the entry of node **5**. Thereafter, the assignment at node **1** can be moved to node **3** and **4**. In the case of node **4** it becomes entirely dead and can finally be eliminated.

Elimination-Motion Effects Such effects show up when the elimination of a dead assignment enables the movement of another assignment as depicted in Figure 6.5(a). Here, the assignment $a := \ldots$ at node **1** cannot be moved to the entry of node **3** without violating the admissibility of this movement.

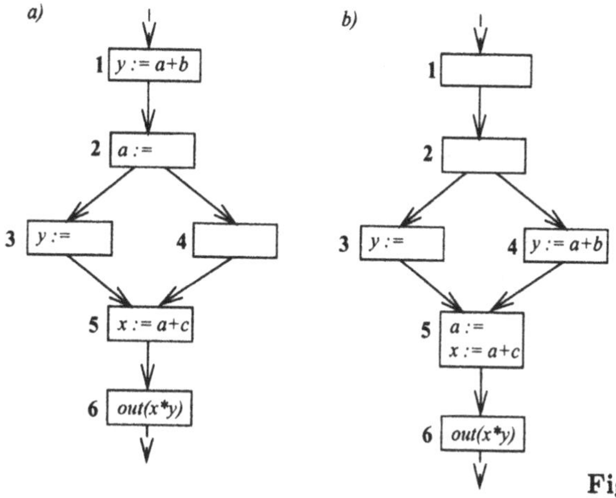

Fig. 6.4. Motion-motion effect

But it can be removed by a dead assignment elimination, since its value is of no further use. Finally, this removal enables the assignment $y := a + b$ to be sunk to node **4** and **5** in order to eliminate further partially dead assignments leading to the resulting program displayed in Figure 6.5(b).

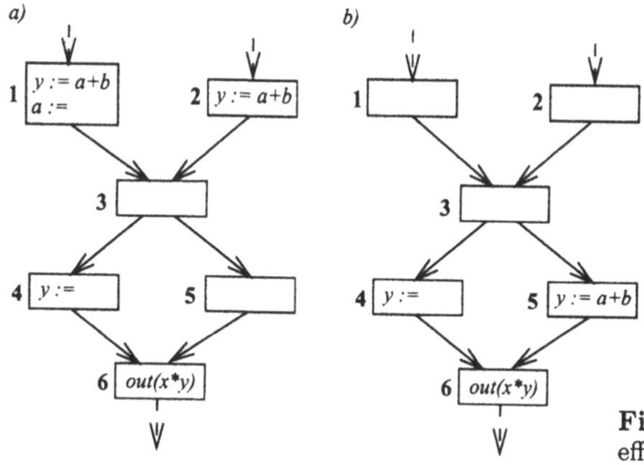

Fig. 6.5. Elimination-motion effect

Elimination-Elimination Effects Such an effect is depicted in Figure 6.6(a). Here, the assignment at node **4** is dead and can be eliminated, since the left-hand side variable y is redefined before it is used on every path leading to the end node. However, the assignment to a at node **1**, which was not dead before due to its usage at node **4**, now becomes dead and can be removed as shown in Figure 6.6(b).

The Power of Resolving Second Order Effects We close this section on second order effects with a more complex example that is suitable to illustrate the enormous potential that lies in the exhaustive resolution of second order effects.

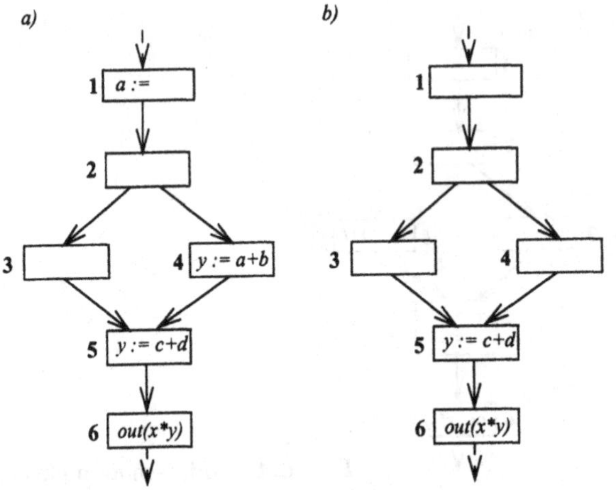

Fig. 6.6. Elimination-elimination effect

The most striking inefficiency in the example of Figure 6.7 is the "loop invariant" code fragment in node **2**. Note, however, that the occurrence of $a + b$ inside of the loop is out of the scope of expression motion, since the first instruction defines an operand of the second one. However, $\mathcal{PDCE}$ can perform the optimisation displayed in Figure 6.8, where no further assignment sinking or dead assignment elimination is applicable.[6]

After removing the second assignment from the loop,[7] the first assignment turns out to be loop invariant, too, and can be removed from the loop as well.

[6] Synthetic nodes are inserted on demand.

[7] Note that this requires two steps. First the assignment $x := a + b$ is moved from node **2** to node **3** and **4**. Afterwards the dead occurrence at node **3** can be eliminated.

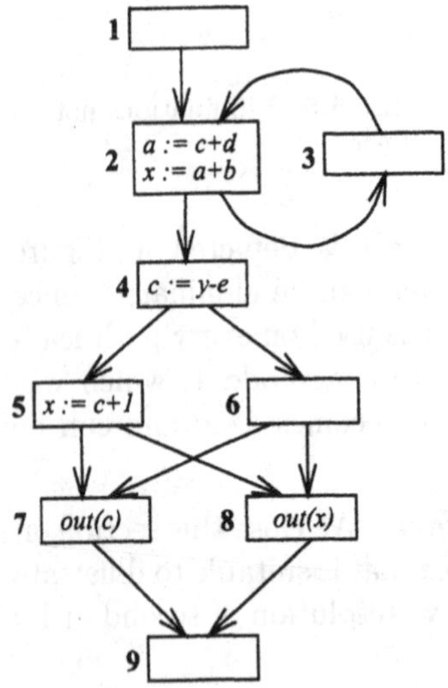

Fig. 6.7. A complex example illustrating the power lying in the exhaustive exploitation of second order effects

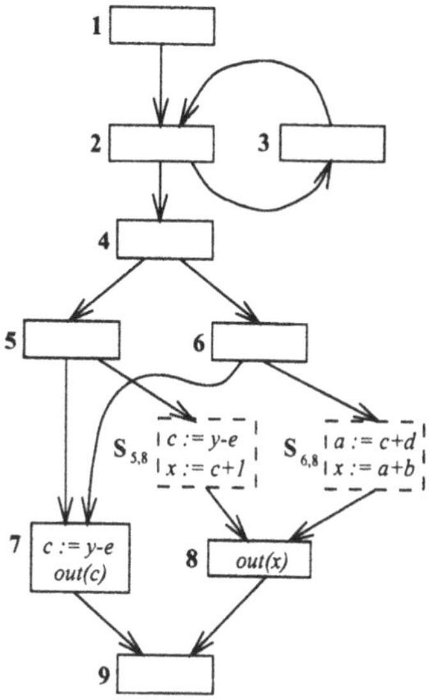

Fig. 6.8. Exhaustive $\mathcal{PDCE}$ applied to Figure 6.7

Thereafter, these two assignments together with the blockade at node **4** can be subjected to further movements and eliminations. Note that the synthetic node $\mathbf{S}_{6,8}$ is finally the only point where the execution of the loop invariant fragment is actually required. In fact, we can see that $\mathcal{PDCE}$ supplies the output instructions at node **7** and **8** exactly with the sequences of assignments that establish the correct output on every path. This significantly reduces the number of assignments in some situations. For instance the number of assignments occurring on the path $\langle \mathbf{1}, \mathbf{2}, \mathbf{3}, \mathbf{2}, \mathbf{3}, \mathbf{2}, \mathbf{4}, \mathbf{5}, \mathbf{7}, \mathbf{9} \rangle$ is reduced from 8 to 1.

6.3 Partial Faint Code Elimination

The definition of deadness (cf. Definition 6.2.1) is too narrow in order to characterise all assignments that are of no use, i. e. that do not contribute to the evaluation of an immobile statement, like for instance an output statement. In [HDT87, GMW81] deadness is weakened towards a notion of *faintness*, which is given in terms of a recursive definition (cf. Definition 6.3.1). Faintness of assignments not only covers all situations that can be detected through the iterated elimination of dead assignments, but in addition also captures some unnecessary assignments that are out of the scope of iterated dead assignment elimination. This is illustrated in Figure 6.9 which is taken from [HDT87]. The point here is that the assignment to x inside of the loop cannot be eliminated by classical dead assignment elimination, since the assignment itself is a use site of its left-hand variable.

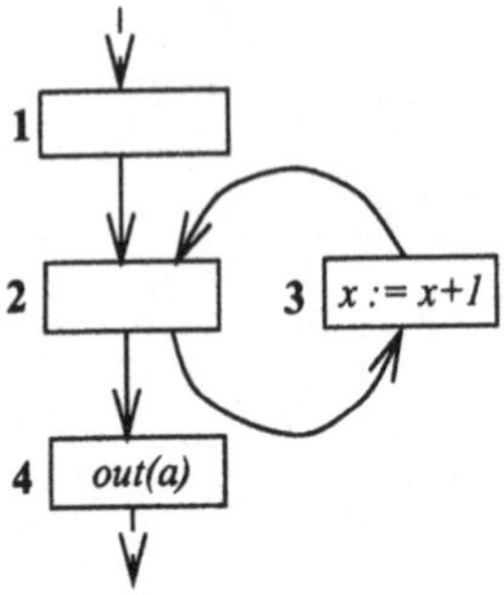

Fig. 6.9. A faint but not dead assignment

Definition 6.3.1 (Faint Assignment Elimination).

1. *An occurrence of an assignment pattern* $\alpha \equiv x := \varphi$ *at a node* $n \in N$ *is* faint, *if on every program path leading from* n *to* $\mathbf{e}$ *a usage of* x
   – *is either preceded by a redefinition of* x *or*
   – *defines a faint assignment as well.*

   Formally, the property is captured by means of the greatest solution of a recursive predicate:[8]

$$Faint_n^\alpha \overset{\text{def}}{\Leftrightarrow} \forall p \in \mathbf{P}[n, \mathbf{e}],\ 1 < i \leqslant |p|.\ LhsUsed_{p_i}^\alpha \Rightarrow (\exists 1 < j < i.\ LhsMod_{p_j}^\alpha) \lor Faint_{p_i}^\beta,$$

   where β *is an assignment pattern that is associated with node* p_i.
2. *A* faint assignment elimination *with respect to* α *is a program transformation that eliminates some faint original occurrences of* α *in the argument program.*

The notions $G \overset{fae}{\longmapsto}_\alpha G'$ and $\mathtt{FAE}_\alpha(G)$ for $\mathtt{FAE}_\alpha \equiv G \overset{fae}{\longmapsto}_\alpha G'$ are introduced in analogy to the counterparts for dead assignment elimination. The set of all faint assignment eliminations with respect to α is denoted as $\mathcal{FAE}_\alpha$.

Hence formally partial faint code elimination ($\mathcal{PFCE}$) stands for any sequence of:

- admissible assignment sinkings and
- eliminations of faint assignments.

6.4 Partially Redundant Assignment Elimination

Complementary to $\mathcal{PDCE}$ also assignment hoisting can be employed profitably in a straightforward way by introducing the *elimination of partially redundant assignments* ($\mathcal{PRAE}$) as a technique that combines:

[8] Note that the least solution exactly characterises those assignments that can be eliminated through iterated dead code elimination.

– admissible assignment hoistings and
– redundant assignment eliminations

where the latter transformations are defined as below:

Definition 6.4.1 (Redundant Assignment Elimination).

1. *An occurrence of an assignment pattern* $\alpha \equiv x := \varphi$ *at a node* n *is* redundant, *if on every program path leading from* $\mathbf{s}$ *to* n *there is a strictly prior occurrence of* α *such that no instruction in between both occurrences modifies*
   a) *the left-hand side variable* x *or*
   b) *an operand of the right-hand side expression* φ.[9]

   Formally, redundant assignments are captured by means of the following predicate:

$$Redundant_n^\alpha \overset{\text{def}}{\Leftrightarrow} \forall p \in \mathbf{P}[\mathbf{s}, n]\ \exists 1 \leqslant i < |p|.\ AssOcc_{p_i}^\alpha \ \wedge$$
$$\forall i < j < |p|.\ \neg LhsMod_{p_j}^\alpha \ \wedge\ \forall i < j \leqslant |p|.\ \neg RhsMod_{p_j}^\alpha$$

2. *A* redundant assignment elimination *with respect to* α *is a program transformation that eliminates some redundant original occurrences of* α *in the argument program.*

Once more, notions $G \overset{rae}{\longmapsto}_\alpha G'$ and $\mathtt{RAE}_\alpha(G)$ for $\mathtt{RAE}_\alpha \equiv G \overset{rae}{\longmapsto}_\alpha G'$ are introduced in analogy to dead and faint assignment eliminations. The set of all redundant assignment eliminations with respect to α is denoted by $\mathcal{RAE}_\alpha$.

6.5 The Uniform Elimination of Partially Redundant Assignments and Expressions

Unfortunately, in practice the optimisation potential of $\mathcal{PRAE}$ is quite limited, since redundant assignment elimination is based on complete assignment patterns. In contrast, the elimination of redundant expressions only matches right-hand side expressions and dead code elimination even only focuses on the left-hand side variables of assignments. However, the importance of $\mathcal{PRAE}$ lies in its catalytic function with regard to expression motion. This effect was first discovered by Dhamdhere [Dha91], whose solution, however, wastes much of the potential of such a combination, which is caused by an inappropriate mixture of optimisations goals.[10]

---

[9] To exclude recursive assignment patterns like $x := x + 1$ from being redundant the occurrence at node n itself must not modify an operand of φ. In the formal definition this is reflected by means of slightly different ranges to be excluded for left- and right-hand side modifications.

[10] Precisely, the proposal incorporates lifetime considerations of temporaries too early. A more detailed discussion on this aspect can be found in Section 7.4.3.

Principally, $\mathcal{PRAE}$ shows the same mutual dependencies between eliminations and assignment motions as illustrated for $\mathcal{PDCE}$. In addition, there are also strong second order effects between the elimination of partially redundant expressions[11] ($\mathcal{PREE}$) and $\mathcal{PRAE}$, which are listed in the following:

$\mathcal{PREE}$-$\mathcal{PRAE}$ Effects In Figure 6.10(a) the assignment to a at node **5** cannot be hoisted out of the loop, since it is blocked by the assignments at node **3** and **4** that cannot be subjected to a successful $\mathcal{PRAE}$. However, using $\mathcal{PREE}$ the expression $a + b$ can be hoisted to node **1** and to (the synthetic node inserted on) the back edge of the loop, which enables $\mathcal{PRAE}$ to hoist the assignment $a := 1$ subsequently as displayed in Figure 6.10(b).

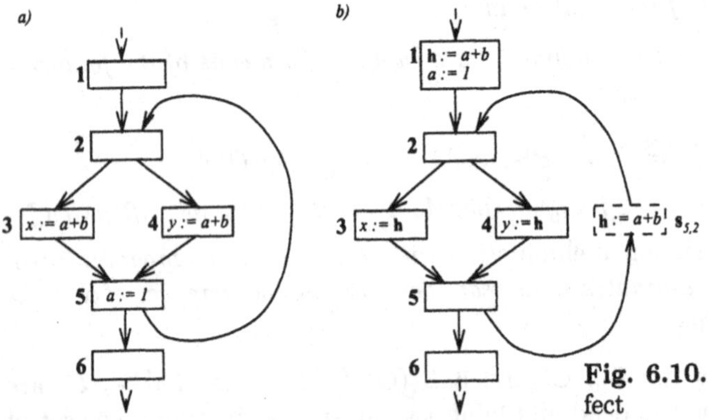

Fig. 6.10. $\mathcal{PREE}$-$\mathcal{PRAE}$ effect

$\mathcal{PRAE}$-$\mathcal{PREE}$ Effects Reversely, $\mathcal{PRAE}$ can also enhance the potential for $\mathcal{PREE}$. To this end we only have to slightly modify Figure 6.10. This leads to Figure 6.11, where first the assignment $a := 1$ at node **2** has to be treated with $\mathcal{PRAE}$ before $\mathcal{PREE}$ can be applied profitably.

In [KRS95] we presented an algorithm for the uniform elimination of partially redundant expressions and assignments ($\mathcal{UPRE}$) that shares the advantages of both $\mathcal{PREE}$ and $\mathcal{PRAE}$, while even enhancing their individual power significantly. Formally, $\mathcal{UPRE}$ stands for any sequence of

- partial redundant expression eliminations ($\mathcal{PREE}$) and
- partial redundant assignment eliminations ($\mathcal{PRAE}$).

To give an impression of the power of $\mathcal{UPRE}$ let us consider the example of Figure 6.12, which is taken from [KRS95].

Figure 6.13 shows the separate results that emanate from an application of pure $\mathcal{PREE}$ and pure $\mathcal{PRAE}$. In particular, both results fail to eliminate the most significant inefficiency in the program of Figure 6.12, the "loop invariant" assignment $x := y + z$ in node **3**. For $\mathcal{PREE}$ this is due to the

[11] $\mathcal{PREE}$ stands as a synonym for expression motion.

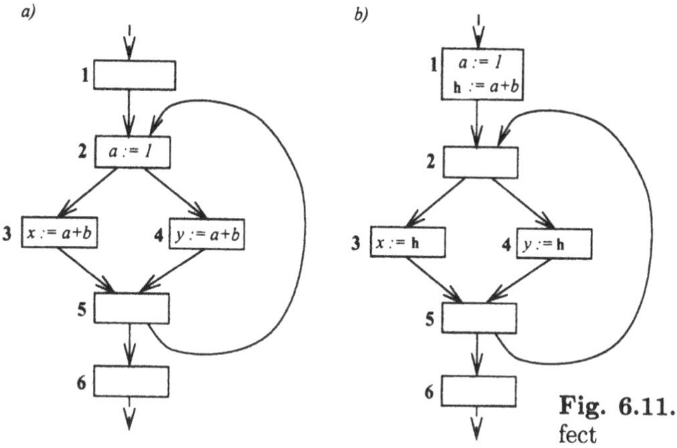

Fig. 6.11. $\mathcal{PRAE}$-$\mathcal{PREE}$ effect

fact that the right-hand side expression $y + z$ is blocked by the assignment to y in node **3** whose elimination is out of the scope of $\mathcal{PREE}$. On the other hand, pure $\mathcal{PRAE}$ does not succeed either, since x is used in the Boolean expression controlling the loop iteration, which cannot be subjected to $\mathcal{PRAE}$.

$\mathcal{UPRE}$ performs the optimisation displayed in Figure 6.14. This optimisation is achieved by the following steps: $\mathcal{PRAE}$ can resolve the redundant assignment $y := c + d$ in node **3**, which is redundant with respect to the corresponding assignment of node **1**. Moreover, $c + d$ can be subjected to $\mathcal{PREE}$, which initialises a temporary $\mathbf{h}_1$ in block **1**. Similarly, $\mathcal{PREE}$ with respect to $x + z$ initialises a temporary $\mathbf{h}_2$ in block **1** and **3**. The original occurrences of $c + d$ in node **1** and **4** are replaced by $\mathbf{h}_1$, and the original occurrence of $x + z$ in node **2** is replaced by $\mathbf{h}_2$. This finally eliminates the blockade of the assignment $x := y + z$ within the loop. Thus, as a second order effect, the assignment $x := y+z$ can now be removed from the loop by hoisting it (together with the corresponding assignment at node **4**) to node **1**.

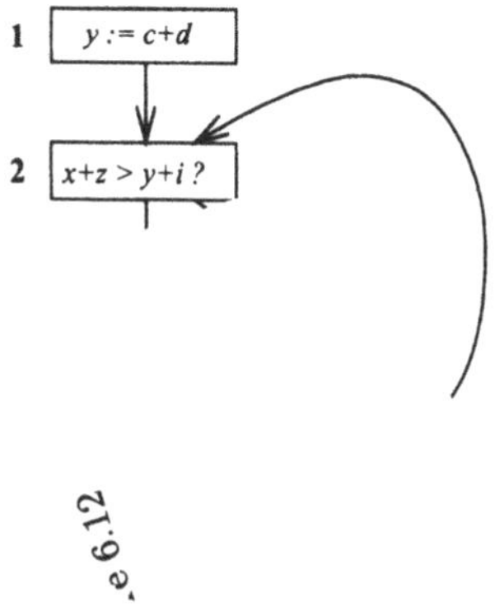

Fig. 6.12. Illustrating the power of $\mathcal{UPRE}$

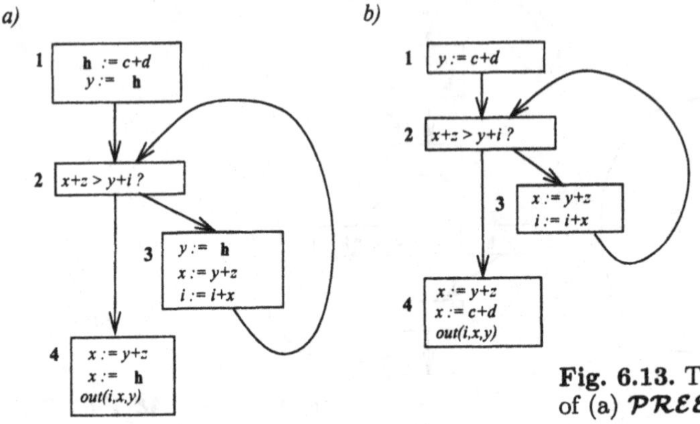

Fig. 6.13. The separate effects of (a) $\mathcal{PREE}$ and (b) $\mathcal{PRAE}$

Note that neither the assignment $i := i+x$ in node **3** nor the computations of $y+i$ and $i+x$ in nodes **2** and **3** are touched, since they cannot be moved profitably.

However, the previous example does not suggest a general way, how $\mathcal{PREE}$ and $\mathcal{PRAE}$ have to be employed in order to take maximal benefit from each other. This problem was solved in [KRS95] where we succeeded in developing an algorithm that, at least for the primary goal of partial redundancy elimination, which is to avoid recomputations of expressions, is solved as well as possible. A key point in this algorithm is the fact that $\mathcal{PREE}$ can completely be simulated by means of $\mathcal{PRAE}$ using a simple preprocess (cf. Lemma 7.4.1). Beside computational optimality, secondary optimisation goals are taken into account which are to minimise the number of (trivial) assignments and to minimise the lifetimes of the temporaries introduced by expression motion. In [KRS95] we showed that these goals cannot be solved optimally, since distinct, incomparable solutions may exits. As a heuristics, a *final flush phase* moves assignments forwards in the direction of control flow as far as possible. However, this solution suffers from two drawbacks: first, like in lazy expression motion interdependencies between distinct life-

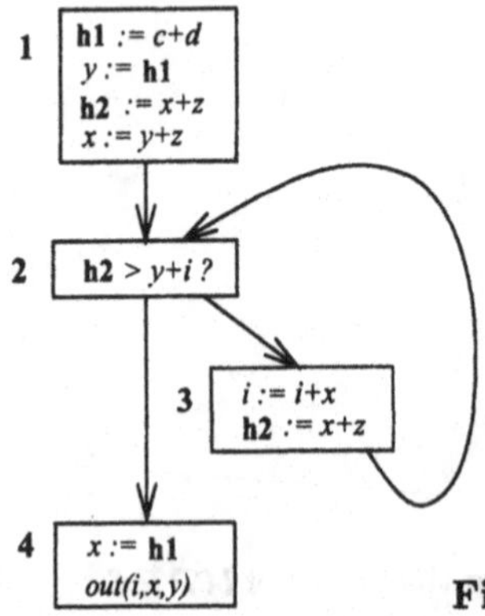

Fig. 6.14. Result of $\mathcal{UPRE}$ with respect to Fig

time ranges are not taken into account. Moreover, lifetimes of temporaries that are already introduced in advance for the purpose of decomposing large expressions are distinguished from the ones introduced by expression motion. To this end, in Chapter 7 we sketch a more ambitious algorithm for $\mathcal{UPRE}$ that uniformly copes with all kinds of temporaries and incorporates trade-offs between lifetime ranges by adapting the techniques of Chapter 4, which finally results in a lifetime optimal solution for $\mathcal{UPRE}$.

7. A Framework for Assignment Motion Based Program Transformations

In this chapter we present a general framework for assignment motion based program transformations that covers all the applications considered in Chapter 6: $\mathcal{PDCE}$, $\mathcal{PFCE}$, $\mathcal{PRAE}$ and $\mathcal{UPRE}$. Within this framework the interleaving of admissible assignment motions and eliminations can be investigated in a general setting. Section 7.1 presents the foundation for this framework. The instances of the framework, motion-elimination couples, combine assignment motions with eliminations. As the presence of second order effects requires to apply the component transformations repeatedly, this process raises the following questions of primary interest:

- Is the process *confluent*, i. e. is the final result independent from the application order? Section 7.2 is devoted to this question.
- What are the additional costs (compared to the elementary transformations) in terms of *computational complexity*? This question is addressed in Section 7.3.

Section 7.4 finally considers $\mathcal{UPRE}$ as a more ambitious application for reasoning within the framework.

7.1 The Setting

7.1.1 Motion-Elimination Couples

The program transformations considered in Chapter 6 share that they are composed of

- assignment motions and
- eliminations

that mutually influence each other. More formally, we define:

Definition 7.1.1 (Motion-Elimination Couple).
A motion-elimination couple *(MEC) is a pair* $(\mathcal{T}_{am}, \mathcal{T}_{el})$*, where*

- $\mathcal{T}_{am}$ *is a set of admissible assignment motions as defined in Definition 6.1.2, i. e.* $\mathcal{T}_{am} = \bigcup_{\alpha \in \mathcal{AP}(G)} \mathcal{AAS}_\alpha$ *or* $\mathcal{T}_{am} = \bigcup_{\alpha \in \mathcal{AP}(G)} \mathcal{AAH}_\alpha$.

– *$\mathcal{T}_{el}$ is a set of elimination transformations of a type as introduced in Chapter 6, i. e.* $\mathcal{T}_{el} \subseteq \bigcup_{\alpha \in \mathcal{AP}(G)} \mathcal{DAE}_\alpha \cup \mathcal{FAE}_\alpha \cup \mathcal{RAE}_\alpha$.

Note that MECs are mainly parameterised by their eliminations $\mathcal{T}_{el}$, since for assignment motions only the direction of movement is indeterminate. The restriction to either sinkings or hoistings ensures that non-trivial assignment motions can be undone by other movements, which would allow non-terminating sequences of assignment motions. Moreover, the usage of equality rather than containment ensures that we can find assignment motions that progress sufficiently fast.

7.1.2 A Note on the Correctness of Motion-Elimination Couples

The elementary transformations of an MEC as they are defined in Chapter 6 are intended not to modify relevant aspects of the program behaviour. However, there are significant differences between them, which the user should be aware of. Transformations introduced so far *preserve total correctness* [DGG+96] of a program, i. e. a terminating execution in the source program has a corresponding terminating execution in the transformed program both coinciding in their visible behaviours. On the other hand, all transformations apart from partial dead code elimination and partial faint code elimination also preserve *partial correctness* [DGG+96]: each terminating execution in the transformed program has a corresponding terminating execution in the original program such that the visible behaviours in terms of their output sequences coincide.[1] $\mathcal{DAE}_\alpha$ or $\mathcal{FAE}_\alpha$ do not preserve partial correctness, as the elimination of a dead or faint assignment like $x := 1/0$ may cause regular termination on a program path that did not terminate in the original program. However, we can easily overcome this defect, since it is obviously caused by the elimination of assignments whose right-hand sides contain partially defined operators. This should particularly be distinguished from the case where partial correctness is violated because a non-terminating loop is made terminating. Fortunately, this can be excluded for dead (faint) code elimination. Essentially, this is due to the fact that branching instructions are classified as immobile statements, which makes it impossible to eliminate any assignment on which such an instruction may depend even indirectly. Therefore, to accomplish the preservation of partial correctness for $\boldsymbol{\mathcal{PDCE}}$ and $\boldsymbol{\mathcal{PFCE}}$, too, we only have to exclude any assignment pattern which contains partially defined operators as a feasible optimisation candidate. Since most of the operators are totally defined on the source level this does not diminish these techniques too much. Finally, static analysis techniques for

[1] Note that neither of these notions implies the other one. The transformation that maps each program to a non-terminating one preserves partial, though not total correctness. The other way round, as explained in the following, $\mathcal{DAE}_\alpha$ is an example for a transformation that preserves total but not partial correctness.

range checking [Har77] could be employed to discover additional cases, where assignments with partially defined operators do no harm, i. e. definitely evaluate to defined values.

7.1.3 Notational Conventions

Since the MEC $(\mathcal{T}_{am}, \mathcal{T}_{el})$ under consideration is always obvious from the context, the following notions are understood relatively to this MEC, which helps to avoid a highly parameterised notation.

Elementary Transformation Steps In accordance to the notation of the elementary transformations introduced in Chapter 6 we use a generic notation for the transformations of the underlying MEC $(\mathcal{T}_{am}, \mathcal{T}_{el})$, which refers to the respective type of assignment motions and eliminations under consideration:

- $G \overset{am}{\longmapsto}_\alpha G'$ is used instead of $G \overset{as}{\longmapsto}_\alpha G'$ or $G \overset{ah}{\longmapsto}_\alpha G'$ according to the type of assignment motions used in $\mathcal{T}_{am}$ and
- $G \overset{el}{\longmapsto}_\alpha G'$ is used instead of $G \overset{dae}{\longmapsto}_\alpha G'$, $G \overset{fae}{\longmapsto}_\alpha G'$ or $G \overset{rae}{\longmapsto}_\alpha G'$ according to the type of eliminations that is responsible for the $\mathcal{T}_{el}$-transition from G to G'.

Moreover, the notion $G \longmapsto G'$ is used as an abbreviation for any of the elementary transformations, i. e.

$$G \longmapsto G' \overset{\text{def}}{\Leftrightarrow} \exists \alpha \in \mathcal{AP}(G).\ G \overset{am}{\longmapsto}_\alpha G' \in \mathcal{T}_{am} \ \vee \ G \overset{el}{\longmapsto}_\alpha G' \in \mathcal{T}_{el}.$$

Source- and Destination-Occurrences Let $\mathtt{AM}_\alpha = G \overset{am}{\longmapsto}_\alpha G' \in \mathcal{T}_{am}$. As already mentioned, Definition 6.1.2 establishes a one-to-one correspondence between the original occurrences on a program path $p \in \mathbf{P}_G[\mathbf{s}, \mathbf{e}]$ and the inserted occurrences on the associated path $p' \equiv p_{\mathtt{AM}_\alpha} \in \mathbf{P}_{G'}[\mathbf{s}, \mathbf{e}]$. Therefore, we can define for $occ_{\alpha,p} \in Occ_{\alpha,p}(G)$ and $occ'_{\alpha,p'} \in Occ_{\alpha,p'}(G')$:

$Src_{\mathtt{AM}_\alpha}(occ'_{\alpha,p'})$: The p-occurrence corresponding to $occ'_{\alpha,p'}$

$Dst_{\mathtt{AM}_\alpha}(occ_{\alpha,p})$: The p'-occurrence corresponding to $occ_{\alpha,p}$

This notion can naturally be generalised to program occurrences. For occurrences $occ_\alpha \in Occ_\alpha(G)$ and $occ'_\alpha \in Occ_\alpha(G')$ we have:

$$Src_{\mathtt{AM}_\alpha}(occ'_\alpha) \overset{\text{def}}{=} \{occ_\alpha \mid occ_{\alpha,p} = Src_{\mathtt{AM}_\alpha}(occ'_{\alpha,p'}),\ occ'_{\alpha,p'} \in Occ_{\alpha,p'}(G')\}$$
$$Dst_{\mathtt{AM}_\alpha}(occ_\alpha) \overset{\text{def}}{=} \{occ'_\alpha \mid occ'_{\alpha,p'} = Dst_{\mathtt{AM}_\alpha}(occ_{\alpha,p}),\ occ_{\alpha,p} \in Occ_{\alpha,p}(G)\}$$

Finally, for sets of α-occurrences M_α we define:

$$Src_{\mathtt{AM}_\alpha}(M_\alpha) \overset{\text{def}}{=} \bigcup_{occ_\alpha \in M_\alpha} Src_{\mathtt{AM}_\alpha}(occ_\alpha)$$

$$Dst_{\mathtt{AM}_\alpha}(M_\alpha) \stackrel{\text{def}}{=} \bigcup_{occ_\alpha \in M_\alpha} Dst_{\mathtt{AM}_\alpha}(occ_\alpha)$$

For convenience, we simply identify occ_α with $Dst_{\mathtt{AM}_\alpha}(occ_\alpha)$, if occ_α is not moved at all. Moreover, it is easy to extend the notions to elimination transformations in $\mathcal{T}_{el}$ yielding definitions for $Dst_{\mathtt{EL}_\alpha}(occ_\alpha)$ and $Src_{\mathtt{EL}_\alpha}(occ_\alpha)$, respectively. The only difference is that $Dst_{\mathtt{EL}_\alpha}(occ_\alpha)$ can be empty. Again post-elimination occurrences are identified with their corresponding original occurrence. Finally, the notions defined above can also be extended to sequences of eliminations and assignment motions. Therefore, for transformations $\mathtt{TR}_i \equiv G_{i-1} \longmapsto G_i \in \mathcal{T}_{am} \cup \mathcal{T}_{el},\ i=(1,\dots,k)$ we use $\mathtt{TR}_1;\dots;\mathtt{TR}_k(G)$ as a shorthand for $\mathtt{TR}_k(\dots(\mathtt{TR}_1(G_0))\dots)$. On the other hand, sequences of transformations are sometimes implicitly specified by using a notion $\mathtt{TR}_1;\dots;\mathtt{TR}_k$, which stands for a program transformation from G_0 to G_k being composed out of appropriate elementary transformations. In the light of this convention we define:

$$Src_{\mathtt{TR}_1;\dots;\mathtt{TR}_k}(occ_\alpha) \stackrel{\text{def}}{=} Src_{\mathtt{TR}_1}(\dots(Src_{\mathtt{TR}_k}(occ_\alpha))\dots)$$

and

$$Dst_{\mathtt{TR}_1;\dots;\mathtt{TR}_k}(occ_\alpha) \stackrel{\text{def}}{=} Dst_{\mathtt{TR}_k}(\dots(Dst_{\mathtt{TR}_1}(occ_\alpha))\dots)$$

As a special case of the above notion we define the *origins* of an occurrence occ_α, for which the sequence of program transformations $\mathtt{TR}_1;\dots;\mathtt{TR}_k(G)$ applied to the initial program G is understood.

$$Orig(occ_\alpha) \stackrel{\text{def}}{=} Src_{\mathtt{TR}_1;\dots;\mathtt{TR}_k}(occ_\alpha)$$

Eliminability

Finally, we introduce a predicate *eliminable*$(G,\ occ_\alpha)$ that indicates, if an occurrence occ_α of an assignment pattern α is eliminable in G:

$$eliminable(G,\ occ_\alpha) \stackrel{\text{def}}{\Leftrightarrow} \exists\, \mathtt{EL}_\alpha \equiv G \stackrel{el}{\longmapsto}_\alpha G' \in \mathcal{T}_{el}.\ Dst_{\mathtt{EL}_\alpha}(occ_\alpha) = \emptyset$$

7.1.4 Uniform Motion-Elimination Couples

As mentioned, MECs are mainly parameterised by their eliminations. In addition, reasonable MECs like the ones presented in Chapter 6 have in common that the eliminations involved are uniformly characterised by the set of eliminable occurrences, i. e. every subset of eliminable occurrences can be eliminated on its own. More formally, we define:

Definition 7.1.2 (Uniform Motion-Elimination Couples). *An MEC* $(\mathcal{T}_{am}, \mathcal{T}_{el})$ *is a* uniform motion-elimination couple *(UMEC), if and only if for any* $\alpha \in \mathcal{AP}(G)$ *and* $M \subseteq \{occ_\alpha \in Occ_\alpha(G) \mid eliminable(G,\ occ_\alpha)\}$

$$\exists\, \mathtt{TR}_M \in \mathcal{T}_{el}\ \forall\, occ_\alpha \in Occ_\alpha(G).\ (Dst_{\mathtt{TR}_M}(occ_\alpha) = \emptyset) \Leftrightarrow occ_\alpha \in M$$

7.2 Confluence of Uniform Motion-Elimination Couples

In this section we investigate under which circumstances different exhaustive iteration sequences with respect to a given UMEC lead to a unique result. This addresses the question of the *confluence* of the $\longmapsto$-relation. Though we usually cannot assure true stabilisation, since local reorderings of independent assignments may lead to infinite sequences of assignment motions, we always have stabilisation up to local reorderings within basic blocks. Fortunately, we can abstract from these local reorderings, which allows us to prove confluence via the weaker property of local confluence. As the central result we provide a simple criterion for local confluence, *consistency* of a UMEC.

7.2.1 The General Case

In general UMECs are not confluent as the following example illustrates. To this end we consider a UMEC that interleaves

- admissible assignment sinkings with
- the elimination of locally redundant assignments.

The elimination of locally redundant assignments is defined as follows: an occurrence occ_α of an assignment α is locally redundant, if it is redundant in the sense of Definition 6.4.1, where in addition the program points p_i occurring in this definition must all belong to the same basic block as $\dot{n}$.

Intuitively, the reason for non-confluence is that the application of eliminations may reduce opportunities for assignment motion and vice versa. This is illustrated in Figure 7.1 where two different maximal results are possible that cannot be subjected to any further transformation.

It should be particularly noted that the resulting programs G_2 and G_3 in this example are even incomparable in terms of the number of assignments being executed on program paths. For instance, in G_2 there are two occurrences of the assignment $x := a + b$ on the path $\langle \mathbf{1}, \mathbf{3}, \mathbf{5} \rangle$ as against only one in G_3. For the path $\langle \mathbf{2}, \mathbf{3}, \mathbf{4} \rangle$, however, the situation is exactly contrary.

7.2.2 Consistent Motion-Elimination Couples

In this section we impose a condition on the interference of motion and elimination transformations that is sufficient to establish local confluence. This condition, which we will call *consistency*, essentially means that both, eliminations and assignment motions, preserve the potential for eliminations:

Definition 7.2.1 (Consistent UMECs). *A UMEC* $(\mathcal{T}_{am}, \mathcal{T}_{el})$ *is* consistent, *or for short a CUMEC, if for any* $\alpha, \beta \in \mathcal{AP}(G)$ *(not necessarily different) the following conditions are satisfied:*

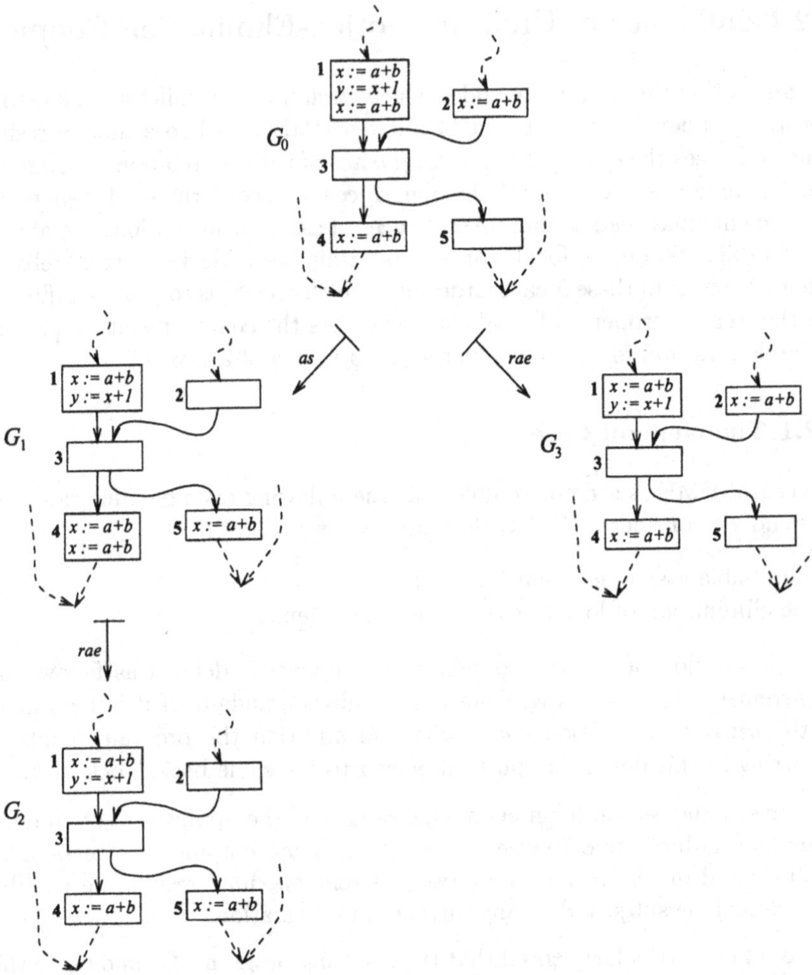

Fig. 7.1. Non-confluence of the combination of assignment sinkings and locally redundant assignment eliminations

1. *Eliminations preserve the potential for other eliminations, i. e. for any elimination* $\mathrm{EL}_\beta \equiv G \overset{el}{\longmapsto}_\beta G' \in \mathcal{T}_{el}$ *and every occurrence* $occ_\alpha \in Occ_\alpha(G)$ *we have:*

$$eliminable(G,\, occ_\alpha) \Rightarrow \forall\, occ'_\alpha \in Dst_{\mathrm{EL}_\beta}(occ_\alpha).\ eliminable(\underbrace{\mathrm{EL}_\beta(G)}_{G'},\, occ'_\alpha)$$

2. *Assignment motions preserve the potential for eliminations, i. e. for any assignment motion* $AM_\beta \equiv G \overset{am}{\longmapsto}_\beta G' \in \mathcal{T}_{am}$ *and occurrence* $occ_\alpha \in Occ_\alpha(G)$ *we have*[2]*:*

[2] Note that in contrast to point (1) this assumption is an equivalence. Implicitly, this means that non-eliminability is preserved at least partially.

$$eliminable(G,\ occ_\alpha) \Leftrightarrow \forall\ occ'_\alpha \in Dst_{\mathtt{AM}_\beta}(occ_\alpha).\ eliminable(\underbrace{\mathtt{AM}_\beta(G)}_{G'},\ occ'_\alpha)$$

If only Condition 1 of Definition 7.2.1 is fulfilled the UMEC is called *weakly consistent.*

Before we are going to present the main result of this section, namely that consistency implies local confluence, it should be noted that consistency does not force the stronger type of modular confluence as it is illustrated by means of $\mathcal{PDCE}$ in Figure 7.2. Besides that, this example provides a deeper insight for the technically difficult proof of Case 6 in the forthcoming Theorem 7.2.1. The point of this example is that the dead assignment at node **2** can be subjected to both a dead assignment elimination as well as to an assignment sinking. Whereas in the latter case the moved assignment remains dead and can be eliminated afterwards, in the former case, however, this still requires to apply both an assignment sinking and a dead assignment elimination. The central result then is:[3]

Theorem 7.2.1 (Consistency Theorem). *A CUMEC* $(\mathcal{T}_{am}, \mathcal{T}_{el})$ *is locally confluent, i. e. whenever two transformations* $\mathtt{TR}_1, \mathtt{TR}_2 \in \mathcal{T}_{am} \cup \mathcal{T}_{el}$ *are applicable to a program* $G_0 \in \mathfrak{FG}$*, then there exists a program* G_3 *such that the diagram can be completed as shown below:*[4]

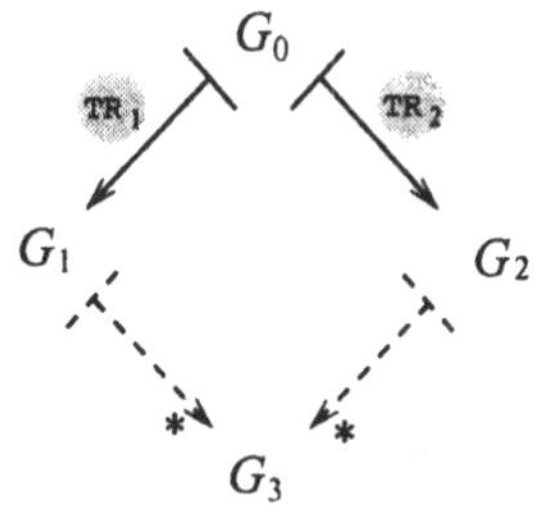

Proof. Without loss of generality we can assume that $\mathcal{T}_{am}$ refers to assignment sinkings. The proof proceeds by an exhaustive case analysis investigating all possible choices for $\mathtt{TR}_1$ and $\mathtt{TR}_2$.

Case 1: $\mathtt{TR}_1 \equiv G_0 \overset{el}{\longmapsto}_\alpha G_1$ and $\mathtt{TR}_2 \equiv G_0 \overset{el}{\longmapsto}_\alpha G_2$.
In this case condition (1) of Definition 7.2.1 ensures that the elimination potential for the α-eliminations of $\mathtt{TR}_1$ is preserved by $\mathtt{TR}_2$ and vice versa.

---

[3] In [GKL+96] an alternative proof of the confluence of $\mathcal{PDCE}$ can be found, which is based on the concept of *delay-monotonicity.*

[4] Here and in following illustrations the "arrows" are labelled by their associated transformation names, which are emphasised by a grey circle.

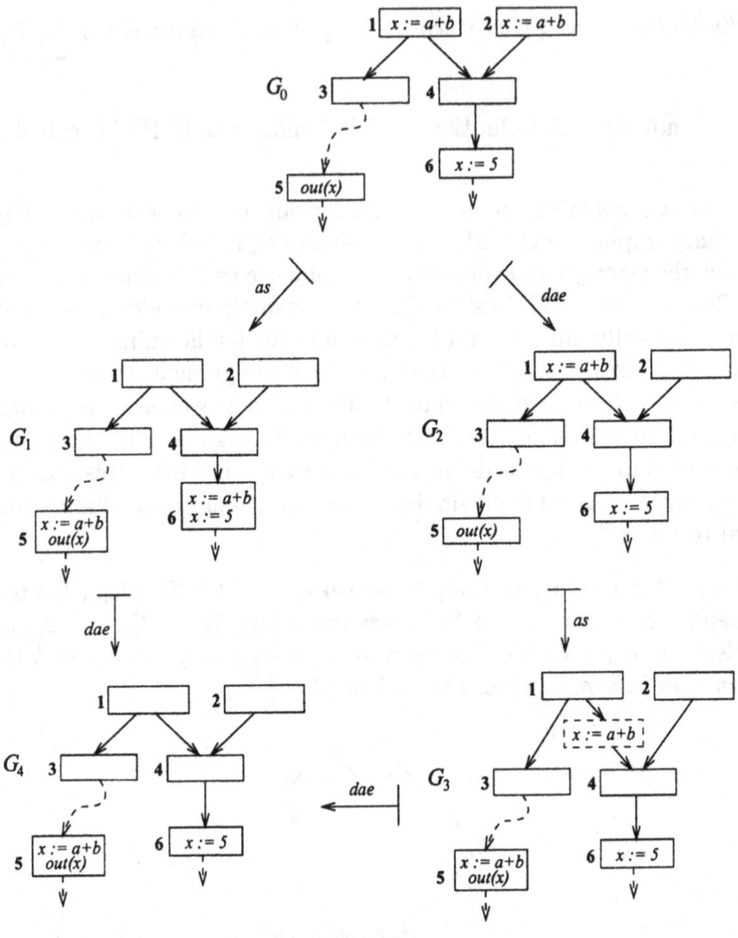

Fig. 7.2. Non-modular confluence of PDCE

Since the MEC is assumed to be uniform, there are elimination transformations TR_3 and TR_4 that eliminate exactly the remaining α-occurrences that are also eliminated by TR_2 and TR_1, respectively. In fact, there is even a "direct" elimination transformation from G_0 to G_3.

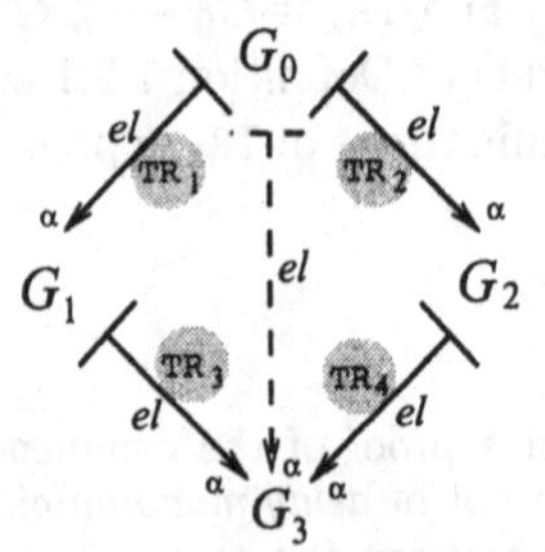

Case 2: $\text{TR}_1 \equiv G_0 \overset{am}{\longmapsto}_{\alpha} G_1$ and $\text{TR}_2 \equiv G_0 \overset{am}{\longmapsto}_{\alpha} G_2$.
An assignment motion TR_5 that dominates both TR_1 and TR_2 can be constructed in the following way: $\text{TR}_5(G_0)$ results from G_0 by removing every original occurrence of α and inserting new occurrences at program points where justification with respect to the original occurrences would get violated by further movement, i. e.

$$\text{TR}_5\text{-}Insert^{\alpha}_{\dot{n}} \;\Leftrightarrow\; OrigJust^{\alpha}_{\dot{n}} \wedge (Blocked^{\alpha}_{\dot{n}} \vee \exists\, \dot{m} \in succ(\dot{n}).\ \neg OrigJust^{\alpha}_{\dot{m}}),$$

where $OrigJust^{\alpha}_{\dot{n}}$ is a slight modulation of the justification predicate of Definition 6.1.2. As opposed to justification this predicate is not parameterised by an assignment sinking, but rather takes all original occurrences into account.

$$OrigJust^{\alpha}_{\dot{n}} \overset{\text{def}}{\Leftrightarrow}$$
$$\forall\, p \in \mathbf{P}[\dot{\mathbf{s}}, \dot{n}]\ \exists\, 1 \leqslant i < |p|.\ AssOcc^{\alpha}_{p_i} \ \wedge\ \forall\, i < j < |p|.\ \neg Blocked^{\alpha}_{p_j}$$

It can easily be checked that TR_5 defines an admissible assignment sinking. Moreover, we can establish assignment sinkings TR_3 and TR_4 such that the diagram below commutes:

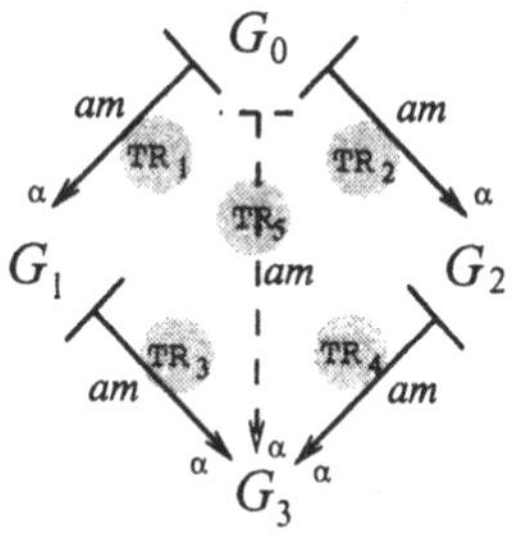

Case 3: $\text{TR}_1 \equiv G_0 \overset{el}{\longmapsto}_{\alpha} G_1$ and $\text{TR}_2 \equiv G_0 \overset{el}{\longmapsto}_{\beta} G_2$, $\alpha \neq \beta$.
In this case condition (1) of Definition 7.2.1 ensures that the elimination potential for β-eliminations is preserved by TR_1, while the potential for α-eliminations is preserved by TR_2. Exploiting uniformity we have straightforward elimination transformations $\text{TR}_3 \equiv G_1 \overset{el}{\longmapsto}_{\beta} G_3$ and $\text{TR}_4 \equiv G_2 \overset{el}{\longmapsto}_{\alpha} G_3$ completing the diagram in a modular way:

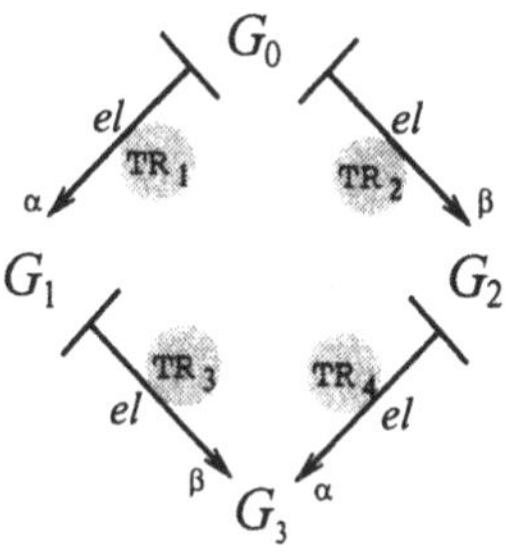

Case 4: $\text{TR}_1 \equiv G_0 \overset{am}{\longmapsto}_\alpha G_1$ and $\text{TR}_2 \equiv G_0 \overset{am}{\longmapsto}_\beta G_2$, $\alpha \neq \beta$.
If α and β are non-blocking, modular confluence follows trivially. Otherwise, the definition of admissible assignment motions (cf. Definition 6.1.2) ensures that no instances of β are inserted into the region of TR_1-justified program points. Hence TR_1 and TR_2 can straightforwardly be sequentialised in an arbitrary order.

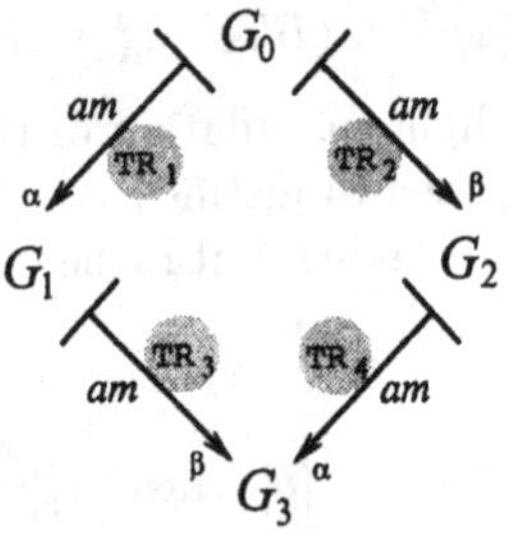

Case 5: $\text{TR}_1 \equiv G_0 \overset{am}{\longmapsto}_\alpha G_1$ and $\text{TR}_2 \equiv G_0 \overset{el}{\longmapsto}_\beta G_2$, $\alpha \neq \beta$.
Due to assumption (2) in Definition 7.2.1 assignment motion TR_1 preserves the opportunities for β-eliminations. Hence we can choose $\text{TR}_3 \equiv G_1 \overset{el}{\longmapsto}_\beta G_3$ as the transformation that eliminates exactly the G_1-occurrences in $Dst_{\text{TR}_1}(occ_\beta)$, where the corresponding G_0-occurrences occ_β are eliminated by TR_2. The argument for the construction of $\text{TR}_4 \equiv G_2 \overset{am}{\longmapsto}_\alpha G_3$ is similar to the one in Case 4. Obviously, β-eliminations do no add blockades within the range of TR_1-justified program points.

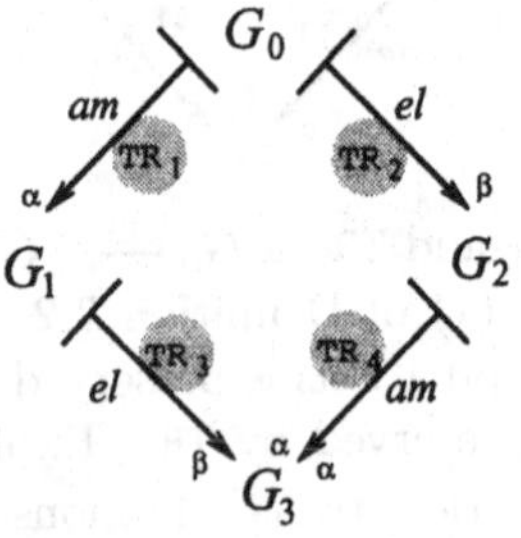

Case 6: $\text{TR}_1 \equiv G_0 \overset{am}{\longmapsto}_\alpha G_1$ and $\text{TR}_2 \equiv G_0 \overset{el}{\longmapsto}_\alpha G_2$. In this case the situation gets more intricate. Here we are going to show that there are a program G_2' and transformations

$$\text{TR}_3 \equiv G_1 \overset{el}{\longmapsto}_\alpha G_3$$
$$\text{TR}_4 \equiv G_2 \overset{am}{\longmapsto}_\alpha G_2'$$
$$\text{TR}_5 \equiv G_2' \overset{el}{\longmapsto}_\alpha G_3$$

such that the diagram as displayed below commutes (for a concrete example reconsider Figure 7.2):

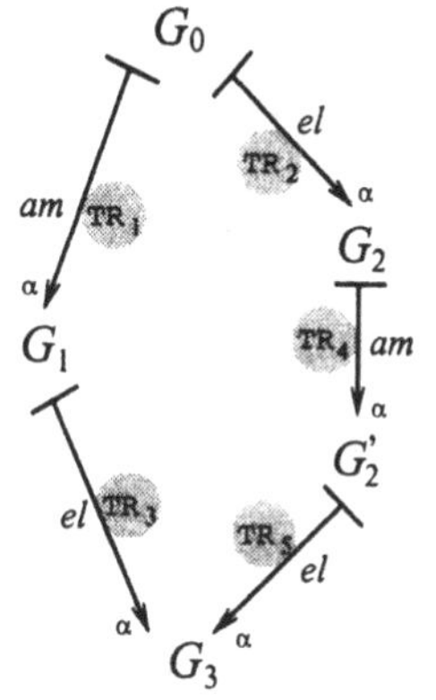

In the following we are going to elaborate the construction of these transformations in detail. Two sets of α-occurrences play a central role:

- The set of G_0-occurrences of α that are not eliminated by TR_2

$$S \stackrel{\text{def}}{=} \{occ_\alpha \in Occ_\alpha(G_0) \mid Dst_{TR_2}(occ_\alpha) \neq \emptyset\}$$

- The set of G_1-occurrences of α whose source occurrences do not participate in TR_2.

$$T \stackrel{\text{def}}{=} \{occ_\alpha \in Occ_\alpha(G_1) \mid Src_{TR_1}(occ_\alpha) \subseteq S\}$$

As a first result we have

$$\forall\, occ_\alpha \in Occ_\alpha(G_0).\ occ_\alpha \notin S \Rightarrow eliminable(G_0,\, occ_\alpha) \qquad (7.1)$$

$$\forall\, occ_\alpha \in Occ_\alpha(G_1).\ occ_\alpha \notin T \Rightarrow eliminable(G_1,\, occ_\alpha) \qquad (7.2)$$

Implication (7.1) is trivial. To show also implication (7.2), consider a G_1-occurrence $occ_\alpha \notin T$. According to the construction of T there exists at least one $occ'_\alpha \in Src_{TR_1}(occ_\alpha)$ such that $occ'_\alpha \notin S$. Due to (7.1) this implies $eliminable(G_0,\, occ'_\alpha)$. Using the $\Rightarrow$-direction of assumption (2) in Definition 7.2.1 together with the fact that $occ_\alpha \in Dst_{TR_1}(occ'_\alpha)$ finally delivers $eliminable(G_1,\, occ_\alpha)$.

Then TR_3, TR_4 and TR_5 are constructed as follows:

Construction of TR_3: Elimination transformation TR_3 is easy to describe: it eliminates all occurrences of α that are not elements of T. This construction is sound due to (7.2) and the assumption of uniformity.

Construction of TR_4: This is the crucial point in the construction of this case. As a first step let us identify S and T with their corresponding program points in G_2. Then I shall denote the set of program points in between S and T:

$$\dot{n} \in I \overset{\text{def}}{\Leftrightarrow} \exists p \in \mathbf{P}.\, p_1 \in S \wedge p_{|p|} \in T \wedge \exists 1 \leqslant i < |p|.\, p_i = \dot{n}$$

Informatively, I is the set of intermediate program points along which a relevant TR_1-movement is propagated, i. e. a movement that is not just the result of a propagated elimination. Now TR_4 is determined through the transformation that
- removes all S-associated occurrences of G_2
- inserts occurrences at program points $\dot{n}$ satisfying

$$\dot{n} \in T \quad \text{or} \tag{7.3a}$$

$$\dot{n} \notin I \ \wedge\ \exists \dot{m} \in \mathit{pred}(\dot{n}).\ \dot{m} \in I \tag{7.3b}$$

Hence TR_4 coincides with TR_1 for the T-associated insertions, while introducing new insertions at program points leaving I without reaching T. This situation is roughly sketched in Figure 7.3(a).

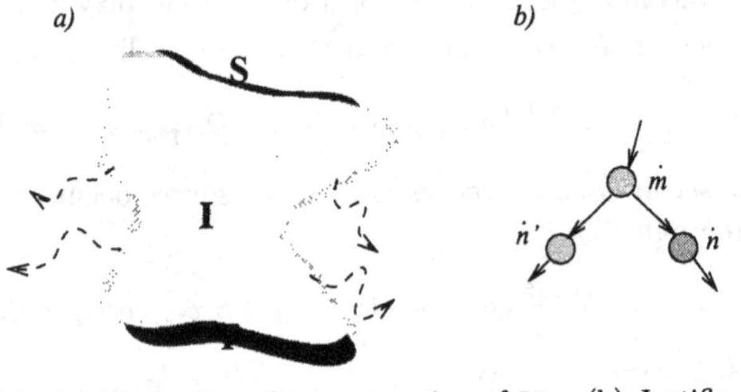

Fig. 7.3. (a) Illustrating the construction of TR_4 (b) Justification of insertions at the border of I

Next, we have to convince ourselves that TR_4 defines indeed an admissible assignment motion. First, the removed occurrences of α are substituted, since every path leading from a site with a removed S-associated occurrence eventually passes an insertion site of TR_4.
Thus it is only left to show that the inserted occurrences are justified as well. For the T-stipulated insertions justification simply carries over from the admissibility of TR_1.[5] To show that the insertions at the border of I are justified as well it is sufficient to prove that Condition (7.3b) already implies $\forall \dot{m} \in \mathit{pred}(\dot{n}).\ \dot{m} \in I$, which grants that $\dot{n}$ can only be entered from the inside of I. To this end, let us assume a program point $\dot{n}$ that meets the requirement of Condition (7.3b). By definition $\dot{n}$ has a predecessor $\dot{m}$ that is element of I. By the construction of I this implies that $\dot{m}$ has another successor $\dot{n}'$

[5] Note that by construction the insertions at the border of I do not introduce blockades for the T-based insertions.

that is element of $I \cup T$. This, however, excludes that $\dot{m}$ has other predecessors besides $\dot{n}$, since this would imply that the edge $(\dot{m}, \dot{n})$ would be a critical one (see Figure 7.3(b) for illustration).

Construction of TR_5: Like TR_3 the transformation TR_5 is simply determined to eliminate all occurrences of α not being contained in T.[6] To prove that this definition is sound we have to show that any occurrence not in T can be eliminated in G_2'. Due to the assumption of uniformity this means that we are left to prove that

$$\forall occ_\alpha \in Occ_\alpha(G_2').\ occ_\alpha \notin T \ \Rightarrow\ eliminable(G_2', occ_\alpha) \qquad (7.4)$$

To this end, we introduce an auxiliary program G_4 which results from G_2' by reinserting the occurrences that have been eliminated by means of TR_2. In fact, we can establish some relations between G_4 and the programs as constructed before, which are shown below.

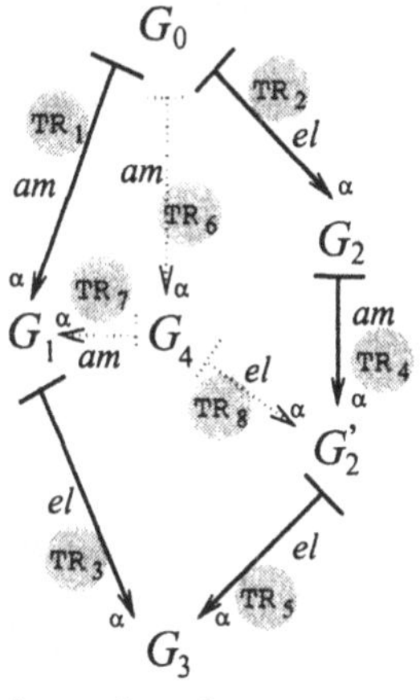

We now have to take a close look at these transformations in order to justify that they are actually well-defined:

- $\mathrm{TR}_6 \equiv G_0 \overset{am}{\longmapsto}_\alpha G_4$: the insertions and removals of TR_6 are chosen exactly as in the construction of TR_4, which is sound as this transformation solely depends on source occurrences of S.
- $\mathrm{TR}_7 \equiv G_4 \overset{am}{\longmapsto}_\alpha G_1$: G_1 coincides with G_4 for the insertions belonging to T. Moreover, no admissible assignment motion with argument program G_0 and T-associated insertions can also have insertions within the range of I as introduced in the construction of TR_4. Therefore, those insertions in G_1 that do not belong to T are justified with respect to the G_4-occurrences that do not belong to T.
- $\mathrm{TR}_8 \equiv G_4 \overset{el}{\longmapsto}_\alpha G_2'$: this transformation eliminates all occurrences being reinserted into the program of G_2'. Due to uniformity it is

[6] We identify the G_1-occurrences of T with their counterparts in G_2'.

enough to show that any reinserted occurrence $occ_\alpha \in Occ_\alpha(G_4)$ is eliminable. By construction, occ_α is also a G_0-occurrence satisfying $eliminable(G_0, occ_\alpha)$. Then consistency and the admissibility of TR_6 yield that also $eliminable(G_4, occ_\alpha)$ must hold.

For the proof of Property (7.4) let us assume an occurrence $occ_\alpha \in Occ_\alpha(G'_2) \setminus T$. Since occ_α is also a G_4-occurrence of α, the fact that occ_α is an occurrence outside of I delivers:

$$Dst_{\mathrm{TR}_7}(occ_\alpha) \cap T = \emptyset \tag{7.5}$$

Then the proof can be completed as follows:

$$\begin{array}{rll} \text{[Property (7.5)]} & & \forall\, occ'_\alpha \in Dst_{\mathrm{TR}_7}(occ_\alpha).\ occ'_\alpha \notin T \\ \text{[Property (7.2]} & \Rightarrow & \forall\, occ'_\alpha \in Dst_{\mathrm{TR}_7}(occ_\alpha).\ eliminable(G_1,\, occ'_\alpha) \\ \text{[Def. 7.2.1(2)]} & \Rightarrow & eliminable(G_4,\, occ_\alpha) \\ \text{[Def. 7.2.1(1)]} & \Rightarrow & eliminable(G'_2,\, occ_\alpha) \end{array}$$

Having defined the transformations it is now easy to see that both sequences

1. $\mathrm{TR}_1; \mathrm{TR}_3$ and
2. $\mathrm{TR}_2; \mathrm{TR}_4; \mathrm{TR}_5$

result in the common program G_3, which evolves from G_0 by removing all original occurrences, while inserting new occurrences corresponding to T. □

7.2.3 Confluence of Consistent Motion-Elimination Couples

So far we established local confluence for CUMECs. According to Newman's Theorem, however, local confluence implies confluence only for terminating relations [New42]. Unfortunately, assignment motions are only terminating up to local reorderings of independent, i. e. non-blocking, assignments inside of basic blocks. Nonetheless, in this section we demonstrate that for our application local confluence is sufficient, since the reasoning on confluence can be transfered to equivalence classes of programs abstracting from local reorderings. To this end we introduce the following equivalence relation on the occurrences of assignment patterns, which reflects the similarity of programs up to local rearrangements.

Definition 7.2.2 (Equivalent Programs). *For an MEC $(\mathcal{T}_{am}, \mathcal{T}_{el})$ the equivalence of programs $\doteq \subseteq \mathfrak{FG} \times \mathfrak{FG}$ is defined by:*

$$G \doteq G' \overset{\text{def}}{\Leftrightarrow} G \longmapsto^* G' \wedge G' \longmapsto^* G$$

Since by definition neither eliminations nor global assignment motions are reversible, equivalent programs are particularly easy to characterise:

Lemma 7.2.1 (First $\stackrel{\circ}{=}$-Lemma). *Let $(\mathcal{T}_{am}, \mathcal{T}_{el})$ be an MEC and $G, G' \in \mathfrak{FG}$ such that $G \stackrel{\circ}{=} G'$. Then G and G' only differ in the local ordering of occurrences of (non-blocking) assignment patterns within basic blocks.*

Using this property we can easily see that elementary transformations are compatible with $\stackrel{\circ}{=}$ unless the potential of eliminations is affected by local reorderings. Hence:

Lemma 7.2.2 (Second $\stackrel{\circ}{=}$-Lemma). *Let $(\mathcal{T}_{am}, \mathcal{T}_{el})$ be a weakly consistent UMEC and G, G', $G'' \in \mathfrak{FG}$. Then*

$$G \stackrel{\circ}{=} G' \ \wedge \ G \longmapsto G'' \ \Rightarrow \ \exists\, G''' \in \mathfrak{FG}.\ G' \longmapsto G''' \ \wedge \ G'' \stackrel{\circ}{=} G'''$$

As a consequence of Lemma 7.2.2 we may restrict our reasoning on $\longmapsto$ to equivalence classes of programs, since the relation induced by $\longmapsto$ does not depend on the particular choice of a representative. Denoting the equivalence class of G with respect to $\stackrel{\circ}{=}$ by $[G]_{\stackrel{\circ}{=}}$ we define:

Definition 7.2.3 ($\circ\!\!\longrightarrow$). *Let $(\mathcal{T}_{am}, \mathcal{T}_{el})$ be an MEC. The relation $\circ\!\!\longrightarrow \ \subseteq \mathfrak{FG}/\!\stackrel{\circ}{=} \times \ \mathfrak{FG}/\!\stackrel{\circ}{=}$ is defined by:*

$$[G]_{\stackrel{\circ}{=}} \circ\!\!\longrightarrow [G']_{\stackrel{\circ}{=}} \ \stackrel{\text{def}}{\Leftrightarrow} \ G \longmapsto G' \ \wedge \ G \stackrel{\circ}{\neq} G'.$$

Note that the term $G \stackrel{\circ}{\neq} G'$ forces irreflexivity of $\circ\!\!\longrightarrow$, which is important for termination. Then Lemma 7.2.2 provides the following correspondence between $\longmapsto$ and $\circ\!\!\longrightarrow$:

Lemma 7.2.3 ($\circ\!\!\longrightarrow$-Lemma). *For a weakly consistent UMEC $(\mathcal{T}_{am}, \mathcal{T}_{el})$ we have*

$$\forall\, G, G' \in \mathfrak{FG}.\ G \longmapsto^{*} G' \ \Leftrightarrow \ [G]_{\stackrel{\circ}{=}} \circ\!\!\longrightarrow^{*} [G']_{\stackrel{\circ}{=}}$$

An immediate consequence of this lemma is:

Corollary 7.2.1. *Let $(\mathcal{T}_{am}, \mathcal{T}_{el})$ be a weakly consistent UMEC. Then*

$$\longmapsto \text{ locally confluent } \Rightarrow \ \circ\!\!\longrightarrow \text{ locally confluent}$$

Combining the previous results and using the obvious termination of $\circ\!\!\longrightarrow$ we finally obtain as the main result:

Theorem 7.2.2 (Confluence of CUMECs).
For a given CUMEC $(\mathcal{T}_{am}, \mathcal{T}_{el})$ the relation $\longmapsto$ is confluent.

Proof. Let us assume a situation as sketched in Figure 7.4(a), where programs G_1 and G_2 result from G_0 by the application of an arbitrary number of $\longmapsto$-steps. Then we have to show that there is a program G_3 which completes the diagram as displayed in Figure 7.4(a).

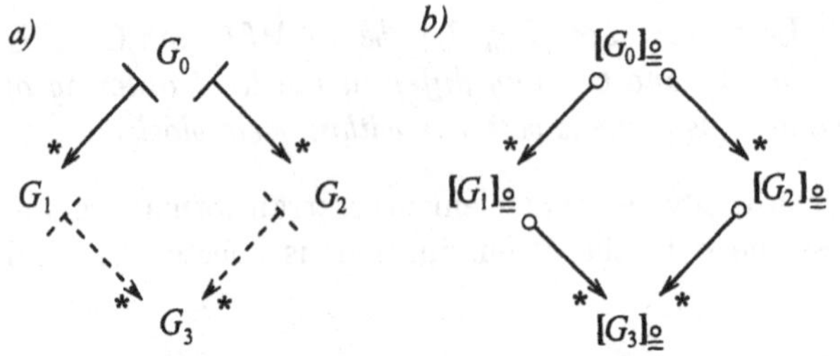

Fig. 7.4. Illustrating confluence

Due to Theorem 7.2.1 consistency implies local confluence of $\longmapsto$. According to Corollary 7.2.1 this also establishes local confluence of the corresponding relation $\circ\!\!\longrightarrow$. Since $\circ\!\!\longrightarrow$ is terminating, $\circ\!\!\longrightarrow$ is also confluent according to Newman's Theorem [New42]. This can be used in order to complete the diagram of Figure 7.4(a) along the following lines. Due to Lemma 7.2.3 the initial situation[7] of Figure 7.4(a) carries over to a corresponding initial situation in Figure 7.4(b), where $[G_0]_{\doteq} \circ\!\!\longrightarrow [G_1]_{\doteq}$ and $[G_0]_{\doteq} \circ\!\!\longrightarrow [G_2]_{\doteq}$ hold. Using the confluence of $\circ\!\!\longrightarrow$ there is a class $[G_3]_{\doteq} \in \mathfrak{FG}/_{\doteq}$ such that the diagram of Figure 7.4(b) commutes. Applying Lemma 7.2.3 once more yields also completion of the diagram in Figure 7.4(a). □

The Universe of an MEC The latter theorem particularly gives rise to a characterisation of maximal programs in a universe that can be reached from an initial program. Therefore, we define:

Definition 7.2.4 (G-Universe of an MEC). *The G-Universe of an MEC $\mathcal{M}$ is given by*

$$\mathfrak{U}_{\mathcal{M}}(G) \stackrel{\text{def}}{=} \{G' \in \mathfrak{FG} \mid G \longmapsto^* G'\}$$

Using Theorem 7.2.2 it is easy to see that maximal elements of the universe are unique up to local reorderings:

Corollary 7.2.2. *Let $(\mathcal{T}_{am}, \mathcal{T}_{el})$ be a CUMEC. Then all programs being maximal up to local reorderings in $\mathfrak{U}_{\mathcal{M}}(G)$, i. e. programs G' such that*

$$\forall G'' \in \mathfrak{FG}.\ G' \longmapsto G'' \ \Rightarrow\ G' \doteq G'',$$

are $\doteq$-equivalent.

Obviously, for a given MEC $\mathcal{M}$ the relation $\longmapsto^*$ is a preorder on $\mathfrak{U}_{\mathcal{M}}(G)$ whose kernel is given by $\doteq$. In addition, we also have preorders to measure the quality of programs within $\mathfrak{U}_{\mathcal{M}}(G)$. In accordance with the Definition of $\precsim^{\varphi}_{exp}$ in Section 3.2.1 and the Definition of $\precsim^{\Phi}_{exp}$ in Section 4.2.2 we introduce a "computationally better" preorder which, for $G', G'' \in \mathfrak{U}_{\mathcal{M}}(G)$, is defined by:[8]

---

[7] That is the non-dashed part.

[8] For $G' \in \mathfrak{U}_{\mathcal{M}}(G)$ we denote the path in G' that corresponds to $p \in \mathbf{P}_G[\mathbf{s}, \mathbf{e}]$ by $p_{G'}$.

- $G' \precsim_{exp} G''$, if and only if for any $p \in \mathbf{P}_G[\mathbf{s}, \mathbf{e}]$ the number of computations occurring on $p_{G''}$ is equal or less than the number of computations on $p_{G'}$.[9]

Analogously, also an "assignment-better" preorder can be defined:

- $G' \precsim_{ass} G''$, if and only if for any $p \in \mathbf{P}_G[\mathbf{s}, \mathbf{e}]$ the number of assignments occurring on $p_{G''}$ is equal or less than the number of assignments on $p_{G''}$.[10]

Finally, we would like to point out a quite obvious result that applies to preorders that harmonise with $\longmapsto$.[11]

Lemma 7.2.4 (Optimality Lemma). *Let $\mathcal{M}$ be an MEC and $\precsim \subseteq \mathfrak{FG} \times \mathfrak{FG}$ a preorder such that $\longmapsto \subseteq \precsim$. Then, if G' is $\longmapsto^*$-optimal in $\mathfrak{U}_{\mathcal{M}}(G)$, this also implies that G' is $\precsim$-optimal in $\mathfrak{U}_{\mathcal{M}}(G)$.*

7.2.4 The Applications

In this section we apply the results of Section 7.2.2 and Section 7.2.3 to the MECs presented in Chapter 6. Here we have:

Theorem 7.2.3 (Confluence of $\mathcal{PDCE}$, $\mathcal{PFCE}$ and $\mathcal{PRAE}$).

1. *$\mathcal{PDCE}$ is a confluent UMEC.*
2. *$\mathcal{PFCE}$ is a confluent UMEC.*
3. *$\mathcal{PRAE}$ is a confluent UMEC.*

Proof. All proofs are applications of Theorem 7.2.2. Obviously, $\mathcal{PDCE}$, $\mathcal{PFCE}$ and $\mathcal{PRAE}$ are UMECs. Therefore, it is left to show that in each case consistency is fulfilled.

Consistency of $\mathcal{PDCE}$: Let us consider an occurrence occ_α of an assignment pattern $\alpha \equiv x := \varphi$ at a program point $\dot{n}$ of G. Starting with the first condition of Definition 7.2.1, we have to show that deadness of occ_α is preserved, if the occurrence survives a dead assignment elimination. Therefore, let us assume a dead assignment elimination $\text{EL}_\beta \equiv G \overset{dae}{\longmapsto}_\beta G' \in \mathcal{DAE}$ with respect to the assignment pattern $\beta \equiv y := \psi$ that does not eliminate occ_α. According to the definition of deadness (cf. Definition 6.2.1) on every path leading from $\dot{n}$ to $\dot{\mathbf{e}}$ a use site of x must be preceded by a site at which x is modified. More specifically, this means:

$$\forall p \in \mathbf{P}[\dot{n}, \dot{\mathbf{e}}],\ 1 < i \leqslant |p|.\ LhsUsed^{\alpha}_{p_i} \ \Rightarrow\ \exists\, 1 < j < i.\ LhsMod^{\alpha}_{p_j} \qquad (7.6)$$

We have to show that this condition still holds after applying the elimination transformation EL_β. Therefore, let us assume a path $p \in \mathbf{P}[\dot{n}, \dot{\mathbf{e}}]$ with

[9] The number of computations is determined by the number of operator symbols.
[10] The number of assignments is determined by the number of operator symbols.
[11] Informatively, this means that no elementary step can impair the quality of programs.

a use site at node p_i ($1 < i \leqslant |p|$) such that $LhsUsed^{\alpha}_{p_i}$ holds.[12] According to Condition (7.6) there exists an index $1 < j < i$ such that p_j satisfies $LhsMod^{\alpha}_{p_j}$. Let us choose j as the greatest one among all such indices. Obviously, then p_j is associated with an assignment pattern $x := \ldots$, which is not dead, since it is used at point p_i without a modification of x in between. Hence this occurrence is not eliminated by means of $\mathbf{EL}_{\beta}$, which finally completes the argument, as it forces the preservation of occ_{α}'s deadness.

Next the second condition of Definition 7.2.1 has to be proved. Therefore, let us assume an admissible assignment sinking $\mathtt{AS}_{\beta} \in \mathcal{AAS}$, and show
i) that all occurrences in $Dst_{\mathtt{AS}_{\beta}}(occ_{\alpha})$ are dead, if occ_{α} is dead and
ii) that at least one occurrence in $Dst_{\mathtt{AS}_{\beta}}(occ_{\alpha})$ is not dead, if occ_{α} is not dead either.

Since the line of argumentation is similar to the first part of the proof, we concentrate on sketching the essentials rather then going into technical details. Starting with (i) let us assume that occ_{α} is dead at program point $\dot{n}$. Without loss of generality let us further consider a program path from $\dot{n}$ to $\dot{\mathbf{e}}$ with a use site of x at a point strictly following $\dot{n}$. According to (7.6) the left-hand side variable x has to be modified in between $\dot{n}$ and this use site. However, a modification site of x particularly means a blockade for the movement of occ_{α}. Since this blockade is still present after application of $\mathtt{AS}_{\beta}$,[13] deadness is preserved for all occurrences in $Dst_{\mathtt{AS}_{\beta}}(occ_{\alpha})$.

Point (ii) is proved analogously. Assuming that occ_{α} is alive yields that $\dot{n}$ is followed by a use site of x on some program path p such that no modification of x occurs in between. Since the instruction at the use site especially blocks occ_{α}, this implies that some occurrence in $Dst_{\mathtt{AS}_{\beta}}(occ_{\alpha})$ that lies on $p_{\mathtt{AS}_{\beta}}$ is still alive.

Consistency of $\mathcal{PFCE}$: In the case of $\mathcal{PFCE}$ the first condition of Definition 7.2.1 is proved almost identically as the counterpart of $\mathcal{PDCE}$. Assuming a faint assignment $\alpha \equiv x := \varphi$ at program point $\dot{n}$, the only essential difference is that we are faced with an additional case according to Definition 6.3.1. Hence the counterpart of Condition (7.6) now reads as:

$$\forall p \in \mathbf{P}[\dot{n}, \dot{\mathbf{e}}]\ \forall 1 < i \leqslant |p|.\ LhsUsed^{\alpha}_{p_i} \Rightarrow \underbrace{(\exists 1 < j < i.\ LhsMod^{\alpha}_{p_i})}_{i)} \vee \underbrace{Faint^{\beta}_{p_i}}_{ii)} \tag{7.7}$$

[12] The case in which there is no use site on path p trivially carries over to G'.

[13] That means, if $occ_{\gamma,p}$ denotes the path-occurrence that blocks the path occurrence $occ_{\beta,p}$, then $Dst_{\mathtt{TR}}(occ_{\gamma,p})$ still blocks $Dst_{\mathtt{TR}}(occ_{\beta,p})$ and both occurrences precede any use site of x on the path $p_{\mathtt{AS}_{\beta}}$.

with β addressing the occurrence associated with node p_i. In fact, in the case that part (i) of the conclusion in (7.7) applies, the argument is exactly the same as in the case of $\mathcal{PDCE}$. Otherwise, also part (ii) can do no harm, because the elimination of the faint occurrence of β at p_i could at most reduce the cases in which the premise $LhsUsed^{\alpha}_{p_i}$ is true. Hence the implication remains valid after performing a faint assignment elimination. The second condition of Definition 7.2.1 is proved completely along the lines of the $\mathcal{PDCE}$-case.

Consistency of $\mathcal{PRAE}$: Starting with the first condition of Definition 7.2.1 let us assume an occurrence occ_α of α at a program point $\dot{n}$ being redundant. According to Definition 6.4.1 this means:

$$\forall p \in \mathbf{P}[\dot{s}, \dot{n}]\; \exists 1 \leqslant i < |p|.\; AssOcc^{\alpha}_{p_i} \wedge \underbrace{\forall i < j < |p|.\; \neg LhsMod^{\alpha}_{p_j} \wedge \forall i < j \leqslant |p|.\; \neg RhsMod^{\alpha}_{p_j}}_{(\bigstar)} \tag{7.8}$$

Let us now assume a redundant assignment elimination $\mathbf{EL}_\beta \equiv G \stackrel{rae}{\longmapsto}_\beta G' \in \mathcal{RAE}$. Then we have to show that occ_α remains redundant, if it survives the application of $\mathbf{EL}_\beta$. Since $\mathbf{EL}_\beta$ does not add assignments, Part ($\bigstar$) of (7.8) is preserved on every path. Thus only the case, where an α-occurrence at node p_i is eliminated is of interest. In this case, however, Condition (7.8) applies equally to p_i in place of $\dot{n}$, which establishes redundancy of occ_α in G', too.

Similarly, the $\Rightarrow$-direction of the second condition of Definition 7.2.1 follows immediately from the path characterisation in (7.8) using the fact that the p_i-occurrences of α are blockades of occ_α, a fact which is preserved for the destination-occurrences during assignment hoisting. Complementary, by means of (7.8) it is easy to see that non-redundancy of occ_α is preserved at least on one program path, which finally also provides the $\Leftarrow$-direction of Definition 7.2.1(2). □

7.3 The Complexity of Exhaustive Iterations

In the previous chapter we gave a sufficient condition for the confluence of a UMEC. Since $\longmapsto$ is terminating up to local reorderings, the optimisation potential can always be exhausted completely. However, we did not yet answer the question what is the cost of a suitable exhaustive iteration sequence. Although for partial redundancy elimination exhaustive approaches based on assignment motion have been proposed and implemented before, no serious estimation of their complexities have been given. Dhamdhere [Dha91] briefly discusses assignment hoisting as an instrument to enhance partially redundant expression elimination, but does not address its complexity. Similarly,

Dhamdhere, Rosen and Zadeck [DRZ92] discuss the presence of second order effects in an algorithm for partial redundancy elimination that employs sparse slot-wise iteration techniques as opposed to bit-vector iterations. However, they neither provide an argument for stabilisation of the process nor address the run-time behaviour. Besides, there are a few implementations that report the usage of an iterated version of Morel's and Renvoise's algorithm [MR79]. These implementations employ a restricted kind of assignment hoisting based on the idea that large expressions are decomposed following a strict naming discipline: the same right-hand side expressions are always assigned to a unique symbolic register. This way expression motion of large expressions is simulated by assignment motion, a phenomenon we will also exploit by our algorithm. The most prominent examples are probably implementations that are based on the work of Chow [Cho83]. Moreover, Rosen, Wegman and Zadeck [RWZ88] also mention the PL.8-compiler of IBM [AH82] as an implementation that iterates Morel's and Renvoise's algorithm.[14] In fact, for acyclic control flow they even state a linear asymptotic upper bound on the number of iteration steps, which, however, is not further elucidated.

Besides there are alternative approaches based on special intermediate representations of dependencies like SSA-form [RWZ88, BC94], the program dependency graph [FOW87, FKCX94], and the dependency flow graph [JP93]. Common to all approaches is that they are limited in capturing second order effects. For example, the SSA-based approaches of [RWZ88, BC94] introduce rankings among the occurrences that are moved, which only guarantees a reasonable ordering for acyclic programs.

In this chapter we examine the complexity of exhaustive iteration sequences in a UMEC. Essentially, there are two levels of iteration that contribute to the overall transformation. The inner level is caused by the fixed point iterations of global data flow analyses which are employed for gathering information to be used for the component transformations. In contrast, the outer level is forced by the exhaustive application of the elementary transformations. Whereas the complexity of the inner iterations is well-understood (cf. Section 4.6), the complexity of the outer iteration process has not been investigated yet.

In this chapter we therefore consider the penalty costs of the outer iteration process, i. e. the additional factor that is caused by the outer iteration compared to a one-step application of the component transformations. In essence, a one-step application means the simultaneous application of a certain type of transformations to all code patterns of interest. It turns out that a quadratic penalty factor always succeeds. Nonetheless, such a compile-time penalty is hardly acceptable in practice. However, most practically relevant UMECs do stabilise considerably faster. In fact, for $\mathcal{PDCE}$ which is implemented in Re-

[14] Unfortunately, this does not seem to be reported in a first-hand reference.

lease 4 of the Sun SPARCompiler[15] measurements indicate that the average iteration count is only 4 to 5 [Gro95].[16] In this chapter we present the theoretical foundation giving evidence for this observation. All our applications are shown to fall into a class of UMECs where the penalty factor is linear and can even be expected to be reasonably small in practice. The central property that characterises this class is that all elimination-elimination effects are restricted to initial ones. Surprisingly, as opposed to the inner level of iteration the penalty factors are independent from the branching structure of a program, i. e. there is no difference in the iteration behaviour of simple straight-line programs and intricate irreducible programs.

7.3.1 Simultaneous Iteration Steps

To give a reasonable estimation on the costs that are associated with an exhaustive iteration sequence, we have to choose the basic components appropriately. In practice, the elementary transformations are typically implemented by means of bit-vector algorithms (cf. Section 4.6). Nonetheless, even for non-bitvector analyses like the elimination of faint assignments we consider iteration steps that apply elementary transformations with respect to all assignment patterns.[17] In a more abstract view we impose two requirements reflecting the sketched situation:

- The elementary transformations have to be reasonably powerful in order to avoid unnecessarily slow convergence.
- All transformations of a given type are assumed to be performed simultaneously for all assignment patterns of a program.

More formally, the first requirement is captured by the usage of maximal component transformations which, at least for the class of UMECs, are guaranteed to exist.

Maximal Transformations Let $(\mathcal{T}_{am}, \mathcal{T}_{el})$ be a UMEC and $\alpha \in \mathcal{AP}(G)$. A maximal assignment motion $\mathtt{AM}_\alpha^\mu(G) \in \mathcal{T}_{am}$ and a maximal elimination $\mathtt{EL}_\alpha^\mu \in \mathcal{T}_{el}$ with respect to α are determined in the following way:

1. $\mathtt{AM}_\alpha^\mu(G)$ is constructed as described in Case 2 of the proof of Theorem 7.2.2.
2. $\mathtt{EL}_\alpha^\mu(G)$ results from G by eliminating every G-occurrence occ_α of α satisfying $eliminable(G, occ_\alpha)$.

[15] SPARCompiler is a registered trademark of SPARC International, Inc., and is licensed exclusively to Sun Microsystems, Inc.

[16] That means 4 or 5 iterations of both assignment motion and eliminations.

[17] In practice, one can speed up the simultaneous iterations by identifying those patterns that are candidates for a successful transformation in advance. However, this does not reduce the costs in terms of worst-case computational complexities.

It is easy to see that both $\mathtt{AM}^{\mu}_{\alpha}(G)$ and $\mathtt{EL}^{\mu}_{\alpha}(G)$ are well-defined, i. e. $G \overset{am}{\longmapsto}_{\alpha} \mathtt{AM}^{\mu}_{\alpha}(G) \in \mathcal{T}_{am}$ and $G \overset{el}{\longmapsto}_{\alpha} \mathtt{EL}^{\mu}_{\alpha}(G) \in \mathcal{T}_{el}$. Obviously, $\mathtt{AM}^{\mu}_{\alpha}$ and $\mathtt{EL}^{\mu}_{\alpha}$ can be regarded as functions from $\mathfrak{FG}$ to $\mathfrak{FG}$.

For our reasoning only one property of maximal transformations is of relevance. If the maximal transformations get stuck any other transformation gets stuck as well. More specifically, we have:

Lemma 7.3.1 (Stability Lemma). *Let $(\mathcal{T}_{am}, \mathcal{T}_{el})$ be a weakly consistent UMEC. Then*

1. $\mathtt{AM}^{\mu}_{\alpha}(G) \doteq G \;\Rightarrow\; \forall\, \mathtt{AM}_{\alpha} \equiv G \overset{am}{\longmapsto}_{\alpha} G' \in \mathcal{T}_{am}.\ \mathtt{AM}_{\alpha}(G) \doteq G$
2. $\mathtt{EL}^{\mu}_{\alpha}(G) \doteq G \;\Rightarrow\; \forall\, \mathtt{EL}_{\alpha} \equiv G \overset{el}{\longmapsto}_{\alpha} G' \in \mathcal{T}_{el}.\ \mathtt{EL}_{\alpha}(G) \doteq G$

Simultaneous Transformations In the proof of Case 3 and Case 4 of Theorem 7.2.1 we saw, how in a weakly consistent UMEC two transformations of the same type operating on distinct assignment patterns can be performed in arbitrary order without affecting each other. This construction can straightforwardly be extended to finite sets of elementary transformations. Let $(\mathcal{T}_{am}, \mathcal{T}_{el})$ be a weakly consistent UMEC, $\mathcal{AP}(G) = \{\alpha_1, \dots, \alpha_k\}$ with $k \geqslant 1$ and $\mathtt{TR}_{\alpha_1}, \dots, \mathtt{TR}_{\alpha_k} \in \mathcal{T}_{am}$ or $\mathtt{TR}_{\alpha_1}, \dots, \mathtt{TR}_{\alpha_k} \in \mathcal{T}_{el}$ a family of transformations operating on the argument program G. Then the program that results from a simultaneous execution is denoted by:[18]

$$(\mathtt{TR}_{\alpha_1} \parallel \dots \parallel \mathtt{TR}_{\alpha_k})(G)$$

Our reasoning again only uses one property of this definition, namely that the simultaneous executions can be sequentialised in an arbitrary order. Under the situation of the above definition this means:

Lemma 7.3.2 (Sequentialisation Lemma). *Let $i \in \{1, \dots, k\}$. And π be a permutation of $\{1, \dots, k\}$. Then there are transformations $\mathtt{TR}'_{\alpha_1}, \dots, \mathtt{TR}'_{\alpha_k}$ such that*

$$(\mathtt{TR}_{\alpha_1} \parallel \dots \parallel \mathtt{TR}_{\alpha_k})(G) \;=\; \mathtt{TR}'_{\alpha_{\pi(1)}}; \dots ; \mathtt{TR}'_{\alpha_{\pi(k)}}(G)$$

In particular, the first transformation coincides exactly with its component transformation, i. e. $\mathtt{TR}'_{\alpha_{\pi(1)}} = \mathtt{TR}_{\alpha_{\pi(1)}}$.

Now we can define the components of the exhaustive iteration process:

Definition 7.3.1 (Simultaneous Iteration Steps).
Let $(\mathcal{T}_{am}, \mathcal{T}_{el})$ be a weakly consistent UMEC and $\mathcal{AP}(G) = \{\alpha_1, \dots, \alpha_k\}$.

1. *A* maximal simultaneous assignment motion step *with respect to G is defined by*

$$\mathtt{AM}^{\mu}_{\parallel}(G) \overset{\mathrm{def}}{=} (\mathtt{AM}^{\mu}_{\alpha_1} \parallel \dots \parallel \mathtt{AM}^{\mu}_{\alpha_k})(G) \ \textit{and}$$

[18] For assignment motions we choose the program, where insertions of independent assignments at the same program point are ordered in accordance to their indices.

2. A maximal simultaneous elimination step *with respect to G is defined by*

$$\mathrm{EL}^{\mu}_{\|}(G) \stackrel{\mathrm{def}}{=} (\mathrm{EL}^{\mu}_{\alpha_1} \parallel \dots \parallel \mathrm{EL}^{\mu}_{\alpha_k})(G)$$

7.3.2 Conventions

For the sake of presentation the reasoning on complexity is exemplified for MECs with assignment sinkings.

As noted in Section 7.2.3 iteration sequences only stabilise up to local reorderings within basic blocks. Therefore, the term stabilisations always addresses stabilisation modulo program equivalence as introduced in Definition 7.2.2. This means, a program G is stable up to local reorderings, if and only if for any elementary step $G \longmapsto G'$ being applicable $G \doteq G'$ is satisfied. Note that in the case of consistent UMECs this always guarantees that the result of this process is unique up to local reorderings (cf. Corollary 7.2.2).

The complexity of an exhaustive iteration sequence with respect to an underlying MEC is stated in terms of a penalty factor that captures the additional costs in comparison to a single application of a simultaneous iteration step. A factor that is of particular importance is the length of a maximal chain of blockades that occurs in a program:

Definition 7.3.2 (Chain of Blockades). *Let* $p \stackrel{\mathrm{def}}{=} \langle p_1, \dots, p_k\rangle \in \mathbf{P}_G$.[19] *A* (forwards directed) chain of blockades *on p is a subsequence $\langle p_{i_1}, \dots, p_{i_r}\rangle$ of p such that for any $1 \leqslant j < r$ the nodes p_{i_j} and $p_{i_{j+1}}$ are associated with assignment patterns α and β, respectively, such that*

- *β blocks α and*
- *the subpath $(p_{i_j}+1, \dots, p_{i_r})$ does not contain an immobile instruction like $out(\varphi)$ that blocks α.*

For MECs with assignment hoistings chains of blockades are defined dually.[20] Let us denote the length of the longest chain of blockades on a path p by Δ^{block}_p.

In contrast to the presentation up to this point the reasoning on the complexity takes advantage from the basic block view of a flow graph, since the general structure of the basic block flow graph does not change throughout the repeated application of transformation steps.

7.3.3 The General Case: Weakly Consistent UMECs

First, we are going to examine the convergence behaviour under the most general assumption that guarantees the existence of simultaneous iteration steps, that is weak consistency.

[19] i. e. a path with elementary nodes.

[20] Actually, the direction of assignment motion is only relevant for the condition on the absence of immobile blockades.

The Upper Bound Even under this assumption the iteration process is guaranteed to stabilise within a quadratic number of iteration steps. Essentially, this is due to the fact that every basic block **n** in the flow graph can "absorb" no more assignments than there are on any path leading from **s** to **n**. This gives rise to the following definition:[21]

$$\Delta^{block}_{\mathbf{n}} \stackrel{\mathrm{def}}{=} \min_{p \,\in\, \mathbf{P}[\mathbf{s}, last(\mathbf{n})]} \Delta^{block}_{p}$$

$$\Delta^{block} \stackrel{\mathrm{def}}{=} \max_{\mathbf{n} \,\in\, \mathbf{N}} \Delta^{block}_{\mathbf{n}}$$

In particular note that the value of Δ^{block} is determined by an acyclic path. Since the blockade relation among moved occurrences is preserved, there are at most $\Delta^{block}_{\mathbf{n}}$ occurrences that are moved to the basic block **n** during the exhaustive iteration including the assignments at **n**. Hence the overall number of initial assignments and of assignments that enter a new basic block due to assignment motion can be estimated by $|\mathbf{N}|\,\Delta^{block}$. Since every simultaneous elimination and assignment motion step influences at least one of these assignments before stabilisation we have:

Theorem 7.3.1 (A General Upper Bound). *For every weakly consistent UMEC an alternating sequence of simultaneous elimination and assignment motion steps, i. e. the iteration sequence* $(\mathtt{EL}^{\mu}_{\parallel};\, \mathtt{AM}^{\mu}_{\parallel})^*(G)$*, stabilises within*

$$2\,|\mathbf{N}|\,\Delta^{block}$$

of both kind of simultaneous iteration steps,[22] *i. e.*

$$(\,\mathtt{EL}^{\mu}_{\parallel};\, \mathtt{AM}^{\mu}_{\parallel}\,)^{(2\,|\mathbf{N}|\,\Delta^{block})}(G)$$

is stable up to local reorderings.

The Lower Bound Unfortunately, the estimation given in Theorem 7.3.1 would mean a compile-time degradation considered unacceptable in practice. Whereas the factor Δ^{block} can be expected to be reasonably small in practice, though in the worst case it may even reach $|Occ_{\mathcal{AP}}(G)|$, the more serious inefficiency is given by the factor $|\mathbf{N}|$. Unfortunately, a linear dependency on this parameter may even show up for simple acyclic programs. In the following we show that the upper bound given in Theorem 7.3.1 is asymptotically tight. To this end, we reinvestigate our example that combines assignment sinking with the elimination of locally redundant assignments (cf. Section 7.2, page 157). Figure 7.5 provides a scheme of programs, where any stabilising iteration sequence is of quadratic order.

---

21 Again the dual notions for MECs with assignment hoistings are straightforward.

22 In practice, one additional step of both kinds of transformations may be required in order to recognise stabilisation.

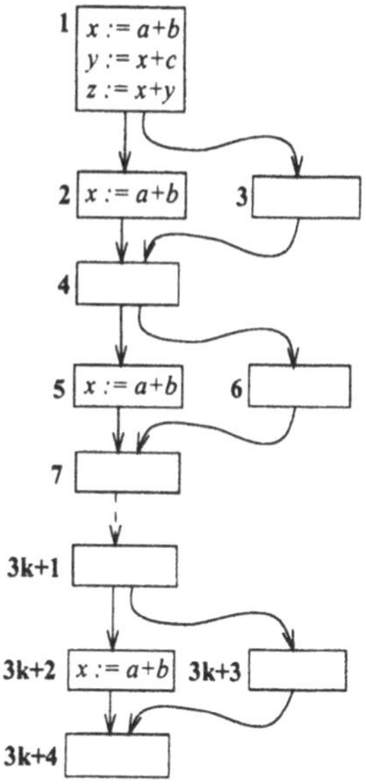

Fig. 7.5. Illustrating slow stabilisation

Essentially, this program scheme is built of the start block **1** being followed by a sequence of $k \geqslant 1$ identical program parts.

The point of this example is that the sequence of blockades in the first node can successively be sunk to the entry of basic block **3i+2** with $0 \leqslant i \leqslant k$, each movement requiring three simultaneous assignment motion steps.[23]

Figure 7.6 displays the situation after the first two iteration steps; two assignments have been moved from block **1** to block **3** and to the entry of block **2**, respectively, where in the latter case they are blocked by the assignment $x := a+b$. In the next iteration step the occurrence of $x := a+b$ at block **1** can also be sunk enabling the elimination of the original occurrence of $x := a+b$ at this site, since it becomes locally redundant. In fact, as displayed in Figure 7.7 the assignment sequence has moved from block **1** to block **2** and **3**, where essentially the same procedure applies in order to resolve the next blockade at node **5**.

In the program scheme of Figure 7.5 the value of Δ^{block} is 4 being determined by the chain of blocking assignments on the path $\langle \mathbf{1}, \mathbf{2} \rangle$. Hence by increasing the number of blockades in node **1** we can easily manage to set Δ^{block} to any value we want to. Thus we have:

Theorem 7.3.2 (A General Lower Bound). *There is a weakly consistent UMEC and a family of acyclic programs $(G_{i,j})_{i,j \in \mathbb{N}}$, where $G_{i,j}$ has i basic blocks and $\Delta^{block} = j$ such that the number of simultaneous iteration steps that are necessary in order to reach a stable solution is of order $\Omega(i\,j)$.*

---

23 In this example assignment sinking cannot take advantage of the simultaneous transformations; at most one assignment pattern can be moved at a time.

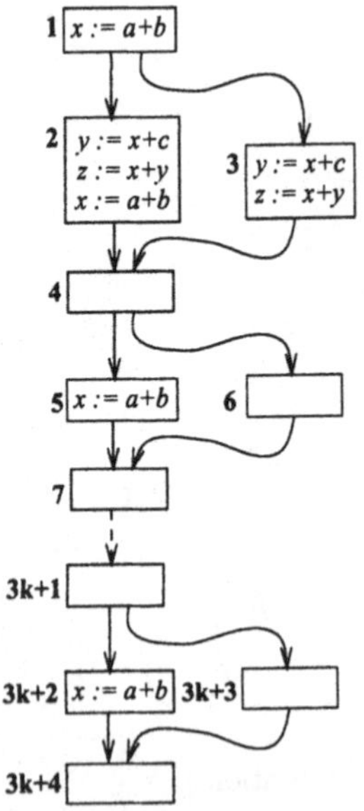

Fig. 7.6. After the second simultaneous iteration step

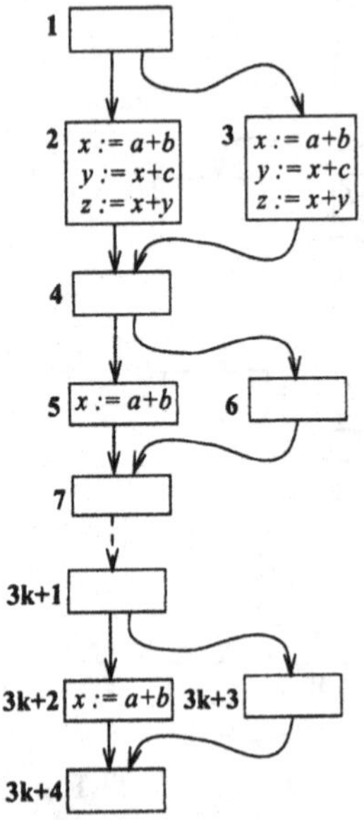

Fig. 7.7. After the fourth simultaneous iteration step

7.3.4 Consistent UMECs

Fortunately, the "odd" behaviour of the previous section does not occur in practically relevant, and thus consistent UMECs. In the following we are going to provide two additional conditions ensuring that a CUMEC stabilises significantly faster. The bounds are given in terms of a linear parameter. In fact, we get completely rid of the "bad" parameter $|\mathbf{N}|$, while only slightly increasing the second parameter Δ^{block}. The most striking advantage of CUMECs is the fact that their motion-elimination effects are particularly simple: assignment motion only increases the elimination potential for assignments that are actually moved. In the light of this property the pathological behaviour of the example from Figure 7.5 to Figure 7.7 is excluded, since this example is based on the effect that the "unmoved" occurrences of $x := a+b$ become eliminable through other movements causing late resolution of blockades.

7.3.4.1 Absence of Elimination-Elimination Effects. First we will examine the situation, where a CUMEC is free of any elimination-elimination effect (EE-effect), i. e. for any elimination $\mathbf{EL}_\beta \equiv G \overset{el}{\longmapsto}_\beta G'$ and any occurrence $occ_\alpha \in Occ_\alpha(G)$ there holds:

$$eliminable(\underbrace{\mathbf{EL}_\beta(G)}_{G'},\ occ_\alpha) \Rightarrow eliminable(G,\ occ_\alpha) \tag{7.9}$$

In UMECs without EE-effects the number of iterations mostly depends on the assignment motions involved. However, even in this case an improved upper bound compared to the situation in Section 7.3.3 is not obvious, since all other second order effects, i. e. motion-motion, motion-elimination, elimination-motion effects (cf. Section 6.2.3), are still present. It should also be noted that the consistency requirement cannot be omitted, since the effect discussed in Figure 7.5 to Figure 7.7 does not depend on the presence of EE-effects.

The key for proving our new bound is a projection from the iteration behaviour to the syntactical structure of the original program. The point is to show that code being moved within the i-th iteration is caused by an acyclic chain of blocking assignments in the original program with length greater than i.

Lemma 7.3.3 (Iteration Lemma for EE-Effect Free CUMECs). *Let us consider a CUMEC without EE-effects and an iteration sequence*

$$\underbrace{(\mathtt{EL}^{\mu}_{\|};\ \mathtt{AM}^{\mu}_{\|})^{i}(G)}_{G_i},\quad 0 \leqslant i \leqslant r$$

Let $i \geqslant 1$ and α be movable across the entry of a basic block $\mathbf{n}$ within the i-th, $i \geqslant 1$, assignment motion step, i. e. we have $OrigJust^{\alpha}_{\dot{n}}$, where $\dot{n}$ is the entry point of the node $first(\mathbf{n})$ in the intermediate program $\mathtt{EL}^{\mu}_{\|}(G_{i-1})$.

Then there exists a path $p \in \mathbf{P}_G[\mathbf{s}, first(\mathbf{n})[$ such that an acyclic prefix of p contains a chain of blockades[24] *that*

- starts *with an occurrence in $Orig(occ_\alpha)$ and*
- *is* at least *of length i.*

Proof. We proceed by induction on i. The induction base $i=1$ is trivial, since on every path $p \in \mathbf{P}_{\mathtt{EL}^{\mu}_{\|}(G)}[\mathbf{s}, first(\mathbf{n})[$ the substituted occurrence of α itself defines a chain of blockades of length 1.

Thus let us assume that $i > 1$ and an occurrence of α that is moved across the entry of $\mathbf{n}$ within the i-th simultaneous assignment motion step. According to the definition of admissible assignment sinkings[25] there is an occurrence of α on every path leading from $\mathbf{s}$ to the entry of $\mathbf{n}$ as shown in Figure 7.8. Due to the maximality of the assignment sinkings (cf. Section 7.3.1) the situation immediately before the i-th simultaneous elimination step is as illustrated in Figure 7.9: there is at least one path $p \in \mathbf{P}[\mathbf{s}, first(\mathbf{n})[$, where the last occurrence of occ_α is followed by an occurrence occ_β at a block $\mathbf{m}$ such that β blocks α. This blockade is resolved within the i-th simultaneous elimination step. Hence we have:

$$eliminable(G_{i-1},\ occ_\beta) \tag{7.10}$$

[24] Note that this is a chain of blockades in the original program G.

[25] Recall that we are restricted to assignment sinkings for the sake of presentation.

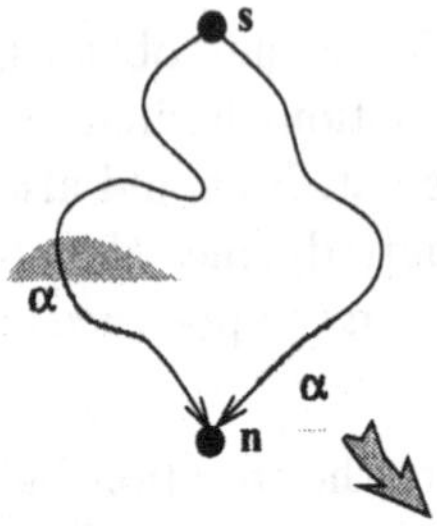

Fig. 7.8. Situation before the i-th simultaneous assignment motion step

Let us now examine the two possible alternatives on the behaviour of occ_β during the i-1st simultaneous assignment motion step:

1. occ_β is moved at most locally within **m** or
2. occ_β is moved globally, i. e. β is moved across the entry of **m**.

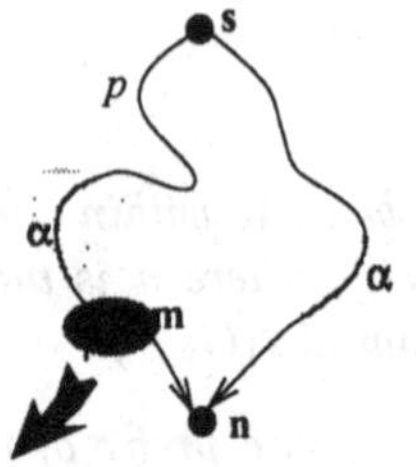

Fig. 7.9. Situation before the i-th simultaneous elimination step

Starting with point (1) we will show that this case cannot happen. Therefore, let us assume

$$Src_{\mathbf{AM}^{\mu}_{\beta}}(occ_\beta) \;=\; \{occ'_\beta\}$$

with occ'_β being located at basic block **m**, too, and lead this assumption to a contradiction. Due to Definition 7.2.1(2) we have

$$\textit{eliminable}(\mathbf{EL}^{\mu}_{\|}(G_{i-1}),\ occ'_\beta)$$

According to Lemma 7.3.2 the simultaneous elimination step can be expressed by means of a suitable sequential representation:

$$\textit{eliminable}(\mathbf{EL}^{\mu}_{\beta}; \mathbf{EL}_{\alpha_1}; \dots ; \mathbf{EL}_{\alpha_k}(G_{i-1}),\ occ'_\beta)$$

where $\mathbf{EL}_{\alpha_i}$ $(i=1,\dots,k)$ refers to elimination transformations with $\alpha_i \neq \beta$. Repeated application of the premise on the absence of EE-effects finally leads to

$$\textit{eliminable}(G_{i-1},\ occ'_\beta)$$

This, however, is in contradiction to the maximality of the elimination transformations involved, since occ'_β is assumed to survive the i-th simultaneous elimination step.

Hence only point (2) remains, which grants that the induction hypothesis becomes applicable. This yields:

Induction Hypothesis: There exists a path $q \in \mathbf{P}_G[\mathbf{s}, \mathit{first}(\mathbf{m})[$ such that an acyclic prefix of q contains a chain of blockades that
- *starts* with an occurrence $occ^0_\beta \in Orig(occ_\beta)$ and
- is *at least* of length $i-1$.

Justification of the α-assignment motion in the i-th iteration step ensures that there is also an occurrence occ'_α of α on q as displayed in Figure 7.10(a).

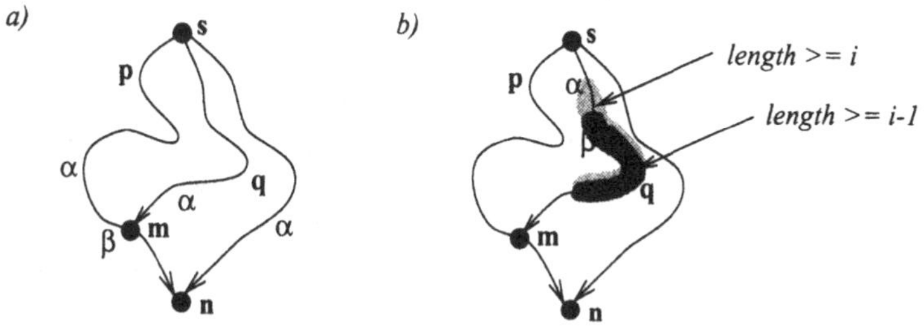

Fig. 7.10. Applying the induction hypothesis

Since occ'_α is blocked by occ_β this blockade must already be present in the original program G yielding an occurrence $occ^0_\alpha \in Orig(occ'_\alpha)$ that precedes occ^0_β. This finally establishes the existence of a chain of blockades on an acyclic prefix of p starting with occ^0_α and having a length that is at least i (see Figure 7.10(b) for illustration). □

Let us now consider a slight variant of the parameter Δ^{block}:

$$\bar{\Delta}^{block}_{\mathbf{n}} \stackrel{\text{def}}{=} \max_{\substack{p \in \mathbf{P}[\mathbf{s}, \mathit{first}(\mathbf{n})[\\ q \text{ acyclic prefix of } p}} \Delta^{block}_q$$

$$\bar{\Delta}^{block} \stackrel{\text{def}}{=} \max_{\mathbf{n} \in \mathbf{N}} \bar{\Delta}^{block}_{\mathbf{n}}$$

The essential difference to Δ^{block} is that $\bar{\Delta}^{block}_{\mathbf{n}}$ is defined by means of the maximum operator, however, restricted to a acyclic paths, which excludes infinite chains of blockades.

An immediate consequence of Lemma 7.3.3 is:

Theorem 7.3.3 (An Upper Bound for EE-Effect Free CUMECs). *For a UMEC without EE-effects the iteration sequence* $(\mathtt{EL}^{\mu}_{\parallel}; \mathtt{AM}^{\mu}_{\parallel})^*(G)$ *stabilises within*

$\bar{\Delta}^{block}$

of both assignment motion and elimination steps, i. e.

$$(\mathtt{EL}^{\mu}_{\parallel};\, \mathtt{AM}^{\mu}_{\parallel})^{\bar{\Delta}^{block}_{G}}(G)$$

is stable up to local reorderings within basic blocks.

This estimation can directly be applied to $\mathcal{PFCE}$ as introduced in Chapter 6.

Theorem 7.3.4 (An Upper Bound for $\mathcal{PFCE}$).
For $\mathcal{PFCE}$ the sequence $(\mathtt{FAE}^{\mu}_{\parallel};\, \mathtt{AS}^{\mu}_{\parallel})^{*}(G)$ stabilises within $\bar{\Delta}^{block}$ simultaneous assignment sinking and faint assignment elimination steps reaching a result that is $\precsim_{ass}$-optimal in the universe $\mathfrak{U}_{\mathcal{PFCE}}(G)$.

Proof. The complexity estimation is an immediate consequence of Theorem 7.3.3 and the fact that, by definition, the elimination of partially faint assignments is free of EE-effects. Hence, we are left to show that the resulting program G_{res} is $\precsim_{ass}$-optimal in $\mathfrak{U}_{\mathcal{PFCE}}(G)$. First Lemma 7.3.1 guarantees that G_{res} is stable up to $\stackrel{\circ}{=}$ under every assignment sinking and faint assignment elimination. Thus according to Corollary 7.2.2 G_{res} is an optimal element of the preorder $\longmapsto^{*}$. Finally, since both assignment sinkings and faint assignment eliminations are compatible with $\precsim_{ass}$, Lemma 7.2.4 yields that G_{res} is $\precsim_{ass}$-optimal within $\mathfrak{U}_{\mathcal{PFCE}}(G)$. □

At this point it should be recalled that the elimination of faint assignments is the only component transformation that cannot take advantage of bit-vector data flow analyses. However, at a later point we will see how to speed up the above iteration sequence by reducing the amount of faint assignment elimination steps to a single one (cf. Theorem 7.3.7).

7.3.4.2 Weak EE-Effects. Unfortunately, some practically relevant problems like $\mathcal{PRAE}$ and $\mathcal{PDCE}$ have EE-effects. However, in these cases we succeed by showing a slightly weaker criterion that guarantees that EE-effects are completely restricted to initial ones. Essentially, assignment motion must not create "new " opportunities for EE-effects. More formally, we call the EE-effects of a UMEC *weak*, if and only if for every $\alpha, \beta \in \mathcal{AP}$ (not necessarily different), $\mathtt{AM}_{\alpha} \equiv G \stackrel{am}{\longmapsto}_{\alpha} G' \in \mathcal{T}_{am}$ and $\mathtt{EL}_{\alpha} \equiv G' \stackrel{el}{\longmapsto}_{\alpha} G'' \in \mathcal{T}_{el}$ such that G does not contain eliminable occurrences of α we have:

$$eliminable(\underbrace{\mathtt{AM}_{\alpha};\mathtt{EL}_{\alpha}(G)}_{G''},\, occ_{\beta}) \;\Rightarrow\; eliminable(\underbrace{\mathtt{AM}_{\alpha}(G)}_{G'},\, occ_{\beta}) \qquad (7.11)$$

The key for fast stabilisation in CUMECs with weak EE-effects only, is the observation that these can be resolved completely in advance. Once such a preprocess has been performed, the iteration sequence behaves like one of a CUMEC without EE-effects, which allows us to adopt the results of Theorem 7.3.3.

Theorem 7.3.5 (Upper Bound for CUMECs with Weak EE-Eff.). *Let us consider a CUMEC with weak EE-effects. Then there is an iteration sequence of the form* $(\mathtt{EL}^{\mu}_{\|})^*; (\mathtt{AM}^{\mu}_{\|}; \mathtt{EL}^{\mu}_{\|})^*(G)$ *that stabilises within*

$\Delta^{init\_elims} + \bar{\Delta}^{block} + 1$ *simultaneous elimination steps and*
$\bar{\Delta}^{block} + 1$ *simultaneous assignment motion steps,*

where Δ^{init_elims} *denotes the number of simultaneous elimination steps that is sufficient to guarantee stabilisation of* $(\mathtt{EL}^{\mu}_{\|})^*(G)$.[26]

Proof. Let G' denote the program that results from G after the initial sequence of simultaneous elimination steps gets stable. As in Lemma 7.3.3 let us further abbreviate the programs resulting from G' by means of further iteration steps in the following way:

$$G'_i \stackrel{\text{def}}{=} (\mathtt{AM}^{\mu}_{\|}; \mathtt{EL}^{\mu}_{\|})^i(G'), \; i \geqslant 0.$$

In order to adopt the reasoning on the number of iterations from Lemma 7.3.3 it is enough to show that for all G'_i, $i \geqslant 0$ there holds:

$$\text{No occurrence in } G'_i \text{ is eliminable and} \qquad (7.12a)$$
$$\mathtt{AM}^{\mu}_{\|}(G'_i) \text{ is free of EE-effects} \qquad (7.12b)$$

We proceed by an induction on the number of simultaneous iteration steps performed on G'.[27] The induction base for G'_0 is trivial. Therefore, we are left to show the induction step. For the proof of Property (7.12a) let us assume that

$$eliminable(G'_i, occ_\alpha)$$

holds for $i > 1$. This can be rewritten as

$$eliminable(\mathtt{EL}^{\mu}_{\|}(\mathtt{AM}^{\mu}_{\|}(G'_{i-1})), occ_\alpha)$$

According to Lemma 7.3.2 the simultaneous elimination steps can be sequentialised as follows:

$$eliminable(\mathtt{EL}_{\alpha_1}; \ldots; \mathtt{EL}_{\alpha_k}(\mathtt{AM}^{\mu}_{\|}(G'_{i-1})), occ_\alpha)$$

---

[26] Note that Δ^{init_elims} is always bound by $|Occ_{\mathcal{AP}}(G)|$, the total number of occurrences in the original program. The factor $\bar{\Delta}^{block}$, however, can even refer to the program $(\mathtt{EL}^{\mu}_{\|})^*(G)$ instead of G.

[27] Because an incrementation of i means two simultaneous iteration steps, this is not an induction on i.

Multiple application of the induction hypothesis that $\mathtt{AM}^{\mu}_{\|}(G'_{i-1})$ has no EE-effects finally delivers:

$$eliminable(\mathtt{AM}^{\mu}_{\|}(G'_{i-1}),\ occ_\alpha)$$

Due to the maximality of the eliminations employed, this would mean that occ_α gets eliminated during the i-1st simultaneous elimination step, which is in contrast to the assumption $occ_\alpha \in G'_i$. Thus we have

$$\neg eliminable(G'_i,\ occ_\alpha)$$

as desired.

For the remaining proof of (7.12b) suppose that

$$eliminable(\mathtt{EL}_\alpha(\mathtt{AM}^{\mu}_{\|}(G'_i)),\ occ_\beta)$$

holds for an occurrence occ_β and an elimination transformation $\mathtt{EL}_\alpha = \mathtt{AM}^{\mu}_{\|}(G'_i) \overset{el}{\longmapsto}_\alpha G''$. Rewriting this expression delivers:

$$eliminable(\mathtt{AM}^{\mu}_{\|};\mathtt{EL}_\alpha(G'_i),\ occ_\beta)$$

According to Lemma 7.3.2 this can be written as

$$eliminable(\mathtt{AM}_{\alpha_1};\dots;\mathtt{AM}_{\alpha_k};\mathtt{EL}_\alpha(G'_i),\ occ_\beta) \tag{7.13}$$

with $\alpha_k = \alpha$. According to the induction hypothesis no occurrences of α are eliminable in G'_i. Repeated usage of the contrapositive of the $\Leftarrow$-direction of Definition 7.2.1(2) delivers that this property still is true for the program

$$\bar{G}_i \overset{\mathrm{def}}{=} \mathtt{AM}_{\alpha_1};\dots;\mathtt{AM}_{\alpha_{k-1}}(G'_i)$$

With this notation the predicate of (7.13) can be rewritten as:

$$eliminable(\mathtt{AM}_\alpha;\mathtt{EL}_\alpha(\bar{G}_i),\ occ_\beta)$$

At this point we can exploit our assumption on the weakness of the EE-effects yielding

$$eliminable(\mathtt{AM}_\alpha(\bar{G}_i),\ occ_\beta)$$

Repeatedly applying the $\Rightarrow$-direction of Definition 7.2.1(2) and using Lemma 7.3.2 we finally obtain

$$eliminable(\mathtt{AM}^{\mu}_{\|}(G'_i),\ occ_\beta) \qquad \square$$

Applications of Theorem 7.3.5 are $\mathcal{PDCE}$ as well as $\mathcal{PRAE}$. Moreover, Theorem 7.3.5 is the key for a surprising improvement on the complexity of $\mathcal{PFCE}$. In order to start with the first point we can immediately prove:

Lemma 7.3.4. *Both $\mathcal{PDCE}$ and $\mathcal{PRAE}$ are CUMECs with only weak EE-effects.*

Proof. Consistency is already proved in Theorem 7.2.3. Therefore, we only have to check the weakness of the EE-effects.

Weakness of EE-effects in $\mathcal{PDCE}$: Let us assume assignment patterns $\alpha \equiv x := \varphi$ and $\beta \equiv y := \psi$ such that no α-occurrences are dead in G. Moreover, let us consider an admissible assignment sinking $\mathtt{AM}_\alpha \equiv G \stackrel{as}{\longmapsto}_\alpha G'$, a dead assignment elimination $\mathtt{EL}_\alpha \equiv G' \stackrel{dae}{\longmapsto}_\alpha G''$ and a G'-occurrence occ_β of β. To prove the contrapositive of Implication (7.11) we are going to show that liveness of occ_β in G' also forces liveness of occ_β in G''. Liveness of occ_β in G' implies the existence of a corresponding use site of x being associated with an occurrence of an instruction γ along a path p leading to $\mathbf{e}$.[28] If $\alpha \neq \gamma$ then liveness of occ_β carries over immediately to G'', as the use site of occ_β is not influenced by $\mathtt{EL}_\alpha$. Otherwise, if $\alpha = \gamma$ the situation gets more sophisticated. Therefore, let us denote the relevant p-path occurrences of β and γ by $occ_{\beta,p}$ and $occ'_{\alpha,p}$, respectively. Obviously, the G-path occurrence $occ'_{\alpha,p} \equiv Src_{\mathtt{AM}_\alpha}(occ_{\alpha,p})$ must follow $Src_{\mathtt{AM}_\alpha}(occ_{\beta,p})$. Due to the general assumption on G we can rely on the fact that occ'_α is not dead. Hence consistency delivers that there is at least one occurrence $occ''_\alpha \in Dst_{\mathtt{AM}_\alpha}(occ'_\alpha)$ that is alive in G'. By construction, this occurrence follows occ_β on some program path such that there are no modifications in between, which finally establishes that occ_β is not dead in G''.

Weakness of EE-effects in $\mathcal{PRAE}$: Let us assume assignment patterns $\alpha \equiv x := \varphi$, and $\beta \equiv y := \psi$ such that no α-occurrences are redundant in G. Moreover, let us consider an admissible asignment hoisting $\mathtt{AM}_\alpha \equiv G \stackrel{ah}{\longmapsto}_\alpha G'$, a redundant assignment elimination $\mathtt{EL}_\alpha \equiv G' \stackrel{rae}{\longmapsto}_\alpha G''$ and a G'-occurrence occ_β of β. In order to prove the contrapositive of Implication (7.11) let us assume that occ_β is not redundant in G' and show that this property carries over to G''. According to the definition of redundancy (cf. Definition 6.4.1) there has to be a program path p leading from $\mathbf{s}$ to occ_β such that every prior β-occurrence on p is followed by a path occurrence $occ_{\gamma,p}$ of an instruction γ that either modifies y or an operand of ψ.[28] Let us denote the relevant p-path occurrence of occ_β by $occ_{\beta,p}$ and define $occ'_{\gamma,p} \equiv Src_{\mathtt{AM}_\alpha}(occ_{\gamma,p})$. Then, by the general assumption on G, occ'_γ is not redundant, and furthermore it is easy to see that $occ'_{\gamma,p}$ precedes $Src_{\mathtt{AM}_\alpha}(occ_{\beta,p})$. Consistency then yields that there is a G'-occurrence $occ''_\gamma \in Dst_{\mathtt{AM}_\alpha}(occ'_\gamma)$ that is not redundant. By construction, occ''_γ defines a modification site for occ_β in G'' that precedes occ_β on some program path such that all prior path occurrences of β are situated before the relevant path occurrence of occ''_γ. This finally prevents that occ_β is redundant. □

[28] Without loss of generality we may assume that $p \in \mathbf{P}[\mathbf{s}, \mathbf{e}]$.

The previous lemma is the key for estimating the complexity of $\mathcal{PDCE}$ and $\mathcal{PRAE}$. Before, let us get more concrete on the number of initial elimination transformations. Fortunately, for both applications this factor is determined through acyclic definition-use chains [W.78, Ken81] that are defined as follows:

Definition 7.3.3 (Definition-Use Chains). *Let $p \stackrel{\text{def}}{=} \langle p_1, \dots, p_k \rangle \in \mathbf{P}$. A* def–use chain *on p is a subsequence $\langle p_{i_1}, \dots, p_{i_r} \rangle$ of p such that for any $1 \leqslant j < r$ the nodes p_{i_j} and $p_{i_{j+1}}$ are associated with assignment patterns $\alpha \equiv x := \varphi$ and $\beta \equiv y := \psi$, respectively, such that*

- *$x \in SubExpr^*(\psi)$ and*
- *the subpath $\langle p_{i_j} + 1, \dots, p_{i_{j+1}} - 1 \rangle$ does not contain an assignment to x.*

In contrast to chains of blockades (cf. Definition 7.3.2) def–use chains need not necessarily lie along acyclic program paths. For instance, in Figure 7.11 the elimination of dead assignments would proceed by eliminating the assignments in order $c := b+1$, $b := a+1$ and $a := a+1$, as it is reflected by the def-use chain in the figure.

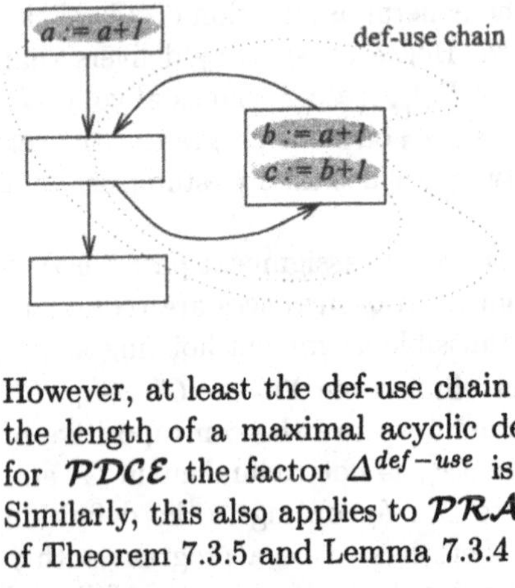

Fig. 7.11. Def–use chain and the elimination of dead assignments

However, at least the def-use chain itself is acyclic. Therefore, let us denote the length of a maximal acyclic def–use chain in G by $\Delta^{def-use}$. Clearly, for $\mathcal{PDCE}$ the factor $\Delta^{def-use}$ is an upper approximation of Δ^{init_elims}. Similarly, this also applies to $\mathcal{PRAE}$. Putting this together with the results of Theorem 7.3.5 and Lemma 7.3.4 we get in analogy to Theorem 7.3.4:

Theorem 7.3.6 (Complexity of $\mathcal{PRAE}$ and $\mathcal{PDCE}$). *For both $\mathcal{PRAE}$ and $\mathcal{PDCE}$ the iteration sequence of the form $(\mathrm{EL}^{\mu}_{\parallel})^*; (\mathrm{AM}^{\mu}_{\parallel}; \mathrm{EL}^{\mu}_{\parallel})^*(G)$ stabilizes within*

$\Delta^{def-use}$ initial elimination steps and

$\bar{\Delta}^{block}$ simultaneous assignment motion and elimination steps

reaching a result that is $\precsim_{ass}$-optimal in the universe $\mathfrak{U}_{\mathcal{PRAE}}(G)$ and $\mathfrak{U}_{\mathcal{PDCE}}(G)$, respectively. This means, the iteration sequence

$$(\mathrm{EL}^{\mu}_{\parallel})^{\Delta^{def-use}+1}; \; (\mathrm{AM}^{\mu}_{\parallel}; \mathrm{EL}^{\mu}_{\parallel})^{\bar{\Delta}^{block}+1}(G)$$

is stable up to local reorderings within basic blocks.

We finish the section by presenting a surprising improvement on the complexity result of $\mathcal{PFCE}$ (cf Theorem 7.3.4). The key for this modification is Lemma 7.3.4, where we proved that $\mathcal{PDCE}$ has only weak EE-effects. Clearly, a program without faint assignments is one without dead assignments, too. In fact, analysing the proof of the weakness of EE-effects in $\mathcal{PDCE}$, we can even show a stronger condition than Implication (7.11). For $\mathtt{AS}_\alpha \equiv G \overset{as}{\longmapsto}_\alpha G' \in \mathcal{AAS}$ and $\mathtt{FCE}_\alpha \equiv G' \overset{fae}{\longmapsto}_\alpha G'' \in \mathcal{FAE}$ such that G does not contain faint occurrences of α we have:[29]

$$Faint(\mathtt{AS}_\alpha;\mathtt{FCE}_\alpha(G), occ_\beta) \;\Rightarrow\; Dead(\mathtt{AS}_\alpha(G), occ_\beta) \tag{7.14}$$

Following the lines of the proof of Theorem 7.3.5 no proper faint code can show up after an initial faint assignment elimination. In other words, faint assignments, which require a more costly analysis, can be treated completely in advance. In practice, this way $\mathcal{PFCE}$ should even be favoured to $\mathcal{PDCE}$, since we get rid of the initial sequence of simultaneous dead assignment eliminations at the costs of a single simultaneous faint assignment elimination step. Hence we have:

Theorem 7.3.7 (An Improved Upper Bound for $\mathcal{PFCE}$).
For $\mathcal{PFCE}$ the iteration sequence of the form $\mathtt{FAE}^\mu_{\|};(\mathtt{AS}^\mu_{\|};\mathtt{DAE}^\mu_{\|})^*(G)$ stabilises within $\bar{\Delta}^{block}$ simultaneous assignment sinking and dead assignment elimination steps reaching a result that is $\precsim_{ass}$-optimal in the universe $\mathfrak{U}_{\mathcal{PFCE}}(G)$.

7.4 $\mathcal{UPRE}$ as an Advanced Application of MECs

As the remaining application of Chapter 6 we are left with $\mathcal{UPRE}$. Unfortunately, $\mathcal{UPRE}$ as introduced is not an MEC, since we have to cope with expression and assignment motions at once. However, we will see that the situations can be reduced in a way such that the central results for $\mathcal{PRAE}$ can be exploited.

As opposed to Chapter 4, here expression motions may be applied at distinct intermediate stages rather than in a closed setting. This new situation leads to two small modifications of the definition of admissible expression motion (cf. Definition 3.1.1) that are only for technical reasons:

1. *Simplification Convention:* if the complete right-hand side expression of an assignment $\mathbf{h}_\varphi := \varphi$ has to be replaced by $\mathbf{h}_\varphi$ then the whole assignment is eliminated in order to suppress the generation of useless assignments $\mathbf{h}_\varphi := \mathbf{h}_\varphi$.

[29] *Faint* and *Dead* are here used in the way like the predicate *eliminable*.

2. *Naming Convention:* the subscript of a temporary is associated with its corresponding original expression rather than the renamed expression that may be the result of previous expression motion steps. For instance, if the original assignment $x := \varphi + \psi$ is turned into $x := \mathbf{h}_\varphi + \mathbf{h}_\psi$ due to expression motion, the temporary associated with the right-hand side term is still called $\mathbf{h}_{\varphi+\psi}$ rather than $\mathbf{h}_{\mathbf{h}_\varphi+\mathbf{h}_\psi}$.

To formalise the latter convention the original shape of an expression φ shall be denoted by $\bar{\varphi}$ which can be defined defined inductively:

$$\bar{\varphi} = \begin{cases} \varphi & \text{if } \varphi \text{ is a constant or variable} \\ \psi & \text{if } \varphi \text{ is a temporary } \mathbf{h}_\psi \\ \omega(\bar{\varphi}_1, \ldots, \bar{\varphi}_k) & \text{if } \varphi = \omega(\varphi_1, \ldots, \varphi_k) \end{cases} \tag{7.15}$$

Furthermore, the notion $G \overset{em}{\longmapsto}_\varphi G'$ shall indicate that G' results from G by an expression motion (in the above sense) with respect to the expression pattern φ.

7.4.1 Computationally Optimal $\mathcal{UPRE}$

The primary goal of the uniform elimination of partially redundant expressions and assignments is to minimise the number of computations on every program path. This intent also fits our intuition that assignment motion is mainly employed as a catalyst in order to enhance the potential of expression motion.

In analogy to the MECs considered before the proof of expression optimality is essentially divided into two steps:

1. Proving confluence of $\mathcal{UPRE}$ and
2. Proving that the elementary steps conform with $\precsim_{exp}$.

Whereas the second point is obvious, the proof of the first point benefits from the confluence of $\mathcal{PRAE}$ by using the trick to simulate expression motion through assignment motion. To this end, we consider a program transformation that

– splits up every instruction α into a sequence of assignments $\mathbf{h}_{\bar{\varphi}} := \varphi;\ \alpha[\mathbf{h}_{\bar{\varphi}}/\varphi]$,

where $\alpha[\mathbf{h}_{\bar{\varphi}}/\varphi]$ results from α by replacing all occurrences of φ by $\mathbf{h}_{\bar{\varphi}}$. For instance, an assignment $x := \varphi$ is decomposed into the sequence of assignments $\mathbf{h}_{\bar{\varphi}} := \varphi;\ x := \mathbf{h}_{\bar{\varphi}}$. Note that splitting transformations are just a special kind of expression motions and, therefore, do not introduce a new type of transformations. We shall write $\mathtt{SP}^\mu_\varphi(G)$ for the program that results from G by means of a (maximal) splitting transformation with respect to φ. Then we have:

Lemma 7.4.1 (Simulation Lemma). $\mathtt{BEM}_\varphi = \mathtt{SP}^\mu_\varphi;\ \mathtt{AH}^\mu_{\mathbf{h}_{\bar{\varphi}} := \varphi};\ \mathtt{RAE}^\mu_{\mathbf{h}_{\bar{\varphi}} := \varphi}$

Proof. Let $G' \stackrel{\text{def}}{=} \mathtt{SP}^{\mu}_{\varphi}(G)$ and $\alpha \equiv \mathbf{h}_{\bar\varphi} := \varphi$. First let us take a look at the close connection between the expression motion related predicates in G and the assignment motion related predicates in G'. In comparison to G the program G' may have some additional program points in between the two assignments of split instructions. Let us identify all other program points in $\dot N_G$ and $\dot N_{G'}$, i. e. all program points apart from the new ones caused by splittings. With this, the proposed correspondences read as:

$$\mathtt{AH}^{\mu}_{\alpha}\text{-}\mathit{Just}^{\alpha}_{\dot n} \;\Leftrightarrow\; \begin{cases} \mathit{DnSafe}^{\varphi}_{\dot n} & \text{if } \dot n \in \dot N_G \\ \mathit{false} & \text{if } \dot n \in \dot N_{G'} \setminus \dot N_G \end{cases} \tag{7.16a}$$

$$\mathtt{AH}^{\mu}_{\alpha}\text{-}\mathit{Subst}^{\alpha}_{\dot n} \;\Leftrightarrow\; \begin{cases} \mathtt{BEM}_{\varphi}\text{-}\mathit{Correct}^{\varphi}_{\dot n} & \text{if } \dot n \in \dot N_G \\ \mathit{false} & \text{if } \dot n \in \dot N_{G'} \setminus \dot N_G \end{cases} \tag{7.16b}$$

$$\mathit{Redundant}^{\alpha}_{\dot n} \;\Leftrightarrow\; \begin{cases} \mathit{UpSafe}^{\varphi}_{\dot n} & \text{if } \dot n \in \dot N_G \\ \mathit{true} & \text{if } \dot n \in \dot N_{G'} \setminus \dot N_G \end{cases} \tag{7.16c}$$

All properties are immediate from the according definitions. Moreover, the definitions of $\mathtt{BEM}_{\varphi}$ (cf. page 25) and the one of maximal assignment hoistings $\mathtt{AH}^{\mu}_{\mathbf{h}_{\bar\varphi}}$ (cf. page 161) provide the following relation between the insertions of the expression and the assignment motion:

$$\forall \dot n \in \dot N_G.\; \mathtt{BEM}_{\varphi}\text{-}\mathit{Insert}^{\varphi}_{\dot n} \;\Rightarrow\; \mathtt{AH}^{\mu}_{\alpha}\text{-}\mathit{Insert}^{\alpha}_{\dot n} \tag{7.17}$$

Hence we are left to show that exactly those $\mathtt{AH}^{\mu}_{\alpha}$-insertions that have a $\mathtt{BEM}_{\varphi}$-counterpart survive the final redundancy elimination:

$$\forall \dot n \in \dot N_{G'}.\; \mathtt{AH}^{\mu}_{\alpha}\text{-}\mathit{Insert}^{\alpha}_{\dot n} \;\Rightarrow\; (\mathtt{BEM}_{\varphi}\text{-}\mathit{Insert}^{\varphi}_{\dot n} \;\Leftrightarrow\; \neg \mathit{Redundant}^{\alpha}_{\dot n}) \tag{7.18}$$

This, however, is straightforward using the equivalences in (7.16). □

Let us now sum up a few properties on the interaction of maximal splittings with other kinds of maximal transformations.

Lemma 7.4.2 (Splitting Lemma). *Let $\varphi, \psi, \rho \in \mathcal{EP}(G)$ and let us consider the following assignment patterns $\alpha \equiv x := \rho$, $\alpha_{ins} \equiv \mathbf{h}_{\bar\varphi} := \varphi$, and $\alpha_{mod} \equiv x := \rho[\mathbf{h}_{\bar\varphi}/\varphi]$.*

1. $\mathtt{SP}^{\mu}_{\varphi}; \mathtt{SP}^{\mu}_{\psi} = \mathtt{SP}^{\mu}_{\psi}; \mathtt{SP}^{\mu}_{\varphi}$
2. $\exists\, \mathtt{AH}_{\alpha_{ins}} \in \mathcal{AAH}_{\alpha_{ins}}.\; \mathtt{AH}^{\mu}_{\alpha}; \mathtt{SP}^{\mu}_{\varphi} = \mathtt{SP}^{\mu}_{\varphi}; \mathtt{AH}_{\alpha_{ins}}; \mathtt{AH}^{\mu}_{\alpha_{mod}}$
3. $\varphi \in \mathit{SubExpr}^*(\rho):\; \mathtt{RAE}^{\mu}_{\alpha}; \mathtt{SP}^{\mu}_{\varphi} = \mathtt{SP}^{\mu}_{\varphi}; \mathtt{RAE}^{\mu}_{\alpha_{ins}}; \mathtt{RAE}^{\mu}_{\alpha_{mod}}$

Proof. Part 1) is trivial if φ and ψ are independent, i. e. neither of the expressions is a subexpression of the other one. Otherwise, without loss of generality, let us assume that $\varphi \in \mathit{SubExpr}^*(\psi)$. In this case the naming convention guarantees that every instruction α that contains an occurrence of ψ is uniquely decomposed into the sequence

$$\mathbf{h}_{\bar{\varphi}} := \varphi;\ \mathbf{h}_{\bar{\psi}} := \psi[\mathbf{h}_{\bar{\varphi}}/\varphi];\ \alpha[\mathbf{h}_{\bar{\psi}}/\psi]$$

Part (2) can be easily checked by means of a careful analysis of the justification predicates triggering the various assignment hoisting transformations along the lines of the proof of Lemma 7.4.1.

For the proof of Part (3) let us assume that $\varphi \in \mathit{SubExpr}^*(\rho)$ and consider a G-occurrence of the assignment $x := \rho$. It is easy to see that $x := \rho[\mathbf{h}_{\bar{\varphi}}/\varphi]$ is redundant in $\mathtt{SP}^{\mu}_{\varphi}(G)$ if and only if $x := \rho$ is redundant itself. In this case all initialisation statements $\mathbf{h}_{\bar{\varphi}} := \varphi$ that immediately precede a redundant occurrence of $x := \rho[\mathbf{h}_{\bar{\varphi}}/\varphi]$ become redundant, too, whereas all other occurrences of $\mathbf{h}_{\bar{\varphi}} := \varphi$ are used. □

This result is the key in order to prove local confluence of $\longmapsto$ which stands for any kind of elementary transformations of type $\overset{ah}{\longmapsto}_{\alpha}$, $\overset{rae}{\longmapsto}_{\alpha}$ and $\overset{em}{\longmapsto}_{\varphi}$. In fact, we have:

Lemma 7.4.3 (Local Confluence of $\mathcal{UPRE}$). $\longmapsto$ *is locally confluent, i. e. two transformations* $\mathtt{TR}_1$ *and* $\mathtt{TR}_2$ *that are applied to a program* G_0 *can be completed as shown below:*

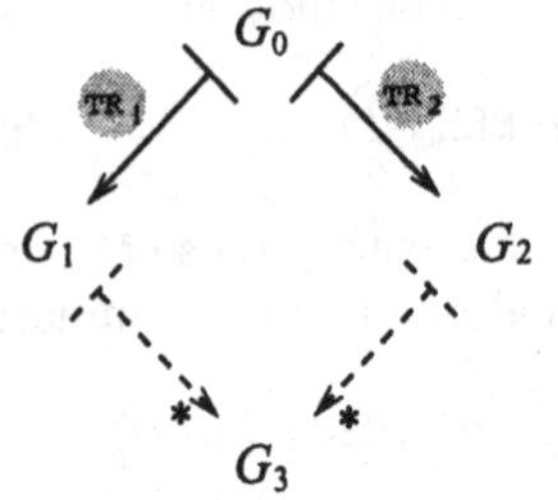

Proof. Most of the work is already done in the proof of Theorem 7.2.2 and Theorem 7.2.3. We are only left with the case that $\mathtt{TR}_1$ or $\mathtt{TR}_2$ refer to an expression motion. Let $\mathtt{TR}_1 \equiv G_0 \overset{em}{\longmapsto}_{\varphi} G_1$. Since $\mathtt{TR}_1$ can be completed to $\mathtt{BEM}_{\varphi}$ by appending a suitable φ-expression motion and $\mathtt{TR}_2$ can be chosen maximal as well, we only have to prove local confluence for the three situations pictured below, where the $\mathtt{BEM}_{\varphi}$-transitions are split up following Lemma 7.4.1:

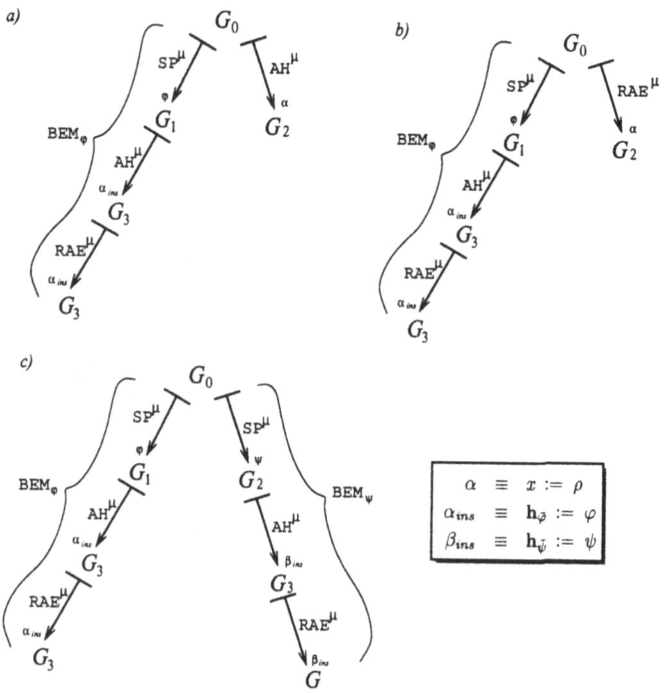

Let us now examine the situation in more detail:

Case a): We demonstrate the most intricate subcase, where $\varphi \in SubExpr(\rho)$. In this case we succeed by "clustering" the plane with patterns for which local confluence is already proved. This is illustrated in Figure 7.12(a), where (I) is due to Splitting Lemma 7.4.2(2), pattern (II) is a simple consequence on the maximality of $\mathtt{AH}^{\mu}_{\alpha_{ins}}$, and patterns (III) and (IV) are due to case 4 and 5 in the proof of Theorem 7.2.2, respectively.

Case b): Again we only give the argument for the subcase, where $\varphi \in SubExpr(\rho)$. Figure 7.12(b) shows the corresponding clustering. Pattern (I) is due to Splitting Lemma 7.4.2(3), pattern (II) is according to case 6 in the proof of Theorem 7.2.2 and (V) is a consequence of the maximality of $\mathtt{RAE}^{\mu}_{\alpha_{ins}}$. Finally all remaining "diamond patterns" (III), (IV) and (VI) are according to cases 3 and 5 in the proof of Theorem 7.2.2.

Case c): In this case the full clustering becomes quite large-scale. However, the interesting part is displayed in Figure 7.12(c). The patterns marked (I), (II) and (III) are according to Splitting Lemma 7.4.2(1)-(3), respectively. The unprocessed part in the middle can easily be completed by using "diamond patterns" according to the cases 3 to 5 in the proof of Theorem 7.2.2. □

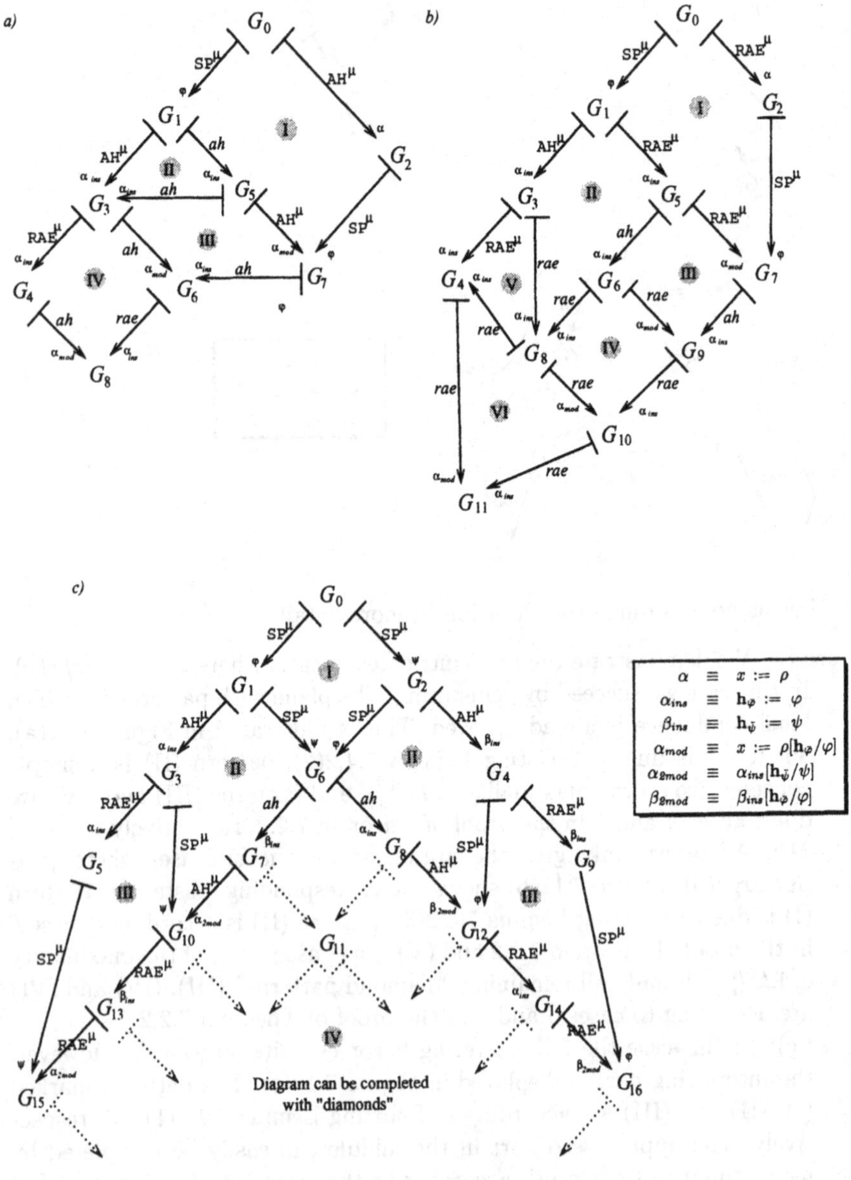

Fig. 7.12. Proving local confluence of $\mathcal{UPRE}$ by clustering

Since no expression motion can be reversed (as opposed to local assignment motions), we can immediately adopt the notion of program equivalence of Definition 7.2.2. Then Lemma 7.2.1 also fits to the new situation, which allows us to use the same line of argumentation as in Section 7.2.3. This leads us to:

Theorem 7.4.1 (Confluence Theorem for $\mathcal{UPRE}$). *$\mathcal{UPRE}$ is confluent, i. e. its associated relation $\longmapsto$ is confluent.*

Up to this point splitting transformations were mainly used on a conceptual level easing, for instance, the reasoning on confluence. Now we show that splitting steps are also useful to obtain a concrete iteration strategy that stabilises reasonably fast. After a preprocess of splitting transformations, expression motion is entirely covered by assignment motion and redundant assignment elimination. According to Lemma 7.4.2(1) the maximal splitting transformations can be processed in any order. Thus in accordance to expression motion, where transformations were extended to sets of expressions, we denote a *complete splitting step*, i. e. a sequence of maximal splittings performed for each expression pattern in $\Phi \stackrel{\text{def}}{=} \mathcal{EP}(G)$, by $\mathtt{SP}^{\mu}_{\Phi}(G)$.[30] Then we have:

Theorem 7.4.2 (Complexity of $\mathcal{UPRE}$). *For $\mathcal{UPRE}$ the sequence $\mathtt{SP}^{\mu}_{\Phi};\ (\mathtt{RAE}^{\mu}_{\|})^*;\ (,\mathtt{AH}^{\mu}_{\|};\ \mathtt{RAE}^{\mu}_{\|})^*(G)$ stabilises within*

- *one initial complete splitting step,*
- *$\Delta^{def-use}$ simultaneous redundant assignment elimination steps and*
- *$\bar{\Delta}^{block}$ simultaneous assignment hoisting and redundant assignment elimination steps*

reaching a result that is $\precsim_{exp}$-optimal in the universe $\mathfrak{U}_{\mathcal{UPRE}}(G)$.

Proof. According to Theorem 7.3.6 the iteration sequence

$$\underbrace{(\mathtt{RAE}^{\mu}_{\|})^*;\ (\mathtt{AH}^{\mu}_{\|};\ \mathtt{RAE}^{\mu}_{\|})^*(\underbrace{\mathtt{SP}^{\mu}_{\Phi}(G)}_{G'})}_{G''}$$

stabilises within the proposed bound if $\mathfrak{U}_{\mathcal{PRAE}}(G')$ is considered as the underlying universe. Hence we are left to show that no expression motion can modify the resulting program. Let $\mathtt{AM}_{\varphi}$ be an expression motion being applicable to G''. Then particularly $\mathtt{BEM}_{\varphi}$ is applicable to G''. According to the Simulation Lemma 7.4.1 we have:

$$\mathtt{BEM}_{\varphi}(G'') = \mathtt{SP}^{\mu}_{\varphi};\ \mathtt{AH}^{\mu}_{\mathbf{h}_{\varphi} := \varphi};\ \mathtt{RAE}^{\mu}_{\mathbf{h}_{\varphi} := \varphi}$$

[30] In practice, $\mathtt{SP}^{\mu}_{\Phi}$ proceeds from large expressions down to more elementary ones.

Since φ only occurs in assignments $\mathbf{h}_{\bar{\varphi}} := \varphi$ after the initial splitting transformations, our naming convention ensures that a further splitting does not have an effect anymore. Hence:

$$\mathtt{BEM}_{\varphi}(G'') = \mathtt{AH}^{\mu}_{\mathbf{h}_{\bar{\varphi}} := \varphi}; \mathtt{RAE}^{\mu}_{\mathbf{h}_{\bar{\varphi}} := \varphi}$$

Due to the stability in $\mathfrak{U}_{\mathcal{PRAE}}$ both steps on the right-hand side leave G'' invariant up to local reorderings of assignments. Finally, according to Lemma 7.2.4 the $\precsim_{exp}$-optimality of G'' is a consequence of the fact that all elementary transformations are well-behaved with respect to $\precsim_{exp}$. □

7.4.2 $\mathcal{UPRE}$ and Code Decomposition

The importance of Theorem 7.4.2 is the fact that expression optimality in the domain $\mathfrak{U}_{\mathcal{UPRE}}$ is actually independent of the decomposition of large expressions. In fact, it does not matter, whether a complex expression is split up in the original program or if it is split up by the algorithm. This is in contrast to the dilemma in expression motion, where splitting expressions simplifies the analyses, but comes at the price of poor results. On the other hand, in practice we are sometimes faced with intermediate languages, where large expressions are already split. Figure 7.13 presents the facets of this problem. The point here is that the loop invariant large expression can be moved out of the loop using the techniques of Chapter 4, if the large expression is part of a structured set of expressions. On the other hand, after decomposing the large expression (perhaps due to generation of 3-address code), expression motion fails in moving all parts of the expression out of the loop, since the assignment to t defines a modification of $t + c$. In contrast, $\mathcal{UPRE}$ succeeds in both cases, where the final programs only differ in the names of variables.

7.4.3 $\mathcal{UPRE}$ with Trade-Offs between Lifetimes of Variables

We conclude this section by showing how the techniques from Section 4.4 can beneficially be employed in order to minimise the lifetimes of variables. In [KRS95] we showed that within the set of computationally optimal results of $\mathcal{UPRE}$ neither the number of assignments nor the lifetimes of temporaries, as secondary goals, can be uniformly minimised. However, like in Chapter 4 the reasoning on lifetimes of temporaries was implicitly based on a notion of lifetime ranges that is not adequate. In this section we therefore develop an adoption of the fully flexible expression motion strategy of Chapter 4 that works for $\mathcal{UPRE}$. In particular, as opposed to the presentation in [KRS95] we make the following assumptions:

- We do not distinguish between temporaries that are introduced by expression motion (or the splitting transformations) and variables of the program. This makes the approach applicable regardless, whether large expressions are decomposed in advance or during $\mathcal{UPRE}$.

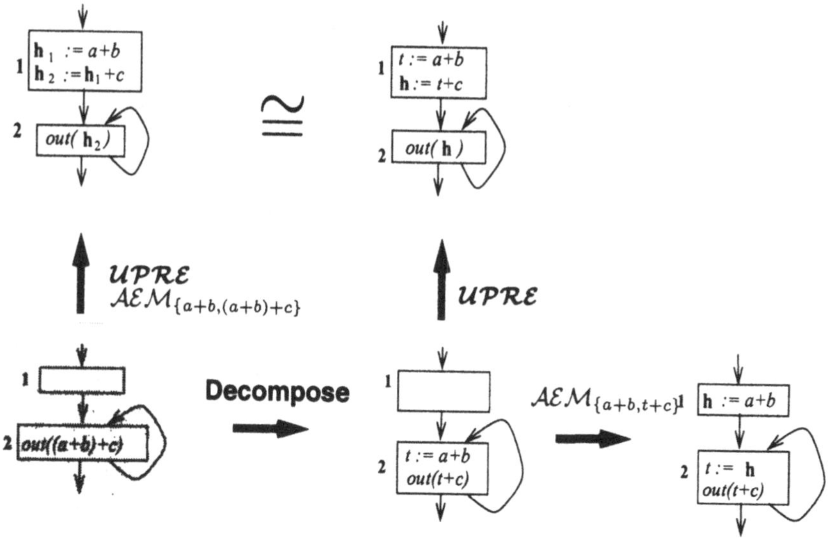

Fig. 7.13. Impact of decomposing large expressions

- End points of lifetime ranges are determined through actual use points of variables. This is in contrast to [KRS95], where the lifetime ranges of temporaries were (implicitly) assumed to end at the original use sites.

Before we are going to sketch the algorithm let us reconsider the notion of a lifetime range. Throughout this section we will not develop a fully formal presentation, but rather sketch the essentials which are sufficient for the construction.

Lifetime Ranges of Variables Essentially we get along with a simple notion of lifetime ranges in the flavour of Definition 3.3.1. However, there are some subtle differences that should be mentioned.

- Lifetime ranges are defined in a uniform way for both program variables and temporaries. In fact, we do not distinguish between these both kinds of variables anymore, and consider them uniformly to stand for symbolic registers.
- Lifetime ranges are determined through the motion invariant program points in the flow graph under investigation, i. e. basic block entries and exits as well as the entries and exits of immobile statements. This is justified, as locally, within a basic block and between such program points, sequences of assignments can move freely.[31]

[31] Note that our reasoning again rests on the assumption that the number of symbolic registers is not bound which strictly separates our algorithm from the NP-complete register allocation problem.

– Variables are assumed to be initialised on every program path leading to a use site.[32]

Using this notion of lifetime ranges a preorder that reflects the overall lifetimes of temporaries can be defined straightforwardly in the style of Definition 4.2.2.

The Algorithm

The basic idea of an algorithm to compute a lifetime optimal representative among the computationally optimal results in $\mathfrak{U}_{\mathcal{UPRE}}(G)$ is completely along the lines of Section 4.5. Again the key is to model situations that can be used for profitable trade-offs between lifetimes of symbolic registers by means of labelled DAGs, where here labelled dependency DAGs play the role of the labelled expression DAGs in Section 4.5.3. However, the construction of labelled dependency DAGs is more complicated than in the expression motion setting, which is reflected by the fact that their construction requires the full process of an exhaustive assignment sinking.

Construction of labelled dependency DAGs: starting with a computationally optimal program $G' \in \mathfrak{U}_{\mathcal{UPRE}}(G)$ maximal assignment sinkings are performed until the program stabilises. At the program points that characterise lifetime ranges, i. e. the entries and exits of basic blocks and immobile statements, the assignments that are moved across such a point successively enter into the construction of the labelled dependency DAG. Leaves of the DAG are annotated by variables[33] and inner vertices are annotated by assignment patterns. Edges reflect the execution-order dependencies. An inner vertex is associated with an assignment that has to be executed after all the assignments of its successor vertices and the leave variables are already assigned (cf. Figure 7.14).

After their construction the dependency DAGs are labelled. To this end, first the assignment sinking is undone establishing the starting situation of program G'.[34] A dependency DAG is labelled with symbols of the set $\{\bullet, \blacksquare, \circ, \square\}$ in the same way as an expression DAG (cf. Section 4.5.3). The first property pair is particularly easy: leaf vertices address register expressions, while inner ones refer to initialisation candidates. The second property pair requires more efforts. In order to tell release candidates from the other ones we have to evaluate, if the variable associated with

[32] This assumption is reasonable for well-formed programs. However, even otherwise we can always assume that the lifetime range starts in **s**, whenever an initialisation is absent on a path leading to a use site. Note, however, that this condition is automatically granted for temporary variables.

[33] That means, program variables or temporaries. Constant type operands are simply ignored.

[34] In practice, the initial situation should be memorised and be reestablished.

a vertex[35] is definitely used at a strictly later program point. Note that this property particularly cannot hold for any vertex whose associated variable also occurs at an upper position in the same DAG. Otherwise, a simple live variable analysis [ASU85] exactly determines those variables that are used later.[36]

Optimal trade-offs: optimal trade-offs of lifetime ranges can be determined along the lines Section 4.5. A labelled dependency DAG is reduced to a bipartite graph whose optimal tight set delivers the optimal trade-off decision for the program point (cf. Theorem 4.5.1).

The transformation: the trade-off information gives rise to a guided variant of exhaustive assignment sinking, where the sinking of assignments is prematurely stopped whenever this is justified by a profitable trade-off between the lifetimes of variables. This can easily be accomplished by adjusting the predicate that drives the sinking process.

Note that the final flush phase of [KRS95] only performs the brute-force sinking of the first step, which here just serves as an intermediate step to gather enough information to guide the "true" sinking in a more "intelligent" way. In fact, adapting the arguments of Section 4.5 we are able to prove:

Theorem 7.4.3 (Lifetime Optimal $\mathcal{UPRE}$). *The $\mathcal{UPRE}$-algorithm described above leads to a lifetime optimal result among all computationally optimal results in* $\mathfrak{U}_{\mathcal{UPRE}}(G)$.

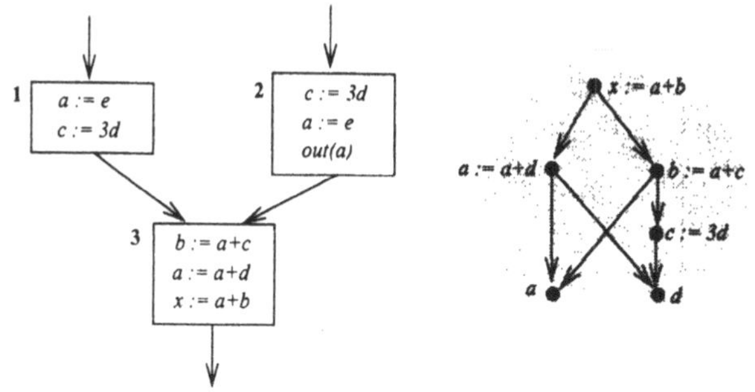

Fig. 7.14. The dependency DAG associated with the exit of basic block **3**

[35] That is the left-hand side variable of the assignment annotated at an inner vertex or the variable annotated at a leaf vertex.

[36] Note that this is an analysis on the original flow graph.

8. Assignment Motion in the Presence of Critical Edges

Analogously to the first part of the book, the final chapter of the second part is also devoted to the impact of critical edges. Unlike in expression motion, where at least some results were already well-known, the situation in assignment motion is completely unexplored. Surprisingly, however, here the presence of critical edges has even more serious consequences than in expression motion. We start this chapter by considering the situation that is characterised by the straightforward adaption of the notion of motion-elimination couples and later also examine enhanced variants revealing an interesting precision-complexity trade-off between both alternatives.

8.1 Straightforward Adaption of MECs

Unfortunately, a straightforward adaption of the notion of MECs from the situation of flow graphs without critical edges is not satisfactorily for different reasons.

8.1.1 Adequacy

The most significant deficiency is that the results that can be obtained in $\mathfrak{FG}_{\mathtt{Crit}}$ are poor compared to the ones in $\mathfrak{FG}$. This is illustrated in Figure 8.1 for $\mathcal{PDCE}$. The point here is that after splitting critical edges, $\mathcal{PDCE}$ would result in the program of 8.1(d). The important observation now is that the resulting program does not actually insert code at synthetic nodes, since the assignment at node $\mathbf{S}_{1,4}$ is dead and thus can be eliminated. However, the transformation is not in the scope of the adapted version of $\mathcal{PDCE}$, since any admissible assignment sinking has to substitute the assignment at node **1** on the path going through node **4**. The absence of the assignment pattern $x := a+b$ on the path that goes through node **2**, however, prevents any movement of the assignment at node **1**. Hence the results that can be obtained by means of a straightforward adaption are not adequate in the following sense.

Definition 8.1.1 ((Uniformly) $\mathcal{M}$-Adequate MECs). *Let $\mathcal{M}_C$ be an MEC in $\mathfrak{FG}_{\mathtt{Crit}}$, $\mathcal{M}$ an MEC in $\mathfrak{FG}$, $G_0, G_{\mathtt{res}} \in \mathfrak{FG}_{\mathtt{Crit}}$ and $G' \in \mathfrak{FG}$. Let*

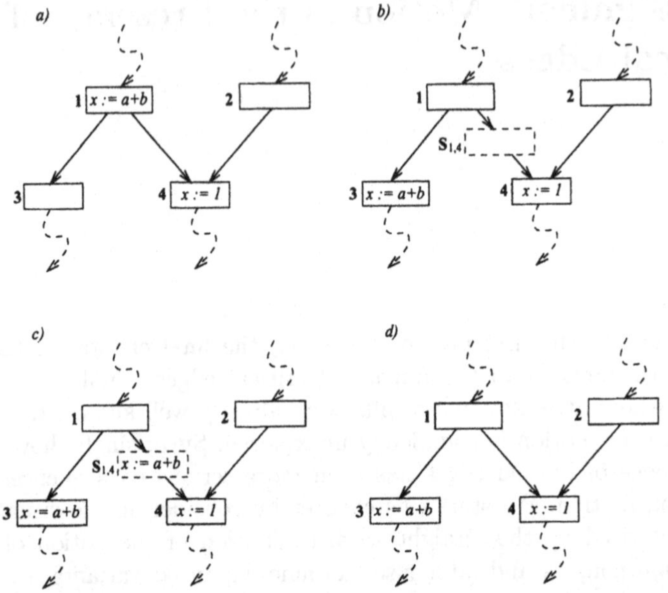

Fig. 8.1. $\mathcal{PDCE}$ and critical edges: a) no transformation are applicable, b) inserting a synthetic node on the critical edge **(1,4)**, c) assignment sinking becomes applicable, d) removing the synthetic node together with a dead assignment

us call a program in $\mathfrak{FG}$ *uncritical, if and only if all occurrences in synthetic nodes are eliminable. Then we define:*

1. $\mathcal{M}_C$ is strongly $\mathcal{M}$-adequate, *if and only if any* $\mathcal{M}$*-result that does not contain code in synthetic nodes can be also obtained in* $\mathcal{M}_C$*. Formally, this means:*

$$G^{\Sigma}_{\mathbf{res}} \in \mathfrak{U}_{\mathcal{M}}(G^{\Sigma}_0) \;\Rightarrow\; G_{\mathbf{res}} \in \mathfrak{U}_{\mathcal{M}_C}(G_0)$$

2. $\mathcal{M}_C$ *is* $\mathcal{M}$-adequate, *if and only if any* $\mathcal{M}$*-result that does not contain code in synthetic nodes and which is uniformly generated via uncritical intermediate results can be also obtained in* $\mathcal{M}_C$*. Formally, this reads as:*

$$\left.\begin{array}{l} G^{\Sigma}_{\mathbf{res}} \in \mathfrak{U}_{\mathcal{M}}(G^{\Sigma}_0) \;\wedge \\ \forall G' \in \mathfrak{FG}.\; G^{\Sigma}_0 \longmapsto^{*}_{\mathcal{M}} G' \longmapsto^{*}_{\mathcal{M}} G^{\Sigma}_{\mathbf{res}} \\ \qquad\qquad \Rightarrow G' \textit{ is uncritical} \end{array}\right\} \Rightarrow\; G_{\mathbf{res}} \in \mathfrak{U}_{\mathcal{M}_C}(G_0)$$

Obviously, strong $\mathcal{M}$-adequacy implies adequacy. However, as seen in Figure 8.1 the adapted version of $\mathcal{PDCE}$ does not meet either of the above notions.

8.1.2 Confluence

The main result of Section 7.2 was that consistency of a UMEC is sufficient to ensure confluence up to local reorderings. This result does not hold any longer, if the underlying domain of programs is extended towards $\mathfrak{FG}_{\mathtt{Crit}}$. As an example we stress again $\mathcal{PDCE}$, which is still consistent (cf. Definition 7.2.1) in the domain $\mathfrak{FG}_{\mathtt{Crit}}$, since the part of the proof of Theorem 7.2.3 that shows consistency does not use the absence of critical edges. On the other hand, Figure 8.2 gives an example, where confluence gets violated. The point of this example is that an initial elimination of the dead assignment at node **2** destroys the opportunity for a further assignment sinking, whereas an initial assignment sinking is the better choice, because the elimination potential is still preserved. This finally leads to a program G_2 being strictly better in the number of assignments than G_3.

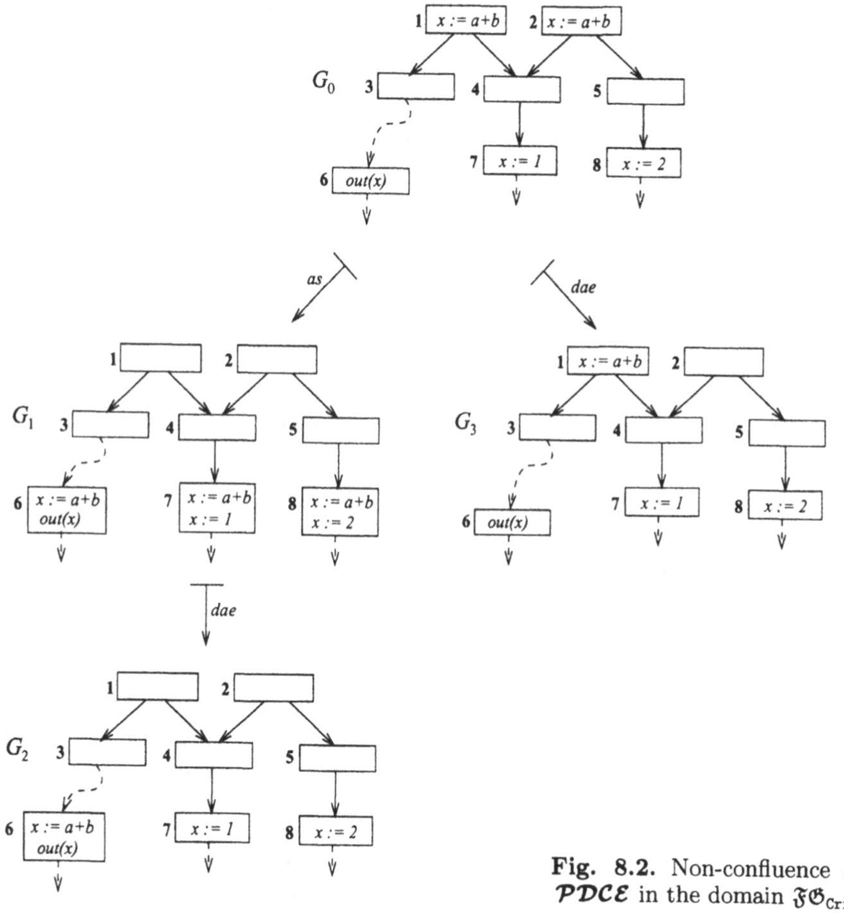

Fig. 8.2. Non-confluence of $\mathcal{PDCE}$ in the domain $\mathfrak{FG}_{\mathtt{Crit}}$

8.1.3 Efficiency

Besides the drawbacks sketched in the previous two subsections, one argument speaks for the straightforward adaption as considered in this section.

This is the fact that all the results on the complexity of $\mathcal{PDCE}$, $\mathcal{PFCE}$, $\mathcal{PRAE}$ and $\mathcal{UPRE}$ carry over to the corresponding MECs operating on $\mathfrak{FG}_{\texttt{Crit}}$. Thus we have:

Theorem 8.1.1 (Complexity of $\mathcal{PDCE}$, $\mathcal{PFCE}$, $\mathcal{PRAE}$ & $\mathcal{UPRE}$). *The complexity results of Theorem 7.3.4, Theorem 7.3.6, Theorem 7.3.7 and Theorem 7.4.2 remain true when applied within the domain $\mathfrak{FG}_{\texttt{Crit}}$.*

8.2 Enhanced UMECs

Fortunately, the deficiencies of the straightforward adaption can be avoided. However, it will turn out that the remedy of both deficiencies has to be paid by a significant increase of the number of iterations. This observation provides a strong and new argument for splitting critical edges that is even more important than the known drawback of higher solution costs of bidirectional data flow analyses (cf. Section 4.6). In fact, the same argument as presented in this section definitely applies to the extensions of Morel's and Renvoise's algorithm [Dha91, DRZ92, Cho83].

The deficiencies of Section 8.1 can be resolved by enhancing the assignment motions under consideration. Conceptually, this is accomplished by incorporating eliminations already into the assignment motions.

Definition 8.2.1 (Enhanced Assignment Motion). *Let $(\mathcal{T}_{am}, \mathcal{T}_{el})$ be an MEC. An* enhanced assignment motion *is a program transformation that (conceptually) results from the following two step procedure:*

1. *Perform an assignment motion $\texttt{AM}_\alpha \equiv G^\Sigma \overset{am}{\longmapsto}_\alpha G' \in \mathcal{T}_{am}$ according to Definition 6.1.1.*[1]
2. *Remove all synthetic nodes in the resulting program G'.*

Obviously, this definition is not sound unless the second step only removes irrelevant code. Therefore, we define:

Definition 8.2.2 (Admissible Enhanced Assignment Motion). *An* enhanced assignment motion *is* admissible, *iff the assignment motion of step 1 in Definition 8.2.1 additionally only inserts assignments at synthetic nodes, if they are eliminable.*

In accordance with the notation for "plain" assignment motions we will write $G \overset{eam}{\longmapsto}_\alpha G'$, $G \overset{eas}{\longmapsto}_\alpha G'$ and $G \overset{eah}{\longmapsto}_\alpha G'$ for the enhanced counterparts, and denote the set of enhanced admissible assignment sinkings and hoistings with respect to $\alpha \in \mathcal{AP}(G)$ by $\mathcal{EAAS}_\alpha$ and $\mathcal{EAAH}_\alpha$, respectively. Finally, enhanced admissible assignment motions induce a notion of enhanced MECs, for short EMEC, and uniform enhanced MECs, for short EUMECs.

[1] That means, an assignment motion in $\mathfrak{FG}$.

8.2.1 Adequacy

Since in CUMECs eliminable code stays eliminable it is easy to see that the eliminable occurrences in synthetic nodes can be removed immediately. Thus we have:

Theorem 8.2.1 (Adequacy Theorem). *For any CUMEC in $\mathfrak{FG}$ the enhanced counterpart is adequate.*

However, even *CUMECs* with enhanced assignment motions need not be strongly adequate. Figure 8.3 shows the reason for this behaviour by means of the enhanced variant of $\mathcal{PDCE}$. In essence, the point of this example is that, although the final program depicted in Part (d) does not contain any code in synthetic nodes, this cannot be achieved without intermediate steps like the ones in Part (b) that place non-eliminable assignments at synthetic nodes.

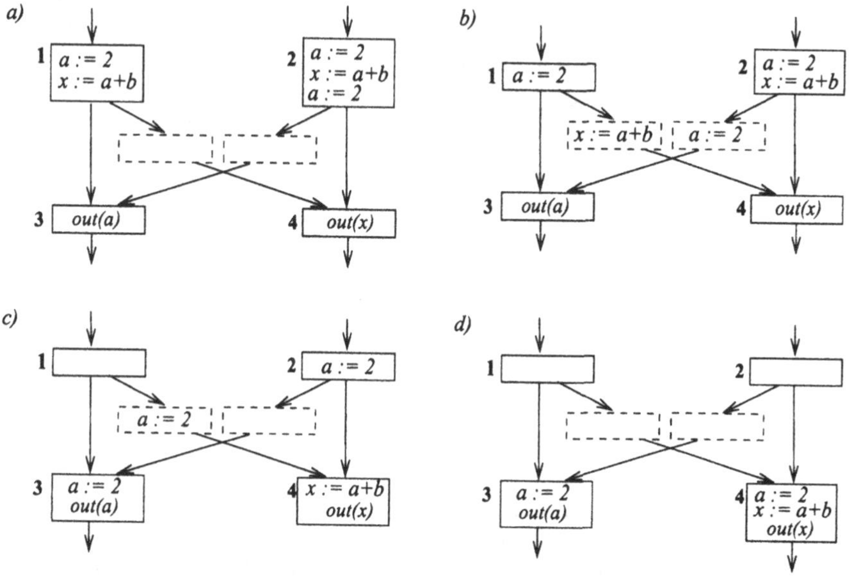

Fig. 8.3. Lack of strong adequacy in enhanced critical $\mathcal{PDCE}$: a) the starting situation, b) after a simultaneous assignment sinking and a simultaneous dead assignment elimination two occurrences remain at synthetic nodes, c) the situation after a further simultaneous assignment sinking and dead code elimination step, d) the resulting program after a final assignment sinking and dead code elimination wrt $a := 2$.

8.2.2 Confluence

Fortunately, the enhanced versions also remedy the loss of confluence being observed for consistent MECS in the straightforward adaption (cf. Section 8.1.2). Thus as the counterpart of Theorem 7.2.2 we have:

Theorem 8.2.2 (Confluence of Consistent EUMECs).
Let $(\mathcal{T}_{am}, \mathcal{T}_{el})$ be a consistent EUMEC. Then $\longmapsto$ is confluent.

Proof. The proof benefits from the construction in the proof of Theorem 7.2.2. This is accomplished by decomposing an admissible enhanced assignment motion $\mathtt{EAM}_\alpha \equiv G \overset{eam}{\longmapsto}_\alpha G'$ into a sequence of an admissible assignment motion $\mathtt{AM}_\alpha \equiv G^\Sigma \overset{am}{\longmapsto}_\alpha G'$ and an elimination step $\mathtt{EL}_\alpha \equiv G' \overset{el}{\longmapsto}_\alpha G''$, where $\mathtt{EL}_\alpha$ eliminates the G'-occurrences of α that are inserted at synthetic nodes. Hence the arguments for confluence can be reduced to its counterparts in the case analysis of the proof of Theorem 7.2.2. We demonstrate this by means of Case 2 which is actually the most interesting one. Assuming the situation of Figure 8.4(a) the decomposition yields a situation as depicted in Figure 8.4(b). Note that the eliminations are assumed to be maximal, which can always be established by appending suitable transformations. Using the

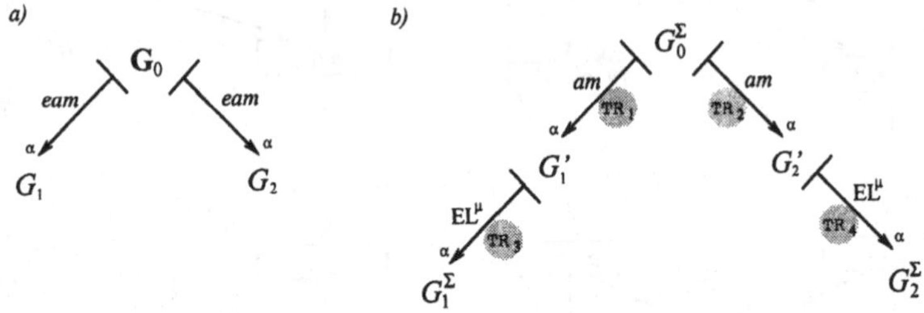

Fig. 8.4. Reducing Case 2 to the situation in $\mathfrak{FG}$

patterns for local confluence as given in the proof of Theorem 7.2.2, the diagram of Figure 8.4(b) can be completed as shown in Figure 8.5(a). The upper diamond is according to Case 2, while the other two situations are according to Case 6. It should be noted that the pattern of Case 6 is slightly modified, as maximal eliminations are used. However, the proof can easily be modified for this additional feature.[2] On the other hand, G'_3 in Figure 8.5(a) can be easily chosen in a way such that every inserted instance of α is an insertion of $\mathtt{TR}_1$ or $\mathtt{TR}_2$. Then consistency ensures that every insertion at synthetic nodes in G'_3 is eliminable. This finally allows to complete the situation of Figure 8.4(a) as shown in Figure 8.5(b). In fact, we even have a "direct" enhanced assignment motion that dominates the other two. □

[2] More specifically, $\mathtt{TR}_3$ and $\mathtt{TR}_5$ in Case 6 of the proof of Theorem 7.2.2 can be chosen maximal, which only eliminates some additional T-occurrences.

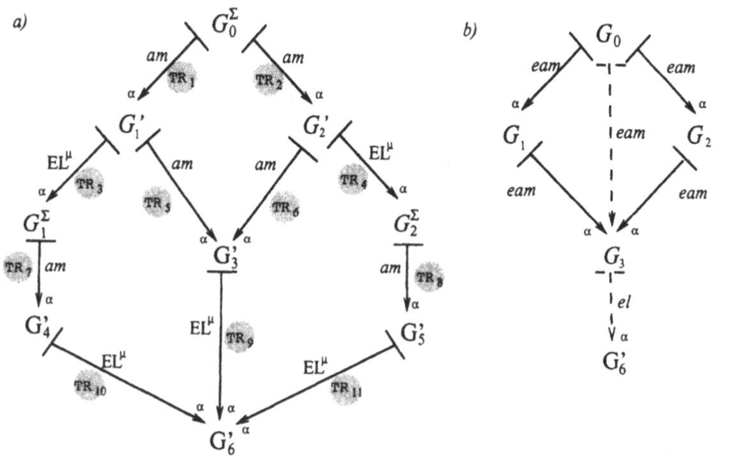

Fig. 8.5. a) Completing the diagram of Figure 8.4(b) b) Completing the diagram of Figure 8.4(b)

8.2.3 Efficiency

Unfortunately, the two positive effects caused by the usage of the enhanced versions have to be paid by a significant slow-down in the convergence speed of exhaustive iterations. To this end, let us start by investigating the maximal component transformations. According to Figure 8.5(b) also for consistent EUMECs maximal representatives exist. Since in this section we are mainly interested in the phenomena caused by critical edges, we will not investigate the construction of such transformations which, in practice, can again be determined by means of bidirectional data flow analyses following the lines of Chapter 5. Denoting the simultaneous execution of maximal enhanced assignment motions by $\mathtt{EAM}^{\mu}_{\|}(G)$ (cf. Definition 7.3.1) the general upper bound of Theorem 7.3.1 still applies to consistent EUMECs.

Theorem 8.2.3 (An Upper Bound for Consistent EUMECs). *For any consistent EUMEC an alternating sequence of simultaneous enhanced assignment motion and elimination steps, i. e. an iteration sequence in* $(\mathtt{EL}^{\mu}_{\|};\ \mathtt{EAM}^{\mu}_{\|})^*(G)$, *stabilises within*

$$(2\,|\mathbf{N}|\,\Delta^{block} + 1)$$

of both kind of simultaneous iteration steps.

The remainder of this section, however, is devoted to the fact that even under the most severe assumption, i. e. for consistent EUMECs without EE-effects, this bound is asymptotically tight. In other words, critical edges reintroduce the "bad" parameter $|\mathbf{N}|$, which means extra costs linearly depending on the size of the flow graph under consideration. We demonstrate that this effect indeed can be observed for the enhanced version of $\mathcal{PFCE}$, which in the uncritical case served as our model class of MECs with maximum convergence speed.

Partial Faint Code Elimination and Critical Edges In Section 7.3 we proved that in $\mathfrak{FG}$ iteration sequences with regard to $\mathcal{PFCE}$ meet a linear bound that is even expected to be sublinear in practice (cf. Theorem 7.3.3). As opposed we will see that for programs in $\mathfrak{FG}_{\mathtt{Crit}}$ the quadratic worst-case bound of Theorem 8.2.3 gets asymptotically tight if we decide to take the enhanced versions for assignment sinking. First let us take a look at the program fragment in Figure 8.6, which is is the basic component of this construction. The point of this Figure is that the assignment $i := i+1$ at node **1** has

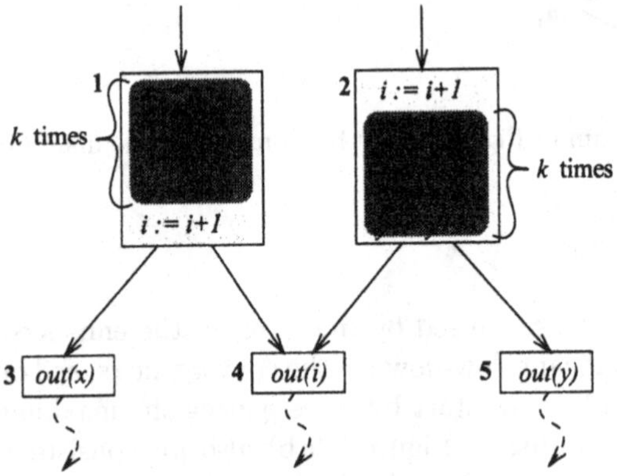

Fig. 8.6. "Synchronisation delays" in enhanced $\mathcal{PFCE}$

to wait k steps for "synchronisation" with its matching counterpart at node **2**. Previously, the chain of increments to y has to be moved along the right branch to node **5**. Note that these sinkings are enhanced ones, as y is dead along a path through node **4**. Afterwards the assignments to i can be sunk to node **4** resolving the blockade at node **1**. This finally enables the sinking of the x-increments along the left path to node **3**.

The above example provides the basic component of a more complex example. The program displayed in Figure 8.7 is essentially composed out of several versions of the program fragment of Figure 8.6 together with a similar starting situation. For the sake of presentation chains of assignments $x := x + i + j$ and $y := y + i + j$ are abbreviated by Δ_x and Δ_y, respectively. The point of this example is that both sequences Δ_x and Δ_y are alternately blocked by assignments $i := i + 1$ and $j := j + 1$, respectively, that are waiting for "synchronisation" with a corresponding assignment. For example, at the beginning the sequence Δ_x is blocked for $k+1$ enhanced assignment motion steps as illustrated in Figure 8.8. Afterwards, the code sequence Δ_y is blocked at node 7 for another $k+1$ enhanced assignment motion steps waiting for the synchronisation of the blocking assignment to i. The situation after $k+2$ iteration steps is displayed in Figure 8.9. Obviously, the above program scheme provides the following result:

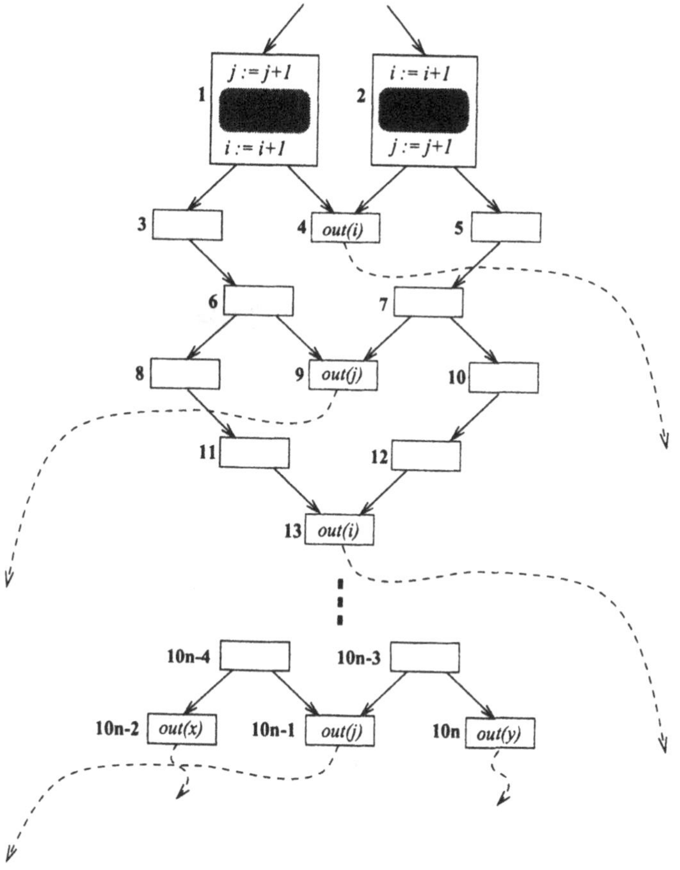

Fig. 8.7. Illustrating slow convergence of enhanced $\mathcal{PFCE}$: the starting situation

Theorem 8.2.4 (A lower Bound for Enhanced $\mathcal{PFCE}$). *There is a family of flow graphs $(G_{i,j})_{i,j \in \mathbb{N} \times \mathbb{N}}$, where $G_{i,j}$ has i nodes and $j = \Delta^{block}$ such that the number of simultaneous iteration steps that are necessary in order to reach a stable solution for $\mathcal{PFCE}$ is of order*

$$\Omega(i * j)$$

Recall that this significantly contrasts from the situation for flow graphs out of $\mathfrak{FG}$, where the dependency on the number of basic blocks in the flow graph is completely absent. Therefore, let us seize the opportunity to take a look on the example of Figure 8.6, if synthetic nodes are inserted on the critical edges. Figure 8.10 shows the situation after $k + 2$ simultaneous assignment sinking and faint assignment elimination steps, i. e. the situation being almost comparable to Figure 8.8. However, in Figure 8.10 the iteration process is already stable. The intuitive reason for this is the fact that synthetic nodes can immediately resolve those situations causing "synchronisation delays". For

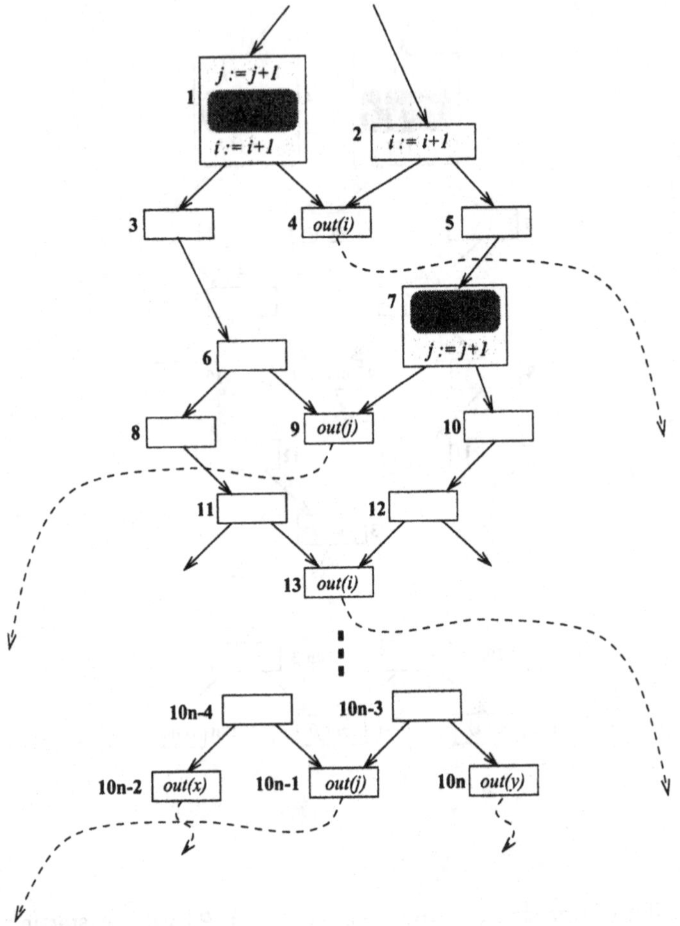

Fig. 8.8. Figure 8.7 after $k+1$ iterations

instance, the assignment $i := i+1$ can move to the synthetic node on the edge $(\mathbf{1}, \mathbf{4})$ in the very first iteration. In fact, this situation has some similarities to Petri-net theory, where the absence of critical transitions is known as *free choice property* [Rei85, Bes87]. Similarly to our application, many problems on Petri-nets, like for instance, determining liveness or reachability, are known to be significantly easier to solve for free choice nets than for arbitrary ones.

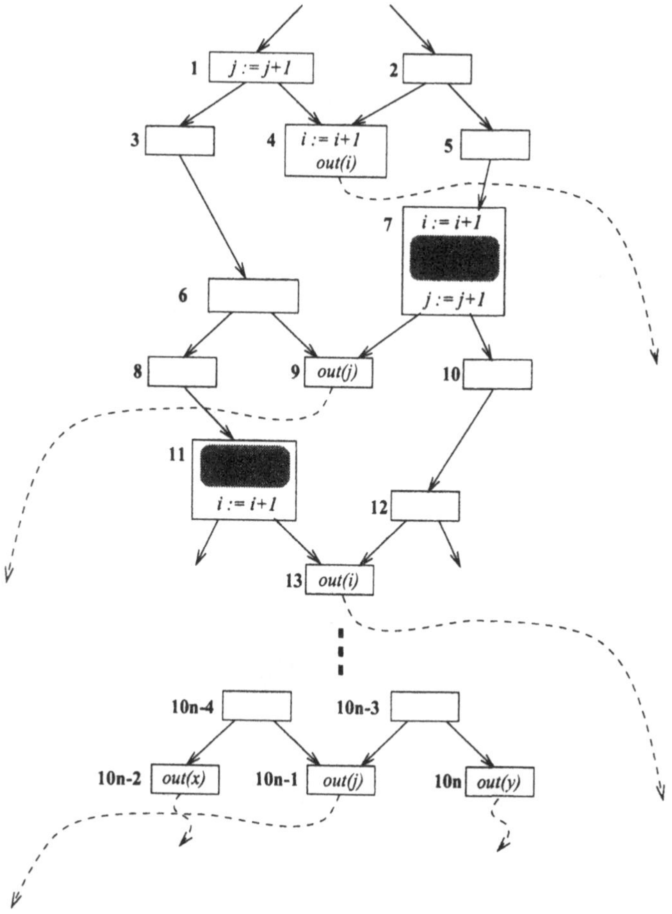

Fig. 8.9. Figure 8.7 after $2k + 2$ iterations

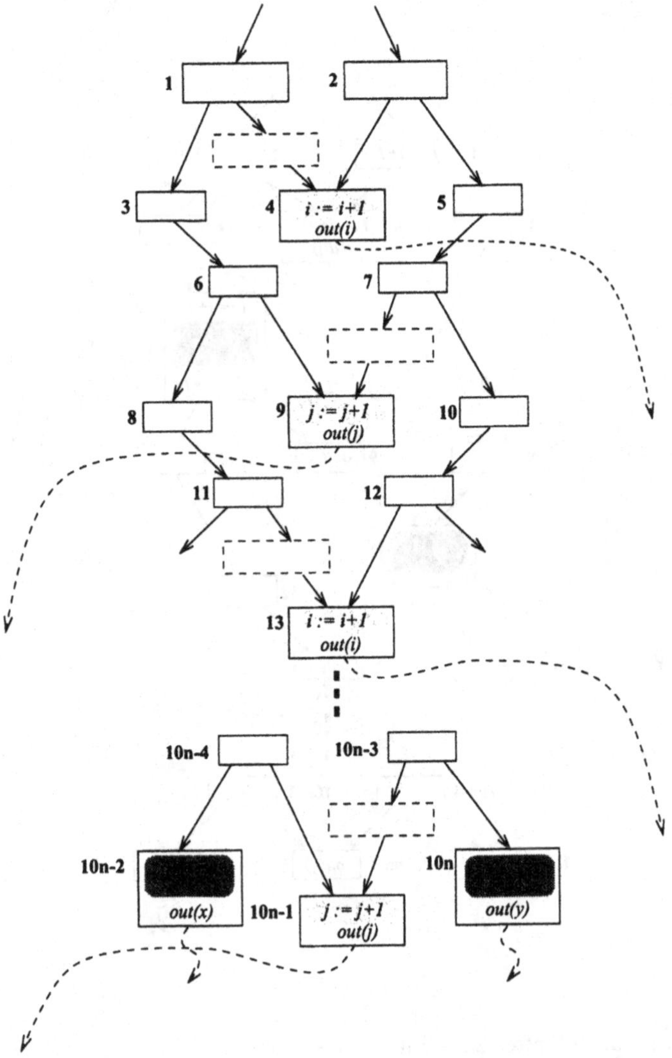

Fig. 8.10. Speeding up convergence in Figure 8.7 through synthetic nodes: stabilisation after $k+2$ iterations

9. Conclusions and Perspectives

In this monograph we examined how to cope with prominent interactions in code motion in a systematic way. Common to all problems we studied was the dilemma that while, on the one hand, exploiting interactions offers a great potential for optimisations this, on the other hand, has to be paid by the increased conceptual and computational complexity of this process. Thus the design of an interacting code motion algorithm requires to capture as much of the optimisation potential as possible, while keeping the schedule as economically as possible. Our work was motivated by the observation that, as opposed to the data flow analysis based design of the component transformations, there is no foundation that deals with the effects of a system of interacting code motion transformations in concert. For a broad class of practically relevant problems in expression and assignment motion this monograph offered rigorous techniques for the design and analysis of aggressive algorithms in the presence of interactions.

9.1 Summary of the Main Results

In the first part of the monograph we investigated the problem of lifetime optimal expression motion in the presence of composite expressions and their subexpressions. Based on the observation that state of the art techniques [Cho83, Dha88, Dha89b, Dha91, DS88, MR79, MR81, Sor89, KRS94a] did not capture the interdependencies between symbolic registers used to keep the values of composite expressions and their subexpressions, we provided the first adequate characterisation of the problem. In a first approximation we tackled a variant of the problem where interdependencies were considered in a levelwise discipline.

This naturally guided us to view the trade-off problem in terms of a graph theoretical optimisation problem on bipartite graphs. Our application turned out to be opposite to the usual matching problem which, in essence, is to find a maximum one-to-one assignment between two sets. In contrast, our problem required to identify the parts (deficiency sets) that prevent the existence of perfect matchings. Lovász's and Plummer's [LP86] excellent monograph on matching theory was of great help to gain the insight in the problem and to find an efficient solution.

The second important finding was that the full, i. e. non-levelwise, problem which at first glance looked significantly harder than the restricted case could be fully reduced to a two-level problem. This finally resulted in our $\mathtt{FFEM}_\Phi$-algorithm for computationally and lifetime optimal expression motion in the presence of composite expressions.

In the second part of the monograph we presented a uniform framework for the reasoning on program transformations that are mainly based on the motion of assignments. As applications we considered partial dead (faint) code elimination, the elimination of partially redundant assignments and the uniform elimination of partially redundant expressions and assignments. Characteristic for assignment motion based transformations are their second order effects which are the reason that the transformations have to be applied repeatedly until the process finally stabilises in order to fully exploit the optimisation potential. Proving that this process is confluent, i. e. independent of a specific application order, turned out to be a quite extensive task when performed for the elimination of partially dead code [GKL+96]. Therefore, we looked for a common confluence criterion that uniformly applies to all our application areas. We found the solution in the consistency property which expresses that the elimination potential is preserved by all transformation steps.

In addition we contributed a criterion that also guarantees that the exhaustive iteration process stabilises reasonably fast. All our applications meet this criterion which, in essence, resulted from the observation that a special class of second order effects, elimination-elimination effects, are restricted to those that are already present in the initial program. In fact, our results provided the theoretical evidence for measurements indicating that in real life programs the iteration process stabilises within a small number of steps.

Finally, all our results were checked for the influence of critical edges. Beside some well-known difficulties, two new massive drawbacks were discovered: critical edges destroy the existence of lifetime optimal solutions in expression motion, and critical edges may seriously slow down assignment motion based transformations. On the other hand, the "classical" deficiency of critical edges, that is that their conceptual and computational complexity is worse than for their unidirectional counterparts, was even diminished in the light of a novel technique whose idea is to entirely eliminate bidirectional dependencies by introducing short-cuts for the information flow along critical edges.

9.2 Perspectives

There is a number of promising directions for future research which could not, or not sufficiently, be treated in this monograph. In the following let us briefly discuss a few of them:

Reducing Register Pressure

The phase of trade-off-guided assignment sinkings as sketched in Section 7.4.3 can be employed as a stand-alone technique to enhance register allocation [Cha82, CH90, Bri92b]. Classical register allocators are pinned to the situation they find when starting their work. A lot of research has been devoted to improvements on the quality of the allocation process. However, even the most sophisticated allocator must fail, if the underlying situation, i. e. the register pressure on the symbolic registers at a program site, is already poor. Using our code motion technique one can probably avoid many potential allocation conflicts in advance leading to better register assignments. It is planned to give empirical evidence for the benefits of this strategy.

Application Areas of the Trade-Off Algorithm

We plan to explore further application areas of the graph matching technique for computing tight sets in bipartite graphs. Essentially, boiled down to its abstract kernel, the problem can be seen as a resource allocation task where the question of interest is to find a most profitable trade-off between some substitutable resources that enter into a process.

Semantic Expression Motion

Finally, the ideas on lifetime optimal expression motion should be directly transferable to the semantic variant of expression motion considered in [SKR90, SKR91, KRS98]. At the moment the semantic algorithms are restricted to busy expression motion. The reason for this is that in the semantic setting there is no chance to succeed with a single object view, as here all relevant values in a program have to be considered simultaneously. We believe that the trade-off algorithm is the key for an adequate semantic variant of lazy expression motion. However, the semantic setting adds an additional degree of difficulty to the problem. Large classes of equivalent expressions can be split at program joins which would force that the number of symbolic registers that are needed to keep the value increases at this program point. The consequences of this phenomenon have to be investigated.

References

[ACK81] F. E. Allen, J. Cocke, and K. W. Kennedy. Reduction of operator strength. In Muchnick and Jones [MJ81], chapter 3, pages 79 – 101.

[AH82] M. Auslander and M. Hopkins. An overview of the PL.8 compiler. In *Proc. ACM SIGPLAN Symposium on Compiler Construction'82*, volume *17*,6 of *ACM SIGPLAN Notices*, pages 22 – 31, June 1982.

[AHU83] A. V. Aho, J. E. Hopcroft, and J. D. Ullman. *Data Structures and Algorithms*. Addison-Wesley, 1983.

[AJU77] A. V. Aho, S. C. Johnson, and J. D. Ullman. Code generation for expressions with common subexpressions. *Journal of the ACM*, 24(1):146 – 160, 1977.

[ASU85] A. V. Aho, R. Sethi, and J. D. Ullman. *Compilers: Principles, Techniques and Tools*. Addison-Wesley, 1985.

[AU75] A. V. Aho and J. D. Ullman. Node listings for reducible flow graphs. In *Proc. 7th ACM Symposium on the Theory of Computing*, pages 177 – 185, Albuquerque, NM, 1975.

[BC94] P. Briggs and K. D. Cooper. Effective partial redundancy elimination. In *Proc. ACM SIGPLAN Conference on Programming Language Design and Implementation'94*, 1994.

[Ber57] C. Berge. Two theorems in graph theory. *Proc. Nat. Acad. Sci. USA*, pages 842–844, 1957.

[Bes87] E. Best, editor. *Theory of Petri Nets: the Free Choice Hiatus*, volume 254 of *Lecture Notes in Computer Science*. Springer-Verlag, 1987.

[BG97] R. Bodík and R. Gupta. Partial dead code elimination using slicing transformations. In *Proc. ACM SIGPLAN Conference on Programming Language Design and Implementation'97*, volume 32, 5 of *ACM SIGPLAN Notices*, pages 159–170, June 1997.

[BGS98] R. Bodík, R. Gupta, and M. L. Soffa. Complete removal of redundant expressions. In *Proc. ACM SIGPLAN Conference on Programming Language Design and Implementation'98*, pages 1–14, Montreal, Quebec, Canada, June 1998.

[BR91] D. Bernstein and M. Rodeh. Global instruction scheduling for superscalar machines. In *Proc. ACM SIGPLAN Conference on Programming Language Design and Implementation'91*, volume *26*,6 of *ACM SIGPLAN Notices*, pages 241–255, Toronto, Ontario, June 1991.

[Bri92a] P. Briggs. Private communication with Preston Briggs. 1992.

[Bri92b] P. Briggs. *Register Allocation via Graph Coloring*. PhD thesis, Rice University, Houston, Texas, 1992.

[CAC+81] G. J. Chaitin, M. A. Auslander, A. K. Chandra, J. Cocke, M. E. Hopkins, and P. W. Markstein. Register allocation via coloring. *Journal of Computer Languages*, 6:47 – 57, 1981.

[CC77] P. Cousot and R. Cousot. Abstract interpretation: A unified lattice model for static analysis of programs by construction or approximation of fixpoints. In *Conf. Record of the 4th ACM Symposium on the Principles of Programming Languages*, pages 238 – 252, Los Angeles, CA, 1977.

[CC95] C. Click and K. D. Cooper. Combining anlyses, combining optimizations. *ACM Transactions on Programming Languages and Systems*, 17(2):181 – 196, 1995.

[CH90] F. C. Chow and J. L. Hennessy. The priority-based coloring approach to register allocation. *ACM Transactions on Programming Languages and Systems*, 12(4):501–536, 1990.

[Cha82] G. J. Chaitin. Register allocation and spilling via graph coloring. *ACM SIGPLAN Notices*, 17(6):98–105, 1982.

[Cho83] F. Chow. *A portable machine independent optimizer – Design and measurements.* PhD thesis, Stanford University, Dept. of Electrical Engineering, Stanford, CA, 1983. Published as Tech. Rep. 83-254, Computer Systems Lab., Stanford University.

[CK77] J. Cocke and K. W. Kennedy. An algorithm for reduction of operator strength. *Communications of the ACM*, 20(11):850 – 856, 1977.

[Cli95] C. Click. *Combining Analyses, Combining Optimizations.* PhD thesis, Rice University, Houston, Texas, 1995. 149 pages.

[CLZ86] R. Cytron, A. Lowry, and F. K. Zadeck. Code motion of control structures in high-level languages. In *Conf. Record of the 13th ACM Symposium on the Principles of Programming Languages*, January 1986.

[CP91] J. Cai and R. Paige. Look ma, no hashing, and no arrays neither. In *Conf. Record of the 18th ACM Symposium on the Principles of Programming Languages*, pages 143 – 154, Orlando, FL, 1991.

[DGG$^+$96] A. Dold, Th. Gaul, W. Goerigk, G. Goos, F. W. Heberle, F. W. von Henke, U. Hoffmann, H. Langmaack, H. Pfeifer, H. Rueß, and W. Zimmermann. Compiler correctness and implementation verification: The *verifix* approach. In *Proc. 6th Conference on Compiler Construction (CC)*, Lecture Notes in Computer Science 1060, pages 106 – 120, Linköping, Sweden, 1996. Springer-Verlag.

[Dha83] D. M. Dhamdhere. Characterization of program loops in code optimization. *Journal of Computer Languages*, 8(2):69 – 76, 1983.

[Dha88] D. M. Dhamdhere. A fast algorithm for code movement optimization. *ACM SIGPLAN Notices*, 23(10):172 – 180, 1988.

[Dha89a] D. M. Dhamdhere. Corrigendum: A new algorithm for composite hoisting and strength reduction optimisation. *International Journal of Computer Mathematics*, 27:31 – 32, 1989.

[Dha89b] D. M. Dhamdhere. A new algorithm for composite hoisting and strength reduction optimisation (+ Corrigendum). *International Journal of Computer Mathematics*, 27:1 – 14 (+ 31 – 32), 1989.

[Dha91] D. M. Dhamdhere. Practical adaptation of the global optimization algorithm of Morel and Renvoise. *ACM Transactions on Programming Languages and Systems*, 13(2):291 – 294, 1991. Technical Correspondence.

[DK93] D. M. Dhamdhere and U. P. Khedker. Complexity of bidirectional data flow analysis. In *Conf. Record of the 20th ACM Symposium on the Principles of Programming Languages*, pages 397–409, Charleston, SC, January 1993.

[DP93] D. M. Dhamdhere and H. Patil. An elimination algorithm for bidirectional data flow problems using edge placement. *ACM Transactions on Programming Languages and Systems*, 15(2):312 – 336, April 1993.

[DRZ92] D. M. Dhamdhere, B. K. Rosen, and F. K. Zadeck. How to analyze large programs efficiently and informatively. In *Proc. ACM SIGPLAN Conference on Programming Language Design and Implementation'92*, volume *27*,7 of *ACM SIGPLAN Notices*, pages 212 – 223, San Francisco, CA, June 1992.

[DS88] K.-H. Drechsler and M. P. Stadel. A solution to a problem with Morel and Renvoise's "Global optimization by suppression of partial redundancies". *ACM Transactions on Programming Languages and Systems*, 10(4):635 – 640, 1988. Technical Correspondence.

[DS93] K.-H. Drechsler and M. P. Stadel. A variation of Knoop, Rüthing and Steffen's lazy code motion. *ACM SIGPLAN Notices*, 28(5):29 – 38, 1993.

[FKCX94] L. Feigen, D. Klappholz, R. Casazza, and X. Xue. The revival transformation. In *Conf. Record of the 21nd ACM Symposium on the Principles of Programming Languages*, Portland, Oregon, 1994.

[FOW87] J. Ferrante, K. J. Ottenstein, and J. D Warren. The program dependence graph and its use in optimization. *ACM Transactions on Programming Languages and Systems*, pages 319–349, July 1987.

[GJ79] M. R. Garey and D. S. Johnson. *Computers and Intractability – A Guide to the Theory of NP-Completeness.* W.H. Freeman & Co, San Francisco, 1979.

[GKL+96] A. Geser, J. Knoop, G. Lüttgen, O. Rüthing, and B. Steffen. Nonmonotone fixpoint iterations to resolve second order effects. In *Proc. 6th Conference on Compiler Construction (CC)*, Lecture Notes in Computer Science 1060, pages 106 – 120, Linköping, Sweden, 1996. Springer-Verlag.

[GM86] P. B. Gibbons and S. S. Muchnik. Efficient instruction scheduling for a pipline architecture. In *Proc. ACM SIGPLAN Symposium on Compiler Construction'86*, volume *21*, 7 of *ACM SIGPLAN Notices*, pages 11–16, June 1986.

[GMW81] R. Giegerich, U. Möncke, and R. Wilhelm. Invariance of approximative semantics with respect to program transformations. In *Proc. of the third Conference of the European Co-operation in Informatics*, Informatik-Fachberichte 50, pages 1–10. Springer, 1981.

[Gro95] V. Grover. Private communication with Vinod Grover, sun inc. 1995.

[Hal35] M. Jr. Hall. On representatives of subsets. *Journal of the London Mathematical Society*, 10:26–30, 1935.

[Har77] A. W. Harrison. Compiler analysis of the value ranges for variables. *IEEE Transactions on Software Engineering*, SE-3(3), may 1977.

[HDT87] S. Horwitz, A. Demers, and T. Teitelbaum. An efficient general iterative algorithm for data flow analysis. *Acta Informatica*, 24:679 – 694, 1987.

[Hec77] M. S. Hecht. *Flow Analysis of Computer Programs.* Elsevier, North-Holland, 1977.

[HK73] J. E. Hopcroft and R. M. Karp. An $n^{\frac{5}{2}}$ algorithm for maximum matchings in bipartite graphs. *SIAM Journal on Computing*, 2(4):225–231, 1973.

[JD82a] S. M. Joshi and D. M. Dhamdhere. A composite hoisting-strength reduction transformation for global program optimization – part I. *International Journal of Computer Mathematics*, 11:21 – 41, 1982.

[JD82b] S. M. Joshi and D. M. Dhamdhere. A composite hoisting-strength reduction transformation for global program optimization – part II. *International Journal of Computer Mathematics*, 11:111 – 126, 1982.

[JP93] R. Johnson and K. Pingali. Dependency based program analysis. In *Proc. ACM SIGPLAN Conference on Programming Language Design and Implementation'94*, pages 78 – 89, Albuquerque, NM, 1993.

[KD94] U. P. Khedker and D. M. Dhamdhere. A generalized theory of bit vector data flow analysis. *ACM Transactions on Programming Languages and Systems*, 16(5):1472 – 1511, September 1994.

[Ken75] K. W. Kennedy. Node listings applied to data flow analysis. In *Conf. Record of the 2nd ACM Symposium on the Principles of Programming Languages*, pages 10 – 21, Palo Alto, CA, 1975.

[Ken81] K. W. Kennedy. A survey of data flow analysis techniques. In Muchnick and Jones [MJ81], chapter 1, pages 5 – 54.

[Kno93] J. Knoop. *Optimal Interprocedural Program Optimization: A new framework and its application.* PhD thesis, Institut für Informatik und Praktische Mathematik, Christian-Albrechts-Universität Kiel, Germany, 1993. To appear as monograph in the series *Lecture Notes in Computer Science*, Springer-Verlag, Heidelberg, Germany, 1997.

[Kou77] L. T. Kou. On live-dead analysis for global data flow problems. *Journal of the ACM*, 24(3):473 – 483, July 1977.

[KRS92] J. Knoop, O. Rüthing, and B. Steffen. Lazy code motion. In *Proc. ACM SIGPLAN Conference on Programming Language Design and Implementation'92*, volume *27*,7 of *ACM SIGPLAN Notices*, pages 224 – 234, San Francisco, CA, June 1992.

[KRS93] J. Knoop, O. Rüthing, and B. Steffen. Lazy strength reduction. *Journal of Programming Languages*, 1(1):71–91, 1993.

[KRS94a] J. Knoop, O. Rüthing, and B. Steffen. Optimal code motion: Theory and practice. *ACM Transactions on Programming Languages and Systems*, 16(4):1117–1155, 1994.

[KRS94b] J. Knoop, O. Rüthing, and B. Steffen. Partial dead code elimination. In *Proc. ACM SIGPLAN Conference on Programming Language Design and Implementation'94*, volume *29*,6 of *ACM SIGPLAN Notices*, pages 147–158, Orlando, FL, June 1994.

[KRS95] J. Knoop, O. Rüthing, and B. Steffen. The power of assignment motion. In *Proc. ACM SIGPLAN Conference on Programming Language Design and Implementation'95*, volume *30*,6 of *ACM SIGPLAN Notices*, pages 233–245, La Jolla, CA, June 1995.

[KRS96a] J. Knoop, O. Rüthing, and B. Steffen. Syntactic versus semantic code motion: Analogies and essential differences. Technical Report 9616, Institut für Informatik und Praktische Mathematik, Christian-Albrechts-Universität Kiel, Germany, 1996. 18 pages.

[KRS96b] J. Knoop, O. Rüthing, and B. Steffen. Towards a tool kit for the automatic generation of interprocedural data flow analyses. *Journal of Programming Languages*, 4:211–246, 1996.

[KRS98] J. Knoop, O. Rüthing, and B. Steffen. Code motion and code placement: Just synonyms? In *Proc. 6th European Symposium on Programming (ESOP)*, Lecture Notes in Computer Science 1381, pages 154 – 196, Lisbon, Portugal, 1998. Springer-Verlag.

[KS92] J. Knoop and B. Steffen. Optimal interprocedural partial redundancy elimination. Extended abstract. In *Addenda to Proc. 4th Conference on Compiler Construction (CC)*, pages 36 – 39, Paderborn, Germany, 1992. Published as Tech. Rep. No. 103, Department of Computer Science, University of Paderborn.

[KU76] J. B. Kam and J. D. Ullman. Global data flow analysis and iterative algorithms. *Journal of the ACM*, 23(1):158 – 171, 1976.

[KU77] J. B. Kam and J. D. Ullman. Monotone data flow analysis frameworks. *Acta Informatica*, 7:309 – 317, 1977.

[LP86] L. Lovász and M. D. Plummer. *Matching Theory*, volume 29 of *Annals of Discrete Mathmatics.* North Holland, 1986.

[MJ81] S. S. Muchnick and N. D. Jones, editors. *Program Flow Analysis: Theory and Applications.* Prentice Hall, Englewood Cliffs, NJ, 1981.

[MMR95] P. M. Masticola, T. J. Marlowe, and B. G. Ryder. Lattice frameworks for multisource and bidirectional data flow problems. *ACM Transactions on Programming Languages and Systems*, 17(5):777 – 802, 1995.

[Mor84] E. Morel. Data flow analysis and global optimization. In B. Lorho, editor, *Methods and tools for compiler construction*. Cambridge University Press, 1984.

[MR79] E. Morel and C. Renvoise. Global optimization by suppression of partial redundancies. *Communications of the ACM*, 22(2):96 – 103, 1979.

[MR81] E. Morel and C. Renvoise. Interprocedural elimination of partial redundancies. In Muchnick and Jones [MJ81], chapter 6, pages 160 – 188.

[Muc97] S. S. Muchnick, editor. *Advanced Compiler Design & Implementation*. Morgan Kaufmann, San Francisco, CA, 1997.

[New42] M. H. A. Newman. On theories with a combinatorial definition of equivalence. *Annals of Math.*, 43,2:223–243, 1942.

[Nie86] F. Nielson. A bibliography on abstract interpretation. *ACM SIGPLAN Notices*, 21:31 – 38, 1986.

[Rei85] W. Reisig. *Petri Nets: An Introduction*. EATCS Monographs on Theoretical Computer Science. Springer-Verlag, 1985.

[RL77] J. H. Reif and R. Lewis. Symbolic evaluation and the gobal value graph. In *Conf. Record of the 4th ACM Symposium on the Principles of Programming Languages*, pages 104 – 118, Los Angeles, CA, 1977.

[RP88] B.G̃. Ryder and M.C̃. Paull. Incremental data-flow analysis algorithms. *ACM Transactions on Programming Languages and Systems*, 10(1):1–50, January 1988.

[Rüt98a] O. Rüthing. Bidirectinal data flow analysis in code motion: Myth and reality. In *Proc. Int. Static Analysis Symposium (SAS'98)*, Lecture Notes in Computer Science, Pisa, Italy, September 1998. Springer-Verlag. To appear.

[Rüt98b] O. Rüthing. Optimal code motion in the presence of large expressions. In *Proc. International Conference on Computer Languages*, pages 216–225, Chicago, Il., May 1998. IEEE.

[RWZ88] B. K. Rosen, M. N. Wegman, and F. K. Zadeck. Global value numbers and redundant computations. In *Conf. Record of the 15th ACM Symposium on the Principles of Programming Languages*, pages 12 – 27, San Diego, CA, 1988.

[SKR90] B. Steffen, J. Knoop, and O. Rüthing. The value flow graph: A program representation for optimal program transformations. In *Proc. 3rd European Symposium on Programming (ESOP)*, Lecture Notes in Computer Science 432, pages 389 – 405, Copenhagen, Denmark, 1990. Springer-Verlag.

[SKR91] B. Steffen, J. Knoop, and O. Rüthing. Efficient code motion and an adaption to strength reduction. In *Proc. 4th International Joint Conference on the Theory and Practice of Software Development (TAPSOFT)*, Lecture Notes in Computer Science 494, pages 394 – 415, Brighton, UK, 1991. Springer-Verlag.

[Sor89] A. Sorkin. Some comments on a solution to a problem with Morel and Renvoise's "Global optimization by suppression of partial redundancies". *ACM Transactions on Programming Languages and Systems*, 11(4):666 – 668, 1989. Technical Correspondence.

[Ste91] B. Steffen. Data flow analysis as model checking. In *Proc. TACS*, Lecture Notes in Computer Science 526, pages 346 – 364, Sendai, Japan, 1991. Springer-Verlag.

[Ste93] B. Steffen. Generating data flow analysis algorithms from modal specifications. *International Journal on Science of Computer Programming*, 21:115–139, 1993.

[Ste96] B. Steffen. Property oriented expansion. In *SAS/ALP/PLILP'96*, volume 1145, pages 22–41, Aachen (D), September 1996. Springer Verlag. Proc. Int. Static Analysis Symposium (SAS'96),.

[Tar79] R. E. Tarjan. Applications of path compression on balanced trees. *Journal of the ACM*, 26(4):690 – 715, 1979.

[Tar81a] R. E. Tarjan. Fast algorithms for solving path problems. *Journal of the ACM*, 28(3):594 – 614, 1981.

[Tar81b] R. E. Tarjan. A unified approach to path problems. *Journal of the ACM*, 28(3):577 – 593, 1981.

[W.78] Kennedy. K. W. Use-definition chains with applications. *Journal of Computer Languages*, 3, 1978.

[WS90] D. L Whitfield and M. L. Soffa. An approach to ordering optimizing transformations. In *Proceedings of the SecondACM SIGPLAN Symposium on Principles & Practice of Parallel Programming (PPOPP)*, volume *25*,3 of *ACM SIGPLAN Notices*, pages 137 – 147, Seattle, Washington, March 1990.

[WS97] D. L. Whitfield and M. L. Soffa. An approach for exploring code improving transformations. *ACM Transactions on Programming Languages and Systems*, 19(6):1053–1084, November 1997.

[WZ85] M. Wegman and K. Zadeck. Constant propagation with conditional branches. In *Conf. Record of the 12th ACM Symposium on the Principles of Programming Languages*, pages 291 – 299, January 1985.

[WZ91] M. N. Wegman and F. K. Zadeck. Constant propagation with conditional branches. *ACM Transactions on Programming Languages and Systems*, 13(2), April 1991.

Index

assignment motion
  enhanced, 204
  maximal, 175

basic block, 12
bit-vector analysis
  elimination technique, 112
  iterative, 112
  node listing, 112
  path compression technique, 112

chain of blockades, 177
code pattern, 13
complexity, 174
  of $\mathtt{BEM}_\varphi$, 35
  of $\mathtt{BEM}_\Phi$, 110
  of $\mathtt{LFEM}_\Phi$, 110
  of $\mathtt{FFEM}_\Phi$, 111
  of $\mathtt{LEM}_\varphi$, 35
  of $\mathtt{LEM}_\Phi$, 110
computationally better, 24
confluence, 159
  local, 161, 168
  modular, 161
correctness
  of replacements, 23
  partial, 156
  total, 156

DAG, 10, 198
  expression, 88, **91**
  labelled expression, 91
deficiency, 51
deficiency set, 51
definition–use chain, 188

edge splitting, 14
EE-effect, 180
elimination
  maximal, 175
  of dead assignment, 143
  of faint assignment, 148
  of redundant assignments, 149
elimination-elimination effect
  weak, 184
equivalence of programs, 168
expression, 10
  level of, 39
expression motion, 22
  admissible, 22, **23**
  busy, 24, 25
  computationally optimal, **24**, **41**
  flat, 38
  fully flexible, 96
  lazy, 26, 28
  levelwise structured, 60
  of a single expression, 22
  profitable, 116
  structured, 40
    busy, 43
    lazy, 46

flow graph, 12
  depth of, 112
  width of, 131

graph, 9
  bipartite, **9**, 62
    induced, 93
    matching, 51
  directed, 10
    acyclic,
      see DAG10
  undirected, 9

initialisation candidate, 88
  relevant, 92
initialisation candidate, 198
iteration
  slot-wise, 174

level, 39

lifetime range, 26, 27
  structured, 47

marriage problem, 52
matching, **51**
  complete, 51
  maximal, 51
motion-elimination couple, 155
  $\mathcal{M}$-adequate, 202
  strongly $\mathcal{M}$-adequate, 202
  uniform, 158
    consistent, 159
    weakly consistent, 161

neighbours
  of a vertex, 9
nodes
  of a flow graph, 12

occurrence
  origin, 158
  sink, 157
  source, 157
optimal
  lifetime, 49
    structured, 49

path
  alternating, 52
  augmenting, 53
  finite, 10
  insertion-replacement, 26
  insertion-use, 47
penalty costs, 174
Petri-net, 210
  free choice, 210
predecessor
  of a vertex, 10
  zig-zag, 123
predicate
  local, 22
preorder, 15, 170
  computationally better, 24
  lifetime better, 27
program point, 12

register
  expression, 88
    relevant, 92
  pressure, 26
  symbolic, 22
register allocation, 51
release candidate, 88, 198

safety
  down-, 23
  homogeneous, 118
  of insertions, 23
  up-, 23
second order effect, **144**
splitting transformation, 190
statement, 11
  assignment, 11
  immobile, 11
  irrelevant, 12
  output, 11
strength reduction, 60
subexpression
  immediate, 10
  mediate, 11
subset
  irreducible, 58, 75
successor
  of a vertex, 10
  zig-zag, 123
superexpression, 11

temporary variable, 22
tight set, 51, 53
tightness
  defect, 58
trade-off candidates
  lower, 50, **61**
  upper, 50, **61**
trade-off pair, 92
  gain of, 92
  optimal, 92

universe
  of an MEC, 170

universe of expressions
flat, 38
structured, 39

variable
temporary, 22

width, 131

Index of Symbols

$\mathfrak{U}_{\mathcal{M}}(\cdot)$, 170
$B_{\dot{n}}$, 93
$D_{\dot{n}}$, 91
$\mathcal{AP}(\cdot)$, 13
$\mathcal{EP}(\cdot)$, 13
$\Phi_{\mathtt{fl}}$, 38
Φ, 39
$\Phi^{<i}$, 39
$\Phi^{\leqslant i}$, 39
Φ^{i}, 39
$\mathcal{E}$, 10
$MaxSubExpr.(\psi)$, 39
$Occ_{\alpha,p}(\cdot)$, 13
$Occ_{\alpha}(\cdot)$, 13
$\dot{N}$, 12
$\Theta_{\dot{n}}^{\mathrm{dn}}$, 93
$\Theta_{\dot{n}}^{\mathrm{up}}$, 93
$\Theta_{\dot{n}}^{\mathrm{dn}(i)}$, 61
$SubExpr^{*}(\cdot)$, 11
$SubExpr(\cdot)$, 11
$\Theta_{\dot{n}}^{\mathrm{up}(i)}$, 61
Δ^{block}, 178
$\Delta_{\mathbf{n}}^{block}$, 178
$\bar{\Delta}^{block}$, 183
$\bar{\Delta}_{\mathbf{n}}^{block}$, 183
$defic(\cdot)$, 51
d, 112
$\langle\,\rangle$, 10
$\ell.$, 91
$Lev_{\Phi}(\cdot)$, 39
$LtRg(\cdot)$, 27
$neigh(\cdot)$, 9
$Orig(\,\cdot\,)$, 158
IRP, 26
$\mathbf{P}_{G}$, 10
$|\cdot|$, 10
$\dot{\mathbf{s}}$, 13
$\dot{\mathbf{e}}$, 13
$\mathcal{R}_{\dot{n}}^{\mathtt{ic}}(\cdot)$, 92
$\mathcal{R}_{\dot{n}}^{\mathtt{re}}(\cdot)$, 92
$SLtRg(\cdot)$, 47
$Dst_{\mathtt{AM}_{\alpha}}(\,\cdot\,)$, 157
$Src_{\mathtt{AM}_{\alpha}}(\,\cdot\,)$, 157
s, 12
e, 12
w, 131
$zpred(\cdot)$, 123
$zsucc(\cdot)$, 123
$pred(\cdot)$, 10
$succ(\cdot)$, 10

Predicates
assignment motion
OrigJust, 163
eliminable(·, ·), 158
AssMod, 140
AssOcc, 140
Blocked, 140
Dead, 143
Faint, 148
•-*Insert*, 140
•-*Just*, 141
LhsMod, 140
LhsUsed, 140
Redundant, 149
•-*Remove*, 140
RhsMod, 140
•-*Subst*, 141
expression motion
Comp, 22
Transp, 22
Hom-Delayed, 120
Hom-DnSafe, 118
Hom-Earliest, 118
LChange, 62
Hom-Latest, 120
Hom-Safe, 118
•-*Insert*, 38, 60
•-*Replace*, 38, 60
A1-Delayed, 61
A1-DnSafe, 61
A1-Latest, 61
A2-Delayed, 62

A2-Latest, 62
UsedLater[$\bullet$], 61
A-Delayed, 96
A-Latest, 96
Change, 96
$\bullet$-*Correct*, 23
Delayed, 27
DnSafe, 23
Earliest, 25
$\bullet$-*Insert*, 22, 40, 97
Latest, 28
$\bullet$-*Replace*, 22, 40
$\bullet$-*Replace*, 96
Safe, 23
UpSafe, 23
UsedLater, 88

Orders and Preorders

$\stackrel{\circ}{=}$, 168
$\precsim_{ass}$, 171
$\precsim^{\Phi}_{exp}$, 38, 41
$\precsim_{exp}$, 171
$\precsim^{\Phi}_{lt}$, 38, 48
$\precsim^{\varphi}_{lt}$, 24, 27
$\sqsubseteq$, 10

Transformations

assignment motion
$\mathcal{DAE}_{\alpha}$, 144
$\mathcal{EAAH}_{\alpha}$, 204
$\mathcal{EAAS}_{\alpha}$, 204
$\mathcal{FAE}_{\alpha}$, 148, 149
$\stackrel{ah}{\longmapsto}_{\alpha}$, 140
$\stackrel{as}{\longmapsto}_{\alpha}$, 139
$\stackrel{am}{\longmapsto}_{\alpha}$, 157
$\stackrel{dae}{\longmapsto}_{\alpha}$, 144
$\stackrel{eah}{\longmapsto}_{\alpha}$, 204
$\stackrel{eam}{\longmapsto}_{\alpha}$, 204
$\stackrel{eas}{\longmapsto}_{\alpha}$, 204
$\stackrel{el}{\longmapsto}_{\alpha}$, 157
$\circ\!\!\longrightarrow$, 169
$\mathtt{EAM}^{\mu}_{\parallel}(G)$, 207
$\stackrel{fae}{\longmapsto}_{\alpha}$, 148
$\mathtt{AM}^{\mu}_{\alpha}(G)$, 175
$\mathtt{EL}^{\mu}_{\alpha}(G)$, 175
$\mathtt{SP}^{\mu}_{\varphi}(G)$, 190
$\stackrel{rae}{\longmapsto}_{\alpha}$, 149
$\longmapsto$, 157
$\mathrm{TR}_{\alpha_1} \parallel \ldots \parallel \mathrm{TR}_{\alpha_k}$, 176
$\mathcal{PDCE}$, 143
$\mathcal{PFCE}$, 148
$\mathcal{PRAE}$, 148
$\mathcal{UPRE}$, 150
CUMEC, 159
EMEC, 204
EUMEC, 204
MEC, 155
UMEC, 158

expression motion
$\mathcal{AEM}_{\varphi}$, 24
$\mathtt{BEM}_{\Phi_{fl}}$, 38
$\mathtt{BEM}_{\Phi}$, 43
$\mathtt{BEM}_{\varphi}$, 25
$\mathtt{CBEM}_{\varphi}$, 118
$\mathtt{CLEM}_{\varphi}$, 120
$\mathcal{COEM}_{\varphi}$, 25
$\mathtt{LFEM}_{\Phi}$, 60
$\mathtt{FFEM}_{\Phi}$, 96
$\mathtt{LEM}_{\Phi_{fl}}$, 38
$\mathtt{LEM}_{\Phi}$, 46
$\mathtt{LEM}_{\varphi}$, 28
$\stackrel{em}{\longmapsto}_{\varphi}$, 190
$\mathcal{AEM}_{\Phi}$, 41
$\mathcal{COEM}_{\Phi}$, 41

Lecture Notes in Computer Science

For information about Vols. 1–1470
please contact your bookseller or Springer-Verlag

Vol. 1471: J. Dix, L. Moniz Pereira, T.C. Przymusinski (Eds.), Logic Programming and Knowledge Representation. Proceedings, 1997. IX, 246 pages. 1998. (Subseries LNAI).

Vol. 1472: B. Freitag, H. Decker, M. Kifer, A. Voronkov (Eds.), Transactions and Change in Logic Databases. Proceedings, 1996, 1997. X, 396 pages. 1998.

Vol. 1473: X. Leroy, A. Ohori (Eds.), Types in Compilation. Proceedings, 1998. VIII, 299 pages. 1998.

Vol. 1474: F. Mueller, A. Bestavros (Eds.), Languages, Compilers, and Tools for Embedded Systems. Proceedings, 1998. XIV, 261 pages. 1998.

Vol. 1475: W. Litwin, T. Morzy, G. Vossen (Eds.), Advances in Databases and Information Systems. Proceedings, 1998. XIV, 369 pages. 1998.

Vol. 1476: J. Calmet, J. Plaza (Eds.), Artificial Intelligence and Symbolic Computation. Proceedings, 1998. XI, 309 pages. 1998. (Subseries LNAI).

Vol. 1477: K. Rothermel, F. Hohl (Eds.), Mobile Agents. Proceedings, 1998. VIII, 285 pages. 1998.

Vol. 1478: M. Sipper, D. Mange, A. Pérez-Uribe (Eds.), Evolvable Systems: From Biology to Hardware. Proceedings, 1998. IX, 382 pages. 1998.

Vol. 1479: J. Grundy, M. Newey (Eds.), Theorem Proving in Higher Order Logics. Proceedings, 1998. VIII, 497 pages. 1998.

Vol. 1480: F. Giunchiglia (Ed.), Artificial Intelligence: Methodology, Systems, and Applications. Proceedings, 1998. IX, 502 pages. 1998. (Subseries LNAI).

Vol. 1481: E.V. Munson, C. Nicholas, D. Wood (Eds.), Principles of Digital Document Processing. Proceedings, 1998. VII, 152 pages. 1998.

Vol. 1482: R.W. Hartenstein, A. Keevallik (Eds.), Field-Programmable Logic and Applications. Proceedings, 1998. XI, 533 pages. 1998.

Vol. 1483: T. Plagemann, V. Goebel (Eds.), Interactive Distributed Multimedia Systems and Telecommunication Services. Proceedings, 1998. XV, 326 pages. 1998.

Vol. 1484: H. Coelho (Ed.), Progress in Artificial Intelligence – IBERAMIA 98. Proceedings, 1998. XIII, 421 pages. 1998. (Subseries LNAI).

Vol. 1485: J.-J. Quisquater, Y. Deswarte, C. Meadows, D. Gollmann (Eds.), Computer Security – ESORICS 98. Proceedings, 1998. X, 377 pages. 1998.

Vol. 1486: A.P. Ravn, H. Rischel (Eds.), Formal Techniques in Real-Time and Fault-Tolerant Systems. Proceedings, 1998. VIII, 339 pages. 1998.

Vol. 1487: V. Gruhn (Ed.), Software Process Technology. Proceedings, 1998. VIII, 157 pages. 1998.

Vol. 1488: B. Smyth, P. Cunningham (Eds.), Advances in Case-Based Reasoning. Proceedings, 1998. XI, 482 pages. 1998. (Subseries LNAI).

Vol. 1489: J. Dix, L. Fariñas del Cerro, U. Furbach (Eds.), Logics in Artificial Intelligence. Proceedings, 1998. X, 391 pages. 1998. (Subseries LNAI).

Vol. 1490: C. Palamidessi, H. Glaser, K. Meinke (Eds.), Principles of Declarative Programming. Proceedings, 1998. XI, 497 pages. 1998.

Vol. 1491: W. Reisig, G. Rozenberg (Eds.), Lectures on Petri Nets I: Basic Models. XII, 683 pages. 1998.

Vol. 1492: W. Reisig, G. Rozenberg (Eds.), Lectures on Petri Nets II: Applications. XII, 479 pages. 1998.

Vol. 1493: J.P. Bowen, A. Fett, M.G. Hinchey (Eds.), ZUM '98: The Z Formal Specification Notation. Proceedings, 1998. XV, 417 pages. 1998.

Vol. 1494: G. Rozenberg, F. Vaandrager (Eds.), Lectures on Embedded Systems. Proceedings, 1996. VIII, 423 pages. 1998.

Vol. 1495: T. Andreasen, H. Christiansen, H.L. Larsen (Eds.), Flexible Query Answering Systems. IX, 393 pages. 1998. (Subseries LNAI).

Vol. 1496: W.M. Wells, A. Colchester, S. Delp (Eds.), Medical Image Computing and Computer-Assisted Intervention – MICCAI'98. Proceedings, 1998. XXII, 1256 pages. 1998.

Vol. 1497: V. Alexandrov, J. Dongarra (Eds.), Recent Advances in Parallel Virtual Machine and Message Passing Interface. Proceedings, 1998. XII, 412 pages. 1998.

Vol. 1498: A.E. Eiben, T. Bäck, M. Schoenauer, H.-P. Schwefel (Eds.), Parallel Problem Solving from Nature – PPSN V. Proceedings, 1998. XXIII, 1041 pages. 1998.

Vol. 1499: S. Kutten (Ed.), Distributed Computing. Proceedings, 1998. XII, 419 pages. 1998.

Vol. 1501: M.M. Richter, C.H. Smith, R. Wiehagen, T. Zeugmann (Eds.), Algorithmic Learning Theory. Proceedings, 1998. XI, 439 pages. 1998. (Subseries LNAI).

Vol. 1502: G. Antoniou, J. Slaney (Eds.), Advanced Topics in Artificial Intelligence. Proceedings, 1998. XI, 333 pages. 1998. (Subseries LNAI).

Vol. 1503: G. Levi (Ed.), Static Analysis. Proceedings, 1998. IX, 383 pages. 1998.

Vol. 1504: O. Herzog, A. Günter (Eds.), KI-98: Advances in Artificial Intelligence. Proceedings, 1998. XI, 355 pages. 1998. (Subseries LNAI).

Vol. 1505: D. Caromel, R.R. Oldehoeft, M. Tholburn (Eds.), Computing in Object-Oriented Parallel Environments. Proceedings, 1998. XI, 243 pages. 1998.

Vol. 1506: R. Koch, L. Van Gool (Eds.), 3D Structure from Multiple Images of Large-Scale Environments. Proceedings, 1998. VIII, 347 pages. 1998.

Vol. 1507: T.W. Ling, S. Ram, M.L. Lee (Eds.), Conceptual Modeling – ER '98. Proceedings, 1998. XVI, 482 pages. 1998.

Vol. 1508: S. Jajodia, M.T. Özsu, A. Dogac (Eds.), Advances in Multimedia Information Systems. Proceedings, 1998. VIII, 207 pages. 1998.

Vol. 1510: J.M. Zytkow, M. Quafafou (Eds.), Principles of Data Mining and Knowledge Discovery. Proceedings, 1998. XI, 482 pages. 1998. (Subseries LNAI).

Vol. 1511: D. O'Hallaron (Ed.), Languages, Compilers, and Run-Time Systems for Scalable Computers. Proceedings, 1998. IX, 412 pages. 1998.

Vol. 1512: E. Giménez, C. Paulin-Mohring (Eds.), Types for Proofs and Programs. Proceedings, 1996. VIII, 373 pages. 1998.

Vol. 1513: C. Nikolaou, C. Stephanidis (Eds.), Research and Advanced Technology for Digital Libraries. Proceedings, 1998. XV, 912 pages. 1998.

Vol. 1514: K. Ohta, D. Pei (Eds.), Advances in Cryptology – ASIACRYPT'98. Proceedings, 1998. XII, 436 pages. 1998.

Vol. 1515: F. Moreira de Oliveira (Ed.), Advances in Artificial Intelligence. Proceedings, 1998. X, 259 pages. 1998. (Subseries LNAI).

Vol. 1516: W. Ehrenberger (Ed.), Computer Safety, Reliability and Security. Proceedings, 1998. XVI, 392 pages. 1998.

Vol. 1517: J. Hromkovič, O. Sýkora (Eds.), Graph-Theoretic Concepts in Computer Science. Proceedings, 1998. X, 385 pages. 1998.

Vol. 1518: M. Luby, J. Rolim, M. Serna (Eds.), Randomization and Approximation Techniques in Computer Science. Proceedings, 1998. IX, 385 pages. 1998.

1519: T. Ishida (Ed.), Community Computing and Support Systems. VIII, 393 pages. 1998.

Vol. 1520: M. Maher, J.-F. Puget (Eds.), Principles and Practice of Constraint Programming - CP98. Proceedings, 1998. XI, 482 pages. 1998.

Vol. 1521: B. Rovan (Ed.), SOFSEM'98: Theory and Practice of Informatics. Proceedings, 1998. XI, 453 pages. 1998.

Vol. 1522: G. Gopalakrishnan, P. Windley (Eds.), Formal Methods in Computer-Aided Design. Proceedings, 1998. IX, 529 pages. 1998.

Vol. 1524: G.B. Orr, K.-R. Müller (Eds.), Neural Networks: Tricks of the Trade. VI, 432 pages. 1998.

Vol. 1525: D. Aucsmith (Ed.), Information Hiding. Proceedings, 1998. IX, 369 pages. 1998.

Vol. 1526: M. Broy, B. Rumpe (Eds.), Requirements Targeting Software and Systems Engineering. Proceedings, 1997. VIII, 357 pages. 1998.

Vol. 1527: P. Baumgartner, Theory Reasoning in Connection Calculi. IX, 283. 1999. (Subseries LNAI).

Vol. 1528: B. Preneel, V. Rijmen (Eds.), State of the Art in Applied Cryptography. Revised Lectures, 1997. VIII, 395 pages. 1998.

Vol. 1529: D. Farwell, L. Gerber, E. Hovy (Eds.), Machine Translation and the Information Soup. Proceedings, 1998. XIX, 532 pages. 1998. (Subseries LNAI).

Vol. 1530: V. Arvind, R. Ramanujam (Eds.), Foundations of Software Technology and Theoretical Computer Science. XII, 369 pages. 1998.

Vol. 1531: H.-Y. Lee, H. Motoda (Eds.), PRICAI'98: Topics in Artificial Intelligence. XIX, 646 pages. 1998. (Subseries LNAI).

Vol. 1096: T. Schael, Workflow Management Systems for Process Organisations. Second Edition. XII, 229 pages. 1998.

Vol. 1532: S. Arikawa, H. Motoda (Eds.), Discovery Science. Proceedings, 1998. XI, 456 pages. 1998. (Subseries LNAI).

Vol. 1533: K.-Y. Chwa, O.H. Ibarra (Eds.), Algorithms and Computation. Proceedings, 1998. XIII, 478 pages. 1998.

Vol. 1534: J.S. Sichman, R. Conte, N. Gilbert (Eds.), Multi-Agent Systems and Agent-Based Simulation. Proceedings, 1998. VIII, 237 pages. 1998. (Subseries LNAI).

Vol. 1535: S. Ossowski, Co-ordination in Artificial Agent Societies. XV; 221 pages. 1999. (Subseries LNAI).

Vol. 1536: W.-P. de Roever, H. Langmaack, A. Pnueli (Eds.), Compositionality: The Significant Difference. Proceedings, 1997. VIII, 647 pages. 1998.

Vol. 1538: J. Hsiang, A. Ohori (Eds.), Advances in Computing Science – ASIAN'98. Proceedings, 1998. X, 305 pages. 1998.

Vol. 1539: O. Rüthing, Interacting Code Motion Transformations: Their Impact and Their Complexity. XXI,225 pages. 1998.

Vol. 1540: C. Beeri, P. Buneman (Eds.), Database Theory – ICDT'99. Proceedings, 1999. XI, 489 pages. 1999.

Vol. 1541: B. Kågström, J. Dongarra, E. Elmroth, J. Waśniewski (Eds.), Applied Parallel Computing. Proceedings, 1998. XIV, 586 pages. 1998.

Vol. 1542: H.I. Christensen (Ed.), Computer Vision Systems. Proceedings, 1999. XI, 554 pages. 1999.

Vol. 1543: S. Demeyer, J. Bosch (Eds.), Object-Oriented Technology ECOOP'98 Workshop Reader. 1998. XXII, 573 pages. 1998.

Vol. 1544: C. Zhang, D. Lukose (Eds.), Multi-Agent Systems. Proceedings, 1998. VII, 195 pages. 1998. (Subseries LNAI).

Vol. 1545: A. Birk, J. Demiris (Eds.), Learning Robots. Proceedings, 1996. IX, 188 pages. 1998. (Subseries LNAI).

Vol. 1546: B. Möller, J.V. Tucker (Eds.), Prospects for Hardware Foundations. Survey Chapters, 1998. X, 468 pages. 1998.

Vol. 1547: S.H. Whitesides (Ed.), Graph Drawing. Proceedings 1998. XII, 468 pages. 1998.

Vol. 1548: A.M. Haeberer (Ed.), Algebraic Methodology and Software Technology. Proceedings, 1999. XI, 531 pages. 1999.

Vol. 1500: J.-C. Derniame, A.B. Kaba, D. Wastell (Eds.), Software Process: Principles, Methodology, and Technology. XIII, 307 pages. 1999.

Vol. 1551: G. Gupta (Ed.), Practical Aspects of Declarative Languages. Proceedings, 1999. VIII, 367 pgages. 1999.